COLLEGE OUTLINE SERIES

A SURVEY OF
ANCIENT, MEDIEVAL
and MODERN HISTORY

by

STEWART C. EASTON

BARNES & NOBLE, INC. · NEW YORK

PUBLISHERS · BOOKSELLERS · SINCE 1873

This book is an original work (Number 115) in the original College Outline Series. It was written by a distinguished educator, carefully edited, and produced in accordance with the highest standards of publishing. The text was set on the linotype in Old Style, Garamond, and Caslon by Hamilton Printing Company (Rensselaer, N.Y.). The paper for this edition was manufactured by S. D. Warren Company (Boston, Mass.) and supplied by Canfield Paper Company (New York, N.Y.). This edition was printed by Hamilton Printing Company and bound by Sendor Bindery (New York, N.Y.). The cover was designed by Rod Lopez-Fabrega.

CONTENTS

MAPS

Tabulated Bibliography of Standard Textbooks

This *College Outline* is keyed to standard textbooks in two ways.

1. If you are studying one of the following textbooks, consult the cross references here listed to find which pages of this *Outline* correspond to the appropriate chapter of your text. (Roman numerals refer to the textbook chapters or units; Arabic figures refer to the pages of this *Outline*.)

2. If you are using this *Outline* as your basis for study and want another treatment of the subject, consult the pages of any of the standard textbooks as indicated in the Quick Reference Table on pp. x–xiii.

Brace, Richard M. *The Making of the Modern World*. 2nd ed. New York: Holt, Rinehart & Winston, Inc., 1961.
I (118–125); II (134–136); III (136–137); IV (128–134); V (138–144); VI (141, 145, 163–164); VII (147–148, 165–166); VIII (146–147, 159–163); IX (152–155); X (148–150, 163–165, 179–181); XI (168–170, 183–184); XII (184–186); XIII (155–157); XIV (158–159, 172–173, 175–177, 187–188); XV (170–174, 186–188); XVI (189, 207–210, 212–213); XVII (190–193); XVIII (188–189, 193–198); XIX (198–200, 203); XX (201–206, 218–225, 228–232); XXI (225–228); XXII (234–236, 242–243, 248–251, 256–258); XXIII (237–241); XXIV (218, 242–245); XXV (226–227, 241–242, 245–248, 258–259); XXVI (210–217); XXVII (311–316, *passim*); XXVIII (211–212, 236–237, 251–258); XXIX (232–233, 264–282); XXX (260–263, 283–290); XXXI (291–293); XXXII (301–305, 311–316, *passim*); XXXIII (291–300); XXXIV (335–337, 349–352); XXXV (305–308); XXXVI (318–329, 331–332, 345–349, 355–356); XXXVII (332–345, 349–355).

Brinton, Crane; Christopher, John B.; and Wolff, Robert Lee. *A History of Civilization*. 2 vols. 2nd ed. Englewood Cliffs, N. J.: Prentice-Hall, Inc., 1960.
I (1–23); II (24–44); III (45–68, 73–75); IV (69–73); V (76–77, 86–96); VI (78–85); VII (98–107); VIII (96–97, 102–103, 112–118, 126–127); IX (81, 108–112, 123–124, 168–169); X (118–126); XI (128–134); XII (138–145); XIII (146–155, 159–160, 163–166); XIV (134–138, 184–186); XV (155–163, 170–174); XVI (159, 169–170, 177–179, 207–209); XVII (175–176, 179–181, 183–184, 186–189, 190–193); XVIII (193–201); XIX (201–206, 218–220, 223–228); XX (208–210, 212–217, 234–235); XXI (211–212, 228–231, 235–237, 248–256); XXII (237–247); XXIII (311–317, *passim*); XXIV (232–233, 259–260, 264–282); XXV (247–248, 260–263, 283–290); XXVI (291–294); XXVII (294–301); XXVIII (301–305); XXIX (305–308, 318–329); XXX (331–334, 345–357); XXXI (334–345); XXXII (311–316, *passim*).

Bruun, Geoffrey, and Commager, Henry Steele. *Europe and America Since 1492*. Boston: Houghton Mifflin Company, 1954.
I (128–134); II (126–127, 170–172); III (120–126, Chapters VIII–IX, *passim*); IV (96–97, 134–138); V (138–145); VI (146–149, 165–166); VII (150–157, 160–161, 163–169); VIII (173–174); IX (170–173); X (161–163); XI (157–159); XII (164–165); XIII (166–170); XIV (184–185); XV (175, 188–189); XVI (186–188); XVII (179–181); XVIII (183–184); XIX (175–179); XX (179, 181–183); XXI (185–186); XXII (190–191); XXIII (185); XXIV (188, 204–206); XXV (189, 207–210); XXVI (191–192); XXVII (193–196); XXVIII (198–201); XXX (201–204); XXXI (192–193); XXXII (220–222, 232); XXXIII (205–206, 212–215);

XXXIV (208–210, 312–313) ; XXXV (211–212, 222–223, 228–230, 270–271) ; XXXVI (224–226, 250–251) ; XXXVII (234–236) ; XXXVIII (227–228, 237–239) ; XXXIX (242–244) ; XL (258–259) ; XLI (230–232) ; XLII (256–257) ; XLIII (314–316) ; XLIV (313) ; XLV (212, 216, 309–310) ; XLVI (216, 236–237, 239–242, 244–245, 251–256) ; XLVII (257–258, 271–273) ; XLVIII (271–273) ; XLIX (245–248, 264–270, 273–282) ; L (247–248, 260–263) ; LI (309–317, *passim*) ; LII (309–310, 314) ; LIII (283–287) ; LIV (287–290) ; LV (291–294) ; LVI (294–295) ; LVII (259–260, 301–302, 304) ; LVIII (302–303) ; LIX (295–298, 300, 305–308) ; LX (303–304) ; LXI (272–273) ; LXII (335) ; LXIII (318–325) ; LXIV (331–334) ; LXV (326–327) ; LXVI (345–349) ; LXVII (336–339, 349–352).

Burns, Edward McNall. *Western Civilizations, Their History and Their Culture*. 6th ed. New York: W. W. Norton & Company, Inc., 1963.
I (1–6) ; III (7–15) ; IV (15–19) ; V (19–20) ; VI (21–22) ; VII (20–21, 23) ; VIII (24–33, 36–41, 44) ; IX (33–36, 41–43) ; X (45–68, 73–77) ; XI (69–73, 76, 86–92) ; XII (78–85) ; XIII (90–91, 93–97, 103–107, 118–122) ; XIV (97–103, 108–115) ; XV (126–132, 134, 170–171) ; XVI (132–134) ; XVII (138–145, 147–148) ; XVIII (125–126, 134–137) ; XIX (107, 121–123, 125, 148–150, 152–163, 169–170) ; XX (170–174, 186–189, 205) ; XXI (188–189, 193–198) ; XXII (198–206, 213, 223–225) ; XXIII (207–211, 213–217, 309–311) ; XXIV (176–177, 211–212, 218–219, 225–226, 228–230, 234–245, 249–256, 258–259, 264–282) ; XXV (190–193, 230–232, 256–258) ; XXVI (312–317) ; XXVII (245–248, 260–262, 283–290, 305–306) ; XXVIII (291–305) ; XXIX (288, 306–308) ; XXX (296–297, 310–311, 318–327) ; XXXI (331–357) ; XXXII (310–311, 313–317, *passim*).

Easton, Stewart C. *The Western Heritage: From the Earliest Times to the Present*. New York: Holt, Rinehart & Winston, Inc., 1961.
II (1–6) ; III (7–23) ; IV (24–44) ; V (45–68) ; VI (69–73) ; VII (73–77) ; VIII (78–85, 124) ; IX (86–91, 93–97) ; X (97–103, 108–112) ; XI (103–108, 118–125) ; XII (91–92, 112–115, 126–127) ; XIII (125–126, 128–146) ; XIV (146–170, 175–186, 190–193) ; XV (170–174, 186–189) ; XVI (193–201) ; XVII (201–204, 218–225, 226–228, 234–247) ; XVIII (207–217, 309–311) ; XIX (224, 228–233, 248–260) ; XX (204–206, 311–317, *passim*) ; XXI (264–282) ; XXII (247–248, 260–263, 283–290) ; XXIII (291–300) ; XXIV (301–308) ; XXV (318–329, 331–334) ; XXVI (334–357) ; XXVII (310–311, 312–317, *passim*).

Ferguson, Wallace K., and Bruun, Geoffrey. *A Survey of European Civilization*. 3rd ed. Boston: Houghton Mifflin Company, 1962.
I (7–23) ; II (24–33, 36–41, 44) ; III (33–36, 41–43) ; IV (45–60) ; V (61–68) ; VI (73–75) ; VII (69–73) ; VIII (75–77) ; IX (78–82) ; X (82–85) ; XI (86–87, 89–90) ; XII (87–89, 91) ; XIII (93–96) ; XIV (90–91) ; XV (97–101) ; XVI (103–106) ; XVII (107–112, 123) ; XVIII (93–96) ; XIX (96–97) ; XX (97–98, 102–103, 112–115) ; XXI (97, 108, 123–125, 164–165) ; XXII (104–107, 118–121) ; XXIII (106–107, 116–118) ; XXIV (125–126) ; XXV (128–132) ; XXVI (132–134) ; XXVII (107, 119, 121–123, 125, 134–136, 152–153, 159–160) ; XXVIII (138–144) ; XXIX (141, 153, 159–160) ; XXX (145–146) ; XXXI (146–148, 153–155) ; XXXII (160–162) ; XXXIII (155–157) ; XXXIV (148–150) ; XXXV (136–137, 184–186) ; XXXVI (170–174) ; XXXVIII (161–163) ; XXXIX (157–159) ; XL (163–166) ; XLI (124, 168–170, 183–184) ; XLII (164, 179–180) ; XLIII (184–186, 190–192) ; XLV (171, 173, 186–188) ; XLVI

(177–183, 188–189, 192–193); XLVII (193–195); XLVIII (195–198); XLIX (198–199); L (199–201, 203); LI (201–203); LII (204–206, 218, 222–225); LIII (208–212, 224–225, 228–230, 234–235); LIV (225–228, 242–243, 250–251); LV (235–237); LVI (237–239, 241); LVII (242–245); LVIII (245–247, 258–259); LIX (209–211, 213–217, 309–313); LX (211–212, 216, 239–241, 251–256); LXI (232–233, 259–260, 264–266, 273–282); LXII (230–232, 256–258, 267–270); LXIII (247–248, 260–263); LXIV (283–288); LXV (288–290, 305–306); LXVI (303–304); LXVII (291–294); LXIX (302–303); LXX (294–295); LXXI (295–297); LXXII (321–322, 335); LXXIII (305–308); LXXIV (318–325); LXXV (326–329, 331–334); LXXVI (347–348, 355); LXXVII (345–355, *passim*); LXXVIII (355–357); LXXIX (334–345); LXXX (310–317, *passim*).

Hayes, Carlton J. H.; Baldwin, Marshall W.; and Cole, Charles W. *History of Western Civilization*. New York: The Macmillan Company, 1962.

I (7–21); II (23–44); III (45–68); IV (21–22, 69–72); V (73–75); VI (75–77, 79–80, 86–87); VII (78–81); VIII (73, 89, 92, 108); IX (82–85); X (81, 87–92); XI (93–96); XII (82–83, 90–92, 105, 108); XIII (93–96); XIV (97–99, 108–109); XV (107–112); XVI (96–97); XVII (100–102, 104–107); XVIII (81, 99–101, 108); XIX (97–98, 102–103); XX (112–114); XXI (114–115); XXII (125–126); XXIII (118–122, 152–153); XXIV (81, 123–125, 164, 166–167); XXV (124, 134–136); XXVI (128–134); XXVII (116–118, 132); XXVIII (125, 159–160, 163–164); XXIX (138–143, 146–147); XXX (143–144); XXXI (145, 170–173); XXXII (147–148, 165–166); XXXIII (136–137, 148–150, 170); XXXIV (160–163); XXXV (164, 166–170, 179–184); XXXVI (178–179, 184–186); XXXVII (173–174, 179–180); XXXVIII (175–176, 180–183, 187–189); XXXIX (155–159, 176–177); XL (190–193); XLI (193–198); XLII (198–202); XLIII (201–203, 222–225, 228–230); XLIV (186–189, 204–206, 218–220); XLV (208–215, 230); XLVI (225–228); XLVII (234–236, 242–243, 245–246, 248–251); XLVIII (237–239, 241–242); XLIX (239–240, 251–254); L (241–244, 246–248); LI (260–261, 264–282); LII (214–216, 310–314, 316–317); LIII (212, 254–256); LIV (244–245, 247–248, 261–263); LV (283–287, 291–293); LVI (287–290, 301–303, 305–306, 314–315); LVII (291–301); LVIII (305–307); LIX (318–325); LX (325–329, 331–334); LXI (355–356); LXII (345–354); LXIII (334–345); LXIV (345–357, *passim*); LXV (315–317).

Neill, Thomas P.; McGarry, Daniel A.; and Hohl, Clarence L. *A History of Western Civilization*. Milwaukee: The Bruce Publishing Company, 1962.

I (1–6); II (7–22); III (23–36); IV (36–44); V (45–68); VI (69–72); VII (72–73); VIII (73–75); IX (75–76); X (76–77); XI (78–82); XII (82–85); XIII (86–87); XIV (87–90); XV (90–91); XVI (93–95); XVII (95–96); XVIII (72, 89, 92); XIX (96–97); XX (108–112); XXI (90, 98–101); XXII (91, 103–105); XXIII (101–102, 105–107); XXIV (97–101); XXV (112–115); XXVI (125–126); XXVII (118–122); XXVIII (107–108, 123–125, 164); XXIX (107, 122–123, 125); XXX (116–118, 132); XXXI (128–134); XXXII (138–141, 159–160); XXXIII (141–143); XXXIV (143–144, 152–155); XXXV (145–146); XXXVI (136–137, 147–148, 154–155, 165–166); XXXVII (130–131, 133–134); XXXVIII (134–137, 184–186); XXXIX (148–150, 163–164); XL (146–147, 160–161); XLI (137, 161–163); XLII (155–159); XLIII (170–174); XLIV (164, 179–181); XLV (168–170, 180, 183–184); XLVI (176–178, 184–186); XLVII (174–176, 178–184, 187–189); XLVIII (190–193,

220–222, 230–232); XLIX (193–198); L (198–201); LI (201–203, 223–224); LII (207–211); LIII (189, 204–206, 213, 218–220); LIV (223–225, 228–230); LV (225–228); LVI (242–243, 248–251); LVII (234–236); LVIII (237–239); LIX (241–247); LX (236–237, 239–241, 251–256, 258–259); LXI (209–211, 309–311); LXII (214–216, 312, 314–317); LXIII (247–248, 260–282); LXIV (283–287); LXV (287–290, 305–306); LXVI (301–305); LXVII (291–294); LXVIII (294–297, 300–301); LXIX (294–295, 297–298, 306–308); LXX (318–325); LXXI (325–329, 331–332, 347–348); LXXII (327, 333, 355–356); LXXIII (332–345, 349–352); LXXIV (309–317, *passim*).

Palmer, R. R., and Colton, Joel. *A History of the Modern World.* 3rd ed. New York: Alfred A. Knopf, Inc., 1965.
I (7–115, *passim*); II (116–118, 122–125, 128–134, 138–145, 152–155); III (134–137, 146–150, 159–161); IV (155–159, 161–163); V (163–165, 167–170, 183); VI (176–179, 181–182, 184–185, 188); VII (170–175, 186–188); VIII (175, 179–184, 188–193); IX (193–198); X (198–206); XI (207–214, 218–220, 223–225, 228–230); XII (214–215, 225–228, 234–235, 248–251); XIII (230–233, 234–239, 241–244, 256–258, 268–270); XIV (211–212, 216–217, 239–241, 251–256, 309–312, 316–317); XV (231–232, 245–248, 264–282); XVI (260–263, 283–289); XVII (291–294); XVIII (295, 301–303); XIX (294–300, 303–308); XX (318–327); XXI (331–357).

Strayer, Joseph R.; Gatzke, Hans W.; and Harbison, E. Harris. *The Course of Civilization.* 2 vols. New York: Harcourt, Brace, & World, Inc., 1961.
I (7–23); II (24–44); III (45–58); IV (58–68, 73–74); V (69–77); VII (76–77, 86–87, 89); VIII (78–85); IX (87–96); X (97–99, 103–104, 108–109, 112–115); XI (96–97, 99–100, 102, 104–106, 112–115); XII (100–102, 104–106, 113–114, 116); XIII (116–122, 124–125); XIV (81–82, 84–85, 108–112, 123–124); XVI (116–118, 128–134); XVII (107–108, 118–123, 125–126, 133–134, 138–145); XVIII (133–136, 146–148, 152–155, 159–160, 165–166); XIX (136–137, 148–150, 155–157, 160–162, 184–186); XX (157–159, 161–170); XXI (170–174, 186–189); XXII (175–184, 190–193); XXIII (193–201); XXIV (201–206, 218–230, 234–235); XXV (207–217); XXVI (235–239, 242–244, 248–254); XXVII (186, 230–233, 256–260, 266–270); XXVIII (211–212, 215–217, 236–237, 239–242, 254–256, 258–259, 309–311, 314–316); XXIX (244–248, 260–266, 270–282); XXX (283–293, 295, 305–306); XXXI (295–305, 312–317, 335–336); XXXII (293–298, 306–308); XXXIII (318–329, 331–334, 345–348); XXXIV (334–357).

Wallbank, T. Walter; Taylor, Alastair M.; and Bailkey, Nels M. *Civilization, Past and Present.* 1-vol. ed. Chicago: Scott, Foresman and Company, 1962.
I (1–23); II (24–44); III (45–68); V (69–77); VI (86–96); VII (78–85); VIII (96–97, 109–111); IX (103–108); X (98–102, 112–115); XI (116–127); XII (128–134); XIII (138–145); XIV (146–157); XVI (134–137); XVII (170–174); XVIII (157–170, 177–186); XIX (176–177, 190–203, 220–222); XX (204–217, 312); XXI (218–220, 222–230); XXII (234–239, 241–253); XXIII (239–240, 244–245, 247–248, 251–252, 254–256, 260–263); XXIV (309–314); XXV (230–233, 256–260, 271–273, 276–278); XXVI (264–271, 273–276, 278–282); XXVII (283–290); XXVIII (291–295, 301–303); XXIX (332, 335, 338); XXX (296–300, 302–308, 318–325); XXXI (326–357); XXXII (310–317).

Wallbank, T. Walter, and Taylor, Alastair M. *Civilization, Past and Present.* 2 vols. 5th ed. Chicago: Scott, Foresman and Company, 1965.
Vol. I. I (1–6); II (7–23); IV (24–44); V (45–68); VII (69–77); VIII (78–82); IX (82–85); XI (86–89, 93–96); XII (89–91, 96–97, 109–111); XIII (91–92, 98–102, 112–115, 125–127); XIV (103–108, 119–124); XV (128–131); XVI (116–118, 132–134, 138–145); XVII (146–157); XIX 134–137); XX (170–173). *Vol. II.* I (159–163, 171–174); II (159–193); III (175–189, 207–208); IV (193–204); V (204–206, 218–220); VI (208–211); VII (220–230, 234–235); VIII (235–239, 241–251); IX (220–221, 230–233, 256–260, 276–278); X (264–271, 273–276, 278–282); XI (309–317); XII (239–256); XIII (212–217, 260–263); XIV (283–290); XV (291–295, 301–303); XVI (332, 335, 338); XVII (295–300, 302–308, 318–325); XVIII (326–357); Epilogue (310–317).

Chapter in Outline	Chapter Title	Brace	Brinton et al.	Bruun & Commager	Burns	Easton
I	Prehistoric Man		Vol. I 9–18	3–5	5–21	11–19
II	The Ancient Near Eastern Civilizations	5–7	18–46	5–7	30–34 38–65 66–85 86–99 100–137	24–50
III	The Civilization of the Ancient Greeks	7–12	49–92	7–9	144–186 188–204	52–86
IV	From City-State to World Empire—The Expansion of Rome	12–14	95–132	9–11	205–238 242–245	89–121
V	The Rise of the Christian Church and the Fall of the Roman Empire	14–20	132–138 141–171 173–180	11–12	238–242 250–262 270–273	125–139 141–156
VI	The Byzantine and Muslim Empires		211–257 345–349 361–369		277–305	158–177
VII	The Early Middle Ages to A.D. 1000	20–21	180–196 204–209		263–269 273–276	184–194 219–223 245–250 276–281
VIII	The High Middle Ages to the End of the Thirteenth Century	21–36	196–204 259–299 301–310 312–342	12–14 35–38 42–43	311–344 346–380	195–217 223–243 250–258 261–265 271–272 281–299
IX	The Late Middle Ages to 1500	39–54 62–63 85–94	310–312 349–361 393–417 426–435	27–29 33–34 39–41	416–417 444–446	258–261 265–271 273–275 299–303 314–317 333–337
X	The Renaissance and the Age of Discovery	58–60 63–83 94–101 102–130 183–186 193–197	417–426 439–475 561–582	18–26 43–58	383–436 484–506	307–333 337–346
XI	The Protestant Reformation and the Wars of Religion	131–154 156–171 175–183 186–193 239–247	479–512 515–537	59–81	438–444 445–475 506–513 533–538	346–371 379–386

TO STANDARD TEXTBOOKS

to pages

Ferguson & Bruun	Hayes et al.	Neill et al.	Palmer	Strayer et al.	Wallbank et al. 1 vol.	Wallbank et al. 2 vols.
3–12		9–24		*Vol. I* 6–10	9–14	*Vol. I* 17–30
14–25	4–15	26–46	3–4	10–37	15–35	33–60 95–101
26–50	17–27	47–77	4–8	40–73	37–63	101–128
51–76	29–39	78–96	8–10	77–114 115–131	64–88	129–160
77–114	41–48 52–75 87–98	97–110 112–133 135–146 149–162 262–267	10–16	114–115 131–135 138–165	120–137	193–216
116–137	77–86 99–109 150–151 222–225 297–298	163–191	16–17	214–238 406–417	159–184	221–240 245–268
138–157 171–174	117–129 141–150	193–232 311–315	17–22	193–212 240–273	139–148 200–201 214–217	240–244 303–319 335–344
158–170 174–180 182–272	131–137 139–140 153–170 174–222 227–259	234–246 248–261 267–278 280–310 315–338 340–353 355–368 370–385 450–453	22–42	276–308 313–340 345–370 417–423	148–157 186–198 201–214 217–220 223–243	319–334 344–391 396–410 414–417 419–421 422–423 426–430
274–322 340–346	264–297 325–333	387–404 406–422 424–440 453–467 469–472	43–49 60–64	371–402 423–436 492–495 500–512	248–265	410–414 418–419 421–422 426–427 431–432 465–470
323–339 343–356 364–370 451–470	299–310 313–323 346–349 407–408	442–450 467–468 473–490 576–587 591–601	49–60 89–104	468–492 495–497 540–553 567–569 572–580	267–289 349–353 362–382	434–465 527–538 554–587
372–387 399–408 413–419 442–450	339–346 351–380 383–389 395–407	492–511 513–575 611–626	64–88 104–117 120–131	512–537 553–559 562–567 598–606	291–323	470–486 499–516

Chapter in Outline	Chapter Title	Brace	Brinton *et al.*	Bruun & Commager	Burns	Easton
XII	The European State System in the Sixteenth and Seventeenth Centuries	55–58 198–238 247–251 267–276 287–296 309–331 346–359	369–391 540–557 597–636 *II*, 26–36	29–33 82–93 98–182	514–533 538–544 546–551 557–558 563–570	374–379 386–394 397–405 407–419 422–440 449–458 461–479 484–485
XIII	The Eighteenth Century —Age of Enlightenment	251–260 263–265 276–286 296–304 331–345 359–369 408–416	*II*, 15–25 36–46 49–80 85–93	186–256 270–317	551–557 558–562 573–582 590–593	386 394–397 405–407 419–422 440–446 458–460 479–484 486–490
XIV	The American and French Revolutions and Their Consequences	260–263 265–266 388–406 416–435 437–458 463–470 492–501	*I*, 582–594 *II*, 80–85 97–143 145–162	318–366 370–405 434–444	593–623 625–642 648–661 768–774	482–518 630–639
XV	The Early Industrial Revolution	370–386 599–612 615–619	*Vol. II* 11–13 187–219	366–370 419–421 428–434 445–452 582–599	663–680 695–709	567–582 588–596
XVI	Reaction, Reform, and Revolution, 1815–1850	470–492 503–518 528–530 535–538 560–565	162–184 224–225	406–415 458–475 480–483 490–495 501–502 512–516 519–537 634–641	643–647 711–721 728–730 774–777	523–545 549–554 559–565 598–605 608–613
XVII	Nationalism, Reform, and Steps toward War, 1850–1914	520–528 538–543 545–559 566–582 583–595 645–659 685–695	226–262 265–310 375–389	475–479 483–489 495–500 502–511 516–518 538–566 600–630 653–663	721–728 730–751 760–765 777–790 838–851	545–549 554–559 605–608 613–628 698–707
XVIII	The Growth of Imperialism in the Nineteenth Century	661–683	343–371	257–269 630–633 642–652 789–791	751–760 790–794	668–695
XIX	The First World War and the Peace Treaties	695–715	389–414	694–712 792–801	851–875	707–721
XX	The Long Armistice	720–742 744–764 778–813 815–830	417–457 459–501 503–535	713–789	877–915 918–937	723–755 757–784
XXI	A Century of Material Progress and Its Cultural Consequences	612–615 621–644 764–776	313–340 663–687	452–457 560–582 668–693	680–695 796–829 938–945 1016–1042	582–588 640–666 853–887
XXII	The Second World War and Its Aftermath	832–871	539–574	806–824	945–967 1002–1007	786–806
XXIII	The Postwar World	873–905	577–616 619–659	824–861	969–1002 1007–1014	807–851

to pages

Ferguson & Bruun	Hayes et al.	Neill et al.	Palmer	Strayer et al.	Wallbank et al. 1 vol.	Wallbank & Taylor 2 vols.
347–364 388–398 409–413 419–441 470–542 565–582	380–382 389–393 408–409 414–438 453–462 477–483 501–512	601–609 626–637 639–700 711–719 729–735	118–120 132–218 259–288	I, 559–562 581–598 II, 3–36 38–56	323–329 388–396 400–410 416–430	I, 488–499 513–519 587–607 II, 1–27 28–35 40–42 46–49 60–61
542–560 582–597	438–451 462–477 485–495 513–514 522–527	700–709 720–728 736–746 748–773	218–258 289–323	56–69 72–100	396–400 410–414 431–443 497–500	27–28 36–38 42–46 49–60 66–88
560–564 597–648 650–656	515–522 529–562 577–580	775–782 794–809 811–843 859–860 868–876	323–420 430–432	100–104 107–140 144–153 154–166	444–462 480–486 502–505	90–117 125–144
665–669 739–742 747–753	587–598 674–676	846–858 986–1000	421–430 432–436 465–468 495–502 567–577 589–596	194–233 337–350	382–384 470–480 486–497	64–73 150–184
656–664 669–688	562–571 580–582 599–608	783–792 843–845 860–868 878–907 924–928 938–940	436–465 469–495	153–154 166–191 284–293	463–466 505–521 597–598	140–148 188–220 262–278
689–736 754–767 780–786 793–804	608–631 637–660 685–692 699–709	908–923 928–936 940–985 1035–1044	502–548 555–567 577–589 607–612 627–635 657–670	236–281 293–313 332–337 367–373 377–385 398–414	523–541 543–565 598–608	211 221–243 359–395
768–779 786–792	660–670	1024–1035	548–554 613–627 635–657	313–329 385–398	594–595 608–610 613–639	260–262 279–313 410–423
806–831	711–734	1046–1080	670–703	414–416 421–434 439–455	644–658 660–662	431–459
832–916	734–736 739–763	1081–1100 1102–1151	704–827	434–439 455–463 466–495 509–549	658–660 662–664 666–687 689–708 710–726	461–486 513–534
742–745 919–932	582–586 671–674 676–683 736–737 853–874	1001–1023 1231–1250	596–607	350–366 495–505	567–590 774–796	597–607
933–948	768–795	1153–1179	827–850	553–584	726–739 744–748	534–549 563–567
949–1005	795–852 874–876	1179–1191 1193–1214 1216–1230	850–902	584–591 595–630 632–639	748–772	487–512 557–596

ABOUT THE AUTHOR

Stewart C. Easton, a native of England, spent two years at Oxford University, followed by a number of years devoted to business and to service in the Canadian army. He then received his B.A. from Ottawa University and his A.M. and Ph.D. from Columbia University. He taught history at City College, New York, from 1947 to 1960, retiring with the rank of Associate Professor. He is the author of *A Brief History of the Western World* (a Barnes & Noble Everyday Handbook), *Roger Bacon and His Search for a Universal Science, The Heritage of the Ancient World, The Heritage of the Past to 1500, The Heritage of the Past to 1715, Twilight of European Colonialism, Western Heritage,* and *The Rise and Fall of Western Colonialism* and co-author of *Charlemagne.*

1 *PREHISTORIC MAN*

By a long-accepted convention history falls into three more or less clearly defined periods—ancient, medieval, and modern. Ancient history begins about 3000 B.C. and ends with the "fall" of the Roman Empire in A.D. 476; medieval history stretches from the Fall of Rome to the end of the fifteenth century; and modern history, with subdivisions according to taste, extends from about the year 1500 to the present. Although objections may be raised to this undoubtedly arbitrary division, it remains in general use and obviously must be maintained in an outline such as the present work.

Distinction between History and Prehistory. Ancient history, however, does not itself begin with the first appearance of man on the earth. History, likewise by convention, in fact begins with man's own record of himself, as expressed through writing. There are several advantages to this convention. Clearly if everything that has ever happened to man anywhere at any time provides the raw material for the historian, then what happened before man began to write of his experiences is no less to be considered as history than what has happened since. But the events of preliterate times are to be inferred only from the material remains left by preliterate peoples, and there will forever be dispute concerning their meaning. Moreover, the discovery of such remains is dependent on the hazards of chance; new discoveries can wreak havoc among long-held inferences and theories. There is therefore legitimate reason to make a distinction between history and prehistory, the latter indeed the province of the separate disciplines of archaeology and anthropology. From the tentative findings of workers in these fields historians try to glean a few of the most probable facts concerning the ancestors, near and remote, of those men and women who built succeeding civilizations.

1

Ages of Prehistory. Prehistory in its turn has its conventional periods, based upon the kinds of tools and the age of the deposits found in the sites which have been investigated. The earliest period, lasting from the date of the first creatures that can properly be called men (say 1,000,000–500,000 B.C.) to about 50,000 B.C., is known as the Lower Paleolithic age. Some archaeologists distinguish a Middle Paleolithic age (about 150,000 B.C. to 50,000 B.C.). Others follow the Lower Paleolithic with an Upper Paleolithic which lasted from about 50,000 B.C. until perhaps 12,000 B.C., when a Mesolithic age is recognized by most archaeologists as a transitional period (12,000–7000 B.C.) between the Paleolithic age and the Neolithic age (7000–3000 B.C.).

The terms *Lower* and *Upper Paleolithic,* meaning earlier and later Paleolithic, refer to the strata of the earth in which the discoveries were made. The word *Paleolithic* itself means Old Stone, *Mesolithic,* Middle Stone, and *Neolithic,* New Stone. The terms have reference to the material from which almost all tools were made. Under such a classification, Bronze and Iron ages would naturally follow. However, it is now very doubtful that this is the most meaningful method of classifying these ages of prehistory since stone continued to be used for tools in some places (for example, Mexico and Peru) long after the science of metallurgy had emerged from its infancy. Moreover, what is called the *Neolithic Revolution,* which consisted of the transition from food gathering to food growing and the domestication of several important animals, is historically far more important than the relatively minor changes that took place in the art of tool making.

The science of geology, with subdivisions such as glaciology, attempts to trace the history of the earth to its remote beginnings in time, which beginnings are constantly being pushed back. It is now widely believed that the earth is close to two billion years old. In comparison with the age of his habitat, man is therefore a very recent newcomer. But in the period since he has been on earth, there have been many changes in its surface. The glaciers have advanced and receded; even now we have little reason to believe the process is at an end, and we may well be in a period which our descendants will think of as "interglacial." In accordance with the changing climate, men have tended to congregate in certain parts of the earth instead of in others. However the last (known as the Würm) glaciation, which took place some 50,000 years ago, marks fairly clearly the division between the Lower and Upper Paleolithic

ages. (All the earlier glaciations took place during the Lower Paleolithic period.) The growth of civilization since the Würm glaciation has been dependent upon the more temperate climate which followed, for it was this change in climate that made by far the greater part of the earth habitable by man.

Lower Paleolithic Men. It is still not at all certain how far back in time man can be traced. It should be understood that no complete human skeletons are available from remote antiquity. The comparative anatomist has therefore to reconstruct a picture of his prehistoric man from a few fossilized bones. This means not only that there is a wide margin for error or even fake (as in the famous case of Piltdown man, exposed in 1953), but also that there can be considerable difference of opinion over whether a particular skull or jawbone belongs to a true man or to a member of the ape family, perhaps no longer extant. Nevertheless, enough has been discovered to establish generally accepted hypotheses about some types.

Recent finds, especially in South Africa, have persuaded some archaeologists that true men did indeed exist before *Pithecanthropus erectus,* or Java man, who for more than a half-century from the discovery of the first jawbone in Java in 1891 was almost universally regarded as having absolute priority. Almost contemporary with Java man was *Sinanthropus pekinensis,* or Peking man, who already knew the use of fire. Best-authenticated among the next groups of men appear to be Swanscombe and Fontéchevade men (so called from the places where they were found in England and France, respectively), both of whom are regarded as very ancient, yet as having some characteristics that are typical of modern men. Widely distributed throughout the world is a later group of men called the Neandertaloid, after the first specimen found in the Neandertal Gorge in Germany and called Neandertal man. These men, who may have appeared as early as 200,000 B.C. though probably much later, differ widely among themselves but are regarded as basically similar to one another. They persisted until the Würm glaciation and may even have been either absorbed into or destroyed by the clearly *homo sapiens* type known as Cro-Magnon man.

All these prehistoric men of the Lower Paleolithic period with the possible exception of Pithecanthropus used tools. Though broken bones were used for tools as early as Peking man, the fundamental tool was a stone hand ax; a variation of this was a kind of all-purpose tool known as the *coup de poing,* something between a pick and an ax that resembled a human fist. The axes were made either by flaking or trimming an original block of stone to the desired shape. The presence of such tools provides sufficient proof that prehistoric men were already using their intelligence to aid them in living. Man being the least specialized of all living creatures, without this intelligence he would have remained at the mercy of the more dangerous and specialized larger animals with which he disputed the possession of his habitat. From Java man onward to Neandertal man, the cranial capacity of men during the Lower Paleolithic period appears to have developed considerably, making possible a larger and presumably more versatile brain—although it should not be thought that there is an exact correlation between brain size and thinking capacity. But the Neandertaloids, with large brow-ridges, low foreheads, and receding chins, differed in many respects from modern man; indeed, it seems probable that they did not walk fully upright. None of these Lower Paleolithic men are believed to have been direct ancestors of modern man.

Upper Paleolithic Men. With the appearance of Cro-Magnon men (30,000–25,000 B.C.) we reach the type that is clearly *homo sapiens*—modern man. As his achievements demonstrate, he had already ceased to devote all his attention to the hard business of providing himself with food, clothing, and shelter. Indeed, it now becomes for the first time possible to differentiate cultural periods and to trace the development and ultimate decline of an art form peculiar to prehistoric man, the painting of animals on the walls of caves, the best-known of which are in northern Spain (Altamira) and southern France (Lascaux). The most technically expert of these paintings were produced during the period known as Magdalenian and may be dated about 10,000 B.C. They evidently represented the culmination of millennia of artistic work. Though their purpose is still, and no doubt always will be, a matter for speculation, it is widely believed that they represent a species of sympathetic magic, by which the artist or magician below ground painted his animals while the hunters above ground attempted to kill them. Other achievements of this age were the improvement of stone tools; the more sophisticated use of bone, antler, and ivory for the making of specialized tools; and the use of the awl and thread.

It is not possible with any certainty to infer from extant discoveries the nature of the religion, if any, of prehistoric man. What is clear is that ever greater attention was given to the burial of the dead, both in the preparation of the corpses for burial and in the manner of their interment. Such practices persisted into historic times, and we know from later written accounts that they were then connected with the belief in an afterlife. Though we shall probably never know anything definite of the actual beliefs of pre-literate men, evidence from the paintings and burial ceremonies does appear to suggest that their horizons were no more circumscribed by the immediately perceptible than have been those of other peoples in the centuries since.

Mesolithic Men. The period immediately preceding the Neo-lithic Revolution was marked by the beginning of the domestication of some animals, notably the dog. Tools were considerably improved, especially with the introduction of microliths, small sharp stones which could be fitted onto hafts made of wood and other materials, thus making possible the manufacture of greatly improved weapons such as the harpoon. The bow and arrow as weapons are also first authenticated from the Mesolithic age. During this period man turned to the sea for additional nourishment, as evidenced especially by the extensive remains of consumed shellfish.

Neolithic Men. While tools continued to be improved during the next period, the outstanding achievement, deserving to be called a true revolution, was the change from food gathering to food grow-ing, accompanied by the domestication of animals used for food and as beasts of burden. Instead of forever wandering in search of food, men could now lead a settled life, thus establishing the basis for civilization. It is not known where the "revolution" began, though it was probably in the Near East, perhaps in present-day Iran. It quickly spread to Egypt (if it did not as is possible begin there). It was however only after many centuries that food growing spread to Europe. Agriculture in America was probably of independent origin. Late in the Neolithic age, no doubt as a result of the in-creased leisure made possible by a settled mode of life, many new techniques were invented, including spinning, weaving, the making of pottery, and the use of the potter's wheel. The wheel, indeed, was probably used in pottery long before anyone thought of using it for transportation. At the end of the period (about 3000 B.C.) writing was invented in the Near East and Egypt, ushering in his-tory, properly so called. By this time tools of materials other than stone were beginning to be made in some places. Copper, which can be used almost in its natural state, was first. Then it was discovered that by the application of heat an alloy could be created which was far more efficient than the unalloyed metal. Bronze, an alloy of copper and tin, thus came into use. It remained supreme for several thousand years until it was replaced by iron, which, although much cheaper and more abundant, required much higher temperatures (reached by man-made devices), before it could be smelted into a usable metal. The plow is first authenticated in the Bronze Age.

Thus by the beginning of history the fundamental inventions and techniques had been discovered which led to the rise of those true civilizations to be discussed in the next chapter.

THE ANCIENT NEAR EASTERN CIVILIZATIONS

It was in the river valleys that the first true civilizations arose. In Egypt, watered by the river Nile, a single civilization flourished from at least 3000 B.C. (the date of the unification of Upper and Lower Egypt is still uncertain) until 525 B.C. (After 525 the country was ruled by alien conquerors until the twentieth century.) In Mesopotamia, watered by the Tigris and Euphrates, several different peoples ruled the land in succession. Sometimes it was not unified at all, but consisted of a number of independent city-states. But until the conquest of Mesopotamia in the sixth century B.C. by the Persians, who already possessed a separate culture and language, the various conquests made little difference in the culture and religion of the inhabitants. All their successors were recognizably indebted to the first settlers, the Sumerians, for their basic law, religion, science, literature, and almost all the components of their cultural heritage.

We, however, are probably more greatly indebted to a relatively minor people of the ancient Near East than to either Egypt or Mesopotamia. To the Hebrews almost all of us in the West owe our fundamental religious concepts and an appreciable part of our law and literature. To the lesser peoples who are considered in this chapter we owe little except our alphabet. But the sum total of our debt to the peoples of the ancient Near East as the progenitors of Western civilization is incalculable and ensures the inclusion of their achievements even in a book otherwise exclusively devoted to the West.

EGYPT

The most remarkable feature of ancient Egypt was the general stability of the country. Although the fall of the Old Kingdom was followed by a period of virtual anarchy and the Middle Kingdom was brought to an end by a conquest by foreigners, these periods were relatively short and involved no fundamental changes in the social structure of the country. As soon as the native monarchy was restored, the old political forms were revived, and the king became once more a king-god as at the time of unification.

The great event from which the Egyptians date their history is the unification of Upper and Lower Egypt by a man whom the Greeks called Menes, but it has not proved possible for scholars to identify him as any particular ruler. The word, indeed, may be a title rather than a personal name. Prior to unification there were many neolithic settlements in the Nile Valley, where pottery was produced that was almost the equal of any that came later. There is evidence that astronomical observations were made that were used by the priests and kings of the later monarchy; the Egyptian calendar, so necessary for agriculture in a land where the great annual event was the inundation of the Nile, was probably in use long before unification. But the great ruling concepts of all Egyptian civilization cannot be traced back for certain any further than "Menes."

The unification of Egypt and the establishment of Memphis in Lower Egypt as the capital of the country brought into being what is always known as the Old Kingdom of Egypt, a period that lasted until about 2200 B.C., a time span of close to a thousand years. Most of the great achievements of Egyptian civilization belong to the Old Kingdom.

Rulers. The government of the country was an absolute autocracy. The ruler, or Pharaoh (meaning "Great House"), was believed to be a god who was divinely inspired. Every official held office only during his pleasure, and he was responsible for securing a blessed afterlife for his servants. It was he who arranged for the rise of the Nile through his divine power. At this period it was customary for Pharaohs to marry their sisters or other close relatives, thus ensuring the continuance of the royal line in the same family. Even so, a particular royal family died out in time, thus giving rise to the numbered dynasties, an invention of later Egyptian historians and unknown to the actual rulers themselves.

The Pyramids. The Old Kingdom, according to these later calculations, comprises the first six dynasties. By the end of the Third Dynasty the Pharaohs were already beginning to build pyramids as the eternal home of their bodies after death. Hence the period from the Third to the Sixth Dynasties, during which each reigning Pharaoh attempted to build a pyramid for himself is known

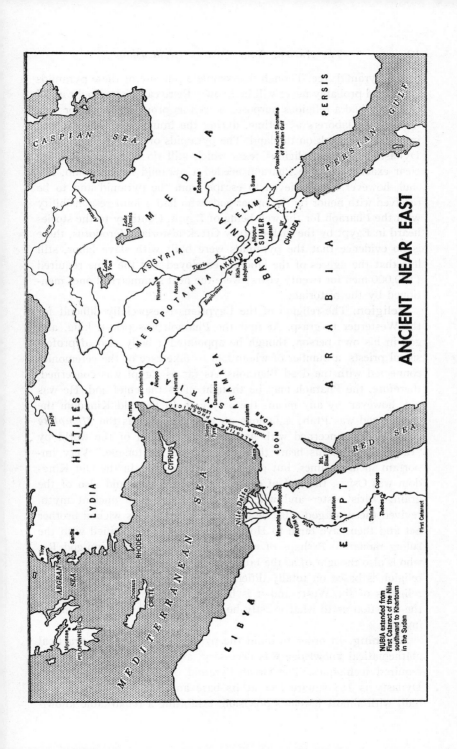

ANCIENT NEAR EAST

NUBIA extended from
First Cataract of the Nile
southward to Khartoum
in the Sudan

as the Pyramid Age. Though the complete purpose of these pyramids is not and probably never will be known, there can be no doubt at all that they had a religious purpose, as well as providing work for vast numbers of laborers at a time, during the inundation, when it was impossible to work on the land. The pyramids of the Fifth and Sixth Dynasties contain religious texts which still do not make it quite clear exactly why the Pharaoh needed a pyramid for his tomb. His soul, however, was believed to escape from the pyramid and to be received with honor by the upper gods who had a joint responsibility with the Pharaoh for the well-being of Egypt. Contrary to the stories heard in Egypt by the fifth-century Greek historian Herodotus, there is no evidence that the pyramids were built with slave labor, still less that the figures of the laborers employed and the time required (100,000 men for twenty years) were the neat symmetrical ones mentioned by the historian.

Religion. The religion of the Egyptians is especially difficult for the Westerner to grasp. At first the Pharaoh was priest, king, and god in his own person, though he appointed a body also of professional priests, a number of whom had to take care of the ceremonies connected with the dead Pharaohs. As far as Egypt was concerned, therefore, the Pharaoh may be thought of as the chief god. He was not, however, by any means the only god. In the Old Kingdom the creator-god was Ptah; a famous document known as the *Memphite Theology* is concerned with him and his creation of the world by "the thought of his heart that appeared on his tongue." Very important in later times, but perhaps less important in the Old Kingdom was Osiris, the god of death and resurrection, and also of the grain. Osiris' sister and wife Isis, according to an ancient myth, revived the dead god after he had been killed by his wicked brother Set and then gave birth to Horus, who is always identified with the ruling monarch. Perhaps of equal importance was the sun-god Re, who is also thought of as the father of the Pharaoh. Clearly Egyptian religion is based on totally different premises from the monotheistic religions of the West; and it is likely that to an ancient Egyptian the question as to what exactly he *believed* would have been meaningless.

Learning. In order to build the pyramids a very exact practical mathematical knowledge was necessary, as well as command of the required techniques. The Great Pyramid of Khufu of the Fourth Dynasty is 755 square feet at its base and 481 feet high, and is built with almost jeweler's precision, exhibiting a remarkable knowledge of astronomy as well as of geometry. However, ancient mathematical treatises are extant, from which it is clear that the Egyptian mathematician had not yet learned to theorize and generalize, though his practical knowledge was unique. A system of writing was also developed which took two forms, the *hieroglyphic* (picture writing) used when stone had to be chiseled, and *hieratic*, a cursive form of the same writing made with a reed on papyrus, which soon became stylized so that the original pictures could no longer be recognized. In late Egypt a still more rapid script was invented, known as the *demotic*. The writing in time came to incorporate the "rebus" principle, under which each symbol represents a syllable or sound. But the Egyptians themselves did not go so far as to produce an alphabet. (The Egyptians were fortunate in that they had good writing materials, including the papyrus made from a reed that grew in the marshes. The use of a stylus and papyrus was far less cumbersome than the cuneiform method developed by the Sumerians and their successors.)

In Old Kingdom Egypt promotion depended on the favor of the Pharaoh, and noble birth was not a requirement for the attainment of even the highest positions in the land. Egyptian documents suggest that the relatively small population was able to live with a fair degree of comfort on the fertile land, that even a poor man could hope for evenhanded justice from the Pharaoh and his officials, and that the ordinary man wished for nothing better than that the afterlife should be a replica of this.

First Intermediate Period and the Middle Kingdom (*c*. 2200–1792 B.C.). Throughout the Old Kingdom the Egyptian provinces, or *nomes*, were ruled by nobles who were the nominees of the Pharaoh. During the Sixth Dynasty—especially during the later years of the long reign of Pepi II (died about 2200 B.C.)—the control exercised by the central government weakened, and these nobles began to make their own decisions without reference to the Pharaoh. It does not appear that they ever made a concerted rebellion against their master, but royal absolutism began to collapse. The country was no longer effectively defended against encroaching neighbors, and for almost two hundred years the Pharaoh ceased to wield any substantial authority in the periphery of his territories. Abandoning Memphis, he moved his capital to Heracleopolis in central Egypt, while Thebes, the leading city of Upper Egypt, was virtually independent. Eventually a prince of Upper Egypt put an end to the rule of the feeble titular monarchs and reunified the kingdom. The

Eleventh and Twelfth Dynasties which thus began comprise the Middle Kingdom, whose capital was Thebes.

It seems clear from the evidence that the nobles who had exercised the power during the Intermediate Period never altogether lost it during the Middle Kingdom, and the absolutism of the former Pharaohs was somewhat modified. Nobles were now buried with a ceremony formerly reserved for their masters, and they copied some of the Pyramid Texts for their own obsequies. After an effort by two of the Middle Kingdom monarchs to build pyramids, this type of enterprise was abandoned forever. The country was once again prosperous under the unified rule, and on the whole the Middle Kingdom achievements in the field of art and especially in craftsmanship were never equaled in Egyptian history. There is also a considerable body of literature extant from the period, most of it composed of popular stories from daily life.

The Hyksos and the New Kingdom (c. 1800–1090 B.C.). The last kings of the Twelfth Dynasty, like the kings of the Sixth, were feeble rulers who could not hold their kingdom together. But this time, after a short period of semianarchy, a successful invasion was launched against Egypt by a people from Asia known as the *Hyksos,* or Foreigners. The Hyksos were never accepted by the Egyptians as legitimate rulers, nor did they establish their complete authority over Upper Egypt, whose princes paid them a merely nominal allegiance. The Thirteenth through the greater part of the Seventeenth Dynasties were Hyksos dynasties. Again it was a prince of Thebes, Ahmose I, who overthrew the alien rulers and once more unified the country. He was the founder of the great Eighteenth Dynasty, which began to rule in 1570 B.C.

For many years the monarchs of the New Kingdom (Eighteenth to Twentieth Dynasties) occupied themselves in consolidating their rule. It was during this period that the famous queen Hatshepsut ruled the country through several rather shadowy Pharaohs (about 1520 to 1480 B.C.). Then Thutmose III, nominal coruler with his stepmother Hatshepsut from the beginning of the century, made the decision to expand the frontiers of Egypt, perhaps for strategic reasons and to prevent another such debacle as the Hyksos conquest. This monarch was uniformly successful, conquering as far as the river Euphrates in Mesopotamia. His successors, however, had to restore some of the conquered territories, as their resources were overextended. In particular Amenhotep IV (1375–1358 B.C.), the religious revolutionary who took the name of Akhenaton, paid far less attention to the military needs of his empire than to his own building and religious programs. He gave so little support to his governors that they were hard put to maintain their positions. The so-called Tel-el-Amarna correspondence between the governors and the Pharaoh gives a vivid picture of conditions during his reign. The military position was somewhat restored by Horemhab, founder of the Nineteenth Dynasty and his successors, especially Rameses II (1292–1225 B.C.). But the latter monarch, whose mania for building used up resources Egypt could no longer spare with impunity, was almost defeated by the Hittites at the Battle of Kadesh, and thereafter made the first written treaty known to history (1271 B.C.), which was more favorable to the Hittites than to the Egyptians. Rameses III (1198–1167 B.C.) had difficulty in repulsing a new group of invaders, the "Peoples of the Sea," and after his reign Egypt was confined more or less within her ancient boundaries. With the end of the Twentieth Dynasty the New Kingdom came to an end and the period of foreign invasions and precipitous decline began.

The Last Period (*c.* 1090–525 B.C.). Successive dynasties followed during which Libyans, Nubians, and Ethiopians ruled the country, though they did not actually conquer it. The Assyrians, expanding from their base in northern Mesopotamia under Esarhaddon, conquered Egypt in 671 B.C. and formed it into an Assyrian province. But an Assyrian-appointed governor made himself independent after the destruction of Assyria by the Babylonians and their allies. This Dynasty (Twenty-sixth) even tried to rebuild the Egyptian empire, but failed somewhat ignominiously. In 525 B.C. Egypt was subjugated by Cambyses, king of Persia, who made it a Persian province. During the next century some adventurers succeeded for a period in shaking off Persian rule (Twenty-eighth and Twenty-ninth Dynasties), but the country returned to Persian suzerainty until it was conquered without bloodshed by Alexander the Great in 336 B.C. Thereafter it was ruled by one of Alexander's generals who took the name of Ptolemy I. Thus began the Thirtieth Dynasty, which lasted until the final conquest in A.D. 30 by the Romans, who made it the most prosperous province of their empire.

Consequences of the Imperial Phase. The winning of an empire by the Egyptians had a profound effect on the social and religious life of the country. There was a great increase of slavery, since prisoners of war were usually enslaved, thus depressing the standard of living of the free Egyptians who had to compete with them. The rich grew richer and the poor poorer. Power tended to gravitate into the hands of the priests, not only those of Amon-Re, who was the patron of the Egyptian monarchy during the Empire and supported Egyptian arms, but also those of Osiris, lord of the dead. Though the Pharaoh was still regarded as a god, this was probably a myth supported by the priests rather than a matter of belief on the part of the people. Too many rulers in the not far distant past had clearly lacked the powers of the gods, having even to submit to conquest by foreigners. Nevertheless, Amon-Re as imperial war-god had to be worshiped; and when Egyptian arms were successful the priests were enriched by the monarch, to the extent that they came to own a sizable proportion of the land. During the last period of Egyptian independence some priests even became Pharaohs themselves. The Pharaoh Akhenaton attempted to abolish the worship of Amon-Re in favor of a single supreme god of his own preference, Aton, the sun-disc. Though his power was enough to compel this reform for his own lifetime, as soon as he was in his grave the priests restored the worship of Amon-Re.

Meanwhile the cult of Osiris was increasing. Everyone who could afford it arranged for his body to be mummified after death. His mummy was provided with charms and spells purchased from the priests to ensure successful passage past the dangers of the underworld and beyond the judgment hall of Osiris, in which a man's heart was weighed and sentence pronounced. The Egyptian was taught especially the Declaration of Innocence, which enabled him to give the right answers to the gods who inquired whether he had perpetrated certain offenses during his lifetime. The Declaration is valuable insofar as it depicts those offenses considered socially reprehensible in ancient Egypt *—especially since no code of Egyptian laws is extant such as exist for many periods of Mesopotamian history. When Herodotus visited Egypt it was his opinion that no people was more "religious" than the Egyptians, as evidenced by the enormous number of ceremonies, including the mummification of cats, that he observed there.

Cultural Life of Late Egypt. There was little innovation of any other kind in late Egypt. Medical knowledge, however, was con-

---

* For example: I have not defrauded the oppressed one of his property; I have not done that which is an abomination to the gods; I have not defrauded the temples of their offerings; I have not driven off the cattle from the property of the gods—as well as such general disclaimers as: I have not done evil to mankind; I have not caused pain; I have done no murder, nor ordered murder to be done by others.

siderable and surgical techniques advanced—furthered by the cult of the dead and the process of embalming. The rulers of the New Kingdom were great builders, with a special taste for the colossal. Art continued to be formal, and the statues stylized, especially those of the monarchs—with the notable exception of the religious reformer Akhenaton, who sponsored a naturalistic movement in art and had no apparent objection to being depicted as he was in life. There was a marked taste for antiquarianism in late Egypt and for the copying of old documents and inscriptions. Egypt was now a poor country, and tomb robberies were frequent. It is perhaps not surprising that a people which had ceased to be culturally creative should also have succumbed to foreign conquest. The people, indeed, were probably more interested in the afterlife than in the present one and could not muster the self-confidence needed to defend what they had remaining to them against their more dynamic contemporaries.

MESOPOTAMIA

In the land between the great rivers, the Tigris and the Euphrates, many different peoples lived in the millennia prior to the Persian conquest in the sixth century B.C. This land, which has no natural boundaries, was frequently fought over, and several empires with a high degree of unity flourished for limited periods. The various conquerors mingled with the older inhabitants, but all except the Sumerians can be safely regarded as Semitic peoples.

The Sumerians. The earliest inhabitants of the Tigris and Euphrates valleys were a people who called themselves the "black-headed people" and are known to us as the Sumerians. We first hear of them living in temple communities ruled by a priest-king as the representative of the city god, who was the real owner of the land. These communities evolved into true city-states, each with its own laws, some of which are extant and constitute the earliest known law codes. In time the rulers (*ensi*) by aggression or peaceably united their cities with others. Thus came into existence the *lugal*, or ruler of several cities, with ensis under him. Each city continued to have its own god, while the god of the lugal became the chief god of the area.

The Sumerians were the founders of Mesopotamian civilization, and almost all their beliefs and practices were transmitted to their successors. The Sumerians had a creation story, according to which man was created for the purpose of serving the gods (and thus was in a sense their slave). This story was elaborated by the Amorites and Assyrians but never fundamentally changed. Likewise the Epic of Gilgamesh contains the prototype of the Flood story that appears in the Bible and is found also in Amorite and Assyrian versions. The epic is concerned with the adventures of a Sumerian ensi, Gilgamesh, who wanders over the earth and through the underworld in search of the plant of immortality and wins it, only to have it stolen from him by a serpent.

The Sumerians invented cuneiform writing, which was used for many centuries by the later Mesopotamian peoples. It consisted of symbols (originally derived from pictures but quickly stylized) cut into damp clay and then baked for permanence. Ultimately a cuneiform alphabet was invented; but the cumbersome nature of cuneiform records made inevitable their replacement by papyrus and other forms of paper, on which symbols could be made with writing instruments. The Sumerians divided the circle into 360 degrees, a method followed by all later peoples, and devised a mathematical system of symbols based on the number 60, which was the forerunner of our own decimal system based on the number 10.

The religious notions of the Sumerians, though they appear primitive to us, greatly influenced those of the Hebrews. The importance of the Sumerian and later Mesopotamian religions lies in the fact that the peoples believed that the gods were concerned with the doings of their servants on earth, even though they were not especially interested in what the Hebrews thought of as morality. Since men were believed to be servants or slaves of the gods it was essential for them to discover what the gods desired of them. This was accomplished by means of various forms of divination, the examination of the entrails of animals and birds, and the interpretation of dreams, especially those of the gods' representative on earth, the ensi. These efforts ultimately led to the use of astrology as the best means of ascertaining what was likely to happen, enabling the king and people to make efforts to avert presaged disaster. Since astrology required accurate observation of the stars, this pseudo-science led to astronomy, in which the later Mesopotamian peoples excelled. The pyramidical structure known as the *ziggurat,* the temple of the Sumerians and other Mesopotamian peoples, was especially useful for obtaining correct astronomical observations.

The existence of many early law codes in the Sumerian cities makes it clear that there was a high degree of political and social organization in the city-states, and many enjoyed considerable prosperity. The Sumerians were skilled metal workers, and textiles were woven, especially in factories connected with the temples. Numerous business records are extant, showing that there was a considerable seaborne traffic, especially from the city of Ur, which is now more than a hundred miles inland but was then a seaport. The Sumerians used the wheeled cart and the plow; they were evidently skilled husbandmen; and dairying was a common small business. Irrigation was extensively used, and canals had to be kept in working order by the peasants, about whose lives naturally little is known —though it is clear that both slaves and freemen worked on the land, most of the latter as tenant farmers. This Sumerian social and economic structure persisted with little change throughout Mesopotamian history in spite of the many changes of rulers in the area.

The Accadians. In the middle of the third millennium B.C., Sargon of Agade subjugated all the Sumerian city-states and built an empire that stretched to the Mediterranean. This empire, however, did not endure very long. It was succeeded by a loose rule by a barbarian people known as the Guti, who effectively controlled only a part of the country. Most of the Sumerian city-states recovered their independence. Ur, a Sumerian city, was able to subjugate some of the other cities and rule them, thus in part inheriting the empire of Sargon. Sargon had been a Semite, and the language of his people, known as Accadian, gradually replaced the Sumerian language, which became extinct.

Amorite Rule of Mesopotamia. Soon after 2000 B.C., a desert people called the Amorites conquered all Mesopotamia and established Babylon as their capital. The sixth king of this line, Hammurapi, or Hammurabi, attempted to establish a legal system applicable to the whole of his dominions. This code is of great interest because it is the only complete legal codification extant from the ancient Orient, and for scope was not equaled until the great codes of the Roman Empire. Lacking the refinements of the Roman codes, it assumes that the king's duty is to provide laws and establish legal procedures for all fields of human activity. Judges, petitioners, and defendants were all expected to go to the code to discover what was required of them and what protections they possessed. The code regulated numerous commercial practices, including the treatment of debts and debtors, the behavior of tavern keepers, inheritance and adoption, the responsibilities and fees due to doctors and builders, the payment of damages in case of accident and similar matters, together with the punishment for crimes against individuals and the state. In general the code adopted the strictest principles of retributive justice, "an eye for an eye and a tooth for a tooth," though it made distinctions between punishments meted out to nobles, commoners, and slaves. Crimes committed by nobles might be more severely punished than those committed by members of the lower classes—though if slaves or commoners assaulted their betters they were treated more severely, possibly because they lacked the means to make money payments in compensation. Fines, amputation, and the death penalty were used as punishment, since as yet there was no thought that mere deprivation of liberty through imprisonment was a suitable retribution for crimes against property or the state.

The Hammurabi Code was obviously designed for use in a centralized empire, which was now provided with a valuable instrument for unity. But the empire did not survive for long after Hammurabi's reign. It was overthrown by the Kassites about 1600 B.C. or somewhat earlier. The Kassites, however, could not establish effective rule over the old Babylonian Empire, although they continued to control Babylon. Much of the old empire enjoyed relative independence until the rise of the warlike Assyrians, formerly a weak pastoral people in the north.

The Assyrian Empire. A succession of Assyrian rulers early in the first millennium B.C., perhaps tired of being at the mercy of their southern neighbors, undertook to build the most powerful war machine in the Near Eastern world. They were thus able over the course of three hundred years to build and administer a mighty empire. At the height of their power they ruled all Palestine except for tiny Judah, which paid tribute to them; Egypt at least as far south as Thebes; and the valleys of the Tigris and Euphrates. Their numbers, however, were too small to enable them to withstand a coalition of Babylonians, Medes, and Scythians organized against them. The Assyrian capital, Nineveh, fell to the coalition in 612 B.C., and the remainder of the empire was destroyed in 606.

The Neo-Babylonian Empire. The conquerors proceeded to partition the territory, Babylon falling to the share of the people usually called the Chaldeans, who were in fact the same people that had been subjected by the Assyrians. Under King Nebuchadnezzar (605–561 B.C.) they rebuilt an empire based on Babylon and this time incorporated Judah into their domains. This empire achieved a short-lived prosperity during which the monarchs re-built Babylon, including the famous "hanging gardens." The last king, Nabonidus, showed more interest in religion than in defense, and the output of religious literature during the period was considerable, suggesting interests similar to those of the later Egyptians. At all events the Chaldeans did not offer much resistance to the next conqueror, Cyrus, king of Persia, who captured Babylon in 538 B.C.

THE PERSIAN EMPIRE

After the breakup of the Assyrian Empire, the Medes, who belonged to the victorious coalition, kept for themselves the eastern parts of the empire. But after a short time they were absorbed by the Persians, a people from the east with an Indo-European language, whose leader Cyrus became king of the Medes and Persians (550–530 B.C.). In addition to the whole of the Babylonian Empire, Cyrus conquered Asia Minor, while his successor Cambyses added Egypt. The remaining Jews were allowed to return to Palestine by Cyrus and his successors, though the land remained under Persian suzerainty. When Darius I (the Great) became king in 521 B.C., he consolidated the whole of these vast dominions into the most efficient and largest empire known up to this time.

Copying much of his system from his Assyrian predecessors, Darius established four capitals, including one at Sardis in Asia Minor (formerly belonging to Lydia), between which he established an imperial postal system carried along well-maintained roads. Local governors called *satraps* exercised his authority in the provinces, watched by imperial officials responsible directly to the monarch. A relatively small permanent and well-trained army known as the Immortals was ready for duty anywhere in the empire, while levies could be pressed into service for major expeditions, including those made against the Greek mainland in the fifth century B.C.

The Persians brought with them into their empire a new religion, developed in their eastern territories, which differed in all respects from the older religions of Mesopotamia. Though they left these religions intact, in due time the Persian religion became predominant in most of the empire. To the Persians there was one great god Ahura-Mazda, the god of light and the sun, who was interested in the moral deeds of humanity. Over against him was a wicked god Ahriman of almost equal power. The world was the scene for an epic struggle between these two powers, and it was the task of men to help Ahura-Mazda to defeat the lord of darkness. In contrast to the views set forth in the religions of Mesopotamia, there was a future life of happiness awaiting the righteous, and punishment awaiting the wicked in the realm of Ahriman. A great prophet, Zoroaster, who probably lived in the seventh century B.C., preached this religion; and his teachings have been incorporated in the Persian holy book, the Avesta.

The Persian Empire survived for a little over two centuries, to be overthrown by Alexander the Great as described in Chapter 3.

LESSER PEOPLES OF WESTERN ASIA

Meanwhile other peoples had built civilizations in the lands outside the Tigris and Euphrates valleys. Most powerful were the Hittites (or Hattians) in Asia Minor in the second millennium B.C. For a time they disputed possession of Palestine with the Egyptians, and at one period they even conquered Babylon, though they were not strong enough to keep it. They are noted for developing the use of iron, of which they had a virtual monopoly for a long time. The light war chariot appears to have been one of their inventions. They had law codes equal or superior to those of Mesopotamia. It is not yet known why the Hittite Empire collapsed in the thirteenth century B.C.; after that time there does not appear to have been any organized Hittite kingdom, though the people survived as a group under other rulers.

The Lydians, another people of Asia Minor, are credited with the invention of coined money. More important were the Phoenicians and Aramaeans, the great traders of the Near East, the former mainly by sea and the latter by land.

The Phoenicians ruled the coastal cities of Tyre, Sidon, and Byblos and voyaged extensively throughout the Mediterranean. They are even credited with the feat of circumnavigating the continent of Africa. A Phoenician colony, Carthage, survived to contest the power of Rome.

The Greeks believed that the Phoenicians had invented the alphabet. Modern research, however, does not support this claim, though the Greeks may have taken their own from the incomplete Phoenician one. In fact, the Greek alphabet itself is the first complete one, including a full complement of consonants and vowels. But, as far as is now known, the original alphabet was developed by a Canaanite people to the south of the Phoenicians at least as early as the middle of the second millennium B.C. The oldest extant writings making use of an alphabet are from Ugarit, one of the small ancient kingdoms of the Canaanites.

The Aramaean capital was Damascus, the oldest continuously inhabited city in the world, and the Aramaeans were the people known as the Syrians in the Bible. With or without a capital under their control, they made their living from the caravan trade, traveling especially into Mesopotamia. The Semitic language of Aramaic, the common language of the area, was spoken by Jesus Christ.

THE HEBREWS

The Hebrews would not merit special attention if it were not for their unique religious and literary heritage. They were a Canaanite people, a number of whom, the descendants of the patriarch Abraham, migrated to Egypt, where after perhaps a few centuries of freedom they were enslaved by the Pharaohs. Led out of Egypt by Moses, they had been promised the land of Canaan by their God Yahweh. But in the time of Moses they were unable to enter Canaan and had to remain in the bordering desert lands. Thereafter under the leadership of Joshua and others they conquered Canaan by the sword and established a kingdom there, bringing their fellow Canaanites under their sway. They established a united monarchy under David and his son Solomon (*c.* 973–933 B.C.), but after the death of Solomon, the country was divided into two. The larger and more prosperous northern kingdom of Israel was incorporated into the Assyrian Empire at the end of the eighth century; a century and a half later the mountainous but more easily defended (as well as less desirable) southern kingdom of Judah fell to the Chaldeans, who took most of the inhabitants of its capital Jerusalem into exile in Babylon. At first only the leading citizens were deported (597 B.C.), but after a rebellion by King Zedekiah, who had been placed on the throne by Nebuchadnezzar, all but the poorest peasants were taken to Babylon to join their compatriots (*c.* 586 B.C.).

When the Persians captured Babylon in 538 B.C., they allowed most of the surviving Jewish exiles to return. These men built a priestly state, which existed by courtesy of the Persian rulers. In 332 B.C. Alexander the Great took the country without difficulty from the Persians, and for a time his successors adopted the Persian policy of noninterference with the Jewish state and religion. When Antiochus (Epiphanes) IV attempted to force Greek customs on the country, a successful full-scale rebellion broke out under the Maccabean family (168 B.C.), and the country maintained a precarious independence until it fell to the Roman Pompey in 63 B.C. Thereafter it was incorporated into the Roman Empire.

Though several of the Canaanite peoples had approached closely to the idea of one God, and though Akhenaton of Egypt insisted that his god Aton was the supreme lord of the universe, it was the Hebrew belief that has prevailed in the Western world. No doubt the Hebrew concept of monotheism developed slowly, as the tribal god of the wilderness gave place to a God to whom all men are responsible, who had created the universe and all that was in it. This idea was voiced most strongly by the prophets, religious leaders directly inspired by Yahweh to proclaim his messages, often directed to the monarchs who had succumbed to the temptation of worshiping the gods of the Canaanite peoples. The God worshiped by the Hebrews was very different from other gods in that he demanded righteousness from men and he gave his "chosen" people the Law, a series of commandments, some ritual and some ethical, which they were enjoined to keep. The Hebrews, as God's people, were expected to retain a higher standard of ethical behavior than other gods expected of theirs. All the Biblical stories, though some were clearly based on Mesopotamian originals, had a moral basis which changed their character. All have passed into the heritage of Western civilization, through Christianity, which has adopted the Old Testament as its own. Monotheism, as developed by the Hebrews (called Jews following their return from Babylon), passed likewise into the religion of Islam.

After the exile in Babylon, the Jewish leaders gave profound thought to the problem of why, in spite of God's promises, they had lost their kingdom and had apparently been singled out for punishment rather than for rewards. Out of this thought arose the idea of the Messiah, or Redeemer, whom the Christians took to be their Founder, Jesus Christ. But also as a result of the Exile came the belief that the people had been punished because they had strayed from the path laid out for them by God. On their return to Jerusalem, therefore, the leaders made the people swear an oath to obey the Law, and the new state became a theocratic one, with its head the high priest. The ritual also was carefully systematized, and those books (especially the first five, known as the Torah or Pentateuch) of the Bible which contained the Law, the history of the people, and the teachings of the prophets, were re-edited and canonized as sacred. They were passed on to the West through Christianity.

THE MINOAN CIVILIZATION

Last to be discussed in this chapter is an important civilization based on the island of Crete, about which relatively little is known. The writings from the later period of Cretan civilization (called Minoan after a semimythical king named Minos) have now been deciphered, and it is clear that the language of this period is an archaic form of Greek. It now seems that the earlier writings are in a Semitic language akin to Phoenician. What we know of Minoan civilization is however almost all derived from archaeology.

We know that the civilization existed at least as early as 3000 B.C. and that it knew the use of bronze but not of iron. It was a commercial civilization which spread out through the whole Aegean area, while retaining links with Egypt to the southeast, whose trade products it carried throughout this area. It seems probable that certain mainland cities in Greece, including Greek Mycenae, and in Asia Minor were colonized by the Cretans—even though in the last centuries of Cretan independence, the period from which the writings have been deciphered, the mainland peoples (known collectively as the Achaeans) dominated the island. Probably the Achaeans dominated Crete from about 1400 B.C. In due time they fell to the Dorians, who had invaded Greece and conquered most of the Peloponnese.

The Cretans had a very well-developed material civilization, with a sanitation system superior to anything that appeared among the later mainland Greeks. They evidently already possessed the Greek love of sports, and their achievements in some arts, especially painting, were superior to those of the earlier Greeks. The Greek story of Theseus and the Minotaur is laid in Crete. Greek tales speak of bull-worship in the island; but we know little of the details of the Cretan religion. Though the decipherment of the earlier script will certainly yield some new and important information, as yet there are relatively few finds available for study, and it is probable that most of our knowledge of this civilization will continue to be inferred largely from the surviving artifacts and interpreted with the tools of the archaeologist rather than those of the historian.

3 THE CIVILIZATION OF THE ANCIENT GREEKS

With the Greeks we enter a totally different world from that of the ancient Near East. Though some elements of our civilization can be traced back in a continuous line through the Hebrews to Mesopotamia, almost everything else in our Western world is Greek in origin, so much so that we can almost think of our civilization as a continuation of theirs. Most of us are direct descendants not of the Greek peoples but of barbarians such as the Romans, Germans, and others who entered the mainstream of Western civilization and absorbed the Greek cultural heritage. But it is difficult to point to any political or social problem of ours to which the Greeks did not devote some thought, any philosophical problem to the solution of which they did not offer some contribution. Greek art and architecture, and even the language, continue today to influence our own. In a word, the ancient Greeks were the greatest *innovators* that the world has yet seen. Indeed, because they began so much, there is relatively little for their inheritors to do except to continue on the lines set forth by them, attempting on the basis of more complete knowledge and wider experience to provide new explanations for the problems that puzzled them.

THE SETTLEMENT OF MAINLAND GREECE AND THE COLONIES

The origin of the Greeks is still not fully known. They were certainly not the prehistoric inhabitants of the land but invaded it in historic times, probably not earlier than 2000 B.C. They came in waves of different peoples, the Achaeans, Ionians, Aetolians, and Dorians, the last-named penetrating into the Peloponnesus in the second half of the second millennium B.C. In historic times these various peoples regarded themselves as different from one another.

The Ionians, the people who settled Athens, looked upon the Dorians as somewhat uncouth though they conceded their military prowess. To the Ionians the Aetolians were a bucolic and phlegmatic people, unlike themselves, who were mercurial and sanguine. But all the Greeks, or Hellenes, as they called themselves, were to be distinguished from barbarians, or foreigners, who were not truly civilized or indeed capable of self-government.

From quite early times there was a severe overpopulation in Greece in relation to available resources. Only a few areas of the land were especially fertile; the remainder was rocky and mountainous, suited for goat pasture and for little else. The life of the peasant was always difficult. Not even at the height of her prosperity did the citizens of Athens, the richest city, have a high standard of living. As early as the eighth century B.C. adventurous Greeks were colonizing the islands of the Aegean, the coast of Asia Minor, the shores of the Mediterranean, the island of Sicily, and the mainland of southern Italy. The various city-states supported these enterprises, even though the colonies thus founded were from the beginning independent and connected with their mother cities only through their common culture and origins.

THE POLIS

The typical political and social unit of Greece was the *polis,* or city-state, a strong point surrounded by the lands which supplied its needs. City-states frequently warred on one another; each was fiercely independent and resisted being incorporated into another state. No one unified Greece until it was conquered by the Macedonian kingdom in the north at the end of the fourth century B.C. In the fifth century B.C. the Athenians built a maritime empire which grew out of an original defensive alliance. The Spartans conquered and enslaved the Messenians in the seventh century B.C. but thereafter did not add to their empire, contenting themselves with a league of states organized to resist Athenian expansion.

Each city-state had its own form of government. Probably all the city-states started as kingdoms, but fairly soon the kings on the mainland were replaced by oligarchies. Some city-states remained oligarchies until the end of their independence; others, notably Athens, became democracies, with most of the allies of Athens following her example. Each polis sought to be a culturally self-sufficient entity, relying as little as possible on outsiders. There was relatively little communication between the cities, and in most cities the noncitizen, enduring always some form of discrimination, had to take a second place to the native citizens. Few cities, except for limited periods because of special circumstances, granted citizenship to the foreigner whether Greek or barbarian.

The Homeric Age. The first great poet of Greece and one of the greatest, if not the greatest, in all Western civilization was Homer of Chios. In the *Iliad,* Homer, writing probably in the ninth century B.C., described a long-past war between the mainland leaders, joined in an alliance under the Achaean king of Mycenae against Troy in Asia Minor; in the *Odyssey* he portrayed the wanderings of Odysseus, king of Ithaca, a small town in the southwest of Greece. Probably Homer himself used the old minstrel songs and by his personal genius welded them into a coherent poem. The feudal society he described is very far from the society of classical times. The country then was evidently not overpopulated, nor was the city-state as yet the typical political and social unit. This ancient society had long passed away, probably by the time of Homer himself, and certainly by the time of the great agricultural writer Hesiod (eighth century B.C.), in whose time the society was recognizably similar to that in the fairly well-documented classical age. This so-called classical age dates from about the seventh century B.C. to the conquests of Alexander (fourth century B.C.).

SPARTA

Sparta, settled by Dorians, continued to bear the military imprint of that people.

Government. The city with its extremely fertile surroundings was ruled by an elected oligarchy (*ephors*), with two kings at the head who performed ceremonial duties fitted to their rank and title and had as a rule the right to military leadership in time of war. The rulers of the city by the eighth century B.C. were land hungry and felt a need to expand. The Spartans therefore made war on the slightly more numerous Messenians to the west, who were Dorians like themselves. In two murderous wars in which they came close to defeat, they conquered the Messenians and enslaved them. The Messenians as well as other slaves were given the task of providing all the sustenance for the free Spartans, who concentrated upon military activity, honoring only military virtues and neglecting all cultural and even commercial pursuits thereafter.

Society. The slaves (*helots*), having formerly been free men, could be kept at their tasks only by force. Control was provided by the citizens, both men and women, who had received specialized physical training. The boy was taken from his parents at an early age and thereafter lived in barracks for the rest of his active life; the helots, for whom he was responsible, had to perform the menial and agricultural labor, this enabling him to live without playing his normal part in the economy. Such trade as there was fell to the lot of a class of people called *perioeci,* who did not live in the city of Sparta itself but in the surrounding area. The result of the system, which was enshrined in a law code attributed to Lycurgus (a figure about whom nothing further is known) was that the Spartans necessarily curtailed their adventures beyond their homeland but had a strong, if very conservative army, which could be used both to defend the state against invaders and to prevent the helots from revolting. Since physical courage was extolled over all other virtues, the reception that a Spartan soldier could expect to receive at home if he escaped after a defeat was such that he might well prefer to die in battle. Yet at the same time the state could ill afford to lose him. The Spartans were respected by the other Greeks for their courage but secretly despised for their lack of initiative—and no one imitated either their polity or their social and military system.

THE ATHENIANS

The Athenians, on the other hand, were innovators and one of the most venturesome peoples of all history. Many states tried to copy their political and social customs. Even Alexander the Great, when granting political institutions to the new cities that he founded in Asia, took the Athenian state as his model, unsuitable though it was in so many respects for cities that were compelled to obey a monarch as their ultimate overlord. But the expansionist policies of the Athenians brought upon them the enmity of the other Greek states, and in the long war with Sparta and her allies Athens was eventually worsted, largely as the result of the defection of her own allies, whom she antagonized by treating as subjects rather than as free associates.

Early Political Development. When Athens first emerged into the full light of history she was an oligarchy, ruled by the aristocratic families represented in the ruling body, the Areopagus. Land hunger on the part of the peasants resulted in the customary suppression by the aristocratic landowners. In the rocky land of Attica it was difficult for the peasant to make a living, especially when he owed a part of his crop to the landowner. Thus poverty increased and enslavement for debt became common. The Areopagus at first attempted to handle the class struggle by issuing a law code which prescribed severe penalties for violence (Constitution of Draco, 621 B.C.). When this was found to have little effect on the land problem the small middle class in the city of Athens took a hand, and some influential voices especially that of Solon, were raised calling for reform. The aristocracy, to their eternal credit, decided that something constructive must be done and agreed to the election of Solon as archon with full powers to institute reform (594 B.C.).

The Reforms of Solon. Solon thereupon prohibited enslavement for debt and encouraged the peasants who had lost their land to migrate to the city. He welcomed the immigration of foreign artisans and granted them citizenship, since it was expected that they would teach their skills to the new inhabitants of the city. He also suggested the growing of vines and olive trees instead of the traditional wheat (which was largely unsuited to the soil) so that wine and olive oil could be exported in exchange for the import of basic foods. On the political side Solon reduced the power of the Areopagus and instituted a Council and Assembly, which would take in most of the citizenry. Lastly he set up popular law courts.

Pisistratus and Cleisthenes. This big dose of reform was evidently too much to be carried out without disrupting the entire society. Before very long Pisistratus, taking advantage of the possibility for political manipulation given in the new constitution, made himself undisputed ruler of the state (561 B.C.). He appears to have put into full operation the economic reforms of Solon, thereby in a long period of supremacy effectively changing the structure of Athenian society. Many of the disgruntled aristocrats went into exile, and their lands were given to the peasant supporters of the ruler. Pisistratus was one of the more benevolent Greek "tyrants," a term that applied to despots who took power for themselves without having inherited it. He was, however, far from the only one. In most of the cities of Greece and in the Greek colonies elsewhere tyrants held sway for a period. But in few places did they prepare the way for a substantial democracy as well as did Pisistratus in Athens —however little this may have been his intention.

When Pisistratus died his sons attempted to rule with similar absolutism. But they did not have the talent of their father. When one of the sons was murdered and the other became more tyrannous in the modern sense, a number of the exiled aristocrats decided that the time was ripe for their return. Aided by a Spartan contingent, they took the city, but they could not hold it against the opposition of the people. Thereupon, one of their leaders, Cleisthenes, decided to support the people's cause and was granted the power to change the old constitution of Solon in the direction of further democracy (510 B.C.). The constitution that thus resulted was close to a full direct democracy, and within the next few years it did in fact become the first democracy of the ancient world, with all property qualifications being abolished and every male citizen having the right to vote.

Democratic Political Institutions of Athens. The sovereign body was the Assembly, made up of all the male citizens. A Council of Five Hundred elected annually by lot, with fifty members chosen from each tribe, prepared legislation for the Assembly, each of the ten tribal delegations carrying out this responsibility for a tenth of the year. The Council administered the state between the meetings of the Assembly and had a number of other responsibilities. A board of ten generals, elected one by each tribe and eligible for re-election, formed the executive of the state. When the Assembly decided upon war, however, it chose the particular general to head the army, and could if it wished even choose the leader from outside the Board of Ten since it was completely sovereign. The Assembly was supposed to act in accordance with the law, but there was no way of compelling it to do so, though it could be dangerous for anyone who did not gauge correctly the temper of the Assembly even to propose an "unconstitutional" law since his proposal would make him liable for prosecution. In order to prevent anyone again from becoming a "tyrant," the system of ostracism was devised, under which any man could be sent to temporary exile by an adverse vote of the people.

The law courts were further "democratized" in the fifth century B.C. with the introduction of pay for service, and the regular empanelment of large juries of citizens who condemned or acquitted by a majority vote. There were no rules of evidence, no public prosecutor, and no presiding judge with legal qualifications. Most lawsuits for public offenses were initiated by professional informers who hoped for a share of the fine imposed, though any citizen was permitted to bring a charge. If, however, the accuser failed to win a conviction he could himself be fined.

It has often been claimed that Athens was not a true democracy because the free status of the citizen depended upon the presence of numerous slaves who performed the menial work, and because women were subjected to legal disabilities and could neither attend the Assembly nor vote. Though there were, of course, many slaves in Athens, according to the best modern estimate, * even in the fifth century B.c., the period of greatest Athenian prosperity, their number did not exceed one-quarter to one-third of the population. It is also perhaps worth remembering that it was not until the early twentieth century A.D. that women were first granted the right to vote in Europe, and in almost all Western societies man has held a privileged legal position, which he has not altogether lost even to this day. Resident aliens in Athens (*metics*) likewise did not possess the vote, as in most modern countries.

FOREIGN AND INTERNECINE WARS

The Greek city-states were almost always at war, either with one another or with foreigners. The new democratic system at Athens and the fortitude of the Greeks as a whole were put to a severe test in the early fifth century by the invasion of the Persians.

The Persian Wars. In 490 B.c. Darius the Great, king of Persia, wishing to chastise the Athenians, who had dared aid a number of Ionian cities in Asia Minor which had revolted against him, sent a fleet against Athens, expecting a quick victory. But the Athenians reacted immediately and won the important Battle of Marathon (490 B.c.). The Persians, however, did not give up their enterprise. Under Xerxes, son of Darius, they prepared a huge expedition which was to proceed by land and sea. Though slow to organize a united defense, the Greeks, almost too late, decided to resist. The Spartans sent a small army under their king Leonidas to Thermopylae, the pass that commanded the road to Athens and the Peloponnesus. After a heroic defense it was overwhelmed. The Athenians, who under the inspiration of Themistocles had built a fleet, won a great victory at Salamis but were compelled to evacuate Athens itself, which was sacked by the Persians (480 B.c.). The following year a strong army, led by the Spartan king Pausanias, with contingents from most of the other cities, decisively defeated the Persians by land (Battle of Plataea), while the Athenians under a Spartan admiral won a victory by sea at Mycale which destroyed the Persian fleet. Thereafter the Persians were never again a military threat to the cities of the mainland.

The Confederation of Delos. In order to protect themselves against any possible further attacks by the Persians, the Athenians

* W. L. Westermann, *The Slave Systems of Greek and Roman Antiquity* (Philadelphia: American Philosophical Society, 1955), pp. 7–9.

organized a defensive alliance known as the Confederation of Delos (after the tiny island sacred to Apollo where the treasury was kept). Sparta and other mainland powers were invited to join. On their refusal the Athenians went ahead and signed up the majority of the Aegean islands, most of whom contributed money to a common navy, while a few supplied ships. Athens, always the unquestioned leader, eventually converted the islands into an empire by refusing to permit secession, although the Persian menace had receded. Pericles, the leading statesman of Athens for more than thirty years, then used the Confederation to promote his own expansionist purposes and had the treasury removed to Athens. He used the money thus obtained to rebuild the city, making it into the artistic showpiece of Greece.

The Peloponnesian War. Imperial Athens by her policies naturally excited the suspicion of Sparta and the envy of other cities, especially Corinth, a commercial center whose foreign trade was threatened by Athenian expansion. Eventually Sparta, Corinth, and other cities launched a preventive war against Athens and her empire. This war, known to history as the Peloponnesian War, lasted from 431 to 404 B.C.

At the beginning of the war Pericles was still the unquestioned leader of Athens. His military policy was to bring the peasants of Attica within the protection of the Long Walls of the city and fight the Peloponnesian League mainly by sea. But the resulting congestion brought on a plague and serious discontent, and Pericles for a short time fell from power. When the Athenians found they could not do without him, he was re-elected, but he died soon afterward. He was succeeded by Cleon, an able demagogue devoted to the policy of winning the war by all available means. Several times he prevented the Athenians from making peace when it could have been obtained on favorable terms. When he was killed in 422 B.C., the peace party led by Nicias gained the upper hand in the Assembly, and a peace was signed the following year.

However, nothing had been settled; both sides soon broke the peace terms; and the war was renewed. Alcibiades now became the leader of the war party, and he persuaded the Assembly to send a great expedition to Syracuse under the joint command of himself, Nicias, and another general. But soon after it had sailed, Alcibiades' enemies in the Assembly prevailed upon it to depose him for alleged sacrilege, whereupon he transferred his services to Sparta. The expedition under the dilatory command of Nicias was destroyed (413

B.C.), and the Spartans took advantage of Athenian weakness to seize and fortify Decelea, only a few miles from Athens, from which outpost they constantly threatened the city. With the aid of Persian money Sparta built and equipped several fleets, which eventually wore down the resistance of the Athenians, and put an end to the war by the decisive victory of Aegospotami (405 B.C.). With their grain supply from the Black Sea cut off, the Athenians had no option but to surrender.

The Fourth-Century Decline. Although several of her allies wished to destroy Athens, now a hated city, Sparta refused to do this, contenting herself with the destruction of Athenian fortifications and the establishment of an oligarchy to replace the discredited democracy. But the oligarchy behaved so tyrannously that the Athenians soon overturned it. The Spartans accepted the inevitable restoration of democratic institutions in Athens, which, however, was now a second-class power, poor in resources, and for a decade or two unable to play an effective part in Greek affairs. At this time Sparta, though acknowledged as leader of the country, was no longer fitted to exercise leadership. She, too, had suffered severely from the war, and she could afford the loss of her free citizens even less than could the Athenians. Nevertheless, her leaders tried to carry on an imperial policy. Worst of all, Sparta deeply offended Persia by sending an expedition to Asia Minor and hence lost all financial support from that source. Indeed, the Persian king humiliated all the Greeks by summoning envoys and dictating a peace which they were compelled to accept (Peace of Antalcidas, 387 B.C.). Soon afterward under energetic leadership the city of Thebes in Boeotia put into effect a number of political reforms which placed it in control of most of that area. The Thebans defeated the Spartans, and in two important battles put an end forever to Spartan aspirations. They freed the helots, who thereupon founded their own state. Thebes was still the leading power in Greece when Macedonia rose to supremacy in the second half of the fourth century.

Meanwhile Athens had partly recovered her power, and even organized a second, but freer, confederation of Delos. Nevertheless, her resources were not such as to enable her to experience any lasting success. Such success, indeed, as she knew during the fourth century was mainly due to her diplomacy. The people had ceased to be interested in military exploits, preferring to hire mercenary soldiers to fight their wars for them. When Philip II of Macedon built a small but strong and well-trained army, based on a new formation, the phalanx, some Athenian leaders, especially Demosthenes, sensed the danger from him but were unable to instill a warlike spirit into the citizenry. Philip, by a shrewd mixture of force and trickery, played off one city against another and one party in a city against its opponents. He thus managed to reassure those who were ready to be reassured and kept Thebes out of an alliance against him until he was ready to crush her. In 338 B.C. he defeated the combined forces of the Thebans, Athenians, and lesser cities at the Battle of Chaeronea. Though Philip was murdered shortly afterward, he was succeeded by his son Alexander the Great, who quickly consolidated his power in Greece and turned toward Asia in search of new conquests. In 334 B.C. he invaded Asia with a relatively small force, made up of his Macedonian professional army, together with some Greek volunteers who enlisted in the expectation of booty.

THE HELLENISTIC WORLD

During the next few years Alexander by his victories not only destroyed the Persian Empire but also for the first time brought Persia and Asia Minor into intimate contact with mainland Greek civilization. This conquest, which resulted in a totally different culture (usually called Hellenistic), was one of the most fruitful in history.

Conquests of Alexander the Great. Alexander's initial victory at the Battle of the Granicus (334 B.C.). over a Persian satrap was one of his most hard-fought, since he had Greeks as well as Persians to contend with. Following a victory at Issus over the Persian king, Darius III, he turned in the direction of Egypt. After a difficult siege of the Phoenician city of Tyre, he found that Egypt presented no problems, and he captured it, almost without bloodshed (332 B.C.). Returning to Persia, he defeated Darius again in the decisive Battle of Gaugamela (331 B.C.). When the monarch was murdered by his own subjects the following year, Alexander took his title of king for himself. Still not content, he marched toward India and defeated an Indian monarch at the Battle of the Hydaspes (326 B.C.). His exhausted troops, however, refused to follow him further, and he was compelled to return to the Persian capital of Babylon, where he died soon afterward at the age of thirty-three, leaving no obvious successor. A posthumous son was born soon after his death, but the Macedonian generals who divided his territory among them refused to allow him to rule. The great empire was partitioned after considerable fighting between these generals. Macedonia retained

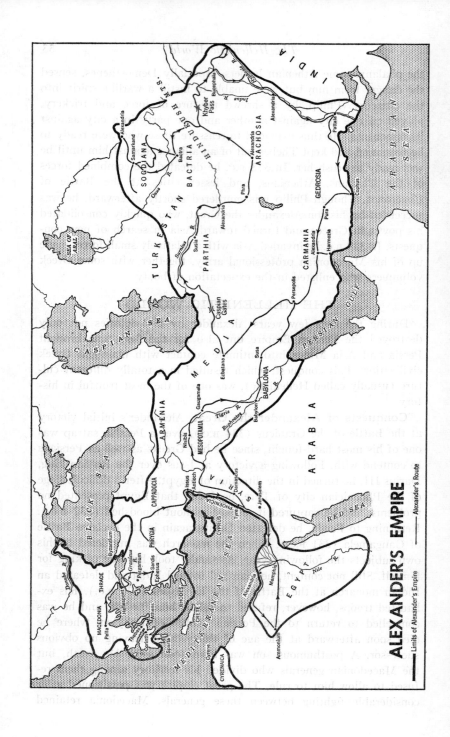

ALEXANDER'S EMPIRE

— Limits of Alexander's Empire
—— Alexander's Route

control over mainland Greece, and a small commercial kingdom of Pergamum was created in northwest Asia Minor. Most of the remainder fell to Seleucus as king of Syria and to Ptolemy I as Pharaoh of Egypt. These kingdoms in turn fell to the Romans in the second and first centuries B.C.

The Consequences for Greece. The Greek cities under Macedonian overlordship retained local autonomy and made many experiments with new political systems in the period before they were absorbed into the Roman Empire. When Macedonia was defeated by Rome, the Greeks were granted independence so long as they refrained from opposing Roman policies. But they never found it possible to build a united country and were thus too weak to stand against the expanding power of Rome. The ephemeral leagues that they formed intrigued with Rome against one another, leading to the eventual fall of the whole country. Their cultural influence on Rome is incalculable, but they were compelled by their political weakness to submit to Roman authority until after the fall of the Roman Empire in the West. Then they inherited their own empire based on Constantinople (the so-called Byzantine Empire), founded by the Roman emperor Constantine I, which contained some Roman elements but at all times was far more Greek than Roman.

Political and Economic Effects of the Conquests. Both Alexander and his generals founded numerous cities in the old Persian Empire. These cities were granted internal self-government with institutions, as already noted, modeled on those of classical Athens. Though they lacked the right to decide on their own foreign policies, their autonomy was real if limited. They were strong enough to survive the Roman conquest and became Roman municipalities. Many were extremely prosperous for some centuries until the Roman tax collectors ruined them, in the declining years of the Empire. The culture of Greek Asia (known as Hellenistic, to be distinguished from Hellenic culture of the earlier classical period) was a mixture of Greek and Oriental. The Greeks who poured into Asia in search of the material advancement unavailable in Greece infused a new spirit of enterprise into the region. Many of them rapidly achieved prosperity. Favored by the administration and aided by their own native gifts, they became an urban upper class. In this class they were joined by some Persians, who had already been granted equality in his army by Alexander. But the great majority of the inhabitants of Alexander's empire no doubt remained as they had always been, while the immigrant Greeks rose to the top. In Egypt a similar situation prevailed. Here the native Egyptians were not granted even equal rights with the Greeks. The Macedonian general Ptolemy became Pharaoh and efficiently exploited his traditional position as owner of all the land and supreme king-god. But the earlier kings of his dynasty at least initiated a considerable number of technical improvements, bringing greater fertility to the land, if not greater prosperity to the peasants who worked on it.

HELLENIC CULTURE

There has seldom been any such galaxy of talent in every field of culture as there was in ancient Greece. It is scarcely possible here to do more than indicate fields in which they excelled and mention the names of some of the great scientists, writers, and philosophers of the Classical Age.

Religion and Tragedy. The traditional religion of the Greeks is usually thought of as anthropomorphic. The gods were conceived of in the likeness of men, with human desires, passions, and frailties. It is, however, open to doubt whether the Greeks actually *believed* in Zeus (the supreme god), his wife Hera, Apollo, Dionysus, Pallas Athena, Artemis, Demeter, and the rest who were supposed to live on Mount Olympus and whose activities in the world of men are described by Homer. Hesiod in his *Theogony* provided the Greeks with a creation story and a series of myths about the beginnings of gods and men. In later times Apollo and Dionysus, representing in a broad sense the virtues of harmony, equilibrium, and wisdom (Apollo), and creative force and emotion (Dionysus), became the favorite gods for worship. Each city had its patron god or goddess, and frequent religious festivals marked the course of the year. It was at these festivals that the Greeks most fully expressed their feeling for the divine.

In general, indeed, it may be said that the Greeks had a remarkable sense for the divinity that lies behind Nature, and this divinity they reverenced. Moreover, they respected the power of the gods— at least until the Sophists began to question both their existence and whether if existing, they really ruled the world and cared about it. Greek tragedy is mainly concerned with the pride of man and the manner in which he is punished if he oversteps the bounds imposed on all human beings. Though there are other themes, this theme more than any other runs through the tragic plays, and there can be no doubt that in the Greek view the greatest "sin" is pride, man's refusal to acknowledge the limits of his powers and the manner in which he offends the gods in striving to make himself equal with them. The Greeks had a strong sense also of destiny, which they called *Moira*, represented by three figures who wove the web of life. These three Fates were regarded by some poets, especially Homer, as stronger than the gods themselves. Even Zeus had to bow to their will. All the three great tragic dramatists, Aeschylus, Sophocles, and Euripides (who was in many respects skeptical of popular belief), recognized that man has only a limited freedom of choice and that his field of action is circumscribed by factors over which he has no control. Man, however, is free in his moral life and he may bear his destiny with dignity as becomes a man or be crushed by it.

History. The two great historians Herodotus and Thucydides show evidence in their work of the religious preconceptions of their time. Herodotus wrote the history of the *Persian Wars* in such a manner as to suggest that Xerxes, the Persian king, was afflicted with excessive pride when he attempted to add Greece to his already huge domains. The theme however is not stressed. Herodotus was an acute observer and indefatigable traveler, the father of anthropology insofar as he describes carefully manners and customs of Egyptians and Persians, contrasting them with those of the Greeks. Though his history of the wars is colorful and he seldom has any method of distinguishing truth from falsehood otherwise than by his personal preference of one version over another, his work is nevertheless an invaluable attempt to provide a consecutive account of what happened —very different indeed from the work of any of the Egyptian or Mesopotamian annalists.

Thucydides' *History of the Peloponnesian War* is both more systematic and critical, and at the same time far more thoughtful. The moral preconceptions of the author, who was himself a general during the war, exiled by the Athenians after a military failure, are much more marked than those of Herodotus. He regards the defeat of the Athenians as the result of their pride and arrogance, and their refusal to curb their ambitions even when attempts at fulfillment constituted a clear offense against the gods. The behavior of human beings and their societies under the stress of war is of prime interest to Thucydides, whose observations remind the modern reader how little humanity has changed in this respect in the centuries since.

Comedy. The great comic playwright Aristophanes, most of whose plays present commentaries upon Athenian life during the Peloponnesian War, attributes the failure of Athens to the moral decadence of the age and the self-seeking of democratic politicians (in contrast to the earlier rule by aristocrats), as well as to the new ideas of the Sophists and their nihilistic philosophy. Most of Aristophanes' plays are full of comic invention, though it is necessary for the modern reader to have considerable knowledge of Athenian life and society of the period if he is to grasp the more subtle points.

Philosophy. Greek philosophy is one of the greatest achievements of the human mind. Indeed, there was no philosophy in the Western world prior to that of the Greeks, and all Western philosophy since their time has been concerned to a greater or lesser degree with the problems first raised by them, although our solutions, in view of our wider knowledge, naturally differ from theirs.

The Cosmologists. It is difficult to classify the early thinkers of Greece who for the first time in recorded history began to try to understand the world. They might be considered scientists insofar as they were occupied with the task of explaining in nonreligious terms the underlying realities beneath the world of material phenomena. But they expressed these in a quite unscientific manner and neglected the actual phenomena themselves. None of these early thinkers was Athenian.

Thales of Miletus in Asia Minor (*c.* 636–*c.* 546 B.C.) claimed that the underlying reality was water, of which all things were made; Anaximenes from the same area preferred air as the fundamental substance. Anaximander produced a theory of evolution, explaining that the different world phenomena, including animals and men, evolve in the process of time from what he spoke of as an indeterminate substance. Heraclitus of Ephesus stressed the harmony of opposites and believed that the underlying substance was fire. Parmenides of Elea in Italy (late sixth century B.C.) stressed that there was no such thing as true change: no coming into being and passing away but only changes in apparent form. Pythagoras (*c.* 586–*c.* 507 B.C.) also from southern Italy, was fascinated by mathematics and claimed that the underlying element was not a substance but number. He discovered the theorem always associated with his name. He and his school also produced an elaborate theory of the origin of the universe, the first one that was not geocentric. Instead, the Pythagoreans held that there was a "central fire," around which ten planets revolved, including the sun, which received its light from the central fire. Empedocles of Sicily spoke of the four elements, earth, air, fire, and water, and held that attraction and repulsion, or, as he called them, love and strife, caused the combination of these elements into material phenomena. Anaxagoras claimed that all motion was caused by mind. Lastly, Leucippus, in the fifth century B.C., and Democritus (*c.* 460–*c.* 370 B.C.) evolved the theory that all phenomena were made up of many tiny finite substances called atoms, each of which had its different characteristics and which in combination produced the almost infinite diversity of material objects. In spite of the fact that all these men leaped to conclusions on the basis of what we should consider totally insufficient data, they were remarkable for the fact that, for the first time in world history, they *theorized* about the world, and did not, like their predecessors, simply *describe* its phenomena as they observed them.

THE SOPHISTS. The Athenians, who had shown relatively little interest in these physical speculations, excelled in the study of man. They were stimulated by the arrival in Athens in the middle of the fifth century B.C. of thinkers from Italy and elsewhere to teach the Athenian upper classes, who proved eager to receive what they brought. Protagoras put forward the proposition that "man is the measuring-rod for all things" and proceeded to criticize in the light of this dictum all that had hitherto been accepted on the basis of belief. Such incipient skepticism evidently pleased the young Athenians, who learned from Protagoras, Gorgias, and others with similar views (all belonging to the group of philosophers called Sophists) how to argue on the basis of logic and how to do such practical things as plead effectively in the law courts. Their criticism began to undermine the accepted religious and political dogmas of the state.

SOCRATES. The great philosopher Socrates, who learned much from the Sophists, went several steps further when he began to develop a method of his own which he called the dialectic, a process of questioning which he used in every sphere of life and conduct to elicit human prejudices and preconceptions. He held that the unexamined life is not worth leading; that man should develop his own ethical standards; and that he should seek to discover the "good" for himself, without necessarily taking into account traditional notions of good. In 399 B.C., Socrates, who had numbered among his pupils some of the leaders of the Athenian oligarchy set up after the Peloponnesian War, was condemned to death by the restored democracy on the charge of having "made new gods" and "corrupted the youth."

PLATO. Plato, the leading pupil of Socrates, was twenty-four years old when his master was executed, and thereafter he devoted his life both to rehabilitating the memory of Socrates and to making the fullest possible use of the Socratic method to arrive at conclusions in every field of thought. Socrates himself wrote nothing, but Plato places him at the center of his own written dialogues as the skilled questioner who attempts to elicit the truth by his method. A profounder thinker than his master, Plato inquired into almost every realm of thought including thought itself. Out of this inquiry he concluded that there was a realm of perfect universal "ideas," the abstractions which are absolute and true, whereas the earthly realm is an inferior copy of these ideas. In his *Republic* he considers the question of what constitutes the perfect state based upon justice; in the *Laws* he considers the best state possible on earth based upon laws which approximate justice. In the *Theaetetus* he considers the question of how man can know anything for certain. In the *Phaedrus* he studies the nature of the human soul and suggests how man arrives at his moral ideas and ideals. In a series of early dialogues which describe the last days of Socrates, he puts in the mouth of his master an eloquent defense of freedom of thought and a number of discourses on immortality. All Plato's work is stimulating to more thought and has always had this effect on later philosophers, even though the majority today would disagree with many of his conclusions.

ARISTOTLE. Aristotle (384–322 B.C.), the chief pupil of Plato, was a much more systematic thinker, and he spread his net even more widely. His written works have in many cases the appearance of lecture notes, making them far more difficult than the literary masterpieces of Plato. He attempted to build a synthesis of all the knowledge of his day, coherently explaining the purposes and functions of all natural phenomena. Thus he was at least as much a scientist as a philosopher. He considered the nature of man, his soul and his body, and the manner in which they interacted (*De anima*), the proper moral tasks of individual men on earth (*Ethics*), and the nature of man's societies and political institutions (*Politics, Constitution of Athens,* and others). He founded the systematic study of logic in several works; he described and tried to explain the animal world and its functioning; he considered the nature of the universe and how it came into being. The sum total of his work is astonishing in its quantity and quality, and his influence extended through the Middle Ages into the early modern period. Only in modern times, with our tremendous increase in mathematical knowledge (in which Aristotle was deficient) and our more systematic observation of natural phenomena have his influence and authority been overthrown.

Medicine. Mention should be made of the doctor Hippocrates of Cos (*c.* 460–*c.* 370 B.C.), who founded a school of medicine based on careful observation and the treatment of the sick by diet and the use of natural remedies. A very considerable corpus of writings by Hippocrates and his colleagues and pupils is extant. His famous oath is still used by graduates of most schools of medicine in the Western world as an ideal expression of the proper relationship between doctor and patient.

Art. Greek architecture was relatively simple, being essentially based on the simple post and lintel construction. But the sense of balance and proportion characteristic of the best Greek work has served to make Greek architecture a model for much of architecture since that day, especially in the time of the Renaissance. Domestic architecture was unimportant to the Greeks because most of their life was spent outdoors. The Greek temple, especially the Parthenon in honor of Athena on the Acropolis at Athens, became a model for public buildings in the West. The temple was considered a home for the god rather than a place of worship such as the Western church.

We do not know as much as we might wish about Greek painting, since little has survived except in the form of painted vases, pottery, and the like. But in sculpture the Greek artistic genius reached its fruition. Even today the Greek masterpieces have seldom if ever been equaled. The Greek artist, who in the Hellenic period did almost all his work for the city and carved his gods in the form of mortal men, was allowed to indulge his taste for the ideal rather than depicting ordinary men. Thus the best of classical Greek sculptures show men and women through the eyes of the imagination and succeed in portraying a harmony between soul and body such has rarely even been attempted in the centuries since.

HELLENISTIC CULTURE

The Greco-Oriental (Hellenistic) culture that resulted from the conquests of Alexander differed from the Hellenic in that it showed awareness of a much larger world than the small city-states, and was to some degree influenced by Oriental thought. Social conditions in the empire tended to favor the growth of competition among individuals in search of wealth and thus led to individualism in thought as well as in practice.

Religion and Philosophy. The old gods of Olympus had never recovered from the assault of the Sophists. On the one hand in the Hellenistic era men turned to the numerous religions of the East, offshoots of Zoroastrianism, the old fertility cults, the religion of Isis and Osiris in Egypt, and even the new cult of Serapis instituted by the Ptolemies. On the other hand, the intellectuals produced their own codes of ethics which were content to minimize or deny the role of gods in human affairs. Stoicism, founded in the early third century B.C. by Zeno of Citium, probably a Phoenician, began a school of thought that exalted the role of Divine Reason and emphasized the universality of reason, and thus eventually the equality of all men. The true Stoics sought to be unmoved by the world, each individual standing firmly against all pressures and seeking neither wealth, renown, nor success. The Epicureans, following their leader Epicurus (c. 341–270 B.C.), who founded a school in Athens, stressed the view that religion leads to fear and discomfort. The gods, Epicurus claimed, created man once and for all, but took no further interest in him. They dwelt far off, at ease. Hence human beings should seek to circumscribe their desires, remaining content with little and enjoying peacefully what came to them, without fear and without ambition. The Cynics, of whom the most famous was Diogenes, who lived in a tub, systematically learned to despise everything that pertained to the world, which for them was a very sorry place. This contempt for the world led, for the Cynic, to self-sufficiency, the only attitude deemed worthy of man. Lastly the Skeptics, or Pyrrhonists after their founder Pyrrho, made it their profession to doubt the possibility of knowing anything for certain, preferring to criticize away the beliefs of others and particularly to show that all religious dogmas were based on nothing but human subjectiveness. The works of all these philosophers can be traced back to ideas first propounded in the Hellenic world, but those ideas were developed more fully in this later age, when they could be used to explain new conditions or to steel men to endure a materialistic and competitive society from which the intellectuals (as so often in our own times) felt themselves alienated.

Science. The Hellenistic period is one of the great ages in the history of science. The opportunity for research and study was provided above all by the Ptolemies in Egypt, who founded the Museum of Alexandria, a kind of research university, which they subsidized from the wealth they acquired as owners of the whole land of Egypt. This Museum contained one of the two great libraries for which Alexandria later won worldwide fame. Earlier Greek science had lacked the careful observations necessary for correct generalizations. These were now provided in good measure with the access of Greek thinkers to the numerous astronomical observations of the Mesopotamian priests. Heracleides of Pontus, Hipparchus, and Aristarchus used these findings in conjunction with their own to formulate theories to correspond with observation—theories which could explain the movements of the heavenly bodies. It was, however, Hipparchus' opinion that prevailed in the ancient world and he who was responsible for the main teachings of the geocentric system (though an astronomer of a later generation, Claudius Ptolemy, gave his name to the system because Ptolemy's writings survived into the Middle Ages). Aristarchus, who held that the earth moved around the sun, gained few adherents in his own day, for lack of any experimental verification of his theory that seemed so contrary to the observed facts.

All the astronomers had command of a growing mathematical technique. Archimedes, in the third century B.C., was the greatest of the theoretical mathematicians and physicists. He was the founder of hydrostatics, and his principle still lies at the basis of this science. Euclid systematized the geometrical knowledge that had grown up during several centuries and invented the basic form and the methods of proof for the proposition or theorem. Eratosthenes, an Alexandrian geographer, made a serious effort to measure the diameter of the earth by trigonometric methods.

Art. Hellenistic art was more realistic than its Hellenic predecessor. In the new age it was no longer the city that commissioned works of art but individual patrons, generally the kings, rich nobles, and merchants. These men were not interested in idealized sculptures; they preferred more nearly exact likenesses either of themselves or of others who served as models. The divine element in sculpture had to a large degree been subordinated to the human. Where the classical sculpture had tended to be static, Hellenistic sculptures stressed movement, as in the famous Nike of Samothrace. In architecture, the wealth of the Hellenistic monarchs enabled them to plan temple complexes on a much larger scale than had been feasible in the small city-state. In this they were perhaps influenced by what they found in Persia and Egypt. At all events the Hellenistic builders were anxious to exhibit their wealth and power at least as much as their piety, and their preoccupations are reflected in the type of work they commissioned. It seems probable that in architecture as in sculpture the greater opportunities in this age had a fructifying effect on the Greek genius. The artistic work of the Hellenistic world shows an ever increasing command of technique, and some of the greatest Greek masterpieces date from this period, including the incomparable Aphrodite of Melos ("Venus de Milo").

CONCLUSION

It is difficult to overestimate the achievements of the Greeks. It was in Greek city-states that democracy first arose; and though democratic self-government did not everywhere survive for long, Athens at least was free and democratic for almost two centuries. The representative principle, though known to the Greeks, was rarely used; but the ordinary citizen has never had greater influence on the policy of his state than he had in ancient Athens. Only in the town-meeting form of government such as that in colonial America, has he had a similarly direct voice in public affairs. The weakness of the Greeks lay in the failure of the states to co-operate with one another, a failure which eventually led to their conquest by outsiders.

In almost every field of culture there were numerous great names, and all were innovators. The Greeks had enough collective genius to inspire the Western world for more than a millennium. Almost all Roman culture was dependent on Greek originals. The Greco-Roman tradition in our own Western civilization was assimilated only slowly, but it has laid its impress on almost everything achieved in the West until very recent times. Indeed, we can say with some truth that the ancient world, with its utterly alien concepts and way of life really ended with the Greeks, and that with the Greeks and Romans the modern world began. Though we adopt the customary division of ancient, medieval, and modern in this book, there is really a greater difference between the world of the Egyptians, Mesopotamians, and Hebrews and the world of the Greeks and Romans than there is between the latter world and our own.

4
FROM CITY-STATE TO WORLD EMPIRE—THE EXPANSION OF ROME

We have seen in the preceding chapter that the Greek city-states were unable to unite and were conquered by Philip II of Macedon. Alexander the Great in turn defeated the Persians and inherited their empire, but it was divided among his generals after his death. However, the Romans from their own base, the city-state of Rome, not only united Greece and the Hellenistic kingdoms under their rule but also added the greater part of western Europe. They maintained their empire intact for several centuries. How this astonishing feat was achieved will be the theme of this chapter.

THE REPUBLIC

From the establishment of Roman independence in the late sixth century B.C. to the Battle of Actium in 31 B.C., when C. Octavianus Caesar, with the title of Augustus, became the sole ruler of the Roman Empire, Rome was governed by an office-holding oligarchy. During those years Rome was a republic, and the period should be distinguished from the years from 31 B.C. to A.D. 476, when the realm was ruled by a monarch under various titles. Although most of the empire was won during the period of the Republic, the term Roman Empire usually applies to the later, monarchical epoch.

The Early Peoples of Italy. According to the archaeological evidence, the Italian peninsula was peopled in the second millennium B.C. by various invaders who arrived at different times, bringing with them first bronze and then iron. It is possible that the Italian peoples were of similar stock to the Greeks and that the first invasions coincided with those of the Achaeans into Greece. Early in the first millennium B.C. a seafaring people, the Etruscans, arrived, probably from Asia Minor. They had their own language, still undeciphered, and a culture somewhat related to that of the early Greeks. They also

45

brought with them customs derived probably from the Mesopotamian peoples, including the practice of divination. Many of these customs were inherited by the Romans. The Etruscans settled in northern Italy and in time extended their sway into central Italy, overcoming the resistance of most of the Latins, the Italian tribe to which the Romans belonged. They could not, however, defeat the Greeks who had arrived in southern Italy as colonists a century or two after the Etruscans.

The Establishment of Roman Independence. The traditional date of the founding of the city of Rome on the Tiber is 753 B.C. This date, however, has little to recommend it to historians, since there is archaeological evidence for a settlement several centuries earlier. The traditional seven kings of Rome, beginning with Romulus have scarcely more historical authenticity. But it is likely that one of them, Tarquin I, an Etruscan monarch, did subject Rome to his rule in the early sixth century B.C. and that the last king of Rome, Tarquin the Proud, likewise an Etruscan, was driven out by a rebellion. The traditional date of this event is 509 B.C.

The Etruscan monarch had ruled Rome with the aid of a Senate made up of the heads of certain patrician families. It is possible that he enjoyed more support from plebeians, who were not of noble birth though they might be men of substance. Nevertheless, the Etruscans were foreigners; and when an incident occurred which excited the animosity of the whole people (traditionally the rape of Lucretia by a son of Tarquin and her subsequent suicide), they were driven out by an angry mob. The patricians then took over the government, choosing two consuls from their own number who held office for a year, replacing the king.

The Struggle between Patricians and Plebeians. At this time the patricians held a monopoly of public office. The election of magistrates was in the hands of the Military Assembly (*Comitia Centuriata*), in which the voting was weighted in favor of men of wealth (of whom there were few outside the ranks of the patricians), and the consuls had to be men of patrician birth. Plebeians were not permitted to intermarry with patricians, and had no way of defending themselves against the arbitrary acts of magistrates. The only check upon the actions of the consuls (who were both civil and military officials but held office only for a year at a time) was the Senate of patricians, in which the consuls sat and of which they remained members after their year of office.

It is evident from the subsequent struggle between the patricians and the plebeians, which fills the domestic history of the next two hundred years, that the latter were far from satisfied with the change-over from kingly to republican rule. Since the Romans had to defend themselves against the Etruscans and local Italian tribes, warfare was incessant. The plebeians, who were of course required to take part in these campaigns, staged a strike against the patricians in 494 B.C. and won the right to have two special plebeian officers of their own (tribunes), who could veto the acts of the consuls. They were also granted an assembly which could pass laws (*plebiscita*) binding on the plebeians but not on the patricians. During the next decades this was converted into an assembly of all the Roman tribes (*Comitia Tributa*), in which patricians as well as plebeians could sit.

In 449 B.C., perhaps by means of another strike, the plebeians compelled a dilatory legal commission set up by the Senate to promulgate a written law code known as the Twelve Tables. These laws, which were of a primitive nature, especially in their criminal provisions, similar to those of the Hammurabi Code (see p. 17), nevertheless represented a considerable achievement for the plebeians. Arbitrary decisions by magistrates would in the future give place to formal trials; and the many provisions regulating such matters as marriage, contracts, debts, and wills already suggest the interest of the Romans in civil law and procedure. Intermarriage between patricians and plebeians was still forbidden, but a law permitting it was passed during the next decade.

In 448 B.C. the Assembly of the Tribes was permitted to legislate for the whole state provided that the Senate accepted the proposals. But this assembly could not debate. It could only accept or reject the proposals of the tribunes or consuls, who had the right to call it into session. Thus effective power continued to rest with the Senate, which alone could debate and amend and among whose members were to be found almost all those in the state who had had executive experience in high office or as generals.

The plebeians therefore made a strong attempt to break the patrician monopoly of the high offices of state. But the Senate, rather than admit plebeians to the consulship, which had taken the place of the Crown, preferred to abolish the office for a time. Eventually, in 367 B.C., they restored it, and thereafter plebeians were admitted successively to all the offices of state, including the Senate itself. By the middle of the third century B.C. these were as follows: two consuls, two praetors (judges and military commanders junior to the consuls), a varying number of aediles (municipal officials), and quaestors (treasury officials). These men were now drawn from all the classes in Rome. In addition there were now ten tribunes, drawn only from the plebs. By this time they were important not only because of their veto but also by virtue of their right to summon the legislature and submit laws to it. It may be noted too that the constitution provided for the election of a dictator in times of grave emergency who was granted supreme power in the state for a period limited to six months. Two censors were elected every five years and assigned the task of taking a census and filling vacancies in the Senate. All officials except the tribunes continued to be elected by the whole people divided into military classes. Since these classes were based upon property ownership, the wealthy, who might be either patricians or plebeians, in fact controlled these elections until late in republican history.

In 287 B.C., after one last strike by the plebeians against the patricians, the Senate lost its veto on legislation, and thereafter the Assembly of Tribes was in theory supreme, and the Roman Republic had formally become a democracy. In practice the Senate, chosen for life by the censors, mainly from among those who had held office, continued to be the most important body in the state. It was the only body that could debate, and its advice was almost invariably accepted by the Assemblies. It controlled the treasury; it appointed the commanding officers in the army and provincial governors; and it alone could declare martial law. Almost everyone who had held important office in the state, including the plebeian tribunes, by this time belonged to it. But, at least in appearance, the long struggle between the classes was over, and no one could be discriminated against merely because of his low birth.

The Unification of Italy. In external affairs the Romans, by a mixture of military valor and tenacity and shrewd diplomacy, had succeeded by the middle of the third century B.C. in winning control of all Italy. They were indeed already engaged in a life-and-death struggle with Carthage for the control of the western Mediterranean.

All Roman citizens who possessed minimum property qualifications were required to do military service from the age of seventeen to forty-six. The organization of the army varied according to the nature of the terrain and the tactics of its enemies. In time it came to be composed of a varying number of legions, each at full strength containing four thousand infantrymen aided by cavalry units. The army was commanded by the consuls, who exercised absolute authority over the troops. Roman armies were in the early centuries noted for their discipline, and even in later times they were usually more disciplined than those of their enemies.

The early years of the Republic were difficult ones. The Romans first were compelled to fight the Latins, who were disinclined to accept the domination of Rome now that the defeat of the Etruscans had freed all the Latins from foreign rule. After three years of fighting (496–493 B.C.), a treaty was made granting the Latins special rights. For a long time thereafter they were firm allies of Rome, though not allowed to pursue an independent foreign policy. There followed wars with other tribes and with the Etruscans until in 396 B.C. the Romans succeeded in subjugating the latter and annexing their territory. By this time Rome was more powerful than her Latin allies and was the leading power in central Italy. Nevertheless, she lost much prestige in 390 B.C., when a raid into Italy by a Celtic people, the Gauls, resulted in a sack of Rome. But the Gauls quickly withdrew, though they were troublesome for several decades thereafter.

The Latins then revolted against Roman domination but were brought back as clearly subordinate allies in 345 B.C. Almost at once the Romans had to fight an important group of tribes known as the Samnites. This war proving indecisive, the Latin tribes again revolted but were defeated in a sharp war (340–338 B.C.). This time they lost almost all their previous privileges and were deprived of some of their lands. From then onward they were in reality autonomous subjects of Rome. They had certain clearly defined rights, such as the right to intermarry and to trade, and they were allowed to rule themselves. But the Romans planted military colonies in the territories of the Latins to ensure that they remained loyal to their alliance to Rome.

Rome was thus strong enough to take on the Samnites again. For over thirty years she competed with them for control of the part of southern Italy that was not Greek. At one time the Samnites founded a confederation of their own, including Etruscans and Gauls, to counteract the Roman alliance. But eventually the Romans with solid Latin help won. They conceded self-government and some other rights to the Samnites, who thereupon became Roman allies. In the course of the wars, however, the Romans had encroached on Greek territory and entered into an alliance with some Greek cities in Italy. This caused the leading Greek city of Tarentum to appeal for help to a Greek king, Pyrrhus, across the Adriatic. Aided by an alliance with Carthage, the Romans after a ten-year war defeated both Pyrrhus and his Greek allies, thereby becoming in 272 B.C. supreme in Italy. The Greek cities were permitted to retain self-government with the status of allies of Rome.

The Wars with Carthage (Punic Wars). Rome was by now a power of the first rank in the western Mediterranean, and probably a war with the other leading power in the area was inevitable. The Romans by their treaties with their defeated enemies, under which the latter were forbidden any independent policy of their own, necessitated that appeals for aid would be made to them. The First Punic War (264–241 B.C.) began when a group of Italian mercenaries in Sicily appealed to Rome for help against the Sicilian king, while others appealed to Carthage for the same purpose. Both powers responded and became involved with one another. Eventually the Romans, though primarily a land power, built fleets effective enough to destroy the Carthaginians. They then took Sicily for themselves, leaving to Hiero, a king of Syracuse, his throne as a client ruler, while the remainder of Sicily became the first Roman province. Rome then seized from the Carthaginians Sardinia, which with Corsica became the second Roman province.

In 218 B.C. Carthage, smarting under her defeat in the first trial of strength with the Romans and having interests in Spain which conflicted with those of Rome, renewed the war (Second Punic War, 218–202 B.C.). The Carthaginian general Hannibal, at the head of a great army including some elephants, crossed the Alps into Italy, defeating several Roman armies, almost annihilating the last of them in 216 B.C. at Cannae. But he did not march on Rome itself, preferring to win the allegiance of the Samnites and others and prepare for an all-out assault later. The Romans continued to fight on, refusing all terms offered by Hannibal, whose armies began to disintegrate. He was unable to obtain any significant aid from home. In the course of the war the Romans seized the rest of Sicily. Eventually, under Scipio Africanus, the Romans took the initiative, invaded Spain, and drove out the Carthaginians. Then at last they attacked Hannibal's home base in Africa. The great general was recalled from Italy, but at the Battle of Zama in 202 B.C. his army was destroyed, even though he himself escaped. The following year Carthage was compelled to make peace. She ceded Spain, which was divided into two Roman provinces.

The Conquest of Greece. Almost at once the Romans became involved in a war with Philip V of Macedon, who had befriended Hannibal after his escape from Africa. Philip had allied himself with

Antiochus III, the Hellenistic king of Syria, who had won a number
of successes in Asia and become the chief power in the eastern Mediterranean. This alliance between Macedon and Syria the Romans
felt was directed against themselves, since several of the Greek
allies would be swallowed up in the process and the independence of
Egypt was threatened. The two Greek leagues and the Hellenistic
state of Pergamum in Asia Minor joined in the Roman attack on
Philip, which was brought to a successful conclusion in 197 B.C. The
Roman consul Flamininus thereupon amidst much enthusiasm proclaimed the independence of all Greece. But this well-meant gesture
did not put an end to intercity rivalry. The Aetolian League (an
alliance controlling much of central Greece) soon solicited the aid of
Antiochus against the Romans. This time Philip remained neutral,
while the Romans defeated Antiochus at the Battle of Magnesia and
took his European and Aetolian territories from him (190 B.C.). In
171 B.C. Perseus, Philip's successor on the throne of Macedon, whose
position in Greece had become increasingly difficult, made war on the
Romans once more, only to be utterly defeated in the Battle of Pydna
(168 B.C.). In spite of the Roman presence, the internecine squabbles
among the Greek cities and their leagues continued until in 146 B.C.
the Romans made Macedonia into a province. The remainder of
Greece followed in 127 B.C. Meanwhile much of the country had been
pillaged by the Roman armies. The booty, indeed, was so great that
internal taxes in Rome were abolished and thereafter Rome lived
from the proceeds of regular provincial taxes. In 146 B.C. Carthage,
which had shown signs of revival, was destroyed on the insistence of
Cato (a die-hard senatorial conservative) and another province
created in Africa.

The Provincial System. By this time the provincial system had
been systematically organized. The governor was appointed by the
Roman Senate from among those who had held high office in Rome
as consuls or praetors. But the governorship was limited to a single
year. Since the governor was unpaid and had been put to considerable expense in winning his elections to his earlier offices, there was
a great temptation for him to make the most of his two years as
governor (one after his praetorship, one after his consulship) and
fleece his province. The Romans tried to prevent this difficulty by
setting up special courts to deal with cases of corruption. But since
they were manned by senators until 121 B.C. and thereafter by
middle-class bankers, who were equally interested in revenues from
the provinces, convictions for bribery were at all times rare. Oppor-

tunities for corruption were numerous, since the governor was in immediate control of the tax collectors, who in turn needed his support. Laws regulating the amount of taxes to be collected from the provincials remained in these circumstances dead letters. From the end of the Second Punic War, expansion had become profitable to the military leaders and to their troops, to the state itself, and to the bankers who handled tax collection, as well as to the governors. Moreover, since few campaigns could now be concluded in one year, the conscript troops, who had formerly been farmers, could not return to their homes in Italy for the harvest. Indeed, when they returned, they usually found that their farms had been taken over by powerful senators and others whom they could not dislodge. They therefore had little option but to remain in the army or swell the ranks of the unemployed and underemployed in Rome.

The Gracchan Revolution. These conditions set the stage for the domestic strife which filled the last century of the Republic. Even while Roman arms continued to be generally successful, a virulent class struggle persisted in Rome itself. In 133 B.C. Tiberius Gracchus was elected tribune on a program for redistribution of lands in Italy to the dispossessed small farmers. The upper classes, now known as the *optimates*, naturally opposed this program but had an even greater objection to popular government, which would become feasible if tribunes could be re-elected and use the Assembly of Tribes to enact legislation over the opposition of the Senate. Against this possibility the optimates had several weapons. But all were dangerous to use against an aroused people, especially when the loyalty of the army and its commanders was doubtful. The Senate still appointed the commanders, but as long as they were militarily successful they would hold the allegiance of their troops, and the Senate could never be sure that they would lay down their commands on demand. The dangers, however, were not yet visible in 133 B.C., and the optimates used their constitutional weapons as long as they could. Tiberius' land law was vetoed by one of the tribunes, as was his right. Tiberius then resummoned the Assembly and had the man deposed and replaced, whereupon the law was passed. This procedure was unconstitutional, but the law went into effect. Much worse, from the point of view of the optimates, was Tiberius' intention to have himself re-elected. To prevent the creation of such a precedent a group of optimates on election day took matters into their own hands and murdered him and many of his supporters.

Ten years later Tiberius' brother Gaius tried again with an extended program of reforms. Tiberius' land law had been shown to be inadequate as a solution to the many problems connected with the expansion of Rome. The Italian allies, who had shared in the hardships of the recent wars, still possessed only limited rights and felt themselves discriminated against by the Romans. The senatorial courts were unwilling to protect the interests of the exploited provincials, and there were still numerous veterans who had not been able to obtain lands in Italy. Palliatives were still necessary to relieve the lot of the unemployed and underemployed in Rome. Gaius Gracchus proposed to grant full citizenship to the Italians, to settle farmers in the provinces in new colonies created for the purpose, to sell grain below market price, and to transfer control of the courts handling cases of provincial corruption to the equestrian order, made up of the middle classes.

This program was not universally popular, even among the majority. Few Romans were willing to share their privileges with the Italians, the down payments insisted on for settlement in the new colonies could not be met by all those in need, and the senators naturally objected to handing over their courts to their social inferiors—many of whom were indeed as deeply involved in the provincial corruption as themselves. A candidate named Drusus, put up by the optimates to oppose Gaius Gracchus, could offer free (not subsidized) grain, promise to abolish down payments in the new settlements, and play upon popular prejudice by opposing the grant of citizenship to the politically powerless Italians. Whether or not he ever intended to carry out his program, it was clearly designed to undermine Gaius' support among the people; and Gaius and his friends deeply distrusted his motives and behavior. Drusus' maneuver was brilliantly successful. Though tribunes by this time could be reelected, and Gaius stood for election three times, the second time he came lower in the poll than Drusus and the third time he failed altogether of re-election.

Neither Gaius nor his followers were willing to see their reform program thus brought to an untimely end. In the disturbances that followed, the Senate declared martial law. Gaius and a large number of his supporters were killed. Little had been won from the reform program except the provision of grain at low prices for the populace. The unemployed were therefore subsidized but had little better means for making a living than before.

The Threat from Marius. The next threat to the Republic arose from the military side. A war in Africa (111–105 B.C.) against a prince, Jugurtha, was going badly for Rome, resulting in charges that the generals had been bribed. Marius, who was a popular officer and a self-made man, obtained enough support in Rome to have himself elected consul and thereupon superseded his superior. With the aid of his lieutenant Sulla, who captured Jugurtha, he won the war. In the process he had reorganized the Roman army on a volunteer basis, removing the former property qualification for service. The new army, which was much more efficient than the old, owed its loyalty no longer to Rome but to its commander, whom it would follow as long as he was successful and could provide booty, while wielding enough political power to compel the state to grant pensions to the soldiers on retirement. This arrangement was the most dangerous instrument yet forged against the integrity of the state.

Immediately after the victory of Marius in Africa, Italy was faced with an invasion by Germanic tribes who poured over the passes and in some places penetrated deep into the country. Marius was the obvious choice for commander of the defending army. To keep him in this post, the people illegally elected him consul for several years. When the menace had receded and Marius had ceased to be indispensable, the optimates wished to return to constitutional government. But Marius with the aid of a political machine had himself reelected consul for the sixth time in 100 B.C. However, he could not control his henchmen. When riots broke out in Rome the Senate declared martial law. Marius as consul was thus called upon to suppress his own followers and did so, thereby discrediting himself with the popular party without endearing himself to the optimates. He thereupon went into exile.

The Social War. Meanwhile the Italian allies had been growing restive. They had been required to take part in all the Roman wars but, not being citizens, had failed to receive their share of the profits and were in other respects discriminated against. Long before, Gaius Gracchus had proposed that they be given full citizenship and the proposal had been frequently made in the years since. But it was unpopular with the Roman people, who did not wish to share their privileges. When a last attempt to pass the law failed in 91 B.C., many of the Italian peoples rose in revolt (Social War, 91–88 B.C.). This revolt the Romans found extremely difficult to suppress, even though they were supported by some of the Italians and had the new professional army. It was brought to an end only by the granting of full citizenship to the Italians.

The Ascendancy of Sulla. Before this war was over, Mithridates

VI of Pontus, a still independent Hellenistic king, declared war on the Romans in Asia, necessitating a new long-term command. Marius and Sulla, who had both aided in the suppression of the Italian revolt, each desired the lucrative position. The Senate preferred the aristo-cratic Sulla, the people Marius. Sulla was able to outmaneuver Marius and leave Rome to join his army. But riots broke out in Rome, com-pelling Sulla to return to the city to restore order. This done, he went off to the East, leaving Rome at the mercy of Marius, who armed the slaves and instituted a reign of terror against the optimates. Though the aging Marius soon died, Rome was in the hands of the popular party until Sulla wound up the war with Mithridates in 84 B.C. and returned to Italy. There he defeated the popular leaders and had himself made dictator, while he instituted reforms intended to take power out of the hands of the populace and place it securely in the hands of the Senate. For a few years, while Sulla lived in retirement but with his army still at his disposal, Rome was quiet and the re-formed Senate ruled constitutionally.

The Rise of Pompey. As soon as Sulla was dead, it became clear that the Senate was both unable and unwilling to rule. A slave re-volt led by Spartacus, one of the slaves, broke out in Italy, while the Spanish provinces seceded under the leadership of a Roman. The result was that once again armies were needed. The two leading commanders, Pompey and Crassus, had themselves made consuls in 70 B.C. though both were under legal age. They used their position to destroy the Sullan constitution and restore to the people and their tribunes and Assembly their old powers. Soon afterward the popular Assembly granted Pompey a long-term command against the pirates in the Mediterranean. This mission accomplished, he was sent, again by the people, to the East where Mithridates had once more raised the standard of revolt. For the next few years Pompey's army, which was uniformly successful, was the crucial factor in Roman affairs, even though he himself was abroad. It was known that at any time he might return, and then Rome would be at his mercy. During these years, the famous orator and lawyer Cicero became consul (63 B.C.) and was instrumental in suppressing a *coup d'état* planned by the demagogue Catiline. But though he achieved this goal by ordi-nary legal means, Cicero earned little thanks from Pompey, who would have preferred to do the job himself.

The First Triumvirate. In 61 B.C. Pompey, his task in the East completed, returned to Italy, expecting the thanks and co-operation of the Senate and people. He needed from the Senate ratification for his acts and pensions for his troops. In order to create a favorable impression, he formally disbanded his army on entering Italy and went to Rome as a private citizen. The senatorial leaders, totally misjudging the situation, refused his reasonable requests, whereupon Pompey turned his support to the consul-elect, Julius Caesar, an ambitious man who had recently returned from a successful campaign in Spain. Caesar had reached his position as a result of financial support from Crassus, the consul of 70 B.C., a Roman capitalist who wished now for a new command as well as for repayment of his debts at public expense. Pompey agreed to their terms, and the First Triumvirate, made up of Pompey, Caesar, and Crassus, was formed (60 B.C.). Its strength lay in Pompey's troops, who were ready to spring to arms as soon as their commander should summon them.

When, therefore, the Senate again refused to meet Pompey's terms, Caesar as consul surrounded the Senate house with troops and the Senate gave way. Thereafter the real rulers of Rome were the triumvirs, though none of them was present in the city. Rome, indeed, was a prey to violence and demagoguery, and often to open warfare in the streets between rival gangs. Caesar, as his share of the bargain, was granted a long-term command in Gaul, in the course of which he not only won the whole of Gaul (58–51 B.C.) and invaded Britain but also built up a powerful professional army loyal only to himself. Crassus in 55 B.C. was granted a similar command in the East but was defeated and killed two years later at the Battle of Carrhae. Meanwhile Pompey, while he continued to hold official command, was not engaged in actual combat—though he was occasionally called in by the Senate to suppress the gang warfare in Rome.

The Dictatorship of Caesar. By 49 B.C. when Caesar's command ran out and he was ready to return, Pompey had in large measure embraced the senatorial cause. The Senate wished to cut short Caesar's career and to hold him to account for various illegal acts of his campaigns. Caesar, with an army he believed to be superior to anything Pompey and the Senate could bring against him, was determined not to submit to their insulting demands and brought his army from Gaul across the river Rubicon into Italy. He was thereupon declared an outlaw by the Senate. But Pompey, the senatorial commander, could not enroll enough troops to defend the country. Preferring to go to Greece, where his name still retained some of its former magic, he was outmaneuvered there by Caesar and defeated at the Battle of Pharsalus (48 B.C.). He fled to Egypt, where he was soon afterward murdered. Caesar followed, aiding Cleopatra to become sole ruler of the country by getting rid of her brothers.

After spending several months in Egypt, Caesar again bestirred himself and mopped up various groups of Pompey's supporters, returning to Rome at last in 45 B.C. as sole dictator. He ruled supreme for the rest of his life and instituted a considerable number of domestic reforms, including the taking of a census, as a result of which he restricted the distribution of free grain to those who needed and were entitled to it. He began several colonization projects both in Italy and in the Empire; instituted a huge public works program, including the construction of much-needed roads; reformed the calendar; and began the reform of municipalities by introducing some uniformity into their charters. In the provinces he made a good beginning by bringing the governors under his personal control and holding them responsible to him for their acts. He substituted a regular annual tax for the arbitrary assessments of the tax collectors, and he made plans for establishing Roman law throughout the whole Empire. In short, he was the first Roman leader to view all the Roman imperial possessions as a whole, ruled from Rome but with all the imperial subjects enjoying substantial equality with one another, unlike most of his predecessors who had regarded the Empire as a preserve maintained for the exclusive benefit of the conquerors.

Caesar does not appear ever to have decided under what permanent forms he himself was to rule. When he was murdered by a group of disgruntled senators and army officers on the Ides of March, 44 B.C., he had barely begun his enormous task of establishing the new order in Rome and the provinces.

The Second Triumvirate. Caesar's murderers had no idea of what they themselves wished to do beyond getting rid of the "tyrant." Caesar's military second-in-command, Marcus Antonius (Antony), who had not been seized by the conspirators, turned the tables on them, with the support of the people, and drove them from Rome. Antony then marched to the north against Decimus Brutus, one of the conspirators, while a young man who had been adopted as Caesar's son and heir under his will, entered Italy and began to raise troops on the strength of his new name and of promises to honor Caesar's bequests—a task neglected by Antony. Gaius Julius Caesar Octavianus, as he now called himself, was then given a command against Antony by the Senate. But after he had won a victory the Senate treated him in an offhand manner, thus driving him into the arms of Antony. The Second Triumvirate was then formed by Antony and Octavian with the addition of Marcus Lepidus, a commander who had joined Antony in his expedition against Brutus. The Triumvirate instituted large-scale proscriptions, in part for the purpose of raising troops from the proceeds of confiscated property and in part as vengeance against their enemies. Antony insisted on the execution of Cicero, who had taken the lead in opposing him after the murder of Caesar. The Triumvirate then proceeded against the murderers of Caesar and defeated their hastily enrolled armies at the Battle of Philippi (42 B.C.). Brutus and Cassius, the leading conspirators, both committed suicide.

The Triumph of Octavian and Establishment of the Principate. Other tasks of pacification remained to be accomplished, especially in the East, where Antony was given the command against the Parthians. Though he won a few victories, he spent most of his time in Egypt with its queen, Cleopatra, by whom he had two sons. This liaison was looked at askance by the Romans, who feared that he was proposing to change the whole character of the Roman Empire, perhaps planning to rule it from Alexandria. Octavian, who turned out to be a master politician, took full advantage of Antony's dubious actions. Quickly shunting off Lepidus and defeating the last of the Pompeians in the person of Pompey's son, he built himself a powerful political party while organizing his own armies under an able general, Agrippa. Though the alliance with Antony was several times renewed, Octavian at last felt himself strong enough to put an end to it. In the naval Battle of Actium in 31 B.C. the forces of Antony and Cleopatra were defeated, and both committed suicide soon afterward.

Octavian was now the unquestioned master of Rome. He set himself to convert the old Roman Republic and its institutions into a disguised monarchy, with himself as *princeps*, or first citizen. He assumed the name of Augustus and the powers of permanent consul and tribune, which placed both military and civil authority firmly in his hands. He reorganized the provincial system by making the commanders of the frontier provinces of the Empire responsible only to himself and subject to recall at any time. He also reorganized the Senate and made membership in it exclusively the reward for holding civil offices. Elections continued to be held for these offices, but of course no one would even have stood for election without Augustus' consent. Thus for a transitional period the forms of the old Republic were retained. But the Republic had in reality ceased to exist, having been effectively replaced by one-man rule. From this time on, it is customary to speak of the realm as the Roman Empire, which lasted from the victory of Augustus in 31 B.C. to the extinction of formal Roman rule in the West in A.D. 476.

Roman Economy and Society Under the Republic. The Roman economy in the last centuries of the Republic was solidly based on slavery, since prisoners taken in the unending wars were customarily sold as slaves. Their price was always low, and free labor in many areas could barely subsist in competition with them. Slaves on the great Italian estates owned by the rich and slaves who were compelled to work in the mines had an unenviable lot; but most of what in our society constitute the professional classes were also slaves, or freedmen (former slaves who had earned their freedom or been freed through the benevolence of their owners). Greek slaves were likely to be better educated and more talented, especially in handicrafts, than Roman and Italian freemen. The pirates who roamed the Mediterranean before Pompey cleaned them up (see p. 55) sold their captives, who might be Greeks or Orientals; such sales were a primary source of income for them. Slaves of this kind could hope to earn money of their own and even acquire property, with which they could purchase their freedom. But this tremendous trade in slaves accounts in large measure for the economic difficulties of the ordinary Roman and Italian workers, who had to compete with them for the available jobs.

Rome always had an unfavorable balance of trade with the outside world. Though there were numerous small industries supplying consumer products, the vast bulk of luxury goods consumed in Rome were imported, as was most of the grain. The payment for these imports was made possible by the immense booty taken from foreigners in the course of Roman expansion and by the heavy taxes laid upon the provinces.

The poor in Rome, as well as the slaves, were regarded as a potential danger by the ruling classes. Slave uprisings were suppressed with the greatest severity. But the poor Roman freemen had the vote and so had to be cultivated by ambitious noblemen who hoped to be elected to office. Hence the general policy of subsidizing the price of grain or even distributing it free, while ambitious noblemen borrowed heavily in order to please the populace by providing sumptuous shows ("bread and circuses"). The gap between the consumption of rich and poor nevertheless was probably greater in the later Roman Republic than at any other time in history. Rich men built

huge villas; even men like Cicero of relatively moderate means possessed several country estates. They submitted to few if any taxes,
and maintained status by every kind of conspicious consumption.
Young noblemen were almost invariably in debt, some of them, like
Catiline, being driven to desperate measures when pressed by their
creditors. Only in the Italian countryside many miles from Rome did
the old virtues prevail, and a small farmer could make a moderate
living on a family farm without owning a single slave.

Roman Culture under the Republic. The Romans on the whole
were not a culturally creative people. Their greatest achievements
lie in the fields of government and law. Though many of the fundamental concepts of Roman law were developed in the time of the
Republic and will therefore be dealt with here, it was the government of the Empire that influenced subsequent Western civilization.
Indeed, it may be said that the government of the Republic has
above all provided us with a case history of how impossible it is for
a city-state, with institutions developed only for such a state, to rule
a large empire.

Most of the other Roman cultural achievements rest upon Greek
foundations. This derivation is true also of the majority of Roman
writers, who modeled themselves on Greek originals, as did, for
example, the Republican playwrights Plautus and Terence. The most
notable Roman orator, Cicero, whose style is usually regarded as
the norm for all Latin writing, modeled his rhetoric on that of the
Athenian orator Demosthenes. His philosophical writings, though
several of them are concerned with Roman political science, owe a
heavy debt to the work of Hellenistic philosophers, especially the
Stoics and Epicureans. Cicero's letters, however, are original, since
this is a form of writing scarcely used among the Greeks. The best
political scientist under the Republic was undoubtedly the Greek
exile Polybius, whose history attempts to study the reasons for the
effectiveness of the Roman Republic in the second century B.C.

The Roman poet Lucretius, who influenced the Augustan writer
Vergil, wrote a long poem *Concerning the Nature of Things (De
rerum naturae),* one of the few philosophical and scientific writings in
history which succeeds in being pure poetry. It is the story of evolution as seen through the imagination of a follower of Epicurus who
had accepted the atomic theory of his master and Democritus.

The Augustan Age. When Augustus assumed power he expressed
a strong interest in culture, and he encouraged his friend Maecenas
to extend patronage to poets and artists, who thus in return glorified

the age. Horace, who wrote many odes to Augustus as well as to his patron, was a kind of poet laureate of the day. But the more serious Vergil was far more greatly honored in later times, especially in the Middle Ages. His *Aeneid* is an epic (partly in imitation of Homer's *Odyssey*) which portrays the wanderings of the Trojan Aeneas after the fall of Troy. Aeneas, according to Vergil, became the ancestor of Romulus, the traditional founder of Rome. Vergil also wrote a long poem (*Georgics*) praising the agricultural life. Ovid, another gifted poet, wrote of the loves and amatory exploits of gods and heroes. Incurring the wrath of Augustus, probably because of a scandal which involved the princeps' family, he was sent into permanent exile. Livy wrote a history of the Republic, glorifying the traditional virtues of the Romans. Vergil, Horace, and Livy, each in his different manner, expressed the idea that the Romans from the beginning had been destined to rule the world and that this destiny was now being fulfilled under the aegis of Augustus, who would usher in a new era of peace.

Roman Law. Reference has already been made to the Twelve Tables of 449 B.C. as the fundamental law code of Rome (see p. 47). Statute law continued to be made by the Assembly in accordance with the demands of the time. This type of law need not concern us further. What was new in Rome was the concept of citizenship as an individual right, which could be granted by the state, and the gradual extension of citizenship to all inhabitants of the Empire, a process completed in A.D. 212. Initially there had been a distinction between the law that applied to a citizen (*jus civile*) and the law that applied in cases where a foreigner was involved (*jus gentium*); but the latter gradually replaced the former.

Lawsuits under the Republic were dealt with by the praetor, assisted by professional jurists. The vast majority of cases were based upon precedent, or the way in which similar cases had been handled in the past. The city praetor, who held office only for a year and who, as a potential general, was probably little interested in his legal work, issued at the beginning of his year of office an *edict* which stated the precedents and principles he would use in his own judgments. Under the emperor Hadrian in the second century A.D., a *perpetual edict* was issued, so that for the future any litigant would know under what laws and precedents his case would be handled. From quite early times it was believed in Rome that the basis of all laws should be equity and justice, a "natural" law (*jus naturale*), to which all man-made laws should as far as possible be required to conform. Eminent legal thinkers under the Empire gave much attention to the content of this "natural" law, and the work of the best of these men was used as an authoritative guide for future cases. In the formulation of this legal theory the Stoics, with their idea of a Divine Reason, were most influential. In the late Empire, views of the leading jurists were frequently collected, and several complete codes were drawn up by the emperors, culminating in the Justinian Code (*Corpus juris civilis*) promulgated by the Byzantine emperor Justinian in the sixth century A.D.

THE EMPIRE (A.D. 14–180)

Augustus, of course, was the real founder of the Empire. When he died in A.D. 14, after a reign of forty-five years as princeps, there was virtually no chance of restoring the old Republic. Though before long the Empire fell into incompetent or tyrannical hands, the solution could only be to place it in better hands, never to overthrow the Empire itself.

The Julian Line. Augustus lived so long that he survived all his direct descendants, each of whom in turn he had wished to succeed him. In his last years he chose his stepson Tiberius, whom he disliked but who was a competent general and administrator. He adopted Tiberius as his son and heir. Then he had his own major powers conferred on him, so that no formidable competitor to Tiberius was available when he died. Augustus therefore in choosing his successor combined the principles of heredity and nomination. (If he had had a surviving son or grandson, no doubt the principle of heredity alone would have prevailed.) This problem of succession was always to plague the Empire, since it required a first-class administrator to govern the huge Roman domains, and not all the sons even of competent emperors would inherit their fathers' abilities.

Tiberius, as expected, proved to be a competent ruler; but he was always unpopular, and a conspiracy, led by the commander of the royal guard (praetorian prefect), the only troops stationed permanently in Rome, almost succeeded. Eventually Tiberius was murdered, and Gaius Caligula, the son of his popular brother, was made princeps. Caligula was weak-minded and frivolous, and soon became totally insane. He too was murdered, to be replaced by his uncle Claudius, a much more competent though pedantic ruler, who began a true civil service, which was to come to its full growth in the second and later centuries A.D. Claudius, however, was never able to assert effective authority in his own imperial household, being ruled and excessively influenced by his successive wives and freedmen. Eventually his last wife, Agrippina, persuaded him to disinherit his son by a former wife in favor of her own son by a former marriage. This latter, the infamous Nero, won the throne without difficulty. For several years he left the government in the hands of effective lieutenants, especially Seneca, his tutor, and Burrus, his praetorian prefect. When the latter died, Nero fell under the influence of his unscrupulous successor and became increasingly tyrannous until he was overthrown by a conspiracy and compelled to commit suicide.

Thus in A.D. 69 the Julian line of rulers came to an end. The Empire under the system established by Augustus and Tiberius remained intact. In the last years of Augustus' reign, the Roman legions had suffered a severe defeat (A.D. 9) at the hands of the Germans which put an end to expansion across the Rhine. Under Claudius the beginning was made of a conquest of Britain, a conquest which took several reigns to complete. The rest of the Empire was consolidated and the frontiers guarded. Nevertheless, in these years it had already become clear that the seat of real power was in the various armies which were held together only by the princeps. The troops frequently mutinied against their own commanders and had to be pacified with donatives. On the death of Nero, leaving no obvious heir to the purple, the various commanders engaged in competition for the throne.

Meanwhile all political power tended to concentrate in the hands of the princeps. The Senate, though it was given considerable tasks by Augustus and his successor and was the official legislature of the state, enjoyed ever less real power. Nero decimated its ranks with executions for treason, and it dared do nothing, not even speak against the will of the princeps. Elections to office by this time were a mere formality. The last vestiges of the Republic had disappeared, and the Senate and the people were now well aware of it. It only remained to be officially recognized in the title of the ruler, to signify his effective powers. This was done during the next dynasties.

The Struggle for Power and The Flavian Dynasty. On the death of Nero, the legions in Spain proclaimed their commander Galba as princeps. He took the throne but was in turn ousted by Otho, with the support of the praetorian guard. The legions in Germany under their commander Vitellius marched on Rome and made him emperor. Vespasian, the commander in the East, taking his time to win impressive support on his way to Rome, secured the throne for himself and bequeathed it to his sons in turn. As the historian Tacitus observed, the fact was noted during this so-called Year of the Four Emperors (A.D. 69) that emperors could be made elsewhere than at Rome.

Vespasian (A.D. 69–79), an Italian of humble birth, proved an efficient ruler. As a soldier he was more personally concerned with the expansion of the Empire and the consolidation of its frontiers than had been his immediate Julian predecessors. At the time that he made his bid for the throne he had been occupied in suppressing a revolt in Judea. His son Titus completed this campaign in A.D. 70 with the capture and destruction of Jerusalem. Vespasian also began a campaign beyond the Rhine and undertook in earnest the complete subjugation of Britain, which was accomplished during the reign of Domitian. Though Titus held the throne for only two years (A.D. 79–81), his energetic brother Domitian continued his father's campaigns with moderate success. At home he was regarded as a tyrant and insisted on being called "lord and god" even during his lifetime. In A.D. 96 he was assassinated, bringing the rule of the Flavian dynasty to an end.

The "Good" Emperors. Thus began the era of the so-called Good Emperors. The murder of Domitian had not been expected by the armies, who willingly accepted the nominee of the Senate, an elderly senator named Nerva. Being childless, he adopted Trajan, the leading general of the Empire, as his son. When Nerva died two years later, Trajan acceded peacefully (A.D. 98–117). As it happened, none of the next several emperors had sons to succeed them. Thus the principle of adoption superseded the hereditary principle. The result was a succession of able men who reached the throne after having demonstrated their capacity. Trajan undertook war in the East, in which he was uniformly successful, expanding the Roman frontiers for the first time north of the Danube by annexing the province of Dacia. Hadrian, his successor (A.D. 117–138) devoted himself with great success to the improvement of the internal administration of the Empire. The reign of Antoninus Pius (A.D. 138–161) was marked by no notable events. The Empire was at peace and enjoyed its greatest period of prosperity. Not until the reign of the Stoic philosopher Marcus Aurelius (A.D. 161–180) did an emperor have to deal with serious disturbances. Marcus spent several of the later years of his reign in fighting the Marcomanni and Sarmatians, and he died while on campaign along the Danubian frontier. Marcus was succeeded by his incompetent son Commodus, thus reverting to the hereditary principle, to the detriment of the Empire. Indeed,

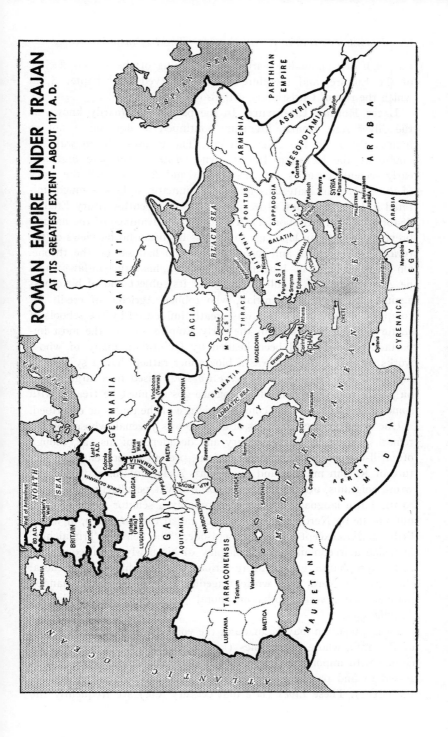

ROMAN EMPIRE UNDER TRAJAN
AT ITS GREATEST EXTENT - ABOUT 117 A.D.

PARTHIAN EMPIRE

ASSYRIA

MESOPOTAMIA

Babylon

ARMENIA

CASPIAN SEA

Carrhae

ARABIA

SYRIA
Palmyra
Damascus
Antioch

PONTUS

CAPPADOCIA

CILICIA

PALESTINE
Jerusalem
JUDAEA

ARABIA

BITHYNIA

GALATIA
Nicaea

ASIA
Pergamum
Smyrna
Ephesus

CYPRUS

LYCIA

PAMPHYLIA

EGYPT

Memphis

Alexandria

BLACK SEA

SARMATIA

Dnieper R.

THRACE

MACEDONIA

EPIRUS

ACHAIA
Corinth
Athens

CRETE

CYRENAICA

Cyrene

MEDITERRANEAN SEA

DACIA

Danube R.

MOESIA

DALMATIA

ADRIATIC SEA

ITALY

Ravenna

Rome

SICILY
Syracuse

Carthage

AFRICA

NUMIDIA

MAURETANIA

PANNONIA

NORICUM

RAETIA

Vindobona (Vienna)

Danube R.

Limes Wall

GERMANIA

Lost in 9 A.D.

Colonia Agrippina

LOWER GERMANIA

UPPER GERMANIA

Rhine R.

Elbe R.

BELGICA

GAUL

ALP. PROVS.

CORSICA

SARDINIA

TARRACONENSIS

LUSITANIA

Toletum

BAETICA

Valentia

NARBONENSIS

AQUITANIA

LUGDUNENSIS

Lutetia (Paris)

Londinium

BRITAIN

Hadrian's Wall

Wall of Antoninus

80 A.D.

HIBERNIA

NORTH SEA

ATLANTIC OCEAN

the reign of Commodus marks the beginning of the serious decline of the Empire, and therefore will be reserved for Chapter 5, in which the rise of Christianity will also be studied.

Later Roman Literature. In the period customarily known as the Silver Age, Roman literature continued to flourish, if not so luxuriantly as in the Augustan era. The greatest figure was undoubtedly the historian Tacitus, who wrote in the late first and early second centuries A.D. His *Annals* and *Histories* tell the story of the early principate. His terse epigrammatic style was much imitated in later centuries, especially by the eighteenth-century English historian Edward Gibbon. Tacitus took full advantage of the natural brevity of the Latin language to express his often biting views of the tyrants, degenerates, and incompetents who had sat on the throne. On the other hand, his biography of Agricola, his father-in-law, whom he greatly admired, is full of praise for its subject and of bitterness against the emperor Domitian, who robbed Agricola of credit for conquest of Britain. Tacitus was greatly influenced by the schools of rhetoric which flourished in the early Empire, one of the most important of which had been headed by Quintilian, many of whose works survive. Suetonius was a biographer rather than a systematic historian. His *Lives of the Twelve Caesars,* based to a large extent on palace records and no doubt palace gossip, must be treated with some reserve as a far from complete picture of the reigns he described.

One of the greatest satirists of all time was Juvenal, whose pointed remarks, especially on the luxury and decadence of his age, though often ill-tempered and perhaps envious, present a very effective picture of Roman middle- and upper-class society of his day. Martial wrote epigrams, often to order, a form of wit peculiarly well suited to the Latin language. Petronius (probably a senator made to commit suicide by Nero) wrote a romance called the *Satyricon,* of which little survives except a humorous episode, "The Feast of Trimalchio" in which a freedman makes a display of his newly acquired wealth to his sycophantic guests. More serious was the philosopher Seneca, the tutor of Nero, who wrote tragedies in a rather heavy-handed manner and several works on moral philosophy, popular in the Middle Ages.

Lastly, mention may be made of the voluminous writings in Greek of Plutarch, whose biographies (known as *Parallel Lives*) are concerned with important Greeks and Romans, in whom Plutarch professed to find parallels (for example, Julius Caesar and Alexander the Great). These *Lives* (late first century A.D.) are frequently the only source we have for many details about the lives of these men, though, having been in most cases written so long afterward, they must be treated with some reserve as history. Plutarch, however, had access to sources forever lost to us. In addition, Plutarch wrote several moral treatises, and his interest in human morality appears also in his biographies.

Though this is naturally an incomplete list of the writers of the time, it comprises the most important among them. It will be noted that almost all appeared in the role of critics rather than admirers of their society—in this differing markedly from the writers of the Augustan age, when the Romans (even Horace, who wrote gentle and usually very good-humored satires) believed that they were living in a great time and that the best was yet to come.

Art and Architecture. In general the early Empire was a more important period for architecture than was the Republic. Though private men of wealth built much in the last years of the Republic, the emperors had considerably more money at their disposal for building programs. Moreover, they regarded it as part of their task to beautify Rome. Augustus virtually rebuilt the whole city. Many emperors also built triumphal columns celebrating their victories—for example, Trajan's column, which still exists. The designs of the new buildings were almost always in the style earlier perfected by the Greeks; and the Romans made few innovations. But their taste ran to the grandiose, as might be expected of an imperial people; they preferred the most ornate of the Greek columns, the Corinthian. On the other hand, the Romans were far more efficient engineers than the Greeks, and in utilitarian works (such as aqueducts), surpass them. The Great Roman amphitheaters, such as the Colosseum at Rome and the Hippodrome at Arles in southern France, although much larger than the Greek theaters, are derived from Greek models.

In sculpture Roman taste ran to realism. In particular facial expressions were studied and character expressed in stone, and as time wore on very special attention was given to such details as the hair. Many of the sculptures, especially in the Empire, were actually Greek.

The recovery of the houses at Pompeii and Herculaneum, overwhelmed by an eruption of Vesuvius in A.D. 79, has shown us that middle- and upper-class Romans were able to decorate their houses in a manner that had been impossible for the less wealthy Greeks. These minor cities were in all respects far more attractive than any medieval town.

CONCLUSION

The first centuries of the Roman Empire were a period of un-broken peace for almost all the inhabitants of the Empire. Men and women were born and died without ever having been in the least danger from an external enemy, nor had they ever feared the out-break of war. Though the central government at times was weak, the provinces continued to prosper. The cities competed with one an-other not in warfare, as had the city-states of Greece, but in such matters as which could build the most attractive public monuments. Rich men were expected to give of their surplus to beautify their home towns, which continued to enjoy municipal self-government under their own elected magistrates. As yet the armies were not too expensive for the Empire to maintain, and taxation was not yet crushing. But Rome, the capital, remained a city with very little in-dustry and was supported by money from the whole Empire. An extravagant emperor could quickly empty the treasury, as did Nero. Economic problems were far from solved; the army was an expen-sive if necessary drain on imperial finances; and the plight of the poor in the great cities, especially in Rome itself, was unenviable. Moreover, at any time a feeble emperor might win the throne and misgovern in such a way that the precarious economic and political structure of the Empire could collapse.

The present chapter has concluded with the succession of Com-modus to the throne. This marked for many of the Romans the end of the era of growth and prosperity and the beginning of the long decline and fall that ended with deposition of the last titular em-peror by a barbarian in A.D. 476.

THE RISE OF THE CHRISTIAN
5 CHURCH AND THE FALL OF
THE ROMAN EMPIRE

The Roman Empire continued in existence for almost three centuries after the death of Marcus Aurelius and the accession of Commodus. During the third century it might have appeared to a contemporary to be in danger of imminent collapse as a result of the failure of any emperors during the period to establish undisputed authority. But the reign of Diocletian (A.D. 284–305) saw a thorough reorganization of the Empire which enabled it to survive for a couple of centuries, though it was progressively weakened by the inroads of the barbarians. In the West the Christian Church and its popes gradually took over many of the functions of the emperor. We shall therefore now consider the rise of Christianity before taking up again the story of the political decline of the Empire in the West which culminated in the Fall of Rome in A.D. 476.

RISE OF CHRISTIANITY

Though Christianity began in Palestine in the heart of the Hellenistic world, and its founder and early leaders were all Jews, with its appeal to all classes of men and women in the Empire, it far transcended its Eastern origins. By the early fourth century A.D. when the emperor Constantine made it his own religion, it was already the most important religion in the Empire. Thereafter only one emperor (known to the Christians as Julian the Apostate) rejected it; and by the end of the same (fourth) century another emperor, Theodosius, had decreed that it was to be the sole religion of the Empire. With the closing of the Platonic School of Athens by Justinian in the sixth century A.D., the last remnants of the old paganism were officially abolished.

Origins. We have already discussed the religion of the Jews as it had developed at the time of the Roman conquest. Judaism had al-

69

ways been exclusive, based as it was on the concept of a chosen people. By the time of Jesus Christ it had become strongly ritualistic, and there was little effort to encourage its spread among the Gentiles —who could in any case hardly have been expected to embrace a religion which made so many demands on its worshipers and usually regarded non-Jews as excluded from God's promises. There were many mystery-religions in the East, some of considerable antiquity, which appealed to those who desired a direct religious experience. A strong salvationist religion called Mithraism, an offshoot of Zoroastrianism, was already making headway and for a long time competed with Christianity—though, since it discriminated against women, it lacked Christianity's universal appeal. Lastly, the old rural religion of Rome had long ago lost its appeal to the sophisticated city-dwellers. The deification of dead rulers established under the Empire was no substitute. It was merely a form of empire-worship, which did not remove the need for a more personal form of belief.

The Gospel of Jesus Christ. The story of the life, death, and resurrection of Jesus Christ is related in the Gospels, which begin the New Testament of the Christian Bible. They tell how his birth conformed to Hebrew prophecy of the Messiah; how he was baptized in the river Jordan by John the Baptist, last of the Hebrew prophets; and how thereafter he began his mission on earth. In the course of the next three years he taught a gospel of love of God and love of one's neighbor; performed miracles of healing, even to the extent of raising the dead; gathered around himself disciples and apostles; and prophesied his own death and resurrection. After a triumphal procession into Jerusalem, he was betrayed to the Jewish authorities, who accused him of blasphemy, and were strong enough to have the sentence of death pronounced by the Roman governor Pontius Pilate, on the grounds that he was guilty of treason against the emperor. He was then crucified and buried, in three days rising from the dead as he had foretold. Thereafter he appeared several times to his disciples and was seen by some of them ascending into heaven.

Paul and the Early Church. The disciples and apostles were for a short while uncertain what to do. Then on an occasion when they were gathered together, suddenly they were filled by the Holy Spirit and felt that it was their mission to preach the good news, especially the gospel of salvation. At first this mission was confined to the Jews. Then after a Jew named Saul (Paul) had been converted by a vision of Christ, at a time when he was trying to eradicate the religion as a danger to Judaism, the mission took on a new urgency. Paul felt that it was his task to preach also to the Gentiles, a course which the apostles at first rejected. Then a compromise was agreed to; and Paul, granted a free hand, made several journeys throughout Asia Minor and Europe, founding churches. To these churches he wrote many letters, some of which are incorporated in the New Testament. They set forth his views on Christian theology as it was developing and on numerous practical matters. Eventually he fell foul of the local Roman authorities; but being a Roman citizen, he was permitted to appeal to the emperor. He was sent to Rome as a prisoner but continued his missionary work without hindrance until, according to tradition, he and St. Peter, the leading apostle, were both put to death at the command of Nero about A.D. 65.

Christianity and the Romans. The Church, however, survived the first series of persecutions, ordered by Nero. Thereafter, though the laws against Christians were still in theory enforced, little in fact was done to hinder them. Church organization gradually became stronger. In almost every city of the Empire there were groups of Christians gathered together into a church, with bishops as leaders, and priests and deacons to assist them. Obviously if the state cult of emperor-worship were taken seriously, the Christians would be suspect, since they refused to make even a formal acknowledgment of the divinity of the emperor. But the first major attack upon them * is attributed to the reign of Marcus Aurelius. This was probably the result of local action by non-Christians, who must have objected to the difference both in religious practices and in ordinary behavior between the Christians and themselves.

In the third century there were many efforts by the emperors to eradicate the growing religion. But by this time the Church had grown too powerful for the secular authorities to succeed in this attempt, even though they were backed by the full force of the law. The emperor Diocletian, who had a religious policy of his own, looking to the serious enforcement of emperor-worship, instituted the most extensive prosecution of the Christians, which was carried on by Galerius, his successor, until just before the latter's death in A.D. 311. In that year toleration was granted. The following year Constantine, a claimant to the throne, faced by an anti-Christian

---

* Early Christian tradition regarded Domitian (A.D. 81–96) as one of the great "persecutors." But modern research has not confirmed this position. Domitian as part of his policy of glorifying the imperial position attacked all Oriental cults which did not accept his divinity, among which were numbered the Christians. But the persecution was brief, since Domitian was murdered less than a year after issuing his edict against the Christians.

opponent, decided, according to Christian tradition, to embrace Christianity if he were granted the victory—whereupon a vision appeared to him of a cross in the heavens on which were inscribed the words, "In this sign conquer." After his victory Constantine and his fellow-emperor in the East issued a joint edict, confirming the edict of Galerius two years earlier.* Constantine throughout his reign displayed much interest in Christianity, and the evidence suggests that he was formally converted quite early. He issued several edicts against various heresies which threatened to undermine the unity of Church belief. He summoned a conference of churchmen which met at Nicaea in A.D. 325. This Council condemned the Arian heresy, which subordinated Jesus Christ to the Father, whereas the view of St. Athanasius, adopted as the "orthodox" (correct) teaching, was that Christ as the Son of God is coequal with the Father and that the Trinity consists of three Persons and one Substance. Nevertheless, some of Constantine's successors continued to hold that the Arian view was the correct one, and many of the barbarian tribes were converted to Arianism rather than to orthodox Catholicism. Those leading Christians whose theological doctrines were considered orthodox became known as the Fathers of the Church. In the West they included St. Ambrose, St. Augustine, St. Jerome, and Pope Gregory I; most important in the East was St. Athanasius.

Organization of the Early Christian Church. The organization of the early Church is still a much-disputed subject, since most reliable evidence dates from the period after Constantine. The various local Christian communities probably each had its bishops and presbyters to minister to its needs, but it is not known whether the bishops or a synod of presbyters including the bishops were the governing body. The Church was certainly divided later into dioceses, each under a bishop. The latter were chosen by their congregations and had almost complete responsibility for them. In time archbishops came to exercise superior authority in a group of dioceses which thus became archdioceses. Deacons in every community ministered to the secular needs of Church members. Some men and women (monks and nuns) who wished to set themselves apart and lead lives exclusively devoted to religion, congregated in monasteries and convents under regulations drawn up by their founders. The most widely followed and famous of the rules were those of the sixth-century St. Benedict in the West and the fourth-century St. Basil in the East.

---

* It was formerly supposed that there was an Edict of Milan issued in 312 or 313, but no such edict is now accepted by scholars.

The Pope as Leader of Christianity. The oldest centers of Christianity in the East for a long time vied with Rome for supreme leadership in the Church. The patriarchs of Constantinople, Antioch, Jerusalem, and Alexandria regarded themselves as the equal of the bishop of Rome. But the latter had several advantages over the patriarchs. It was widely held that St. Peter, who had been granted "the keys of heaven" by Christ himself, who had also said that upon this rock (Peter) he would build his Church (Matthew 16: 18–19) had become the first bishop of Rome, and that his successors in the bishopric inherited his authority. Such authority could not be matched by that of any other bishop or patriarch if the theory of Apostolic Succession were accepted.

Political events tended to enhance the authority of the bishop of Rome. Not only was Rome the capital of the Roman Empire, but by the fifth century no emperor wielded effective authority in Rome. In Constantinople the patriarch was to a large degree subject to the authority of the Eastern emperor who appointed him. But in Rome the bishop was the recognized leader and Emperor Valentinian III during the barbarian invasions (A.D. 445) formally granted authority to him by allowing papal decisions to have the authority of law. The word *pope*, as applied exclusively to the bishop of Rome, dates probably from the seventh century A.D. Previous to that time the word, which means *father*, had been used for all bishops, though this usage tended to die out from the fifth century onward. Pope Leo I, the Great (A.D. 440–461), used his authority to secure terms from the barbarian invaders such as Attila and Gaeseric, and it was in large measure due to the vigorous actions of fifth-century popes that the Church was able to survive the collapse of the Roman Empire and in some degree to inherit its power and organization. At the end of the sixth century Pope Gregory I was treated by the barbarian Lombard chiefs as a prince in his own right, with lands separate from theirs under his control in Italy.

DECLINE AND FALL OF THE EMPIRE

The Empire at all times was too extensive to be ruled effectively by a single man unless he possessed quite exceptional ability. After a century of almost continuous civil war the Empire was formally divided into two parts, with emperors ruling both in Rome and in the new Eastern capital of Constantinople.

The Barrack Emperors. The murder of Commodus in A.D. 192 was quickly followed by the murder of his successor after another short reign. Then Septimius Severus, an able soldier, seized the throne and quickly eliminated all his rivals. Though he ruled effectively for eighteen years, it was clear to all by this time that the army was the dominant power in the state, and all pretense of civilian supremacy was abandoned. But for almost a hundred years no other emperor was able to establish his rule in such a manner that he could administer the Empire efficiently and protect its boundaries. The acceptance of an emperor by one army did not mean that armies on other frontiers would accept him. Almost every emperor was murdered, usually by his troops, and for much of the third century the Empire was a prey to anarchy while the armies consumed the substance of the state. Peasants entered the army rather than have their crops sequestrated. The tax-paying middle classes suffered equally from the anarchy. Taxation was often erratic and arbitrary, and always oppressive. Moreover barbarians were already exerting pressure on the frontiers, frequently penetrating deep into the Empire before some general or emperor could defeat them. The Persians in the East meanwhile were reviving their own empire beyond the Roman frontiers, and frequent incursions had to be repelled. The emperor Aurelian (A.D. 270–275) abandoned Trajan's province of Dacia (beyond the Danube), which had become indefensible; but by a series of brilliant victories he drove off the German barbarians and restored order in the East. Then he, too, was murdered, and the process of disintegration was resumed.

Reforms of Diocletian and Constantine. At last in A.D. 284, Diocletian, an able soldier and administrator, won the throne, and lived long enough to reorganize the Empire. His reforms and those of his successor Constantine gave it a new lease of life, though at the expense of such remaining prosperity as remained in the West, its progressive barbarization, and ultimately the division of the Empire into East and West.

DIOCLETIAN. Diocletian reformed the army through the admission of volunteers among the barbarian troops. Thereafter as professional soldiers they defended the Empire against their former compatriots. He divided the Empire into four prefectures, subdivided into dioceses, and associated a coemperor with him. He and his coemperor (both called Augusti) took two Caesars as their heirs apparent. It was intended that the Augusti after twenty years' rule should give way to the Caesars. To pay for the armies, Diocletian and his successors greatly improved the efficiency of the tax-collecting system and made it difficult for civilians to leave their occupations. In short

Diocletian established a system usually compared to Oriental despotism; it may well be called totalitarianism, since the state exercised supreme control in every sphere of life to see that there was sufficient production and tax money to support the army. In the hopes of centering the loyalty of the citizens on the Crown, Diocletian established an elaborate court ceremonial with himself at the center. The emperor maintained an aloof and unapproachable magnificence of the type usually associated with Oriental empires.

CONSTANTINE. When Diocletian in due course abdicated, and persuaded his coemperor to do the same, civil war quickly broke out among their successors. This was brought to an end by the accession of Constantine in A.D. 312. As we have noted, Constantine granted toleration to the Christians and won their support. In a reign of twenty-five years he completed the system inaugurated by Diocletian and fastened the imperial yoke even more oppressively upon the citizens of the Empire. Only the military (including in time the barbarians) remained a privileged class. The soldier was free from taxation and able to rise as high as his abilities could take him, whereas all the other classes were deprived of even the hope of rising out of the class and occupation to which they had been born.

One of the most significant acts of Constantine was the founding of Constantinople, named after him, on the Bosporus. This new city had an incomparable site; it was a seaport located in the most prosperous sector of the Empire. Quickly it grew to surpass Rome in size and wealth, and in due course it became the Eastern capital of the Empire. During the next fifty years there were always at least two corulers, although one was in theory senior to the other. The last emperor to assert his authority over the whole was Theodosius the Great (A.D. 379–395). After his death there was scarcely any pretense that a single ruler governed. But the Eastern Empire, based on Constantinople, survived the barbarian assaults which were to prove fatal to Rome and the West. (The history of the Eastern or Byzantine Empire will be considered in Chapter 6.)

"The Barbarian Invasions." In part as the result of pressure from Asia, especially from the Huns who were migrating westward, various Germanic peoples, particularly the West Goths (Visigoths), the East Goths (Ostrogoths), and the Vandals, had been pushing against the frontiers of the Empire, both in the east and the west. As early as A.D. 376 the Visigoths, who had been tolerated in the neighborhood of the Danube by the Eastern emperors, suddenly crossed the river, defeated an army led by the emperor Valens, and killed him. Though they did not take Constantinople, they ravaged the Balkans for some years with impunity until Theodosius I made a treaty recognizing them as allies. Later a large band of Visigoths under Alaric were expelled from Greece or persuaded to leave it, whereupon they marched westward toward the much less well-defended lands of the Western emperor. Vandals and others penetrated into Gaul about the same time (A.D. 406). The following year Roman troops were withdrawn from Britain, which soon fell prey to Picts and Scots from the north and to the Germanic tribes of Angles and Saxons who invaded the defenseless country by sea. Meanwhile the Huns under Attila ravaged central European territories of the Empire and penned the Ostrogoths within the lands north of the Black Sea.

In A.D. 409 Alaric with his Visigoths invaded Italy, took Rome, and sacked it. But he died soon afterward and his Visigoths moved north again into Gaul and Spain, driving the Vandals, who were by then in possession, across the Straits of Gibraltar into Africa. During all this time the emperors, safely ensconced in Ravenna, were unable to check the barbarian inroads until 436, when the Roman general defeated the Visigoths in Gaul. He could, however, do nothing about the Vandals in Africa, who set up their own kingdom, completing their conquest in 439. In 450 Attila with his terrifying Huns moved into Gaul. Against this menace the Visigoths in Gaul were willing to join the Romans. The allied army defeated and turned back Attila at the Battle of Chalons (451), but the Hun decided to invade Italy instead. Reaching Rome, he was met by Pope Leo I, who probably saved the city by buying him off. Attila died the following year, and his horde swiftly disintegrated.

But the Empire was by this time in such a state of disintegration that nothing could save it. The Vandals under Gaeseric came over from Africa in 455 and once more Rome was sacked. All the pope could do for the helpless city was to negotiate with the barbarians for the personal safety of the citizens. The titular emperors were completely in the hands of their barbarian generals until at last, in 476, Odovacar, a Herulian, deposed the last holder of the title, Romulus Augustulus. Odovacar did not proclaim himself emperor, but he ruled for seventeen years (476–493) as virtual king, with the title of *patricius,* recognizing the overlordship of the emperor in Constantinople. He did not live to found a dynasty. In 488 Theodoric, leader of the Ostrogothic people, who were free to move elsewhere once the threat from the Huns had been removed, was assigned by the Byzantine emperor the task of reconquering Italy from Odovacar. In 493 he took Ravenna, treacherously killed Odovacar, and became king of Italy. The Ostrogothic kingdom of Italy lasted until its conquest by the Byzantine Empire under Justinian in the middle of the sixth century.

By the end of the fifth century, Africa was in the hands of the Vandals; Spain was controlled by the Visigoths; Gaul was in the process of being subdued by the Franks; and Italy was ruled by the Ostrogoths. The Angles and Saxons had made their first inroads into Britain and were gradually conquering the country. (These barbarian successor states of the Romans will be dealt with in Chapter 7.)

CONCLUSION

The Roman Empire in its heyday had unified much of Europe and given it a civilized and frequently enlightened government unified by Roman law and administration. It had endowed its territories with a universal language spoken and written by all educated men. Though the impact of Roman rule had been least in the areas furthest removed from the center, the Romans and their system had always exercised some civilizing influence which remained to soften in some degree the rule of the barbarians who succeeded them. Nowhere was this influence more marked than in the Church, which adopted Roman imperial organization as its own, used the Latin language, and thus in a very real sense became the most eminent successor of Rome. The Church in the barbarian kingdoms remained the only organized and literate body, and as such it was instrumental in aiding the barbarian rulers in their administration and modifying some of their customs, even though in the process it could not avoid being influenced in its turn. Above all, the new peoples of western Europe continued to retain the memory of Rome and hold to the idea of a great Empire which was in their view the only natural form of government for Europe—and the Germanic empire that stalked through medieval and early modern history under the name of the Holy Roman Empire, owes not only its name but its sole reason for existence to its illustrious forebear.

6 THE BYZANTINE AND MUSLIM EMPIRES

While the Roman Empire in the West was falling to barbarian invaders, the Empire in the East maintained its independence until the beginning of the thirteenth century despite barbarian attempts to destroy it. As an outpost of civilization it was instrumental in spreading a form of Western culture among the Slavs, Avars, Bulgars, and others who came under its influence even while they were attempting to conquer it. Meanwhile, another empire, based upon the new religion of Islam, was being established and exerting its influence.

THE BYZANTINE EMPIRE

At first the Byzantines (so called after Byzantium, the ancient name of the city on the Bosporus which was replaced by Constantinople) regarded themselves as Romans and their state as the legitimate heir of Rome. In fact they inherited the form of centralized government developed in the late Roman Empire, and they used a modified form of Roman law. In all other respects their culture was Greek, as was their language, and the Byzantine emperors were of Greek rather than Roman stock. The emperor maintained a strict ceremonial, similar to that of the last Roman emperors but increasingly modified by Oriental influences. The state remained authoritarian and centralized; many industries were state monopolies, and all industry was subjected to some government control. Taxes were high, since it was essential for the emperor to maintain a powerful standing army for defense against the barbarians and the expenses of the court were considerable. But the Empire as a whole (whose extent varied very greatly through the centuries in accordance with the progress of Byzantine arms, but which originally included all the Roman imperial provinces east of Illyria) was prosperous. It could successfully meet the expenses of defense and the court, and in all the centuries of its existence it never went bankrupt. The capital city of Constantinople, unlike Rome, was a center for trade and industry, and was at all times the most prosperous city in the Empire as well as its seat of government.

Church and State. The Church in Constantinople was headed by a patriarch appointed by the emperor, who could also dismiss him. Hence though he sometimes opposed the emperor, he usually acted as an instrument of imperial policy. At times the patriarch acknowledged the authority of the pope as the successor of St. Peter, but papal influence in Constantinople remained largely nominal. During the centuries when there was no emperor in the West and the Byzantine emperor was the highest ranking ruler in Europe, it was difficult for the papacy to exercise any influence on the patriarch, protected as he was by his master. A controversy which arose in the eighth century between East and West over the use of icons (sacred pictures and images) in the churches strained the relations between popes and emperors for more than a hundred years. This Iconoclastic Controversy, as it was called, stemmed from an attempt by the Byzantine emperor Leo III to purify the Church, which had, in his view, been becoming idolatrous. He ordered the icons to be destroyed, thus greatly offending the monks who made them, and the pope, who regarded them as an aid to devotion.

When, from the ninth century onward, papal power began to increase in the West (which, with Charlemagne and his successors, also acquired its own emperors) other controversies arose over theological questions and over the allegiance of newly converted barbarians. In 1054 the two churches separated, ostensibly over a point of theology, and they have never since been united except for a short period (in the thirteenth century) during which Constantinople was ruled by Westerners. The Eastern Church is called the (Greek) Orthodox Church. It has a different liturgy and ritual from that in use in Roman Catholic countries, and it does not acknowledge the pope as head of Christendom.

Reconquest of the West. For several decades after the Fall of Rome, Constantinople was fully occupied in consolidating her own territories and in keeping the barbarians out of the Empire. But hope had not yet been abandoned that the Roman Empire could be reconstituted. The emperor Justinian I (527–565) at last felt himself strong enough to undertake the reconquest, in spite of the fact that a revived Persian empire threatened him on his eastern flank. In 532 he signed a peace with the Persians and turned his considerable armies against the barbarian kingdoms of the West. His first campaigns, led by Belisarius, destroyed the Vandal kingdom of North Africa; then in a long and bloody campaign the Ostrogothic kingdom of Italy was gradually worn down by Belisarius and Narses. Soon afterward, southeastern Spain, ruled by the Visigoths, was also added to the Empire.

The cost of these conquests was heavy. The Persians seized the opportunity to invade the imperial dominions in the East, necessitating another long war, which ended in 562 with an agreement by Justinian to pay tribute for fifty years. Huns and Avars at times raided far into Greece and right up to Constantinople, and were driven off only with great difficulty. Moreover, the conquest of Italy proved to be ephemeral. The destruction of the Ostrogothic kingdom meant that Constantinople became responsible for the defense of Italy against any further barbarian invasions. After the death of Justinian, she was not strong enough to wage wars on so many fronts. In 568 the Lombards invaded Italy and won most of the Byzantine possessions (see p. 89). Only Ravenna and Naples remained under effective Byzantine rule, while Rome, though nominally under Byzantine suzerainty, was in reality ruled by the papacy, which made its own arrangements with the Lombards that had little reference to Constantinople.

Persian and Muslim Wars. The arrangements with Persia lasted a bare ten years, while the Avars and other barbarians were far from subdued. In the early sixth century the Persians took almost all the Byzantine possessions in Asia and confronted the new emperor Heraclius (610–641) across the Bosporus. The emperor, who had just lost his last territories in Spain, thought of escaping to Africa and abandoning his capital. But he was dissuaded by his patriarch Sergius, who eventually organized the successful defense of Constantinople against the advancing Avars, while Heraclius himself undertook a campaign in Asia in which the Persians were utterly defeated and their empire almost destroyed. But during the long war a new power (the Muslims) had arisen in Arabia, strengthened by the new religion of Islam. Later Byzantine emperors had constantly to defend themselves against the Muslims, while the Persian Empire succumbed to their attacks and became a Muslim state (see p. 83).

In spite of numerous attempts the Muslims did not succeed in capturing Constantinople, which was too strong to be taken from the sea. Only many centuries later after the city had been greatly weakened by a Latin conquest achieved by treachery, did it fall to the Muslim power of the Ottoman Turks, who had first taken most of its European hinterland (1453). But most of the Byzantine possessions in the East were captured by the Muslims without great difficulty, as were the last of Justinian's possessions in Africa.

Bulgarian Wars. By the tenth century the tide of Muslim advance had receded, and Constantinople was occupied in defending herself against the Asiatic Bulgars, who disputed the Byzantine European territories with the emperor. The Bulgars finally submitted to the emperor Basil II (Bulgaroktonus—the Bulgar-killer) in 1018, after a murderously destructive war, and their territories, most of which had at one time belonged to the Empire, were again incorporated in it.

Latin Conquest of Constantinople. In the late eleventh century the Byzantine Empire was threatened both by the Muslim Seljuk Turks and by Christians from the rising Western kingdoms (usually collectively called "Latins"). The emperor Alexius Comnenus (1081–1118) called in the Christians to help him against the Turks, from which initiative resulted the Crusades (see Chapter 8), which established a number of Western enclaves in Palestine. The Crusades brought Constantinople into increasing conflict with the Westerners, especially with the aggressive commercial city of Venice, formerly a Byzantine vassal state. In 1204 the Fourth Crusade, planned for the reconquest of Jerusalem, turned aside to Constantinople, where there was a disputed imperial succession. The crusaders, many of whom were admitted to the city peaceably, suddenly turned upon it and sacked it, driving out the imperial rulers and establishing a new kingdom ruled by a Flemish noble. The Byzantine emperors, exiled to some of their territories in Asia which were not conquered by the Latins, staged a counterattack in 1261 and were able to restore their old Empire. But it was always feeble and had to defend itself first against the Serbs and then against the Ottoman Turks. In 1453 it fell to the latter, whose descendants still control Constantinople (Istanbul), though since the First World War their possessions have been almost entirely in Asia.

Byzantine Culture. In art and architecture the Byzantine achievement was considerable. The church of Santa Sophia in Constantinople, commissioned by Justinian, greatly influenced Muslim architecture, as well as church building in European centers such as Venice and Ravenna that came under Byzantine rule. Byzantine art, always influenced by religion, was distinctive, especially the religious paintings and the unique Byzantine mosaics. Byzantine craftsmanship for centuries was greatly superior to that of western Europe. But in other fields of cultural activity the Byzantine achievement was largely derivative. No writers or thinkers arose who were the equal of those of classical Greece, though the Greek language and many of the Greek classical masterpieces were preserved in Constantinople. Most Byzantine thinkers were more interested in theological controversy than in original creative work. Roman law was codified by Justinian in the sixth century in the *Corpus juris civilis,* which incorporated various Christian ideas unknown in the earlier secular codes of Rome (as did codes issued by later Byzantine emperors). It was through the medium of the Justinian Code that the full principles of Roman law became known to the West in the Middle Ages. But on the whole it may still be said that the Byzantine cultural achievement, in spite of many features of outstanding interest, was remarkably small in view of the long period of political independence enjoyed by the Empire—one of the most long-lived in the history of mankind hitherto.

THE MUSLIM EMPIRE

The expansion of the Muslims into Asia, Africa, and Spain stemmed from the work of the prophet Mohammed and is inseparably connected with the rise of the new religion of Islam. Before Mohammed's time, Arabia, only a small part of which had been included in the Roman Empire, was a disunited country of constantly warring tribes. Mohammed and his religion unified them into a powerful fighting force strong enough to build and maintain an extensive empire.

Religion of Islam. When Mohammed, who began his career as an Arab trader, was forty years old, he began to experience visions and received instructions from God, conveyed to him, as he claimed, by the archangel Gabriel. These teachings were later collected into the Koran, which became and remained the single holy book of the religion, though sayings attributed to Mohammed were also compiled (the *hadith*) and regarded as scarcely less authoritative. The chief article of belief is that there is a single God (Allah), whose prophet on earth was Mohammed. Converts to the religion formed a single brotherhood whose members were expected to support one another, especially against the world of the infidels. Such duties as almsgiving were prescribed and the customary virtues of the desert, such as hospitality to strangers, were extolled. There was to be no professional priesthood; but since prayers were offered at set hours there could be prayer-leaders (*imams*) and public criers who summoned the faithful to prayers (*muezzins*). It was held that infidels should if possible be converted to Islam, and force could be used against those who, unlike Jews and Christians, had no sacred book of their own. A holy war (*jehad*) could be proclaimed against enemies who threatened the religion. After death the faithful Muslims, especially those who died in battle for their religion, could expect to go to a paradise which was pictured in appealing terms, whereas the unfaithful were consigned to Gehenna, the place of torment. Clearly the religion owes much to both Judaism and Christianity, differing from Judaism in its desire for converts and from Christianity in its emphasis on the unity of God (Muslims regarded Christians as polytheists in view of their belief in the Trinity).

Expansion of Islam. At first Mohammed won few converts in his native city, Mecca, gaining little support even from his own family, of which he was but a minor member. In 622 he escaped to Medina (this escape is known as the Hegira, from which event dates the Muslim era), where he was more successful, returning in 630 to his home city with enough reinforcements to persuade the Meccans to accept conversion. Thereafter Mecca became Islam's holy city, to which all good Muslims should make a pilgrimage at least once in their lifetime. Before the death of Mohammed in 632, much of Arabia had been converted. Soon afterward the Muslims began to expand into the neighboring countries, capturing in quick succession Syria from the Byzantines (640), Mesopotamia and Persia (641), and Egypt (642). During the following century North Africa and Asia as far east as the borders of India were added to the empire. The Muslims then crossed the Straits of Gibraltar and by 715 had conquered Visigothic Spain. Their westward expansion was checked in central France (732) by Charles Martel, the Frankish mayor (see p. 87), and thereafter they retreated into Spain. In the ninth century Sicily and Crete were added to the Muslims' rule, giving them the command of most of the Mediterranean.

Most of the conquests had not proved to be difficult. Converts from the non-Arab peoples were treated as equals, and even those "peoples of the Book" (Christians and Jews) who refused to convert were not molested, though they were subjected to heavier taxation than were the Muslims. The pagan Berbers of North Africa presented the stiffest opposition to the advancing tide of Islam, but after conversion they often became even stricter Muslims than the Arabs themselves. In the Byzantine territories Muslim rule was, on the whole, easier than that of the Byzantines, and the taxes imposed were lighter. Probably many Byzantine subjects were not sorry to change masters. The Persian Empire, greatly weakened by the wars with Constantinople, could not put up an effective resistance. But after the conquest the superior Persian culture gradually absorbed its conquerors, and the Muslim Empire ruled by the Abbassid Dynasty of Bagdad was far more Persian than Arabic; and even the Shiite religion of most Persians differed in many respects from traditional Islam as held by the Sunnite majority.

Ommeyad and Abbasid Caliphates. On the death of Mohammed, no provision had been made for a successor, who was expected to be both the protector of Islam and a secular ruler. The Muslims therefore chose Abu Bekr, father-in-law of Mohammed, as "caliph." When he died after two years of rule, he was succeeded by other disciples of the prophet until Ali, cousin and son-in-law of Mohammed, obtained the throne in 656. Soon afterward a civil war broke out and Ali was murdered by a relative of his predecessor who was not related to the prophet but succeeded in making himself caliph and founding the new Ommeyad Dynasty. The Shiite and other sects of Islam have ever since refused to recognize this usurpation, believing that the rulership should have passed by heredity to the line of Mohammed.

The Ommeyads ruled the expanding empire from Damascus in Syria until 750, when the Abbasid family, which claimed to be descended from the prophet, seized the throne, shortly afterward removing the capital to Bagdad in Mesopotamia. The Abbasid Dynasty remained in power until the beginning of the twelfth century and continued to rule in name until the Mongol conquest of Bagdad in 1258. But its authority was never recognized in Spain or Morocco, where a scion of the Ommeyad Dynasty continued to rule. In the tenth century the Fatimid Dynasty won control of Egypt and ruled independently of Bagdad. Thus the once great empire dissolved into its component parts; but the religion has remained to this day as a unifying force among Muslims, whatever their political differences.

Muslim Culture. The conquering Arabs who provided the dynamism for the expansion of Islam contributed the Arabic language (in which the Koran is written) but little else to the amalgam of Muslim culture. On the other hand, they were perhaps the greatest assimilators the world has yet seen. They learned from every people they conquered, but the specifically Arab contribution is not easily to be distinguished from those of these peoples. The Muslims excelled especially in the sciences, notably astronomy, mathematics, chemistry, and medicine, and in these fields they worked upon the foundations laid by the Hellenistic Greeks. Their few philosophers, especially the Persian philosopher-physician Avicenna and the Spaniard Averroës, looked upon the Greek Aristotle as their master. Since representations of the human form were strictly forbidden by their religion, the Muslims concentrated on delicate decorative work, especially the incomparable arabesques, and in fine craftsmanship they were unexcelled in their time. In architecture they developed the graceful minaret; and the Taj Mahal, widely regarded as the most beautiful building in the world, was designed and constructed by Muslims who had penetrated from Persia into northern India. Perhaps the most famous of all Muslims in the West was the poet-mathematician Omar Khayyam, who won his fame posthumously in the nineteenth century when his poem the *Rubáiyát* was translated by Edward Fitzgerald. Omar Khayyam, however, holds no such exalted position in his native Persia, where he was one of many poets and far from the greatest of Persian mathematicians.

During the heyday of Muslim culture Westerners visiting the Muslim world astonished their contemporaries with descriptions of their greatly superior artistic and scientific achievements. When the Christians reconquered Spain in the eleventh century, they fell with avidity upon the Muslim works of learning, which were quickly translated into Latin, thus providing impetus to similar study in the West. So eventually much of the Muslim heritage was absorbed by the West, where it has become a part of the foundations of Western civilization, even while learning was decaying in the Islamic lands themselves.

7 THE EARLY MIDDLE AGES TO A.D. 1000

The Middle Ages is a conventional term invented in early modern times to describe a transitional period between the great age of antiquity and the "Renaissance," which has little real meaning today. It was once widely believed that nothing of significance happened during this transitional period; that "civilization" remained in a state of suspended animation during the Middle Ages and resumed its march when men lost their excessive preoccupation with the here-after and began to turn once more to a secular way of life. Though the term continues to be used, its original meaning is largely forgotten, and the Middle Ages are generally regarded as the seedtime of Western civilization, on whose accomplishments, slow as they were, later civilization has been built.

THE FRANKS AND THE CAROLINGIAN ERA

One of the last of the barbarian peoples whose invasions of western Europe are described in Chapter 5 were the Franks. This Germanic people followed the Goths and Vandals into Gaul and gradually consolidated most of modern France under a single monarchy, known as the Merovingian kingdom.

Merovingian Kingdom. The leader responsible for the unification was Clovis, whose grandfather Meroveus gave his name to the monarchy. From being a relatively minor chief of one branch of the Frankish people, Clovis gradually became the virtually absolute ruler of much of the country. He was aided in this achievement not only by his undoubted military and political talent but also by his willingness to be converted to Catholic Christianity, unlike other barbarian leaders, who had earlier been converted to the heresy of Arianism (see Chapter 5). This decision won Clovis the support of the

Catholic Church (which possessed a strong organization in his territories) as well as the good will of the papacy.

The kingdom founded by Clovis lasted for almost three hundred years, but his successors were unable to hold it together as a single unit, and civil wars were endemic throughout the period. By the beginning of the eighth century, power was being exercised not by the titular Merovingian kings of the two major subdivisions of the country, Neustria and Austrasia, but by the managers of their households, usually known as "mayors of the palace." Charles Martel, who defended France against the invading Muslims, as mayor of the palace, united the whole country under his control. Upon his death in 741, he bequeathed his position to his two sons, Pepin the Short and Carloman.

When his brother entered a monastery in 747, thus abandoning his position as ruler, Pepin determined to put an end to his unsatisfactory position as mayor under a powerless king. But he could not simply depose his predecessor; he needed some backing not only from his lords but also from a recognized higher authority. Such an authority existed in the person of the pope, who was in need of assistance against the encroaching Lombards threatening his capital. As the result of an agreement with the pope, Pepin sent a military expedition to Italy which compelled the Lombards to cede the exarchate of Ravenna and other territories to the papacy (Donation of Pepin, 756). Meanwhile in 751, with papal sanction, Pepin had become king of the Franks. When he died in 768, dividing his kingdom between his two sons, Charles and Carloman, he was by far the most powerful ruler in western Europe.

The Carolingian Empire. For a few years there was serious rivalry between the two brothers. Then Carloman died, and Charles, usually known as Charlemagne (Carolus Magnus), was the undisputed ruler of the Frankish kingdom, able to compel all his lords, including high officials of the Church, to obey him. He undertook wars on the northern frontier with the Saxons, whom he forcibly converted to Christianity, and with other border peoples. As a result, by the end of his reign, in 814, he ruled an extensive empire, far larger than the Byzantine Empire of the period. Though the pope was the nominal ruler of most of Italy as far south as Rome, Charlemagne maintained his own ultimate responsibility in that area also, and he ruled a small part of northern Spain which he had wrested from the Muslims (or Saracens).

Charles was greatly interested in the administration of his realms and kept a close supervision over all his subordinates. He appointed officials known as counts of the march (*margraves*) who undertook the defense of his frontiers. He issued numerous decrees called *capitularies,* regulating all aspects of life in his territories; and at intervals he sent out inspectors (*missi dominici*), one lay and one clerical, to see how his officials were fulfilling their duties. Though his relations with successive popes were correct, Charles did not hesitate to show that he, not the pope, was the master of western Europe, occasionally interfering even in ecclesiastical controversies. He granted asylum to Pope Leo III when he was driven from his see by disgruntled Italians and allowed him to establish on oath his innocence of charges brought against him, thereby maintaining him in office. This same pope rewarded Charles by crowning him as emperor on Christmas Day, 800.

Charles, it is recorded by his contemporary biographer Einhard, was offended by the pope's action, which was taken without consulting him. Not that he did not wish to be emperor; almost certainly he intended to make himself emperor in due time. But the pope's action could be interpreted as meaning that the pope was *entitled* to make and not only to crown emperors (and, possibly, could refuse the honor if he wished). Moreover, the action was premature and embroiled Charles with the emperor in Constantinople. To win the latter's recognition he had to restore some Italian cities his troops had captured from the Byzantines and make other concessions. Nevertheless, before his death his title was recognized by all, and henceforth there were to be two emperors in Europe.

In addition to his political and military exploits, Charles was deeply interested in education and learning. Though illiterate himself, he invited Alcuin of York in England to take charge of the palace school at his capital of Aachen, and he commanded all his bishops to institute schools in their dioceses. There was little scholarship in the Europe of his day, but Charles made the most of it, and a regular curriculum of the so-called Seven Liberal Arts became the norm. A new kind of cursive writing, the Carolingian minuscule, prepared the way for the production of far more legible and easily written manuscripts than had been available in the past.

The End of the Carolingians. When Charles died, the only one of his sons who survived him, Louis the Pious, inherited the entire empire. In spite of the fact that his father had crowned him emperor before his death, Louis insisted on being crowned also by the pope, for which he had to pay a price in concessions. When he died, his surviving sons fought for their share of the empire, which according to Germanic custom should have been divided among all three of them. The two younger sons, Ludwig (Louis) and Charles the Bald, compelled the eldest, Lothair, to content himself with the title of emperor and a shapeless and indefensible territory (which included Rome) between their own territories, roughly present-day France and Germany (Treaty of Verdun, 843). Thereafter the once great empire was frequently subdivided. Each ruler had difficulty in establishing his authority over rebellious subordinates, and few were even crowned emperor. The direct Carolingian line died out in 911. (See Chapter 8 for a discussion of the feudal system that developed during this period.)

ITALY IN THE EARLY MIDDLE AGES

When the Lombards invaded Italy in 568, the pope naturally appealed for help to his nominal overlord in Constantinople. But the Byzantine emperors were much too occupied with their own troubles to give the aid. It therefore fell to the popes to make their own arrangements with the Lombards. Pope Gregory I (the Great) in particular came to a *modus vivendi* with the Lombard nobles, in the sixth century, under which he retained substantial power in Rome and the surrounding areas. This pope was even strong enough to send out missionaries to distant lands, including Britain, in the attempt to convert them to Catholic Christianity. Britain, hitherto a partly Christian land under the influence of the semi-independent Irish Church, was successfully converted and organized by St. Augustine of Canterbury, the emissary of Gregory, and the Irish Church at the Synod of Whitby in 664 accepted the supremacy of Rome. The Lombards, on the other hand, were slow to convert to Catholic Christianity, and retained their Arianism for many generations.

Fall of the Lombard Monarchy. By the early eighth century the Lombards had consolidated their own rule under the king who replaced the numerous nobles previously in power. But his strength was far from equal to that of the Frankish rulers, who defeated him whenever they sent an expedition across the Alps. He could, however, menace the pope, who commanded little military force and had no reliable protector, since the Byzantine emperor showed only sporadic interest in his nominal possession, and opposed the papacy on the question of images (see p. 79). Pope Zacharias was therefore no doubt happy indeed to find a genuine protector in Pepin and to send his own emissary to crown him in France, as described above. When Pepin attempted to fulfill his own part of the bargain, the Lombard king quickly agreed to terms and ceded his lands but took possession of them again as soon as Pepin had returned home over the Alps. It was not until the reign of Charlemagne that the Lombard monarchy was abolished and the pope obtained secure control over his Donation. With the breakup of the Carolingian Empire the nobles assumed their old power, and for more than a century few popes exercised much authority in Italy.

RESTORATION OF THE EMPIRE IN GERMANY

After the Treaty of Verdun, the German sector of the old empire developed in substantial independence from the remainder. The German monarch was traditionally elected by his nobles and held little power unless he could win it by his military might. The opportunity to exercise power over all Germany was presented by the renewal of the barbarian invasions in the late ninth century: first by the Northmen from Scandinavia, who did not trouble Germany as much as they troubled the rest of Europe, and then by Magyars, from the east, and, to a lesser degree, by the Slavs, the brunt of whose attacks was borne by the Germans. Henry I, the Fowler (919–936), inflicted a decisive defeat on the Magyars in 933. His son Otto I, the Great (936–973), profited by his father's prestige to exert his authority over the German nobles, feeling powerful enough in 962 to have himself crowned emperor. Thus began the German empire which was to become known in later centuries as the Holy Roman Empire. Otto and his successors took their role as emperors of Italy so seriously that they insisted on exercising a veto over the election of the popes. Whenever the Italian nobles and clergy attempted to assert their independence and chose a pope unacceptable to the emperor, the latter intervened by force to put his own nominee on the papal throne. Not until 1059 did the cardinals succeed in defying the imperial power with impunity, as will be discussed in Chapter 8. The emperors likewise controlled the Church in Germany without difficulty, appointing all the higher clergy and using them for their own purposes.

INVASIONS OF NORTHMEN

Before the end of the eighth century, a new wave of invasions from the north by sea had begun, which persisted throughout the ninth century. The Scandinavian Vikings became masters of the sea and for a long time the hard-pressed Europeans were unable to find any means of effective defense. Raiding the towns on the sea-coast and penetrating up all navigable rivers, the Vikings took back with them to the north everything their boats could carry and at times made orderly government impossible in the lands that they plundered.

Settlement of the Northmen. In the early tenth century one of the Viking leaders, Rollo (Hrolf), did feudal homage for that part of northern France later called Normandy, from which center Viking descendants known as Normans conquered England in 1066. At about the same time, a number of Norman adventurers led by Robert Guiscard captured southern Italy from the Byzantines, later establishing a kingdom in Sicily, which they took from the Saracens. Another group of Vikings from Sweden, known as Varangians penetrated Russia and founded the city of Kiev, thereafter even threatening Constantinople from the sea. Kiev, ruled by descendants of the Vikings, was for several centuries the leading city of Russia.

The "Danes" in England. The impact of the Northmen was strongest in England, where the Angles and Saxons, who had gradually been subjugating the country since their first arrival from Denmark and western Germany in the fifth century, proved unable to resist the repeated Viking raids. The Danes, as these new invaders were called, took a large part of eastern England, known as the Danelaw. But the Danish invasions had also the effect of uniting England under Alfred the Great (871–899), king of Wessex, whose sons, inheriting a unified realm, were the first true kings of England. Alfred, after first buying time by paying tribute (*Danegeld*) to the Danes, ultimately succeeded in compelling them to make peace on the basis of a division of the country. His sons conquered the Danelaw, and the Northmen then became a part of the English population. At the end of the tenth century, the invasions were renewed, and though Danegeld was again collected and paid by Ethelred the Reedless (or Unready), the country was conquered, and Knut (Canute), king of Denmark, ruled England as part of a considerable empire. Seven years after his death, his line became extinct and England was once more ruled by a descendant of Alfred (Edward the Confessor, 1042–1066). After his death, England was invaded by another Viking, King Harold Hardrada of Norway, but he was defeated and killed by Harold the Saxon, the choice of the English magnates, at the Battle of Stamford Bridge. A few weeks later Harold, in turn, was killed by Duke William of Normandy, himself also a descendant of the Vikings, who became William I of England (see p. 103).

EARLY MEDIEVAL CULTURE

During the period covered by this chapter, learning reached its lowest ebb in western Europe. As early as the reign of Theodoric (489–526) in Italy, scholars perceived the likelihood that a knowledge of Greek would disappear, and the philosopher Boethius translated as much as he could of the works of Aristotle and wrote many simplified textbooks which became standard fare in the schools. Bishop Isidore of Seville wrote an *Etymology,* which was a mixture of accurate information and popular misinformation, ostensibly concerned with the origins of words. Alfred the Great patronized learning in England during his reign and attempted to improve English education. The Venerable Bede wrote a useful *Ecclesiastical History of England;* and the invaluable source book for the history of the following centuries, the *Anglo-Saxon Chronicle,* was begun under his inspiration. One original philosopher, John Scotus Erigena, flourished at the court of Charles the Bald in the ninth century. Gerbert of Aurillac, who was pope (Sylvester II) from 999 to 1003, had the reputation of being the most learned European of his day, but much of his knowledge had been gleaned from the Muslims. Indeed, in these centuries Muslims and Byzantines had almost a monopoly of scholarship in Europe, and the only way for others to acquire it was to make a journey to either Spain or Constantinople.

But the seeds for the future had been planted, especially in the educational reforms of Charlemagne. Before the eleventh century was over, the major Muslim works had been translated into Latin, and original scholarship was beginning; by the following century medieval art and architecture were already flourishing and on the way to attaining their full original creativeness. What has so often been called the Dark Ages had ended.

8 THE HIGH MIDDLE AGES TO THE END OF THE THIRTEENTH CENTURY

During the period of semianarchy which followed the breakup of the Carolingian empire, central authority could no longer be effectively enforced. As a result, the local landowners found themselves saddled with the sole responsibility for law and order in their territories. They could not rely upon outside help against barbarian invaders, nor was there usually any monarch who could compel them to do his bidding. In these circumstances their relations with their fellow-landowners became more important to them than their relation with the king, who was himself a landowner, with a higher rank than theirs but not necessarily with any great power. The relations among these nobles were regulated by a series of customs and mutual obligations collectively known as the feudal system. Relations between the landowners and the workers on their estates were likewise composed of reciprocal duties and obligations, which are collectively known as the manorial system. From these systems the institutions of church and state gradually emerged and were consolidated.

FEUDALISM AND MANORIALISM

The origins of the feudal and manorial systems are to be found in both the later Roman Empire and in tribal Germany. Heavy taxes in the fourth and fifth centuries had crushed the Roman middle classes, leaving only a few aristocrats at the top and a mass of poor people at the bottom. The large estate of the later Roman Empire, known as a *villa*, was more easily defensible against marauding bands of barbarians than were cities or smaller agricultural units. The landowner agreed to protect smaller landowners on condition that they yielded their lands to him. The smaller free farmers, forbidden by imperial legislation to leave their land, gradually sank to the condition of unfree workers, the precursors of the medieval serfs. In Germany it was a tribal custom for certain powerful warriors to gather around themselves groups of warriors to whom they provided leadership. In return these followers swore allegiance to their leader. This system, known as the *comitatus* (companionship) is believed to be the origin of the particular type of feudalism, based on the ceremony of homage and the oath of allegiance, that grew up in the Middle Ages among all the Germanic peoples.

Under the feudal system every landowner belonged to the upper ranks of society and possessed a certain number of *fiefs*, or grants of land. For these he either did homage to another noble who had issued the grant and to the king, or to the king alone, since the latter was the theoretical owner of all the land in his realm. If he did homage to another lord, he was that lord's *vassal*.

Mutual Obligations of Lords and Vassals. The condition of vassalage entailed certain definite obligations which differed in each fief. As a rule, a vassal had to supply a stipulated number of armed men if called upon to do so. He had to pay certain *reliefs* and *aids* on special occasions. A relief was a sum paid upon the death of a vassal by his heir to the feudal arrangement. Aids were other money payments. If the vassal's lord were taken prisoner, for example, he would have to contribute toward his ransom; if his lord visited him, he owed him hospitality. He had to make a money payment on the occasion of the knighting of the lord's eldest son and on the marriage of his daughters. If the vassal died leaving only a female heir, his lord had the right to bestow her in marriage and to exercise a wardship over her while she was a minor. Strictly speaking, fiefs were not hereditary possessions, but as long as a vassal's heir was capable of fulfilling his feudal obligations it was customary for a lord to bestow them on him, on the same terms as on his father. Lastly, a vassal had to sit in his lord's court when summoned to do so, and he had to play his part in enforcing its decrees. If a vassal did not live up to his obligations, his land could be *forfeited* by a judgment of the feudal court; if he died without heirs, his fief would *escheat* to his lord, who could then bestow it elsewhere.

In return for all this the lord was obligated to protect his vassals, as well as endowing them with their lands. A minor lord who lacked such protection might find himself dispossessed of his lands. The more powerful lords would thus often be requested to grant protection. In such circumstances the lesser lord would have to give his lands to his protector, receiving them back as fiefs with all the usual obligations (*commendatio, precarium*).

Military Basis of Feudalism. If the feudal system had in practice been as simple as it appeared in theory, it might have worked well. But it was complicated by the facts that most vassals held their fiefs from several different lords and that these lords themselves held fiefs from other lords. By the process of *subinfeudation* lords could also grant some of their lands to new vassals who undertook to fulfill their share of the lord's obligations to their superiors. It therefore often happened that a vassal would find himself faced with conflicting obligations, making it impossible to be "faithful" to all. The only method of settling disputed claims was warfare, and feudal wars were so frequent that the Church tried to intervene to enforce days of peace during which all fighting would cease. The Peace of God and Truce of God proclaimed by the Church, were, as might be expected, indifferently observed.

Since the feudal code was a military one, martial virtues at all times were greatly esteemed; and especially in the later Middle Ages, when kings were beginning to maintain law and order over wide areas, mock battles were staged, marked by single combats between individual nobles on various pretexts, or simply as entertainment. Strict regulations were drawn up governing the behavior of lords and knights. Combats to win the favors of noble ladies, to avenge insults, or even to demonstrate prowess took the place of the earlier and more serious warfare to win land and possessions. These customs were extolled by wandering minstrels and troubadours, and accounts of them formed a considerable part of medieval literature. This military code of behavior became known as chivalry.

Manorial System. The feudal lords of course had to provide for their own sustenance, and in the later Middle Ages they needed an increasing money income to buy the products of the towns. Every lord therefore had to keep some of his lands in cultivation according to his needs. Any surplus lands he could grant as fiefs, thus ensuring military help from his vassals in times of emergency. His personal lands, known as his *demesne*, were divided into manors, to each of which were attached a certain number of free men and a larger number of serfs, who were not free to leave the manor. Serfs and their families, who usually lived in a village on the manor, owed certain kinds of work to their lord and had to pay fees for the use of various facilities provided by the lord (for example, his baking ovens). Once they had fulfilled their obligation to their lord, the serfs could keep the rest of their produce and sell any surplus in the neighboring towns. But they could not marry outside the manor without their lord's permission (for which they would have to pay if it were granted). They could not go to live in a town without permission, nor could they be ordained as priests. The manor, at least in the early Middle Ages, was a nearly self-sufficient economic entity, requiring scarcely any imports. But the method of utilizing land was inefficient, and it was difficult for the lord to increase his income by improving his agricultural practices; nor was there much incentive for the serf to exercise his initiative. When the lords in later times wished to improve their income, they came to find it advisable to emancipate their serfs and rent out their lands for a fixed income, as will be discussed in Chapter 9.

URBAN DEVELOPMENT

There had of course been some towns in western Europe from the beginning of its history, and a few of them had persisted since the days of the Roman Empire. But most had become seriously depopulated during the centuries of the invasions, and even the Italian towns and those dependent on the Mediterranean trade, with few exceptions, had long declined in importance.

The Great Seaports. The first to recover were the towns in northern Italy, where the feudal and manorial systems never became entrenched. Venice, founded after the invasions of the Huns, for a long time had special relations with Constantinople and shared in the Byzantine trade. Genoa, Pisa, and Amalfi on the west coast of Italy were usually able to trade with the Muslims who controlled the Mediterranean, and they later took an important part in ousting the latter from their virtual monopoly. Other towns, such as Milan and Florence, became manufacturing centers whose products were carried into Muslim and Byzantine lands by the seaport towns. Though they often fought among themselves in the twelfth century, many of the northern Italian towns banded together in the Lombard League to resist the efforts of the Holy Roman emperors to impose their rule over the country. After they defeated Frederick I (Barbarossa) in the Battle of Legnano (1178), they enjoyed virtual independence from the feudal lords and could later play the leading part in the Renaissance.

Achievement of Independence by Towns. Elsewhere towns grew up at important river junctions, fords, and similar places where transportation was convenient. In some instances manorial villages increased in size to become real towns. In Flanders there were many towns of importance which lived by processing wool grown in England and elsewhere. Much depended on the attitude of the feudal lord within whose territories the town was situated. If he wished to increase his income by taxing industry, he might grant the town a charter setting forth the terms under which it could function. The kings and emperors especially would grant charters in exchange for payment of fixed sums of money which they could then use for their own (usually military) purposes.

Merchant and Craft Guilds. In the towns were organizations of merchants and of craftsmen known as guilds. Both types of guilds tended to restrict freedom of enterprise and to keep the number of merchants and manufacturers confined to as few men as possible. It was believed that the market for their products was limited and that any newcomers would only spread the available business more thinly. The merchant guilds sometimes grew so powerful that they could take over the governments of their cities, and in the later Middle Ages many of the German mercantile towns joined together in the Hanseatic League. This league for a time was a kind of sovereign state which even waged war against those states that refused to permit members to carry on business with them.

The craft guilds provided for a limited number of masters, who employed journeymen (skilled workers waiting to become masters) and apprentices who were learning their craft. The guilds prescribed conditions of work and policed the quality of their products and the prices for which they were sold. They took care of the social needs of their members and decided on new entries into the ranks of the masters. As long as the market was expanding, it was not too difficult for a journeyman to become a master; in later times, however, the journeymen had to wait long before they were accepted and hence tended to do work outside the guild at cut prices. Thus they were instrumental in breaking the monopoly of the guilds.

THE MEDIEVAL CHURCH AND ITS CONFLICT WITH THE EMPIRE

The most important institution in Europe during the Middle Ages was undoubtedly the Christian Church, which had a monopoly of religion in Europe. Every European (excluding a small minority of Jews and the Muslims in Spain) was at least a nominal Christian.

The Church was the sole dispenser of the sacraments believed to be necessary for salvation. At the same time it performed many functions now reserved to secular states. It had its own legal system (canon law) based on Roman law, its own court (*Curia*) headed by the pope with his secretariat. By the early thirteenth century the papacy appointed and controlled all the high Church officials in Europe, including the archbishops and bishops, many of whom were also cardinals (a position which was solely honorary except that they had the right to participate in the choice of the next pope).

The Investiture Struggle. At the beginning of the period with which we are concerned in this chapter, the papacy lacked the essential power of appointing its own clergy and thus could not pursue a consistent policy. Until the late eleventh century it had to recognize the right of secular rulers to appoint the clergy in their own countries. Even the popes themselves had to be approved by the emperor since he was usually able by the use of military force to compel the appointment of his own nominee. Even when the emperor did not interfere, the Roman nobles and populace exercised a powerful influence on the choice of popes, and they chose unsuitable candidates at least as often as did the German emperor. In Europe the Church was largely a prisoner of the feudal system. Church officials relied for their subsistence on lands granted to them by feudal lords or kings. It was not unnatural that these lords should appoint their own relatives to these lucrative positions (*nepotism*); when they were short of money they might even sell the offices to the highest bidder (*simony*). In any case they did not care to see Church positions filled by members of rival families, nor could they brook outright opposition from powerful priests. For all these reasons they were unwilling to relinquish the right of appointment to the papacy. On the other hand, the popes would have been derelict in their duty if they had permitted the high offices in their Church to be in the hands of worldly men without any claim to sanctity and serving the interests of their feudal relatives.

At the beginning of the tenth century, a French duke bequeathed some land outright to a group of monks without imposing any feudal obligations upon them. These monks and their successors thus were given in perpetuity a means of subsistence independent of the feudal system. This Cluniac Order soon attracted to itself some of the most dedicated clergymen, who carried out a much-needed reform of the Church. Emperor Otto III was so much impressed by the work of these men that he appointed one of them as pope, and for much of the rest of the eleventh century popes were drawn either from the Cluniac Order or from sympathizers with it. In 1056 Emperor Henry III died, leaving as his heir a son who was only six years old. Though he was chosen emperor, the German nobles rebelled against him throughout his reign. The papacy decided to take the opportunity to remove the election of the pope from the hands of the emperor, and a synod decreed that future popes should be chosen by the seven cardinal bishops (later it was provided that he be chosen by all cardinals). When the young emperor Henry IV came of age he refused to recognize the new procedure, but for some time he was powerless to prevent it.

In 1073 a reformer named Hildebrand, who was determined to put an end to the appointment of the higher clergy by laymen, ascended the papal throne and took the name of Gregory VII. His principal target was Henry IV, who continued to sell Church offices, whereupon Gregory excommunicated him (forbade him all services of the Church) and deposed him from his position as emperor. Henry, faced with a rebellion by his magnates and having doubtful support in the German Church, decided to make his peace with Gregory. After doing penance before the pope at Canossa (1077) and receiving absolution, he returned to Germany and at once began to suppress the baronial revolt. As soon as this had been accomplished, he returned to Italy, drove Gregory into exile, and set up his own antipope. But Henry continued to be plagued by rebellions, while Gregory's successors carried on the struggle against lay investiture.

The next emperor, Henry V, after several expeditions to Rome to set up his own popes, at last in 1122 negotiated a settlement (Concordat of Worms) under which the emperor was in the future to invest bishops with their secular power (symbol—the scepter), while the pope made the nomination and invested them with their spiritual power (symbols—the ring and the cross). The papacy on the whole gained more by the compromise, since the emperors' previously exclusive right of appointment was converted to what amounted to only a veto over appointment by the pope. During the same period a similar compromise was accepted for their own realms by the kings of England and France.

The Papacy at the Height of Its Power. For much of the rest of the century the strong emperor Frederick I, Barbarossa, of the Hohenstaufen family sat on the imperial throne. Frederick interfered constantly in Italy, though his main quarrel was not so much with the papacy itself as with the Italian towns which the papacy supported against him. After his defeat by the Lombard League at Legnano in 1178, he agreed to relinquish most of the rights he had claimed in northern Italy, contenting himself with the formal recognition of his sovereignty by the towns (Peace of Constance, 1183). In Germany he overpowered the always rebellious German nobility.

When he was drowned during the Third Crusade, the Empire was inherited by his son Henry VI (1190–1197), who was married to the heiress of the Norman kingdom of Sicily. The new emperor dominated Italy as long as he lived, but he died prematurely, leaving as his heir a boy of three (later Frederick II). Pope Innocent III (1198–1216), although he was Frederick's guardian, thus won the opportunity to weaken the Empire by supporting a candidate for the throne who did not belong to the powerful Hohenstaufen family.

Though Frederick eventually won the imperial crown for himself, Innocent was free to exercise his authority over all the rulers of Europe. He compelled Philip II, Augustus, of France to take back the wife whom he had repudiated. When King John of England refused to accept Innocent's nominee, Stephen Langton, as Archbishop of Canterbury, the pope excommunicated the monarch and laid an interdict on his country (i.e., forbade all religious ceremonies). When he attempted also to depose him, John, faced by a rebellion of his own barons, submitted to the pope and "commended" his whole realm to Innocent, receiving it back as a fief with all the feudal obligations that this entailed. Other countries that were papal fiefs included Aragon, Bulgaria, Denmark, Hungary, Poland, Portugal, and Serbia, all of whose rulers did Innocent homage. In 1215 Innocent summoned a great council attended by most of the kings of Europe or their representatives, together with a huge throng of high clerics. Here he issued a number of decrees and proclaimed the dogma of transubstantiation (see p. 142). Never before or since has any pope wielded so much authority and actual power, because the possibility of exercising it was dependent on factors peculiar to the period of Innocent's reign. The Empire was in a state of confusion with two families warring for the crown, neither able to intervene in Italy. The French and English monarchs were at war with one another, and the English monarch himself was at war with his own lords. Constantinople had just fallen to Western arms, under at least the nominal direction of the pope. Such favorable circumstances for papal supremacy in Europe could not be expected to recur.

Struggles with the Empire. In fact the ruler who was to prove a scourge of the medieval papacy was already king of Germany and

Sicily by the end of Innocent's reign. In 1220 Frederick II became emperor also (1220–1250). His background eminently fitted him for playing the part of an antipapal leader. Influenced by Islamic thought at least as much as by Christian (the result of his upbringing in still partly Muslim Sicily), a patron of secular culture; proficient in many languages, including Arabic; and an extremely efficient ruler in his hereditary kingdom of Sicily, he paid little attention to the fulminations of the popes and did not hesitate to fight against them, even when he was excommunicated. His main task, as he saw it, was to unite his domains of Germany and Sicily by controlling Italy. This meant a life-and-death struggle with the Italian towns, which were backed by the papacy. When Pope Gregory IX, his implacable enemy, died, Frederick was influential in having a personal friend elected as Innocent IV ((1243–1254). But the latter almost at once turned against him and escaped to France, where he tried to arouse Europe against Frederick. However, he had little success until after the death of Frederick, when his appeals and the appeals of his successors to foreign princes finally bore fruit. Charles of Anjou defeated and killed Frederick's illegitimate son Manfred in 1266 and beheaded his last surviving grandson Conradin in 1268. Meanwhile Conrad IV, the last Hohenstaufen emperor, had died in 1254, and the Germans could not agree on a successor till 1273. When Prince Rudolf of Hapsburg, the first of his line, was finally chosen, he proved to be totally uninterested in the Italian territories that were traditionally a part of the Empire.

Thus the papacy had succeeded in destroying the old Empire but at the cost of demonstrating to the world that the papacy was as willing to use political and military weapons as was any secular authority.

Struggle with France. The next trial of strength was with the powerful French monarchy. Pope Boniface VIII (1294–1303) tried to prevent Philip IV of France (1285–1314) from taxing the Church in France. When he issued a bull forbidding the practice (*Clericis laicos*, 1296), Philip retorted by placing an embargo on all money leaving France, whereupon Boniface gave way. After Boniface's finances had been restored by pilgrims to Rome during a papal jubilee held in 1300, he again quarreled with Philip, asserting in the bull *Unam sanctam* (1302) that all Christians owed absolute obedience to the pope in everything if they hoped to be saved. Philip, threatened with excommunication by Boniface, sent his chancellor to Italy to compel the pontiff's resignation. Aided by a group of

Italian nobles opposed to the pope, Chancellor Nogaret burst into the papal apartments at Anagni and so mistreated Boniface that he died soon afterward. The following year a new pope decided that it was unsafe to live in Rome and moved the papal see to Avignon in France, thereby beginning the "Babylonian Captivity."

The Growth of Heresy. The worldliness of the Church produced a strong reaction among faithful Christians. Some groups (such as the Waldensians, founded by Peter Waldo in the twelfth century) criticized the wealth of the Church and refused to accept its authority: others (such as the Cathari [Albigensians]) of southern France set up their own church. The Waldensians were declared to be heretics, and the medieval Inquisition was organized in 1233 to seek them out and compel them to recant on pain of death if they refused. The Inquisition, or Holy Office, was empowered by the papacy to hear all cases of alleged heresy brought before it. The accused could then be questioned, and tortured if necessary, in order to obtain a confession. If he recanted a severe penance could be imposed, but his life was usually spared. If he refused he was "relaxed to the secular arm"; that is, he was delivered to the secular authorities to be put to death by burning. If he recanted and then returned to his heresy, he was condemned as a "relapsed" heretic and put to death. Most of the Albigensians were exterminated in a Crusade called against them by Pope Innocent III in 1208. The remnants of both Albigensians and Waldensians were effectually stamped out by the Inquisition.

The Mendicant Orders. Many good Catholics also felt that the church needed to be reformed. Throughout the first half of the twelfth century, St. Bernard of Clairvaux had constantly attacked the worldliness both of the monks (regular clergy) and of the high Church officials of his day (secular clergy); and he strongly influenced the Cistercian Order, which he refounded, toward austerity and useful labor. In the thirteenth century two new orders of friars arose, both devoted to the ideal of Christian poverty. The Dominicans, founded by the Spaniard St. Dominic (1170–1221), laid emphasis on preaching, and the Franciscans, founded by the Italian St. Francis of Assisi (1182–1226), on healing and other good works. Both lived from free-will offerings and for some time, at least, the Franciscans tried hard to keep from accumulating worldly possessions. Unlike the monks, the friars did not live away from the world but mingled with the people and shared their lives. It was largely due to their efforts that many nominal Christians in the thirteenth century were converted to a serious practice of their religion and that the precipitant decline of the Church was postponed until the fourteenth and fifteenth centuries.

NATIONAL MONARCHIES

The origins of the modern national state can be traced back to the Middle Ages. Although Germany and Italy failed to unite, largely because of the persistence of the imperial ideal in the form of the Holy Roman Empire, other countries had already become true nations by the end of the Middle Ages. Conspicuous among these were England, France, Spain, and Portugal.

The Norman Monarchy in England. When Duke William of Normandy won the Battle of Hastings in 1066, Anglo-Saxon resistance quickly crumbled and William consolidated the country under his rule. Since England was his by right of conquest, his position was much stronger than that of most feudal monarchs. He was the real owner of all the land, unlike the French Capetian monarchs, who possessed France only in theory and became actual rulers of the country through their own efforts over the course of centuries. William gave lands to his followers in exchange for their acceptance of feudal obligations; and these in turn subinfeudated lands to their own vassals. Saxon lords received their lands back on the same terms. But only the king had the right to declare war, and private armies were forbidden. Late in William's reign all his vassals and subvassals took a direct oath of allegiance to him (Oath of Salisbury) and his officials compiled a great book (Domesday Book), in which every fief was recorded, together with the obligations attached to it. Thus by the time of his death in 1087, William's position as king was securely established and rebellion was virtually impossible. His strong monarchy was continued by his sons William II, Rufus (1087–1100), and Henry I. During the latter's long reign (1100–1135) the beginnings of a royal bureaucracy were established. Henry chose many of his officials from men who belonged to the higher nobility and were thus dependent on his favor, instead of being powerful in their own right by virtue of their rank and wealth.

Unfortunately for England, when Henry I died he left no male heir, and it was not yet established that a woman could succeed to the throne. The next nineteen years were largely spent in civil war between Stephen, the nearest male heir, and Henry's daughter Matilda. Eventually a compromise was reached under which Stephen was to reign during his lifetime but was to be succeeded by Matilda's son Henry Plantagenet, who became king in 1154. Henry II, who was the son of a French nobleman and married a French heiress (Eleanor of Aquitaine), ruled more than half of France in addition to England. With the aid of his French vassals he re-established the strong monarchy that his grandfather had begun in England and reduced to obedience the feudal nobles, who had done more or less as they wished during the interregnum.

The Angevin Monarchy in England. During the reign of Henry II (1154–1189) many of the old feudal courts were abolished and a common law for the whole country was gradually brought into being. Jury trials, the earliest of which are known from the time of Henry II, in due course took the place of the customary trials by ordeal and combat. Henry's legal innovations caused a conflict between the monarch and the Church, which had its own ecclesiastical courts and claimed the right to try all clerics, whatever their crimes might be. In the course of the struggle between Henry and Archbishop Thomas Becket, the latter was murdered in his own cathedral at Canterbury. Since Henry was blamed for the crime and public opinion turned against him, he did penance for it and withdrew some of his edicts against the Church. Henry's son and successor Richard I, the Lion-Hearted, was away from England on the Third Crusade for most of his reign, and on his way home was imprisoned by the Holy Roman emperor Henry VI. Richard's English vassals were compelled to raise a huge ransom for him, the payment of which plagued the reign of his successor John (1199–1216).

John was a weak monarch, faced with strong opponents in the persons of the French king Philip Augustus, who coveted the English monarchy's lands in France, and of Pope Innocent III. Philip took almost all John's possessions in France, and Innocent compelled him to become a vassal of the papacy (see p. 100). The English nobles objected so strongly to John's exactions and the failure of his wars that they rebelled and forced him to sign Magna Carta (1215), a document in which John swore that he would observe their traditional rights which they had always enjoyed under the feudal system— especially the rights to be consulted on taxation and to be free from arbitrary use of royal power. Though Magna Carta could not be enforced except by threat of rebellion, it was at least a recognition by the king that there were limits to his right to use his royal power, and later kings could be reminded of it and made to take the same oath.

Henry III, who reigned for most of the thirteenth century (1216–

1272), was little more effective than his father. In addition his feudal obligations to the papacy bore hard on the people of England and he did not refrain from engaging in expensive adventures on the Continent. As a result there was another rebellion in 1258, and this time the barons attempted to limit the king's power by forcing him to consult with them and with representatives of the towns and counties. The first English Parliament was indeed called by the rebellious barons. Though Henry's son Edward eventually suppressed the rebellion (and killed its leader, Simon de Montfort, in 1265), when he himself came to the throne in 1272 he instituted a number of pressing reforms. In 1295 he called a Parliament (known as the Model Parliament), in which all the major classes in England were represented. Thereafter, Parliament was an established institution and gradually came to exercise the functions of a legislature, thus limiting the arbitrary power of the king more effectively than had been possible for the feudal lords with their threats of rebelllion. Nevertheless the tasks of Parliament were limited, and the king with his Council made up of his own chief officials was the effective ruler of England for a long time to come.

France under the Capetians. In 886 when the Carolingian Charles the Fat neglected the defense of Paris against the Northmen, the West Franks chose the gallant defender Odo as their king in his place. Even so, another Carolingian was accepted by others and for most of the tenth century there were two kings in France. This situation was brought to an end in 987 when Hugh Capet was accepted by the whole country, although he was the feudal ruler only of the Île-de-France, a small territory that included Paris. Fortunately for the monarchy, for several centuries the reigning monarch had an eldest son capable of ruling, and the elective kingship of the Germanic peoples gradually fell into disuse.

The early Capetians nevertheless had relatively little power. There were always in France more powerful nobles than themselves; they had to make careful use of the prerogatives belonging to the monarchy which were distinct from those of the feudal lords—especially the right to lead the country in foreign wars, the right to take possession of lands left without heirs, and the right to appoint the higher clergy in areas larger than those of the king's own feudal domains, where alone he exercised undisputed authority. The Capetian monarchs also made effective use of their clerics as advisers and officials, rarely using their feudal barons in responsible positions.

Louis VII (1137–1180) won a huge increase in his territories by his marriage to Eleanor of Aquitaine. But when she failed to present him with an heir and they became estranged during the Second Crusade, on which she accompanied him, the marriage was annulled. Eleanor promptly married Henry, count of Anjou, and her territories became possessions of the English crown when her new husband became Henry II of England in 1154. Louis' son Philip II, Augustus (1180–1223), spent much of his reign trying to win them back by war and intrigue. Since the kings of England did homage to Philip as king of France for their French fiefs, an opportunity was provided for the French monarch to put pressure on his vassal. This he used several times to good effect. When John refused to stand trial in his feudal court for failure to honor his feudal obligations, his lands were declared forfeited, and Philip's other vassals helped him to carry out the sentence. Much of southern France was also added to the royal realm by the Albigensian Crusade (see p. 102). By the time of the accession of Louis IX in 1226, the monarchy was therefore in effective control of almost the whole country. Henry III of England, however, continued the effort to regain some of his possessions until a treaty was signed in 1259. This treaty recognized English rule in Guienne and Gascony in southern France in exchange for the abandonment of all claims elsewhere. During his long reign Louis established a strong bureaucracy, made royal law (Roman) generally supreme over local and feudal law, and legislated uniformly for all his possessions. He also assumed control over many towns to which charters had been granted by his predecessors.

Philip IV (1285–1314) pursued a costly program of expansion which necessitated the discovery of new sources of income, and, as we have seen (p. 101), brought the monarchy into conflict with the papacy. During the struggle with Boniface VIII, Philip summoned the States-General, an assembly of the important classes of the kingdom, as a means of demonstrating public support for his policies. Later in his reign he called it several times for the purpose of winning its assent for new taxation; but, unlike the English Parliament, it did not win control of taxation, and it never in fact became an established institution. Philip failed to add the rich County of Flanders to his kingdom, his old-fashioned feudal troops being soundly defeated by the Flemish townsmen in the Battle of the Spurs (1302). But he gained much in prestige when the papacy moved to Avignon (see p. 102), even though the territory was papal and not royal. Moreover, Philip won the acquiescence of the French pope Clement V to his sequestration of the property of the Knights

Templar, the richest financial organization of Europe, which had been originally founded as a crusading order. The acquisition of so much wealth helped greatly to solve his financial difficulties. By the end of Philip's reign, France was by far the most important and the richest country in Europe, bearing a strong resemblance to modern nations in its centralized form of government and its control over the national economy.

The Iberian Peninsula. The Muslim rule of Spain had been seriously weakened by the eleventh century. Some Christians had never submitted to the Saracens (Moors), and from the eighth century onward they had begun to conquer northern Spain. In the early eleventh century Ferdinand I of Castile won the crown of León, and in 1085 Alfonso VI of Castile captured Toledo from the Saracens. Alfonso called various European noblemen to his assistance, including Henry of Burgundy, whom he made Count of Portugal. The Saracens attempted to obtain reinforcements from Africa, but in spite of temporary reverses the Christians gradually wore down their resistance until the decisive Battle of Las Navas de Tolosa (1212), when Alfonso VIII brought independent Muslim power virtually to an end. A Muslim emir remained only in Granada, as a vassal of the Castilian monarch. Meanwhile northeastern Spain, the Spanish march established by Charlemagne, was not retaken by the Saracens, and in the twelfth century Alfonso of Aragon added Catalonia to his domains. James I (1213–1276) increased his mainland kingdom, and Peter III (1276–1285), who inherited the kingdom of Sicily through his Hohenstaufen wife, made good his claims, thus adding a maritime empire to his mainland possessions. Both Aragon and Castile possessed representative assemblies known as *Cortes,* made up, like the French States-General, of the three estates (nobility, clergy, and burghers), which the monarch consulted on taxation and legislation and which for a long time exercised some restraint on royal power. However, when Aragon and Castile were united at the end of the fifteenth century by the marriage of Ferdinand of Aragon and Isabella of Castile, royal power became too great to be withstood and the Cortes ceased to exercise any effective control.

Henry of Burgundy (*c.* 1057–1112) and his immediate successors in Portugal spent most of their reigns in wars against the Saracens, followed by further wars with Castile to settle the boundaries of the new kingdom. Portugal was not free from Castilian threats until a great victory at Aljubarrota in 1385. Henry's son Alfonso I was proclaimed king by his Cortes in 1143.

The Slavic Kingdoms. Following the missionary efforts of two Byzantine priests, Cyril and Methodius, in the late ninth century, the Slavic peoples were gradually converted to Christianity. The furthest western penetration of the Slavs was into Bohemia and Moravia, where a strong kingdom was established by the thirteenth century. These kingdoms came under the influence of the German clergy and accepted the ecclesiastical authority of the pope. Poland was converted, mainly from Bohemia, and became Roman Catholic also. By the twelfth century, Poland was a fairly strong kingdom, but its monarchy, like that of Bohemia, was elective. The king was therefore greatly dependent on the magnates, who prevented the consolidation of royal power. Hungary was populated not by Slavs but by Magyars from Asia, who created a strong kingdom under Stephen I, later canonized as St. Stephen (997–1038). But in later centuries the nobles robbed the monarch of most of his power. The Hungarians, in spite of several Byzantine efforts, gave their adherence to the Roman Church.

The eastern Slavs of Russia, who were far closer to Constantinople, were converted in the tenth century by the Byzantines and joined the Orthodox Church in the eleventh-century schism between the Eastern and Western churches. The organized Russian state for several centuries consisted of a principality of varying size ruled from Kiev. In the eleventh and twelfth centuries other principalities arose, including the duchy of Moscow and the great northern trading center of Novgorod. All the eastern European states were threatened by the great Mongol invasions of the thirteenth century led by the conqueror Genghis Khan and his successors, who established a vast Asian empire. Poland resisted at the cost of widespread devastation. Hungary was defeated but saved by the departure of the Mongol leaders to take part in the election of a new khan. The Russians suffered most. Except for Novgorod the entire country was subjected to Mongol rule for a century. The Mongolian Golden Horde established its capital at Sarai on the lower Volga and compelled all the Russian princes to pay tribute and acknowledge the suzerainty of the khan. It was during this period that the duchy of Moscow became the chief Russian state; its princes played the leading part in expelling the Mongols in the fourteenth and fifteenth centuries.

THE CRUSADES

Although eastern Europe, which was little-organized for resistance, had to submit to invasions and conquests from Asia, western Europe from the eleventh century onward was itself expanding into the Near East. Though it was unable to maintain its bridgehead in Asia beyond the thirteenth century and at no time controlled very much territory, the contact of the culturally backward West with the still superior Muslim culture had effects on the West that went far beyond the military occupation.

The First Crusade. Christian knights had long been active in conquering Spain from the Saracens when a further opportunity presented itself for action in the East. The Seljuk Turks, a more militant group than the Muslims of the Abbasid Caliphate, began to threaten the Byzantines in the late eleventh century, nearly defeating the Byzantine emperor in 1071 at the Battle of Manzikert. In the meantime they had taken over the rest of the Abbasid possessions, including Jerusalem. The Byzantines had appealed to the pope for help as early as the pontificate of Gregory VII, who had passed on the request to his Norman allies in Sicily (1084). When reports continued to arrive in Rome of the ill treatment of Christian pilgrims to Jerusalem by the Turks, Pope Urban II in 1095 decided to proclaim a Crusade, calling upon all true Christians to aid in rescuing the Holy Sepulcher from the hands of the infidel. The kings and most leading nobles made little response; but enthusiasm was stirred among the poorer classes and the more adventurous and less wealthy of the nobles. Two groups of landless peasants who marched to Constantinople by land were quickly destroyed. But the nobles and their retainers, led by Godfrey de Bouillon of Lorraine, arrived safely in Constantinople, where they somewhat overawed Emperor Alexius Comnenus, who had been expecting merely some military assistance. He made use of them to regain some of his possessions in Asia Minor, then left them. After many hardships they finally reached Palestine, capturing Antioch and then Jerusalem against relatively light resistance (1099). The crusaders divided Palestine into fiefs on the Western model and Godfrey became ruler of Jerusalem. A number of military religious orders were founded which undertook to aid the Christian peoples to retain possession of the country.

Second and Third Crusades. In 1144 the Muslims, better unified than before, recaptured the outlying principality of Edessa, whereupon St. Bernard of Clairvaux preached the Second Crusade, to which the German emperor Conrad III and Louis VII of France responded. This Crusade met with no success and the crusaders returned home. The Muslim position in Syria continued to improve,

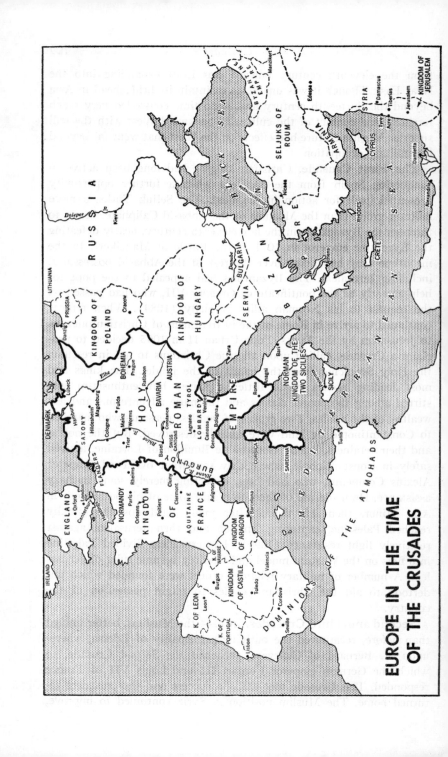

EUROPE IN THE TIME
OF THE CRUSADES

and in 1171 Egypt was captured by the Muslim leader Saladin, whose forces now almost surrounded the Latin kingdoms in Palestine. In 1184 he advanced on Jerusalem, capturing it in 1187. The Third Crusade was a great effort by three monarchs, the emperor Frederick Barbarossa, the French king Philip Augustus, and the English king Richard I, to restore the Western position in Palestine. But Frederick was drowned on the way, while the French and English monarchs, bitter rivals at home, co-operated little with each other. Eventually Richard and his forces were left to fight alone. But he could not defeat Saladin, and though he made an agreement with him, it could not be enforced. Jerusalem therefore remained in non-Christian hands.

Later Crusades. The Fourth Crusade, called by Innocent III, sacked the Christian city of Constantinople. But the Venetians, who financed the Crusade and supplied part of its leadership, were not interested in taking the Holy City of Jerusalem, which by this time contained little of commercial value and was in any case strongly defended. The crusaders therefore returned home after toppling the Byzantine monarchy, except for those who remained to rule the Empire. For the next seventy years other minor Crusades followed. Only one had a measure of success, when Emperor Frederick II tried a different approach and negotiated a treaty with the sultan of Egypt under which the Christians were granted Jerusalem without fighting (1229). It was lost again in 1244. Meanwhile a so-called Children's Crusade had served to discredit the whole crusading movement. In 1212 a number of children from France and Germany began a spontaneous march to the Mediterranean in the belief that the sea would turn into dry land and enable them to rescue the Holy Sepulcher. Though some of the children were sent home, it is probable that most of them were sold into slavery. In 1291 Acre, the last Christian stronghold in the Holy Land, fell to the Muslims, and Palestine thereafter remained securely in Muslim hands.

Consequences of the Crusades. The chief consequences of the Crusades were the cultural contact between the growing Western and the declining Muslim civilizations and the economic effect on Europe of new products which entered into European trade. The papacy won prestige for the successful First Crusade, which was due to its initiative, but its reputation suffered when it could neither control the crusaders nor help them to victory. It debased the title of Crusade when Innocent called the Albigensian Crusade against heretical Christians. By continuing to summon Crusades long after the religious crusading spirit was over, it demonstrated a failure to understand the changed conditions in Europe. The towns, especially Venice, profited most. Ripples of influence from the Crusades spread all through Europe, and the great majority of changes in the next centuries can indirectly be traced back to them; but other causes were at least as important, and it is easy to overestimate the importance of the Crusades.

HIGH MEDIEVAL CULTURE

The interests of medieval people differed so greatly from those of our own time that their achievements have often been underestimated by their successors. In a world dominated by the Church, in which the primary aspiration approved by medieval society was the winning of salvation in an afterlife, obviously the most important scholarly discipline would be theology; and education, which was in the hands of the clergy, would be little concerned with the practical arts and sciences which bulk so large in the modern curriculum.

Education—The Rise of Universities. The curriculum of the cathedral and royal schools was traditional, based on the so-called Seven Liberal Arts: the *trivium,* logic, rhetoric, grammar (Latin); and the *quadrivium,* arithmetic, astronomy, geometry, and music. Textbooks were few and elementary in the early Middle Ages; they improved in later centuries, especially with the new translations of Aristotle from the Greek and Arabic, and translations from the Arabic of some of the Hellenistic masterpieces which were studied in Muslim lands, notably the *Almagest* (describing a geocentric astronomical system) of Claudius Ptolemy. The stress on logic by the faculties of liberal arts in the universities led to great skill in reasoning but a certain reluctance to admit new knowledge based on observation. From the twelfth century onward, many new universities were founded, of which the chief was the University of Paris refounded in 1200 by Philip Augustus on the basis of an original cathedral school. Here theology in particular was studied, especially in the form of discussions of theological questions, many of which had been collected in a book of Peter Lombard called the *Sentences* (Opinions). The University also had an important school for the study of law (Roman and ecclesiastical). The University of Bologna in Italy was founded somewhat earlier than the University of Paris, and its fame was almost as great. The impulse for its founding was the rediscovery of the law code of Justinian, which a series of eminent jurists began to study seriously, commenting on it for the purpose of adapting it to medieval use. Only mature students who needed this law for their careers in the state and Church usually studied at Bologna. They assumed responsibility for running the university, whereas at Paris and most of the other medieval universities the faculty was in charge as in the modern European universities. Medicine was studied at Montpellier in France and Salerno in Italy, in a curriculum influenced by the superior medical science of the Muslims.

Faith versus Reason in Theology. In the twelfth century the questions of how we come to know and what we really know for certain were widely examined. Peter Abelard, the greatest teacher of the century, argued the question of the role of faith and authority in knowledge. In his *Sic et Non* (Yes and No) he propounded certain questions and listed what different authorities had argued on both sides of each question, demonstrating clearly that not all had agreed with one another. Then he himself tried to supply a solution. This *scholastic* method became usual in medieval schools. Peter Lombard applied it to disputed theological questions. A further subject of great interest was the nature of "universals" (abstract ideas), whether the abstraction is more real than the particular. The Realists held with Plato that the universals (Plato's Ideas) were a reality and more real than the particulars (for example, humanity than individual men, the Church than churches). Their opponents, the Nominalists, held that the universals were only a convenient way of describing groups of many particulars.

In the next century, with the rediscovery of Aristotle's books on natural science, students began to consider him to be infallible and regarded him as a supreme authority. But it also became clear that if he were right, then the Bible must have erred. This conflict led to the banning of the teaching of Aristotle in the University of Paris for several decades. Then Albertus Magnus (*c.* 1193–1280) and Thomas Aquinas (1225–1274) attempted to use Aristotle to confirm the teachings of religion. Thomas Aquinas in particular used Aristotle's logic in a very sophisticated manner to prove those tenets of the Christian religion which could be discovered by reason, leaving all those truths which were beyond reason to the realm of faith. After a period during which the Church authorities wavered about permitting reason to have its way in spite of its leading to possible skepticism or heresy, they finally decided that Thomas Aquinas' method was acceptable and he became the *Doctor Angelicus* of the Church.

Science. Scientific writings in the earlier Middle Ages mostly consisted of descriptive books on animals, tales of marvels, and excerpts, sometimes with commentaries, of Roman, Hellenistic, and Muslim writings. But in the later period, partly under Muslim influence, students became interested in such subjects as alchemy, and there is evidence of some schools of experimenters who had a substantial fund of knowledge at their disposal. Albertus Magnus studied botany, alchemy, and mineralogy in addition to his theology. Robert Grosseteste founded a school at Oxford devoted to the study of light and other physical phenomena. In the thirteenth century Roger Bacon publicized the experiments of his associates; did some original work in optics; and in a compendium of knowledge addressed to the pope (*Opus Majus*), called on him to give his approval and financial support to a project of creating a new Christian synthesis of scientific knowledge. But the scientific interest during this period was not great, though some preparation was being made for the future. Science was still held back by too many preconceptions, too little empirical knowledge and experimentation, and excessive theorizing. The last medieval centuries, to be dealt with in Chapter 9, held more promise for the future and eventually saw the work of Copernicus and Galileo.

Medieval Literature. In the early medieval centuries almost all literature was in the Latin language. It included, in addition to works of learning, much interesting and often lively poetry. With the rise of the vernacular tongue there was a greater public to appreciate what was written. The townsfolk liked story and fable; the nobles preferred the work of the minstrels, tales and poems of chivalry and courtly love. The legends of King Arthur and the Grail Cycle with its profound religious content were spread by many poets to whom they appealed; the *Parzival* of Wolfram von Eschenbach is the outstanding example of this type. But the greatest of medieval poems is certainly the *Divine Comedy* of Dante (1265–1321), the vision of the poet as he passes through Hell, Purgatory, and Paradise. Among the masterpieces of prose are the *Decameron* of Boccaccio (1313–1375) and the *Canterbury Tales* of Chaucer (*c.* 1340–1400).

Art and Architecture. The greatest medieval achievement, perhaps still unsurpassed in Western civilization, was the building of churches and cathedrals. From the twelfth century onward every bishop believed it to be his task to build a cathedral in his diocese, a co-operative effort in which every parishioner should play his part. The Romanesque style with its rounded arches, based on the old

Roman basilica, gave place in time to the Gothic, with all its varia-
tions. The Gothic church with its flying buttresses is a stone skeleton
which permits the entry of light through numerous stained-glass
windows, themselves one of the greatest medieval achievements.
Sculpture and much of the work in glass were in the main realistic,
especially in the decorative features. Painting was almost exclusively
religious, and the medieval Madonnas do not have the vividness and
human qualities of the Madonnas of the Renaissance. Only in the late
Middle Ages, with Giotto (*c.* 1276–1337), is the Renaissance foreshadowed; from his time there was no looking back to the still technically somewhat primitive religious art of the earlier period.

As in art, so in almost all other fields of the Middle Ages, there is
a noticeable difference between the medieval and the modern outlook—even though the evolution took place without an obvious well-
defined breach. But in the last centuries of the Middle Ages there is
a clear indication that medieval civilization was coming to an end
and that the ruling ideas that had held medieval Christendom
together were losing their appeal. This becomes especially evident in
social and political life and will be discussed in the next chapter.

9 *THE LATE MIDDLE AGES TO 1500*

The fourteenth and fifteenth centuries in Europe in general mark a period of religious and cultural, and even political, decline (except in the Italian towns to be dealt with in the next chapter). It is this decline which has led some historians to hold that the Middle Ages constituted a separate civilization which was coming to the end of its life span. There is certainly much evidence for this point of view, but it should also be recognized that the great upsurge of cultural creativity known as the Renaissance was not something altogether new but in many respects was dependent on what had been achieved in the Middle Ages as well as in antiquity.

THE PAPACY

When the popes moved their court to Avignon in France (see Chapter 8), they did not lose their control over the clergy that had been won with so much difficulty in the Middle Ages. On the contrary, the papacy was stronger than ever, and the succession of lawyers who occupied the papal throne understood the realities of power and finance on which their position was based—even if too many lacked strong religious convictions. But the struggle between Pope Boniface VIII and Philip IV of France had made it clear to the Avignon papacy that most monarchs were by now too strong to be resisted openly. The higher clergy were compelled to contribute to the papacy, but some of the money flowed into royal coffers also.

The Conciliar Movement. The preoccupation of the popes with the mechanics of administration and the extreme centralization of ecclesiastical authority in the papacy, combined with the almost universal European belief that Rome was the only true center for the Church, led to an increasing movement by the clergy (including some cardinals) and important laymen directed toward taking away some of the power of the popes. They believed that this could be done through the medium of councils, composed of high clerics, leaders in the universities, and secular rulers, who would dictate policy to the pope. Naturally these men tried to exalt the authority of their councils above that of the pope. They had some success while the papacy was divided, and especially during the Great Schism which they were instrumental in bringing to an end at the Council of Constance. But once the popes had returned to Rome, they were able to exploit the differences between the Council members and to reassert their authority.

The Avignon papacy lasted from 1305 to 1378. Pope Urban V (1362–1370) returned to Rome briefly, but finding the city as dangerous as ever and by this time poverty-stricken as well, quickly went back to Avignon. The next pope, persuaded to try again, died while he was still there (1378), whereupon the Italian cardinals chose a pope unacceptable to the French majority, who chose another one for themselves. Thus began the Great Schism which lasted from 1378 until the Council of Constance (1414–1417).

The scandal created by the division of the papacy and a Europe equally divided in its religious allegiance was such that the Council of Pisa was called in 1409. This Council deposed both the French and the Roman popes, and chose another—the highly unsuitable John XXIII—whose election by a council and not by the cardinals has since been regarded as uncanonical (enabling a twentieth-century pope to take the same title). But the other two popes did not accept their deposition, thus compelling the emperor Sigismund to call the Council of Constance. John XXIII was likewise deposed; the Roman pope resigned; and the French pope, who retired to Spain, was ignored by Christendom. The new choice of Martin V, a Roman noble, was eventually accepted by all, and the schism came to an end. The Council of Basel, which met intermittently from 1431 to 1449, though it tried to depose Martin's successor, did not succeed in its aim. The series of notorious Renaissance popes followed, postponing the numerous reforms demanded by both rulers and prelates and probably making inevitable the Protestant Reformation of the next century.

Heresy and the Hussite Wars. At this time the Church had reached its lowest ebb in popular estimation. During the social disintegration of Europe, in part the result of the Black Death (bubonic plague) which had spread through the continent in the fourteenth century, it had done little to help. In fact, many regarded these epidemics as the consequence of the wickedness of the Church and of the loose living of the regular clergy. There was a great increase in popular superstition, especially the belief in witches and in the activity of the Devil and his capacity for entering into human shape. Flagellants marched through Europe, tormenting themselves and calling on the people to repent.

The Franciscan Order, which had held so much promise in the thirteenth century, was by the fourteenth split into two segments, especially on the issue of poverty. The Fraticelli, who had persisted in their demand for the return of the Church and their order to the ideals of their founder, had been persecuted as heretics. Other heretical groups had arisen, notably the Lollards ("poor preachers"), followers of the English reformer John Wycliffe, who went so far as to deny the importance of the sacraments for salvation and stressed the authority of the Scriptures over that of the Church, as well as making the by now customary attacks on the luxury of the clergy. These teachings were spread widely in Europe and for a time had a spectacular success in Bohemia, where John Huss supported most of them. The Council of Constance summoned Huss to give an account of himself. Anxious to defend his doctrine, he received a safe conduct from Emperor Sigismund, who withdrew his support, however, after hearing his defense. Huss, and a supporter, Jerome of Prague, were condemned by the Council and burned at the stake.

This action infuriated their Czech followers in Bohemia, who refused to recognize Sigismund any longer as their king. They then took to arms, effectively resisting papal "crusades" called against them. The Hussite Wars continued for several decades but gradually petered out when the movement divided between Taborites, who were bitter-end opponents of the papacy, and Utraquists, who negotiated a number of important reforms and remained within the Church. The Taborites were decisively defeated in 1452, but the remnants of this group survived to form part of the Protestant movement as the Moravian sect, which continues to this day.

NATIONAL STATES

The national states discussed in Chapter 8 were afflicted by several internecine wars during this period, of which the most important was the Hundred Years' War between England and France which eventually resulted in the almost total expulsion of the English from France. Portugal developed a strong monarchy capable of carrying the small country to leadership in opening up the Orient to European trade, and at the end of the period Spain was at last united, beginning her period of westward expansion. The Empire remained weak until the beginning of the sixteenth century; Germany continued to be a prey to the sectional interests of her nobles.

England—Internal Development. Under Edward I, as we have seen in Chapter 8, England obtained her first Parliament, already composed of two Houses, the Lords and Commons. The House of Lords, made up of the feudal nobles and higher clergy, who held their positions by right, was at first more powerful; but the House of Commons, whose members were elected under a restricted property franchise, grew rapidly in power, since it was the Commons which voted taxes, including those needed for the prosecution of the Hundred Years' War. Parliament obtained the right to present petitions to the king, which if accepted became the law of the land. Such legislation gradually replaced the royal ordinances of the past.

Two monarchs during the late Middle Ages (Edward II [1307–1327] and Richard II [1377–1399]) were compelled to abdicate by baronial conspirators. When Richard II abdicated in 1399, the Lords and Commons gave the crown to Henry of Bolingbroke although he was not the nearest heir to the throne. Thereafter by their consent, he ruled as Henry IV, thus in effect establishing a limited constitutional monarchy. A rebellion under the leadership of the House of York broke out in the reign of Henry's incompetent grandson, Henry VI. This division resulted in a long civil war (Wars of the Roses) between the House of York and the House of Lancaster, to which Henry VI belonged. The war virtually destroyed the power of the feudal nobility, enabling the Yorkist monarch Edward IV (1461–1483) and the new Tudor dynasty begun in 1485 by Henry VII (a Lancastrian who married the daughter of Edward IV, thereby uniting the two Houses), to rule with much more authority than the House of Lancaster had enjoyed. Both Edward and the Tudor monarchs held the support of the middle classes represented in the House of Commons and experienced little trouble from the remnants of the feudal nobility who sat in the House of Lords.

France—End of the Capetian Dynasty. The direct Capetian line of the French kings came to an end in 1328 with the death of Charles IV, who was succeeded by Philip VI of the Valois House, nephew of the late king Philip IV. Edward III, king of England, whose mother Isabella was the daughter of Philip IV, would have been the heir to the French throne if the law of succession of France had been similar to that in England. However, the French nobles in

1328 decreed that the so-called Salic law applied to France and that therefore no woman could succeed to the throne, nor could the crown pass through a woman to her son. (Edward was later to challenge this decision and claim the throne for himself.) The reigns of all the Valois monarchs were dominated by the long intermittent war with England. Not until Charles VII defeated the English and drove them from France would the kings devote themselves again to the consolidation and enlargement of their realm.

Hundred Years' War. Edward III (1327–1377) might never have made any claim to the French throne if he had not become embroiled with the French monarchy over Flanders, where the English merchants who supplied the wool for Flemish industry had important interests. Edward did homage for his French lands in the usual way. But when the French monarchy tried to subject Flanders to a bureaucratic rule, a number of Flemish merchants appealed to him to become their king. When Edward agreed, Philip tried to take English lands in the southwest of France, thus beginning the Hundred Years' War, which was fought entirely in France and on the sea. The Black Prince, son of Edward III, won the two great victories of Crécy and Poitiers in 1346 and 1356, in the latter taking John II, king of France, prisoner. In both battles the English yeomanry combined with the nobility to defeat the outmoded French chivalry. (During several of the years between the two crucial battles, the Black Death raged unabated, killing probably between one-third and one-half of the population of western Europe, including England.)

The defeat, the capture of the king, and the collecting of ransom demanded by the English for his release proved to be disastrous for France. The young dauphin, who tried to govern while his father was being held in England, was compelled to lay more taxes on the people and to summon the States-General to obtain its consent to the imposition. Naturally it attempted to make conditions, but it was too divided to decide on a coherent policy. Moreover there was a peasant uprising (the *Jacquerie*) against the taxes, and severe disorders occurred in Paris. These revolts were suppressed by the nobility and the dauphin with great loss of life. The Peace of Brétigny between the English and the French was finally signed in 1360, thus bringing the first phase of the war to an end. The treaty favored the English since it left their French possessions and conquests intact.

The second phase of the war consisted in the main of successful guerrilla warfare led by Bertrand du Guesclin, constable of France, and the expulsion of the English from all but a few French towns. But this French victory was soon followed by the outbreak of civil war between two groups of nobles, the Armagnacs and the Burgundians, the latter led by a member of the French royal House who had been invested with the important duchy but who had become virtually independent. The king, Charles VI (1380–1422), who was intermittently insane, was unable to exercise his authority over his quarrelsome nobles, thus allowing the English under Henry V (1413–1422) to renew the war and win the notable victory of Agincourt (1415). Burgundy supported Henry against the Armagnacs. Under the Treaty of Troyes (1420), Henry married the daughter of Charles VI and was accepted as the heir to the French throne. The dauphin, later Charles VII, resisted only feebly Henry's continued efforts to conquer the whole of France. But the French monarchy was saved by the premature death of Henry a few weeks before that of Charles. The French crown thus fell to Henry VI of England, who was a child. His regents, still aided by the Burgundians, proclaimed him King of France as well as England and continued the war against the Armagnacs and others who refused to accept him.

It was when the monarchy was in this parlous state that Joan of Arc, a village girl who had been instructed in visions to go to the aid of the dauphin, first offered her services. Granted an army and authority by the dauphin, she succeeded in raising the English siege of Orléans. This victory and the belief that they were led by a saint inspired the dauphin and his supporters to action. With the aid of Joan he was crowned king (Charles VII) at Reims in northern France in the middle of hostile territory. Joan herself was taken prisoner by the Burgundians and sold to the English, who allowed her to be tried by an illegal Inquisition court, then burned her as a relapsed heretic and a witch. But Charles finally broke up the alliance between England and Burgundy, at the cost of the recognition of Burgundy's independence. Thereafter he reformed the army with the aid of new taxes granted to the monarchy in perpetuity and expelled the English from the whole of France except the port of Calais.

Consolidation of France under Louis XI. This work had just been completed when Louis XI (1461–1483) inherited the French throne. A competent and careful ruler, he greatly improved administration and won from the States-General its complete acquiescence in the right of the king to rule absolutely and legislate as he wished. Several territories in the hands of important nobles escheated to the

Crown during his reign. Though he was at odds with Burgundy for
most of his reign and was frequently worsted in their encounters,
his Swiss allies defeated and killed Charles the Bold, duke of Burgundy, at the Battle of Nancy in 1477, and Louis incorporated the
greater part of the duchy into his own kingdom. But he lost Flanders,
a Burgundian possession, forever. This important county fell to Mary
of Burgundy (daughter of Charles the Bold), who married Maximilian of Hapsburg. Maximilian shortly afterward became Holy
Roman emperor, and his grandson, later Charles V, Holy Roman
emperor, was brought up as a Fleming, though he ruled the greater
part of Europe as will be discussed in Chapter 11.

Unification of the Spanish Monarchy. Throughout much of the
fourteenth and fifteenth centuries the Castilian crown was weak,
though Alfonso VI defeated the Muslims who were trying to re-
conquer the country from Africa. He put an end to this menace for
good in 1340. But nobles and townsmen both exercised considerable
influence, especially during the reign of Henry IV (1454–1474).
This situation changed after the accession of Isabella to the throne in
1474. By agreement with the pope she set up the Spanish Inquisition
in 1478, which was thereafter used as the tool of the monarchy. But,
most important of all, she had married Ferdinand the Catholic, heir
of Aragon in 1469, and in 1479 he came to the throne of that country
as Ferdinand II. The result was that the power of the two monarchs
became irresistible and a centralized royal rule gradually took the
place of feudal semianarchy. The conquest of Spain was completed
by the capture of Granada from the Moors in 1492, followed by the
expulsion of the Jews in the same year and the Moors (from Castile)
in 1502. The Aragonese monarchs, prior to this personal union, had
been more successful than those of Castile in subduing the nobility.
But they had dissipated much more of their strength in efforts to
retain the crown of Naples and Sicily. After the union these foreign
territories again became a bone of contention, but they were ultimately retained as an appanage of the Spanish crown until the
eighteenth century.

The reign of Ferdinand and Isabella was marked also by the rediscovery of the Americas in 1492 by Christopher Columbus, a Genoese sailor whose voyage had been commissioned by the monarchs.
This was followed by other expeditions which eventually resulted in
the foundation of the huge Spanish empire in North and South America. The joint rule was cut short by the death of Isabella in 1504.
Castile thus fell to the share of Joanna (daughter of Ferdinand and

Isabella), who was married to the Hapsburg archduke Philip. Ferdinand, unwilling to relinquish Castile, was able to make an agreement with Philip by which he himself remained as regent. When Philip died in 1506, Ferdinand continued as regent for Joanna, who soon became insane, and for her son Charles, who later became Charles I of Spain and Charles V of the Empire.

Portugal. Portuguese independence was secure after the decisive victory of Aljubarrota in 1385 against Castile. John I (1385–1433), founder of the Avis dynasty, signed a permanent treaty of alliance with England in 1386 and married an English princess. One of John's half-English younger sons, Henry the Navigator, founded a school in Sagres near Lisbon, where he trained a generation of mariners and subsidized voyages down the coast of Africa and into the Atlantic. Before Henry's death in 1460, Madeira, the Azores, and Cape Verde Islands had been discovered and added to the Portuguese realm. John II (1481–1495), the greatest Portuguese royal patron of discovery, renewed the quest for an all-sea route to India. Bartholomew Diaz rounded the Cape of Good Hope in 1488. But it was not until Vasco da Gama's voyage of 1497–1499 that India itself was reached. John was faced by a feudal rebellion at home but suppressed it vigorously, leaving a secure throne to his son Manuel I (1495–1521).

Eastern Europe. The late Middle Ages in eastern Europe were marked by the expansion of the Teutonic Knights eastward from Germany. This militant religious order, founded in the time of the Crusades, became the spearhead of German expansionism from the middle of the thirteenth century, and all the territories that it conquered became fiefs of the papacy. The Knights first subdued and converted Prussia (a conquest completed by 1285), then subjugated much of the Baltic region. The fourteenth century was marked by their conflict with Poland, and their expansion was brought to an end by a decisive defeat by the Poles and Lithuanians in 1410. In 1466 the Knights lost West Prussia to Poland but retained East Prussia, which ultimately became a fief of the Hohenzollern family, who also ruled Brandenburg.

Following the death of Casimir III in 1370, the Polish monarchy became elective, thereafter becoming one of the great prizes available to ambitious west European princes. The major result was the failure of the monarchy to control the great nobles, who exercised a veto over royal policy and gradually reduced the free peasantry to serfdom—a trend diametrically opposed to that in western Europe, where the serfs gradually won their emancipation. Though the country was almost constantly at war, the wars were rarely beneficial to Polish interests, and Poland never became an effective national state. In 1386, however, the elected queen of Poland (Jadwiga) married the duke of still heathen Lithuania (Jagellon), who promised to allow his people to be converted to Christianity. The huge ramshackle state of Poland-Lithuania stretched from the Baltic to the Black Sea in the fifteenth century. But though it remained under a single monarchy until the seventeenth century, it was never a strong state and was further weakened by wars with its neighbors, especially Russia.

The duchy of Moscow, on the contrary, continued to grow in strength as the Mongols were finally driven out. Ivan III, the Great (1462–1505), who completed the destruction of the Mongol invaders in 1480, had already added much of present-day European Russia to his realm in earlier wars. He married the niece of the last Byzantine emperor—Constantinople had fallen to the Turks in 1453 —and thereafter pictured himself as the Christian successor of the Byzantines. He called Moscow the "Third Rome" and regarded it as the center of the Orthodox Church. Like the Byzantine emperors, he considered himself the supreme autocrat. Ivan and his successors fostered the growth of the "gentry" class, which owed their position to their rulers, as against the boyar class of hereditary nobles who possessed certain traditional rights which they guarded jealously. Ivan IV in the next century used the gentry to break the power of the boyars and establish his own absolute rule. In the process, as in Poland, the free peasantry was reduced to serfdom.

Hungary likewise was weakened by having an elected monarchy, usually in the hands of German princes, and a powerful nobility. For a short period in the fifteenth century it was ruled by a native Hungarian, Matthias Corvinus (1458–1490), who made his country the most powerful kingdom in central Europe. But in 1526 at the Battle of Mohacs the Turks decisively defeated the Hungarians and thereafter ruled most of the country until the end of the seventeenth century.

The Holy Roman Empire. After its long struggle with the papacy, the Holy Roman Empire remained weak for a long time. A few emperors tried to assert imperial claims in Italy and sent expeditions to Rome, but in view of their failure to achieve anything of permanence, the claim was tacitly abandoned. Emperors ceased even to be interested in a coronation in Rome, the last to be crowned in

Rome by the pope being Frederick III of Hapsburg (1440–1493). The first Hapsburg emperor was Rudolf I, prince of Swabia, who won Austria for his family in warfare but abandoned all imperial claims in southern Italy and the papal states. In 1438 with the election of Albert II, the imperial throne became virtually hereditary in the Hapsburg family, although the system of election was maintained and was formalized under the Golden Bull of 1356. Under this system three electors were Catholic archbishops (of Trier, Mainz, and Cologne); three were German princes (the count palatine of the Rhine, the duke of Saxony, and the margrave of Brandenburg); and the seventh was the king of Bohemia, who was himself elected by the Bohemian diet. In spite of the electoral system, once the Hapsburg family was established on the throne, it was never found possible by other claimants to obtain enough votes for their own election. Secure in their ancestral lands, the Hapsburgs arranged their marriage alliances so carefully that their possessions were continually increased until Charles V divided them into two in the middle of the sixteenth century, thus creating two separate monarchies (see p. 148). But Germany could not be united under Hapsburg rule while so many nobles, determined to prevent unification, ruled their own territories. The country was not united until 1871, when Bismarck completed the process by, as he called it, "blood and iron."

Italy. Italy likewise could not be unified in the Middle Ages or early modern times. It was a hodgepodge of duchies, free cities, kingdoms, and papal states. Although Italy was the unquestioned leader of European culture during the Renaissance, it was constantly fought over for centuries and was far surpassed in power by the unified national states.

LATE MEDIEVAL ECONOMY

It was in Italy, however, that most of the modern economic developments originated. The great trading cities invented most of the devices of modern capitalism, including the draft, the bill of exchange, the practice of discounting bills, and the system of double-entry bookkeeping. Though the earliest known public-deposit bank of Europe was founded in Barcelona, Genoa soon had its Bank of St. George. This type of bank later became much more common, but during the Middle Ages the private banking houses, often family enterprises, were the usual providers of credit, especially to kings and popes who alone could hope to pay the high rates of interest. The Medici family, to be discussed in Chapter 10, headed the most

important Florentine banking house from the fifteenth century onward. Another great banking family was the Fuggers in Germany.
Italian banking practices spread elsewhere in Europe. The Frenchman Jacques Coeur for a time rivaled the great German and Italian
houses, though he prospered only from the favor of the French
monarchy and was ruined when he lost it. Paper came to Europe in
the Middle Ages from the Orient, as did printing, the technique of
which was perfected in Europe by Johann Gutenberg in the middle
of the fifteenth century.

In agriculture the Black Death and its consequent shortage of labor
hastened the emancipation of the serfs in western Europe. Landlords
in search of larger incomes began to "enclose" the common land and
turn it into sheep pastures, which not only employed fewer persons
than had worked the lands but also robbed the peasants of their
traditional right to graze their own animals on them. As a consequence there were numerous peasant revolts throughout Europe, one
of the most serious of which (Wat Tyler's rebellion) occurred in
1381 in England, where it was stimulated by efforts to force emancipated serfs back into servitude. Efforts were also made to fix wages
and prices although there was a shortage of labor, caused by the
Black Death. No legislation, however, could prevent the trend toward
the free movement of labor and the abolition of serfdom.

LATE MEDIEVAL CULTURE

Church building continued during the late Middle Ages; the Gothic
style tended to become more flamboyant and more attention was
paid to decoration. Many more universities were founded, but there
was little innovation in the curriculum. Aristotle, no longer the con-
troversial figure of the thirteenth century, by this time had become
enthroned as the great master of knowledge. Scholasticism had largely
degenerated into barren argumentation with ever more subtle technical refinements and ever finer distinctions. Only in science was there
much done that pointed toward the future. Here Aristotle's authority
was ceasing to be absolute. His theory of motion was discovered to
be, if not inaccurate, at least incomplete. Jean Buridan at the University of Paris proposed a new concept of "impetus," while at the
University of Padua in Italy much thought was given to the problem
of acceleration, and Arabic numerals at last became acceptable in
the West. Bishop Nicholas of Oresme disputed the long-held theory
of the movement of the sun around the earth and in the process
hit upon the fundamental techniques of analytical geometry, later

developed independently by Descartes. Nicholas of Cusa, a cardinal, was equally sure that the Ptolemaic theory was wrong. All these efforts led to the great work of Copernicus (1473–1543) and Galileo (1564–1642), whose teachings on astronomy and motion overthrew the medieval world conception and ushered in the modern scientific outlook.

10 *THE RENAISSANCE AND THE AGE OF DISCOVERY*

While the social, political, and cultural life of medieval Europe was in so many respects disintegrating, a new movement had arisen in the Italian cities which was a curious combination of looking to the past of antiquity for inspiration and looking to the future for a fresh start and great accomplishment. The Italians of this age felt that they were experiencing a Renaissance, or rebirth, after the long dark night of the Middle Ages.

ITALIAN RENAISSANCE

The Italian towns, which with the aid of the papacy had succeeded in escaping the military threat from German emperors in the thirteenth century, made remarkable progress in the fourteenth and fifteenth centuries. The feudal lords who had formerly exacted their dues from the cities now usually preferred to live in them and to share in the general prosperity, receiving a money income in exchange for the abandonment of their purely feudal rights. By the fifteenth century a new class of nobles had arisen, some of them exclusively by their own efforts and owing little or nothing to their birth. Such men were often soldiers of fortune (*condottieri*) who made themselves despots but allowed their subjects a free hand to trade as they wished. Others, like the Medici family, originated as merchants or bankers and acquired their patents of nobility through their financial services to the papacy or to secular lords or monarchs. These despots were the great patrons of Italian art, able to pay for what they wished and regarding themselves as competitors of their fellow despots, not only in warfare but also as patrons whose duty and pleasure it was to adorn their cities.

The Humanists. The economic base for such movements as the Renaissance, which was primarily an artistic and cultural phenomenon, was present nowhere else in Europe in the fourteenth and fifteenth centuries. The cities of northern and central Italy had been growing in prosperity for several centuries. They were pre-eminent not only in trade but also in manufacturing, and their luxury products were in demand everywhere. The great Italian banking houses, such as that of the Medici, grew rich from lending to monarchs and to the papacy as well as to noble families and merchants.

The Renaissance took the form it did in large part because of the presence in Italy of so many monuments of antiquity and the belief among Italian intellectuals that it was their own ancestors who had produced the civilization of ancient Rome. The most important feature of the early Renaissance was this cult of antiquity. Despising all medieval culture as backward and otherworldly, these Italians came to believe that the ancient pagans were the only people who had ever had a proper appreciation of earthly life. Renaissance literature, lacking the religious orientation of the Middle Ages, was more concerned with man in his human aspect, with his mind and body, than with his soul. The "humanists" (as they called themselves) wished to draw attention to the pleasurable aspects of life and to man's inherent possibilities for self-development. They resented all forms of authority, particularly the authority that the Church still wished to exercise over them—even while the papacy was busy at Avignon repairing its finances, enjoying its luxury and wealth, and in other respects concerning itself only minimally with its spiritual tasks.

The humanists therefore began to search for manuscripts in classical Latin and Greek, admiring them inordinately, since such works were examples of an attitude toward life which they thought similar to their own. As a tiny intellectual elite, they kept in constant touch with one another, informing their fellow humanists of all that they found and rejoicing in every discovery rescued from oblivion. They seldom conceded that the possibility of recovering such manuscripts was due to the labors of the monks who had copied them in earlier centuries and whom they now professed to despise. Since the manuscripts were in classical Latin, they wrote to each other in the closest approximation they could manage to the language of Cicero and thus helped to kill off the really universal tongue (medieval Latin), which was still spoken and still capable of modification, even though the humanists considered it "barbaric."

The chief forerunner of the Renaissance was the fourteenth-cen-

tury Italian Petrarch, who wrote learned works in classical Latin
and exquisite love lyrics in Italian, the tongue of Dante. He admired
but could not himself read a Greek manuscript of Homer that he
"recovered." In the next century two of the greatest names were Pog-
gio Bracciolini, an indefatigable hunter of manuscripts, and Lorenzo
Valla, a serious scholar who by his literary criticism proved con-
clusively that the Donation of Constantine, a famous document used
as evidence for papal political authority, was a forgery.

The humanists had considerable influence in the field of education. Greek scholars, imported from Constantinople, tutored the
upper classes. Several pioneers in "progressive" education were hired
by Renaissance princes to tutor their children and the children of
fellow nobles. Though the interest in Greek quickly faded in Italy,
the study of Greek beyond the Alps soon became a part of the
regular curriculum. In Florence for a long time there was a Platonic
academy (founded by Cosimo de Medici) where the works of Plato
and his Neo-Platonic successors were studied. It was headed by
Marsilio Ficino, and one of its leading lights was the humanist Pico
della Mirandola.

Italian Art and Architecture. The greatest glory of the Italian
Renaissance is undoubtedly its art. In architecture the medieval
style was despised as "Gothic" (barbaric), and the Renaissance
architects returned to the classical style, though it was never as
simple in their works as most Greek architecture had been. The
architects preferred to imitate the Roman remains which they saw
around them; but their originality and creativity soon escaped the
bonds thus imposed. They created their own style, similar to, but
distinct from, that of their masters of antiquity. Every Italian city
had its Renaissance palaces and some Renaissance churches. When
the papacy was taken over by a series of humanist popes in the
late fifteenth century, they turned to the building of St. Peter's, for
which they extracted huge donations from the whole of Christendom.
Many of the greatest Renaissance artists, especially Michelangelo,
laid their impress upon this unique cathedral.

In sculpture and painting the tendency was away from the often
symbolic and stylized work of the Middle Ages toward the use of
human models of beauty and strength, in this respect also tending in
the direction of a new individualism so often regarded as the hall-
mark of the Renaissance. Greatest of the sculptors, perhaps the
greatest of all time, was Michelangelo.

Painting, until the Renaissance almost a minor art, now came into its own. The technique of painting in perspective was discovered early in the Renaissance and thereafter adopted by all. The thirteenth- and fourteenth-century painters, especially Giotto, continued to paint religious subjects, but they were rapidly humanized. Schools of painters arose familiar with each other's work, and workshops turned out painting to meet the ever increasing demand from munificent patrons.

Most but by no means all Renaissance works remained religious in inspiration and content. Botticelli, who excelled in painting the human figure, nevertheless also painted Madonnas with exquisite little angels—though they are perhaps more human than angelic. The "big three" of the High Renaissance in Italy are Leonardo da Vinci, Raphael, and Michelangelo. Raphael, in his own time regarded as a perfect painter, has never been excelled for his Madonnas, equally human and spiritual. Leonardo painted relatively little in his tremendous life. But his few paintings, including the now almost obliterated "Last Supper" and "La Gioconda" ("Mona Lisa") are among the world's greatest masterpieces. In the later years of the Renaissance the Venetian Titian, who painted to almost the end of his ninety-nine-year life span, excelled in portraits of notables, both men and women; but his religious inspiration was not equal to that of his predecessors, though his technical equipment was superior.

In craftsmanship Italy also gave the lead to Europe. The workshops of the greatest artists such as Benvenuto Cellini turned out huge numbers of exquisite and often noble pieces, which were bought by all the princes of Europe.

The ideal of the Renaissance was "the universal man" (*uomo universale*) who excelled in everything he undertook. Such men were Lorenzo de Medici, ruler of Florence, scholar, statesman, warrior, poet; and Leonardo da Vinci, scientist, craftsman, painter, engineer, whose services were in demand everywhere and who regarded the whole field of human activity as his own. At one time he was thought of as a great pioneer scientist and inventor, who filled his notebooks with wonderful original drawings of such things as flying machines. Today it is recognized, that, like Roger Bacon in the thirteenth century, he was in close touch with others working in this field and that probably few of the inventions he recorded were his own. But nothing can detract from our admiration of the care with which he studied, the fertility of his imagination, his attention to detail, his meticulous observation of all that he examined, and the manner in which he developed his own technical ability.

The Church. The Church during the Renaissance became increasingly worldly. From the middle of the fifteenth century when a humanist, Pius II (1458–1464), was elected to the papacy, the Holy See was filled by princes who for the most part regarded their work in administering the papal states and as patrons of art as more important than their religious duties. Rome became once more a great city, but the luxury of the papal Curia was regarded as a scandal by those who wished a religious reform of the Church. Martin Luther was greatly shocked by an early visit to Rome.

RENAISSANCE BEYOND THE ALPS

Though the Renaissance was at first a purely Italian phenomenon, it soon spread beyond the Alps to all the other countries of western Europe, influencing them in many different ways according to the characteristics of the various peoples and the character of the existing cultures which it penetrated. An expedition launched by the French king Charles VIII in 1494 with the avowed purpose of making good a claim to the crown of Naples was especially influential in bringing the progress of Italian culture to the attention of the French, who were greatly impressed by reports of those who had been to Italy. Though the expedition itself was a failure, its cultural influence was immense.

Renaissance in France. The Renaissance was slow in reaching France but its influence was profound, in part due to the support it won from the monarchs, especially Francis I (1515–1547). Francis used the resources of his national state, the strongest and wealthiest in the Europe of his day, to patronize first the Italian artists and craftsmen whom he invited to France, and later his own subjects, who learned from them. He founded a new center of learning, the Collège de France, built a great new palace at Fontainebleau, purchased numerous manuscripts, and exemplified in his own person the Renaissance gusto for living. François Rabelais (*c.* 1490–1553) in his *Gargantua and Pantagruel* ridiculed the pretensions of monks who mortified their flesh in preference to enjoying the good life on earth, and he depicted a beautiful Renaissance city where the only motto was to "do what thou wilt." Michel de Montaigne (1533–1592), a more serious sixteenth-century writer, used the form of the essay to express his own tolerant views on life. A religious skeptic, he was deeply interested in man and his behavior, and his writings are full of wise aphorisms and observations. In architecture France for a long time retained her attachment to the Gothic, and French architects continued to build castles and churches in a modified Gothic style. Most of the Loire castles date from the Renaissance period, during which the Italians were returning to "classical antiquity."

Humanism in Germany and Holland. The Germans were early influenced by Italian humanism and took to the study of Greek with more tenacity than did the Italians. One of the earliest German humanists was Johann Reuchlin, who devoted himself to the study of the New Testament, finding numerous errors in the Latin translation of the Greek original. From Greek he passed on to Hebrew for the purpose of studying the Old Testament. Other German thinkers wrote influential books on education, and Sebastian Brant in his *Ship of Fools* castigated the weakness of mankind. German Renaissance art is best represented by Albrecht Dürer, famous for his wood engravings as well as for his religious paintings, and Hans Holbein the Younger, who painted excellent portraits in the Renaissance manner, notably the well-known one of Henry VIII.

The Flemish artists were influenced by the Italians in technique but their subject matter for a long time continued in the Flemish religious tradition. In a later century Frans Hals (*c.* 1580–1666) was a typical Renaissance painter; but the greatest of the Flemish artists, Rubens and Rembrandt, are better classed as baroque (see p. 173).

Desiderius Erasmus (*c.* 1469–1536), born in Holland though living much of his life elsewhere, was the most gifted of the humanist intellectuals. Tolerant as Montaigne, he found his greatest secular hero in Socrates, who had allowed himself to be killed in preference to abandoning his right to freedom of speech and expression. Erasmus' book *In Praise of Folly* was a satire on scholastic learning and monkist behavior. Erasmus maintained an immense correspondence, couched in elegant Latin, with other European humanists, who acknowledged him as their leader. He also prepared the first printed Greek edition of the New Testament.

Humanism in England. The Italian Renaissance influenced English poetry (including the form of Edmund Spenser's *Faerie Queene*) and much of the subject matter of Shakespeare's plays. It also influenced English studies, including those of the universities. Sir Thomas More, chancellor of Henry VIII, who was executed for refusing to acknowledge Henry's overlordship of the English Church, wrote *Utopia* (Greek for *nowhere*), which pictured a new society based on Renaissance ideals. The Renaissance won its greatest hold in England during the great Elizabethan age, marked not only by

Marlowe and Shakespeare, whose grasp of human character has never been excelled, but also by the great individualist sea captains like Sir Francis Drake and Sir Walter Raleigh—a time when enjoyment of life was as yet undimmed by the spread of Puritanism.

Spain. Lastly the unique work of Miguel de Cervantes (1547–1616) should be mentioned. *Don Quixote de la Mancha* is the picaresque tale of a knight of chivalry born out of his age who wanders through his country attended by his simple but hardheaded squire Sancho Panza. The book is in part an attack on outmoded chivalry and the feudal romances still popular in Spain. The often ridiculous but always pathetic figure of the noble knight is one of the truly great character studies of the Renaissance.

Renaissance Science. The age was one of preparation rather than achievement. In the Italian High Renaissance there was considerable medical advance, especially in the field of anatomy, to which an epoch-making work was contributed by Andreas Vesalius, professor at Padua. The Swiss Paracelsus practiced in Germany as a doctor, winning a considerable reputation as a healer, in spite of the unusual methods he employed and the often mystical nature of his writings. In other scientific work attention was given to problems of physics, especially the laws of motion; but the great achievements in this field did not come until the end of the sixteenth century and will therefore be considered in another chapter. The work of Nicholas Copernicus (d. 1543) falls within the Renaissance period, but it too will be discussed with that of the later thinkers who provided the evidence for his hypotheses and completed his system.

THE AGE OF DISCOVERY

During the late Middle Ages there had been a considerable growth of knowledge about the world, resulting in part from improvements in navigation, especially the mariner's compass and the astrolabe (for obtaining latitude and longitude), introduced by the Muslims. Medieval scientists had been well aware of this sphericity of the earth, but mariners were still wary of venturing far into unknown quarters; and knowledge of the Americas, at one time widespread among the Scandinavians, had disappeared save for legends and old maps. Much of the credit for the revival of interest in geography and navigation belongs to the Portuguese prince, Henry the Navigator (see p. 123).

Portuguese Discoveries. The voyages of discovery sponsored by Henry and the fifteenth-century Portuguese monarchs, pointed the way to other nations. As a small power Portugal was unable to compete with the great resources of Venice, who had a virtual monopoly of the overland trade with the East. But Henry was sure that an all-sea route could be found. His captains gradually sailed ever further to the south, Gil Eannes rounding Cape Bojador in 1433; Bartholomew Diaz sailed around the Cape of Good Hope in 1488. In 1497 began the voyage of Vasco da Gama which by way of Mombasa took him to Calicut in India. When he reached home with a rich cargo two years later, the Portuguese government decided to back further voyages and the creation of an empire in the East. The city of Goa on the southwest Indian coast became the capital of Portuguese India in 1610, and after several victories over the Arabs and other Muslims, the Portuguese established a monopoly of the Oriental trade with Europe. Their new wealth, however, did not greatly profit their country, which was short of shipping and lacked the manpower to maintain such a large empire against its competitors. When the Spanish and Portuguese crowns were united in 1580, Spain, more interested in her American possessions, neglected the defense of her Portuguese territories, thus permitting the aggressive and efficient Dutch to capture them one by one. The Dutch were followed by the English and French, as will be discussed in Chapter 13.

Spanish Discoveries and Conquests. Christopher Columbus, an imaginative and ambitious Genoese sailor, meanwhile had become greatly interested in the exploration of the western ocean. As early as 1484 he appealed to the Portuguese monarch John II to finance a voyage westward in the hope of opening up trade with China, which had been frequently penetrated from the west (e.g., by Marco Polo in the thirteenth century). John, who may have wished to send a Portuguese expedition in due course, was not impressed by Columbus, and refused. After several fruitless efforts to elicit the support of Spain, he was finally put in command of an expedition by Ferdinand and Isabella.

On his first voyage (1492) Columbus discovered the Bahama Islands, Cuba, and San Domingo (Hispaniola), and he was sent out again a few months later. Soon afterward the Spanish-born pope Alexander VI (Rodrigo Borgia) demarcated a line to the west of which all territories not under a Christian monarch should be Spanish, leaving the territories east of the line to Portugal. In 1494 Portugal and Spain signed the Treaty of Tordesillas, under which the line was pushed westward by a further five hundred miles. By this treaty, Brazil, not yet officially discovered—though its existence and loca-

tion were possibly known to the Portuguese—fell to Portugal and not,
like the rest of the Americas, to Spain. In 1500 the Portuguese captain Cabral took possession of Brazil while on a voyage to India.
More voyages were quickly undertaken by both the Spaniards and
the Portuguese, opening up the whole east coast of Africa and culminating in the great voyage begun in 1519 by Ferdinand Magellan,
a Portuguese in Spanish employ. One of his ships succeeded in circumnavigating the world, though Magellan himself was killed in the
Philippines, which were later (1602) colonized by Spain. After
gradually settling the West Indian islands, the Spaniards moved
against the American mainland. Hernan Cortes in an epic expedition,
with the aid of Indian allies, destroyed the Aztec empire based on
Tenochtitlán (Mexico City) and created the empire of New Spain
(1521). With an even smaller force Francisco Pizarro by a mixture of
guile and military prowess destroyed the Inca empire in Peru (1533),
from which base almost the entire continent of South America was
subjected during the next decades.

The Spaniards, like the Portuguese, established a monopoly of
trade in their empire. Trade, however, was not their main source of
wealth. For more than a century they exploited the mines, thus
greatly increasing the supply of gold and silver in Europe and causing
a price revolution which proved to be little to their own benefit. Every
year the treasure ships set forth to Europe, protected by the Spanish
navy, paid for by the proceeds of the mines (of which a fifth belonged to the Crown). The maritime powers of Europe frequently
attacked the convoys but seldom succeeded in picking off more than
a few ships, the loss of which, valuable though they were, did not
cause much lasting damage to the Spaniards. Throughout the sixteenth century Spain had little competition from other European
powers in the New World save for the sporadic raids on her shipping
and occasional attempts to break her monopoly. The Frenchman
Jacques Cartier explored a section of Canada in the early sixteenth
century, but his settlement had to be abandoned. The English in
the second half of the century tried hard to find a northwest passage
to China but failed. Not until the early seventeenth century did
England, France, and Holland pick up their West Indian islands and
begin to colonize North America.

THE COMMERCIAL REVOLUTION

The influx of precious metals greatly affected the economy of
Europe. The resulting price inflation hit Spain hardest. The Spaniards,

who initially controlled the bullion, used little of it to assist their country's industry. The other countries, competing with one another, tended to sell their products to the Spaniards, who could afford to buy them, using this new capital to improve their own industry. Nevertheless, industry was not greatly advanced until the beginning of the Industrial Revolution in mid-eighteenth century. The new money helped in the distribution of such goods as were produced and undoubtedly caused a considerable expansion of trade. Her new-found wealth enabled Spain to become the greatest military power in Europe, since her monarchs could afford to pay and train the best soldiery. Even so the Spanish troops were frequently in arrears of pay, while Spain tried to live beyond her means on the proceeds of her colonies. Far more attention was given in the sixteenth and seventeenth centuries than ever before to the importance of trade, especially by monarchs who wished to make war. It was believed that each country should try to export more than it imported ("favorable balance of trade"), thereby obtaining a surplus of bullion to pay for troops and royal extravagances.

Thus arose the *mercantile* theory, according to which total trade was limited—as indeed it largely was at that period—and it was the task of each nation to use all available means (tariffs, navigation acts, subsidization of home industries, trade wars) to improve her own trade and lessen the share of her competitors. This theory found its greatest exponent in Jean Baptiste Colbert (1619–1683), finance minister to Louis XIV of France.

Industry, in fact, grew slowly during these centuries. The most usual method of increasing it was simply to persuade more home workers to engage in small-scale manufacture. Under the "putting-out," or domestic, system, a middleman (jobber) provided cottagers with raw materials and collected from them the finished products. In the cities there were small-scale specialized shops manufacturing certain articles for sale. Although the strength of the medieval guilds was declining, it did not evaporate overnight. The journeymen had long been free in most areas to work as they wished; but when all manufacture was carried on by hand or with simple machines, it was impossible for it to be done on a large scale. There was still only a relatively small middle class, which, with the upper classes, constituted the sole market for manufactured goods.

These economic conditions should be borne in mind when we discuss in the next two chapters the Protestant Reformation and the religious wars and the growth of the early modern nation states.

11

THE PROTESTANT
REFORMATION AND
THE WARS OF RELIGION

By the early sixteenth century, dissatisfaction with the Church was so widespread in Europe that only an early and fundamental reform could have saved it from a revolt. Heresies were spreading and opposition was rising against the Church's system of taxation and the way in which the papacy was draining the European countries of money which their leaders, in an age of growing mercantilism, wished to keep at home. Several efforts at internal reform were made by influential and dedicated clergymen, but all failed to move the Renaissance papacy from its preoccupation with worldly affairs. The result was that when Luther was driven, largely against his own will, to raise the standard of revolt, he found a support which earlier heretics had lacked. Unlike his predecessors he was not burned at the stake but lived to lead a schismatic church which is still known by his name and to begin the whole Protestant Reformation.

THE LUTHERAN REVOLT

The Renaissance papacy, as already noted, was engaged in building St. Peter's, which required enormous sums of money over and above what it needed for its vast bureaucracy. Though it taxed the churches in Europe and had its own income from the papal states, these sources proved to be insufficient. The popes therefore resorted to another method of raising money by voluntary contributions. This was what can only be called the "sale" of indulgences.

The Issue of Indulgences. Strictly speaking indulgences were not sold, but the European faithful did not always understand the fine distinctions made by the Church. According to Catholic teaching, many human beings who attained salvation had to spend some time in purgatory, in order to be purged from their sins. If a sinner did penance on earth for his sins, the time he spent in purgatory would be shortened. Penance could be made in a variety of ways. A pilgrimage to Jerusalem was often prescribed during the Middle Ages. But another method, subject to abuse, was to make a money payment, in exchange for which the pope could grant an indulgence either for the sinner himself or for a loved one already in purgatory. From the fifteenth century onward purveyors of indulgences, armed with papal authorization, went through Europe calling upon sinners to "buy" them, and it was common practice to neglect to emphasize the sacrament of penance, of which the indulgence was an essential but not the only part.

Career of Martin Luther. Martin Luther (1483–1546), an Augustinian monk who had noted the corruption in Rome on a mission there during his early manhood, found himself unable to believe that the pope had any power to shorten the period in purgatory. He had long wrestled with his own sinful nature and at last been rewarded with an experience which left him in no doubt that he had been saved by God's mercy in spite of his sins. As a result of this experience he came to the conclusion that no intermediary is required between man and God and that man is "justified by faith" alone. As he was to put it later, every man could be "his own priest." When Tetzel, a Dominican friar, came into Saxony to offer his indulgences, Luther protested strongly and posted on the door of his church in Wittenberg a series of ninety-five theses, attacking the whole principle of the indulgence and especially the way in which it was being abused in Germany. In this he had the support of his own ruler, the elector Frederick the Wise of Saxony.

The Holy Roman emperor Charles V in 1521 summoned Luther to a diet (assembly) at Worms, and commanded him to recant. When Luther refused to do so, with the famous words, "Here I stand. I can do no other. God help me." Charles laid the ban of the Empire upon him, despite the fact that he had some support from other German princes. Luther had been excommunicated by the pope several years earlier. Frederick the Wise, who had given Luther a safe conduct to the diet, honored it and took him into protective custody in one of his castles, where Luther occupied himself in translating the Bible into German. Meanwhile he had written three influential pamphlets (*Address to the Christian Nobility, On the Babylonian Captivity of the Church, Concerning Christian Liberty*), which were widely published in Germany and won him much support from nobles and princes anxious to cast off the yoke of the Church—

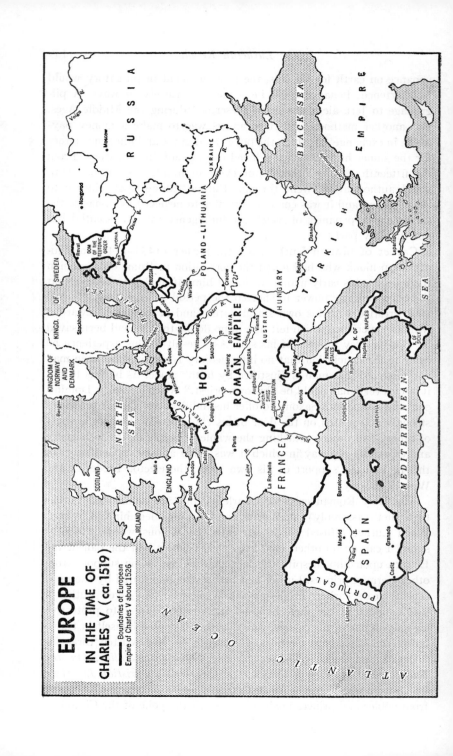

EUROPE
IN THE TIME OF
CHARLES V (ca. 1519)

Boundaries of European
Empire of Charles V about 1526

and incidently to seize Church lands and properties for themselves. Charles, deeply engaged in a war with France, was unable to take effective action against the Protestants, as they were now called. When, however, the German peasants claiming to be followers of Luther, revolted against their overlords, they were ruthlessly suppressed, and Luther himself, dependent on the support of the nobles, showed them hardly any sympathy. Luther and his followers, led by Philip Melancthon, eventually organized a new church with a liturgy in the German language—though Luther continued for a long time to regard himself as a Catholic. Luther married a former nun, devoted his time to church organization and writing, and died peacefully in 1546, the year after the beginning of the Council of Trent, which finally reformed the Catholic Church.

The Religious Peace of Augsburg. By 1530 Charles V had defeated France and been crowned emperor in Bologna. He was now ready to deal with the Protestants, who had produced under Melancthon's leadership the "Augsburg Confession," reaffirming their faith, which they put forward for the emperor's consideration. When he refused to permit any religious innovations, most of the Protestant princes formed the Schmalkaldic League to defend their church. Charles was at first prevented by troubles elsewhere from suppressing them, but in 1546 he began the Schmalkaldic War with the purpose of restoring the unity of the Church and putting an end to the independence of the rebellious German princes. Though he won several victories, he proved unable to achieve his complete ends and in 1555 agreed to the Peace of Augsburg, under which each prince could choose for himself and his land either Lutheranism or Catholicism and the Lutheran princes could retain the church properties they had sequestrated before 1552. The Calvinists were not included in this compromise. During this time Lutheranism had spread into Scandinavia but did not otherwise have much success outside of Germany.

CALVINISM

Only a year after Luther had posted his Ninety-five Theses a reform movement began also in Switzerland under the leadership of the humanist Ulrich Zwingli, whose main difference with Luther was on the question of the Mass. Zwingli regarded it as a symbolic remembrance of the Last Supper, whereas Luther believed that in the Eucharist the body and blood of Christ come together with the bread and wine (consubstantiation).* Zwingli converted a number of Swiss cantons to Protestantism but was himself killed in battle against the Catholic cantons, which had the aid of Charles V's brother, who was in charge of the government of Austria.

John Calvin and the Presbyterian Churches. Much more successful was the branch of Protestantism diverging from Zwinglianism which was founded by John Calvin (1509–1564), whose *Institutes of the Christian Religion* was perhaps the most influential of all the early Protestant works, as it was also the most systematic. Calvin believed that all men before birth have been destined by God for either salvation or damnation (the doctrine of predestination). Those destined to salvation would demonstrate this fact by their life and behavior and thus constitute an elect body of godly men and women. The Puritans who came to America in the early seventeenth century were followers of Calvin, believing strongly in their mission to establish a religious community which would obey God rather than earthly rulers, who seldom could be considered as belonging to the elect. Although a Frenchman, Calvin was entrusted with the government of the free city of Geneva, which under his guidance became a theocracy, with severe laws against the ungodly. Geneva was the headquarters of Calvinism, and most of those who carried Calvin's teachings throughout Europe were trained there. Each of the churches established by Calvin was governed by a group of elders chosen because of their upright manner of life. The Presbyterian Church was a direct outcome of Calvin's teaching, whereas other reformed churches have deviated in certain respects from them, each following its own path.

The Spread of Calvinism. One of the most successful disciples of Calvin was John Knox, who founded the Presbyterian Church of Scotland, which drove Mary, Queen of Scots, from the country when her indiscretions became insupportable to the reformers. In France the Calvinists were known as Huguenots. Many of the great nobles, in part for political reasons, became Huguenots and were strong enough to force toleration upon the monarchy when one of their number became king as Henry IV. Though Henry found it expedient to convert to Catholicism for the sake of ensuring peace in his country, he nevertheless issued the Edict of Nantes in 1598, under which the Huguenots were permitted to exercise their religion. The Edict was revoked by Louis XIV in 1685 and the remaining Huguenots were exiled to Protestant countries. Calvinism also gained many adherents

---

* According to Catholic belief, the bread and wine in the Eucharist change into the body and blood of Christ (transubstantiation).

in Holland and was the motive force behind the Dutch independence movement (see p. 148). It made inroads into Catholicism in several parts of Germany (especially Prussia) and in Hungary, Poland, and Bohemia. But with the exception of Germany, these countries were largely reconverted to Catholicism by the Jesuits, aided by the military might of the Catholic princes.

REFORMATION IN ENGLAND

The English Reformation was in its initial stages carried out with little bloodshed. In the seventeenth century the religious struggle can only with difficulty be distinguished from the constitutional struggle over the supremacy of Parliament and the limitation of the powers of the king. The eventual result of the English Reformation was the establishment of the Church of England, whose ritual and liturgy are closer to Catholicism than are those of any other Protestant Church.

Henry VIII and His Struggle with the Papacy. The conflict between England and the Church arose over the difficulty experienced by Henry VIII (1509–1547) in obtaining from the pope an annulment of his marriage to Catherine of Aragon, who had not given him a male heir (on the ground that since she was his brother's widow, the marriage was not valid). Because his own title to the throne was not too secure, Henry considered it vital to leave his crown to a son. His chancellor, Cardinal Wolsey, could not obtain the necessary dispensation from the pope, who was at the time a virtual prisoner of the emperor Charles V, nephew of Catherine of Aragon. Henry, who like the other Protestant princes, coveted the lands of the Church, which were very extensive in England, therefore took the opportunity to appoint a Protestant, Thomas Cranmer, as Archbishop of Canterbury and Primate of the English Church. He then declared himself to be the Supreme Head of the Church and instructed his new chancellor, Thomas Cromwell, to obtain the consent of Parliament for this action. Parliament thereupon dissolved the monasteries, which were sold for the benefit of the Crown, and agreed to Henry's other demands. Those who refused to accept the position, including Sir Thomas More (author of *Utopia* and a predecessor of Cromwell as chancellor), were executed. Cranmer then dissolved the royal marriage, permitting the monarch to marry Anne Boleyn, who it was hoped would give him a male heir. In fact she became the mother of the later Queen Elizabeth and in due course was herself executed for alleged infidelity.

All this time Henry had not changed his religion. He disliked Luther and his doctrines and wrote a pamphlet against him. Late in his reign he issued the Six Articles, strongly Catholic in their content and even executed some Protestants who refused to accept them. Thus by the end of his reign England was in most respects still Catholic though no longer recognizing the supremacy of the pope.

Reigns of Edward VI and Mary. In the reign of Henry's sickly son Edward VI (1547–1553) Protestantism made considerable headway under the leadership of the King's Council. The First Book of Common Prayer was issued under the authority of the king and Archbishop Cranmer, and the Six Articles were repealed.

When Edward died at the age of sixteen, his eldest half-sister Mary, the daughter of Catherine of Aragon, became queen (1553–1558). A strong Catholic, she attempted to restore Catholicism in England and had about three hundred Protestant clerics (including Cranmer) and laymen burned at the stake. She then appointed a Catholic archbishop of Canterbury and used her influence to have a Catholic Parliament elected, which dutifully legislated the restoration of the old religion. But Mary made an extremely unpopular marriage with Philip of Spain, heir to the most powerful monarchy in Europe, and her efforts did not survive her brief reign.

The Elizabethan Compromise. Elizabeth, Mary's half-sister, who succeeded her (1558–1603), unwilling to see her country divided on the question of religion, negotiated a compromise under which she became Supreme Governor of the Church of England. The Church itself was re-established, with a liturgy substantially the same as that of today, and its creed was promulgated in the form of Thirty-Nine Articles, which are still binding on the Anglican Church. Both Catholics and Calvinists were tolerated by Elizabeth as long as they did not actively oppose her. After her excommunication by the pope in 1570, the Jesuits tried by all means at their disposal to reconvert England. Various Catholic conspiracies attempted to unseat her from the throne, usually with the hope of placing on it the Catholic Mary, Queen of Scots, her prisoner after 1568. (If, as Catholics held, Elizabeth was illegitimate, then Mary was the rightful queen.) Toward the end of Elizabeth's reign, a number of Catholics and even a few extremist Protestants were executed for treason. Opposition from the Calvinists who objected to the residue of Catholicism in the English Church was increasing at the time of her death.

THE CATHOLIC OR COUNTER REFORMATION

The Catholic Church, faced by the challenge of Protestantism, had to make a decision as to whether or not to modify its teachings and act upon some of the Lutheran criticisms. It decided to reform the Church from within but to make no other concessions to the Protestants. With the aid of a new militant order, the Society of Jesus (Jesuits), founded in 1540, and the arms of Catholic rulers, it managed to stem the tide of Protestantism and recover some of the countries it had lost.

The Council of Trent. It was several decades before the reformers could dispossess the Renaissance popes in Rome and set the Catholic Reformation in motion. Under pressure from Charles V, Pope Paul III finally called a great Council at Trent in 1545 which continued to sit at intervals until 1564. The Council at first tried to find some common ground with the more moderate reformers, but it was unable to compromise on the Lutheran doctrine of justification by faith, which would have nullified the role of the Church in winning salvation. When these efforts failed, the Council set itself to make much clearer than before the doctrines held by the Church. These were embodied in the Tridentine Catechism, which priests were instructed to teach to all Catholics. The Index of Forbidden Books was drawn up with the purpose of preventing the faithful from having access to heretical doctrines, and the Inquisition was strengthened for the obdurate. All major Protestant doctrines were declared "anathema" (cursed).

The Society of Jesus. The Jesuit Order (founded, like other orders, by an individual, Ignatius Loyola, and not by the Church itself) was made up of dedicated men who took a vow of obedience to the general of the order, who himself took a vow of obedience to the papacy on behalf of the order. Thus the popes now had at their disposal a militant organization which penetrated into every Catholic country, dominating all education for several centuries and engaging in missionary work throughout the world. In later times many monarchs expelled the Jesuits from their countries, fearing their enormous influence and their subservience to papal policies, which often conflicted with their own. There can, however, be no doubt that their influence in the Counter Reformation was crucial to the success of the whole movement.

THE RELIGIOUS WARS

The Catholic Church had too much at stake to be willing to allow a dangerous schism to split it irrevocably. It believed that it was the only true Christian Church, founded by Jesus Christ, who authorized Peter to be its first head, and that its sacraments, unlike those of the Protestants, were efficacious for salvation. It therefore felt that it had a religious duty to preserve its unity. The Church was also a great landowner, a ruler of the papal states, and as the arbiter of Christendom the high court of appeal for numerous lawsuits, not only on ecclesiastical matters but also on matters that today would fall within the prerogative of secular states. Though no doubt it would have preferred to reconvert the Protestants by peaceful means, it was not prepared to abandon its sources of livelihood, which alone permitted it to carry out its responsibilities. Believing as it did that salvation for Christians depended upon its continued existence, the Church did not shrink from using force if necessary. Catholic princes, holding similar views, were willing to fight to preserve the unity of the Church, even though they might have made greater material gains if they had "nationalized" the Church in their countries. Hardly less important in the monarchs' minds was the thought that Protestants, like the earlier heretics, were rebels as well as dissenters on religious doctrine. It therefore becomes difficult to distinguish between the wars with a genuinely religious cast and wars in which nobles and classes chose their different sides for mainly political reasons. In all the wars both elements were intermingled, and though in most cases religious reasons predominated at the outset, the conflicts soon ceased to be exclusively religious, and secular motives and ambitions were paramount when they were at last brought to a conclusion.

Huguenots and Catholics in France. In 1516 Francis I negotiated an agreement with the papacy under which the French monarch was allowed to appoint bishops and abbots in exchange for the relinquishment of any right over certain monies due to the papacy. Thus in effect the French had a national church of their own (the Gallican Church) which remained Catholic. This Concordat of Bologna was so favorable to French aspirations that the monarchy did not have the grievances against the papacy which led other princes to Protestantism; and French monarchs invariably backed Catholicism against the Protestants.

By the time of the premature death of Henry II (killed in a tournament) in 1559 there were many Huguenots in France, especially in the towns and among the nobility; but though there were some persecutions, they were as yet not systematically conducted, and they had not yet taken on a political aspect. Henry left his wife Catherine de Médicis as his regent, and she dominated her sons, who came to the throne in succession until the extinction of the male Valois line in 1589. If these three children were to die without heirs, the nearest to the throne was the Bourbon family, descended from Louis IX, the thirteenth-century king of France, who was canonized as St. Louis. This family was Protestant, but it was opposed by a far more powerful nonroyal family, the Guises, who were strongly Catholic.

From 1562 onward, while Charles IX (1560–1574) and Henry III (1574–1589) occupied the throne and Catherine de Médicis vainly tried to govern and keep the peace with the aid of an advisory group known as the *politiques,* civil wars were almost continuous. At one time Admiral Coligny, a Protestant, obtained the ear of the young king, and the Catholics, especially the Guises, were afraid that he might decide for Protestantism. On the occasion of the marriage of Henry of Navarre, the Bourbon heir, to a Valois princess in 1572, Catherine and the Guises persuaded the king to permit the Massacre of St. Bartholemew, in which Coligny and numerous other Huguenots were killed throughout France. Henry escaped by feigning conversion to Catholicism, but the Huguenots did not give up the struggle, several times winning toleration for their religion. In 1585 began the so-called War of the Three Henrys (King Henry III, Henry of Navarre, and Henry, duke of Guise), which was brought to an end by the murder of Henry of Guise in 1588. This was avenged the following year by a monk who murdered Henry III. Thus Henry of Navarre, still a Huguenot, became king as Henry IV by hereditary right. When the Catholics, backed by a Spanish army, refused to accept him and chose their own king, Henry IV after winning an important victory decided to abjure his Protestantism ("Paris is worth a Mass"). Shortly afterward he issued the Edict of Nantes, which granted a measure of toleration to the Huguenots and left them some fortified places. These were restored to the monarchy by Henry's successor Louis XIII and Cardinal Richelieu, his chief adviser. The toleration of Huguenots continued until 1685.

The United Provinces. When the Holy Roman emperor Charles V abdicated in 1556, his Spanish and Dutch possessions were inherited by his son Philip II of Spain, who was a strong, even bigoted,

Catholic. Charles himself had taken little action against the Netherlandic Protestants, who had become strong especially in the northern cities. When Philip came to the throne it soon became clear to the Netherlanders that he would be a more faithful servant of the Counter Reformation. Moreover, Philip was engaged in so many wars elsewhere that he increased his taxation of his wealthy Dutch provinces, thus also increasing discontent. When he proposed to introduce the Inquisition into the Netherlands, a number of nobles banded together to resist, while numerous extreme Protestant groups began to engage in attacks on the Catholic churches, in spite of the opposition of the upper classes.

Philip therefore decided to send one of his leading soldiers, the Duke of Alva, to the country. His policy of repression was so severe and the behavior of his often unpaid Spanish soldiery was so atrocious (especially the sack of Antwerp in 1576, known as the Spanish Fury) that all classes, Catholic and Protestant alike, led by William of Orange ("William the Silent") united to resist him. A formal agreement was drawn up called the Pacification of Ghent (1576), under which all the provinces, irrespective of religious affiliations, agreed to remain united until the Spaniards were expelled from the country. The skilled Dutch seamen preyed upon Spanish shipping but could not defeat the Spaniards by land. A new and effective Spanish general, the Duke of Parma, eventually succeeded in restoring the Southern Catholic provinces to Spanish rule. But the northern provinces, almost wholly Protestant, proclaimed their independence in 1579 as the Republic of the United Provinces under William of Orange as hereditary stadholder. With the aid of an English expedition sent by Queen Elizabeth, the Republic defeated all Spanish efforts to destroy it, and it received formal recognition from the powers at the Peace of Westphalia in 1648.

Thirty Years' War. After the abdication of Charles V, his brother Ferdinand became emperor. He and his son took few active steps against the Protestants, and by the opening of the sixteenth century many princes had taken advantage of the Religious Peace of Augsburg to convert to Lutheranism. Calvinism also had made headway, in spite of the fact that Calvinists were not included in the arrangement of Augsburg. Three of the imperial electors were now Protestants, the Duke of Saxony (who was a Lutheran), the Elector Palatine, and the Margrave of Brandenburg (who were Calvinists). Within the Empire, Bohemia was largely Protestant, while Austria and Hungary had at least a strong minority of Protestants. This situation was intolerable to the Jesuits and to many Catholic princes, especially Maximilian, duke of Bavaria.

The approaching death of the emperor Matthias (1612–1619) brought matters to a head. The emperor, a strong Catholic, was childless, and he wished his cousin Ferdinand of Styria to inherit the throne. But Ferdinand could not command enough electoral votes unless he, like Matthias, were also elected king of Bohemia. As their price for this election the Bohemians would certainly insist on toleration for Protestantism and the respect of their traditional rights. But the Protestants were plagued by dissensions between Lutherans and Calvinists; and though they formed a league they were unable to concert a united policy, whereas the Catholic League dominated by Maximilian of Bavaria experienced no such difficulty.

The Bohemian diet, finding itself without a suitable candidate of its own, elected Ferdinand to the throne, relying upon the undertakings given by his predecessors. But Ferdinand proceeded to exercise absolute authority in the country, whereupon the citizens of Prague threw two of his commissioners out of the window (*defenestration*) and deposed him in favor of the Protestant Elector Palatine (thereafter known as Frederick the Winter King), who was married to the daughter of the English king James I. Frederick, however, was unable to stand against Ferdinand and Maximilian, in spite of receiving some English aid, and he was utterly defeated in the Battle of the White Mountain (1620). Thereafter Bohemia was subjugated and forcibly reconverted to Catholicism. As a reward for his loyalty to the Empire, Maximilian was given Frederick's electoral vote.

The German Protestant princes had so far given little aid to the Protestant cause. In the next period of the war Ferdinand hired a leader of mercenary troops named Wallenstein, who, with the aid of Maximilian's general Tilly, held off the attacks of a Protestant coalition, led by King Christian IV of Denmark, and drove the monarch out of the country. After the expulsion of Christian, Gustavus Adolphus, king of Sweden, intervened, backed by French money and aided by an army provided by the Lutheran Elector of Saxony. The French under Richelieu wished to weaken the power of both branches (Spanish and Austrian) of the Hapsburg family each of which was actively engaged in the war not only in central Europe but in northern Italy.

Gustavus Adolphus himself was killed in battle in 1632, but the Swedes continued active in the war. Ferdinand withdrew his confidence from the ambitious Wallenstein and had him murdered as soon as his services could be dispensed with (1634). In the last stages of the war the French intervened actively, as did the Margrave of Brandenburg, and Hapsburg resistance was worn down. The Peace of Westphalia, the first great all-European peace treaty, brought an end to the war with a settlement favorable to France and Sweden and unfavorable to the Empire. The religious Peace of Augsburg was to hold good both for Calvinists and Lutherans in the future. But those areas which had been reconverted to Catholicism during the war could retain it. The Protestants within the Hapsburg lands, however, were unprotected by the treaty and were compelled to accept the Catholicism of their rulers. Under the treaty Sweden received territories in northern Germany and became a member of the German diet. France received some bishoprics in the Empire, captured during the war, and was granted sovereignty over much of Alsace, likewise a former imperial possession.

A separate phase of the war was a struggle between the French and the Spaniards, originally over the control of the Spanish Hapsburg possessions in northern Italy and the passes into Austria, through which the Spanish ruler could have sent direct aid to his brother Hapsburg in Vienna. This war went generally in favor of the French, but it was not brought to an end by the Peace of Westphalia, which the Spanish monarch refused to accept. The war dragged on until 1659, when the Peace of the Pyrenees was signed between France and Spain, under which some of the Spanish Netherlands was ceded to France. This Peace marked the end of the supremacy of the Spanish soldiery in Europe.

The Thirty Years' War was an unmitigated disaster for Germany from which she recovered only very slowly. The whole country had been fought over for thirty years and few areas were undamaged by the rapacious soldiers of Wallenstein, and later by the Swedes and French. But the war at least had had the effect of producing a general sense of exhaustion and numerous questionings as to whether such wars fought in the name of religion were worth what they cost. Thus the war led to the growth of tolerance—even if it was only the tolerance of exhaustion and indifference.

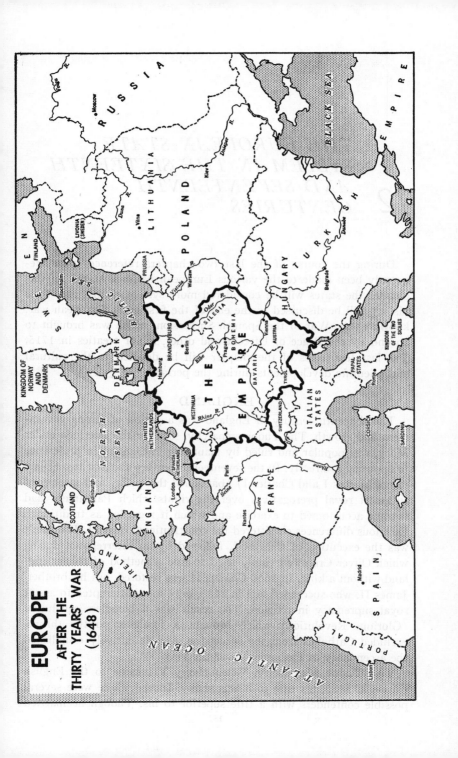

EUROPE
AFTER THE
THIRTY YEARS'' WAR
(1648)

12 THE EUROPEAN STATE SYSTEM IN THE SIXTEENTH AND SEVENTEENTH CENTURIES

During the course of the last two chapters references have frequently been made to the various European national states. In this chapter the states will be considered more systematically, and their history will be discussed to the end of the first great European war, known as the War of the Spanish Succession, which was brought to an end by the Peace of Utrecht and other, minor treaties in 1715. The last few pages of the chapter will be devoted to the cultural and scientific developments during the period.

ENGLAND

The sixteenth century in England was a period of strong government and growth. The Tudor monarchy, save for the interlude under Mary, was popular and ruled by managing Parliament in preference to opposing it directly. In the seventeenth century the first two Stuart rulers (James I and Charles I) abandoned this policy and attempted to assert royal prerogatives over the rights which Parliament had become accustomed to exercise and which it regarded as traditional. Religious differences embittered the constitutional quarrel. The result was the execution of Charles I, followed by an interregnum during which Oliver Cromwell vainly tried to find a method of ruling England without a king. In 1660 Charles II was restored, but his brother, James II, who succeeded him in 1685, once more attempted to assert royal supremacy in religion. The result was a bloodless revolution (Glorious Revolution) which brought a foreigner to the throne, excluded Catholics from the succession, and definitively established the ascendancy of Parliament over the king.

The Tudor Monarchy. When Henry VII came to the English throne in 1485, his title to it was shaky. Indeed, there were several possible contenders with a title superior to his. Though he married the heiress of the House of York, thereby uniting the two families that had fought the Wars of the Roses, he nevertheless had to suppress several minor uprisings during his reign. But since his best title to the throne was the fact that he had brought the Wars of the Roses to an end and been accepted by Parliament and people alike, there was never any serious possibility of his being overthrown —and indeed he used the excuse of the rebellions to punish the rebels and nobles with heavy fines, thus increasing the treasury surplus, which he carefully husbanded all his reign. Henry called Parliament whenever he needed it, and it dutifully did whatever he requested. Since the ordinary law courts too often refused to convict influential persons accused of crime, he obtained from Parliament the right to set up a new royal court composed of a committee of his Council. The Court of Star Chamber became notorious as an instrument of tyranny during the next century. But under the Tudors it was undoubtedly an aid to justice—though, like other courts, based on the Roman legal system, it was empowered to use torture. Henry, one of the first royal mercantilists, also had Parliament pass several acts which were helpful to English trade, notably a Navigation Act which gave competitive advantages in international trade to English shipping. When he died in 1509 Henry left a full treasury to his son Henry VIII (1509–1547), a typical Renaissance monarch who had little sympathy for his father's penny-pinching policies.

Henry VIII, extravagant and authoritarian, nevertheless strengthened the international position of his country and made himself respected and feared at home and abroad. England, however, was still a small country with a population much inferior to that of France. Henry's major achievement was the nationalization of the English Church, described in Chapter 11. Toward the end of his reign difficulties arose over the succession. Edward, his only son (by Jane Seymour, his third wife who had died in childbirth), was not expected to live long. If the annulment of his marriage with Catherine of Aragon was legal, then Mary was illegitimate and could not succeed to the throne. If the annulment was illegal then his marriage to Anne Boleyn was bigamous and her daughter Elizabeth was illegitimate. Since both Mary and Anne were dead by the time Edward was born, he was in any case legitimate. Parliament finally left the question for Henry himself to decide, whereupon he declared that both Mary and Elizabeth were legitimate and that if Edward died prematurely each could succeed in turn. This in fact happened.

Edward VI occupied the throne only from 1547 to 1553. His uncle, the Lord Protector Somerset, at first ruled the country from the vantage point of the presidency of the King's Council. But after losing the support of his fellow councilors, he was ousted by the Duke of Northumberland, who tried when Edward was dying to put the Protestant Lady Jane Grey in a position to inherit the throne in preference to the Catholic Mary. But when Edward died the coup failed, and Lady Jane and Northumberland were both executed by Mary. Though the British were willing to accept Mary as queen, they insisted that her husband Philip II of Spain should not become king. When he inherited the throne of Spain and it was clear that Mary would never bear him a child, he abandoned the country altogether.

Elizabeth, who succeeded to the throne after the death of Mary (1558), was expected to enter a marriage alliance with some foreign prince, or, failing that, at least to take for herself a noble English husband. But she herself had other ideas. She did not wish to favor any Continental country above another; yet at the same time she wished to make use of the possibility of her marriage to aid in her diplomacy. Thus she could not take even an Englishman as her husband. This game she played brilliantly all her reign in the interests, as she saw them, of England.

Like her grandfather she was careful of money and shunned wars as far as she could, even against Spain, who was hated in England, in part for her commercial policies, which hindered English trade with the Americas, and in part because of Philip's support of the Counter Reformation. Nevertheless, Elizabeth encouraged piratical attacks on Spanish shipping, from whose proceeds the Crown took a share. These attacks were immensely popular when successful, especially with the middle classes, whose interests Elizabeth, like her grandfather, did her best to foster, benefiting markedly those companies to whom she granted trade monopolies. In the later part of her reign Parliament complained of the restraint of trade involved in these monopolies, and Elizabeth graciously modified her policy for the sake of good relations with it. Only in the matter of religion she was adamant and refused to abate any of her prerogatives as Supreme Governor of the Church.

When she went so far as to send aid to the rebellious Protestants in the Netherlands, Philip II decided to take drastic action, planning to use the Duke of Parma's forces in the Netherlands to invade England, with the support of a huge Armada, which he sent directly from Spain. But in 1588 the Armada was badly mauled by the light English ships in the Channel, and the rest of the fleet was destroyed by gales in the North Sea and off the coast of Scotland. Parma therefore was unable to invade, the Spanish threat was brought to an end, and England was secured from invasion for an indefinite future.

The Reign of James I (1603–1625). James I (son of Mary, Queen of Scots), who succeeded Elizabeth on the throne, believed in the divine right of monarchies and had written a book on the subject. He had no understanding of the role of Parliament in British political life. He had already been king in Scotland ever since the deposition of his mother, but had been hedged around by numerous restrictions and compelled to listen to Presbyterian elders. He hoped to be freed as ruler of England from all such impediments to his absolutism. Especially he wished, as an amateur theologian, to dictate to the English Church, of which he was the nominal governor. But he was extravagant and needed money for his pleasures and favorites. A pacifist by instinct and policy, he would not undertake Spanish adventures like those that had brought booty to Elizabeth. Moreover, he had no talents for persuading Parliament, preferring to assert his royal prerogative and compel it to obey him.

He was faced in Parliament by a strong Puritan minority, which in time became a majority and which hoped to reform the established Church of England by removing "Popish" survivals, whereas James proposed to discipline the Puritans and make them conform to Anglican practice.

During his reign James was constantly at odds with Parliament. When it desired to continue war with Spain he brought it to an end through dissolution; he supported his daughter (married to Frederick, the Winter King of Bohemia) only feebly during the Thirty Years' War. He insisted on raising money by increasing the rate of customs and excise (tunnage and poundage) duties without the consent of Parliament. He deposed judges who would not give verdicts in his favor; he took action against Puritans which drove many of them abroad and ultimately across the Atlantic to found the Puritan settlements in New England. When Parliament would not give him what he wanted he tried to discipline its members directly by imprisoning them. When this failed he dissolved it. Lastly at the end of his reign he involved the country in war with Spain, for which a disgruntled Parliament now refused to grant him subsidies.

Charles I and the Civil War. Charles I (1625–1649) was if anything more obstinate than his father, and even less successful. Parliament in 1628 forced him to sign the Petition of Right, according to which he promised, like King John before him, not to do certain things he was accustomed to doing: among other things, not to raise taxes without the consent of Parliament, not to billet soldiers in private houses, not to declare martial law in time of peace, and not to imprison anyone without a specific charge. Parliament then went further, and began to insist on interfering with Charles's right to govern the Church, whereupon Charles decided to dissolve Parliament and try to rule without it.

Thus in 1629 began the eleven years of experiment in absolute rule, during which the people were left without a forum for their grievances. Administration was greatly improved, and persons refusing to pay the taxes that Charles imposed were condemned by royal courts and imprisoned if necessary. The period has been variously described as a necessary modernization of the British government along Continental lines and as a tyranny contrary to English traditions. It was in fact both; but since Parliament was the victor and the result was a limited constitutional monarchy which eventually led to democracy, the struggle was of the greatest importance as an example for others when they too in later centuries came to limit the powers of their monarchs without a revolution.

Charles eventually failed because he became involved in a war which he could not wage without new taxes voted by Parliament. Archbishop Laud, a fervent Anglican, tried to introduce the Anglican liturgy into Scotland. At this the Scottish elders called upon the faithful to sign a Solemn League and Covenant, and an expedition was sent into England which defeated the feeble royal forces. Charles thereupon called Parliament, which refused to vote supplies unless he agreed to redress grievances. Charles, preferring to dissolve Parliament, then tried to raise troops on his own. The Scots this time advanced far into England and defeated the king, imposing an indemnity, which he could not pay without the aid of Parliament. Thus the Long Parliament (1640–1660) came into being; it was able to compel Charles to consent to the execution of his chief minister and to accept the dismantling of almost all the instruments he had used for his absolute rule. Parliament was also to be allowed to call itself at least once in three years if the king refused to do so (Triennial Act). Parliament, by this time having a small Puritan majority, then tried to impose Presbyterianism on England. Charles refused and tried to arrest the leading members of Parliament, who escaped to the City of London. He then realized there was no alternative to civil war, which broke out in 1641.

In the war the king was supported by most Anglicans and by the bulk of the upper and the rural classes and the north and west of England. These were the so-called Cavaliers. The forces of Parliament (Roundheads) held most of the remainder of the country. The Puritan groups in Parliament and the country were not, however, united. The Presbyterians had the support of the Scottish, but several independent sects gradually took over the army, in which extreme democratic ideas also found a home. Its most effective leader was Oliver Cromwell, who organized a "model army" of "Ironsides," which decisively defeated Charles at the Battle of Naseby (1645). During the next few years Charles tried to play the Scots off against Cromwell by agreeing to accept Presbyterianism. But Cromwell defeated the Scots also at the Battle of Preston in 1648, captured the king, and purged the Parliament of Presbyterians as well as of Anglicans. The remainder, known as the Rump Parliament, condemned Charles to death and executed him (1649).

There followed the Commonwealth and Protectorate, dominated by Cromwell and his army, which he refused to disband. It was on this issue that he was opposed by each Parliament that he called, even when it was packed by his own nominees. Eventually the country was ruled by Cromwell as Protector backed by the army. Though Cromwell was respected abroad and pursued an effective foreign policy, he was unable to establish any form of government which held hopes of being permanent; and his son, who succeeded him as Protector, had no interest in the position. This left the generals with no better alternative than to call back Charles Stuart, son of Charles I, who was restored to the throne as Charles II in 1660.

The Restoration Era. Charles II, much more intelligent and realistic than his father, realized that he could not oppose Parliament directly. But the monarchy still had many powers in reserve which could be used to good effect to enable him to do what he wished. He was favored on his accession by his Parliament (Cavalier Parliament), anxious to please him and to restore England to what it had been before the Civil War. Strongly Anglican in religion, it legislated against the Calvinist and Catholic churches alike. Charles himself inclined toward Catholicism. He recognized that he could never restore the old religion, but he hoped to remove the political and other disabilities from which the Catholics still suffered. Unfortunately for him, the people were still wary of the Jesuits and the Counter Reformation, and Charles found it difficult to achieve any measure of toleration for Catholics. For the later part of his reign he was at least a secret Catholic, and he probably made a promise to the

Catholic king Louis XIV of France that he would choose the right moment to declare himself. He also made a secret treaty (Treaty of Dover) with Louis, under which he agreed to go to war with the Netherlands when called upon by Louis to do so, for which action he would be rewarded by a subsidy. Much of this devious policy was due to the determination of Charles, who had no legitimate children, to ensure the succession of his brother James, a known Catholic convert.

In 1672 Charles issued a Declaration of Indulgence for the benefit of Catholics, to which Parliament retorted in the following year by a Test Act, requiring all Catholics to declare themselves and preventing them from holding governmental office. Parliament then tried to pass a bill excluding James from the throne, which Charles prevented by dissolving Parliament whenever there was danger that the bill would be passed. He duly went to war with Holland, according to his agreement with Louis XIV, and received his subsidy. But his arms were unsuccessful and the war unpopular. Louis, however, was later willing to continue the subsidy to England in exchange for Charles's neutrality, enabling him to continue to defy Parliament safely over the succession.

In 1678 the Whig majority party in Parliament, in most matters opposed to the king, overreached itself by exploiting a "Popish Plot" to put James on the throne, which was in fact the invention of a notorious informer named Titus Oates. A succession of executions of supposed conspirators disgusted the people, allowing Charles to strike suddenly by arresting Oates and compelling him to confess his false witness. Charles, backed by the Tory party, which in general supported the king and opposed the Whigs, revised the electoral districts to make the election of another Whig majority virtually impossible. Soon afterward he died, leaving James to ascend the throne peaceably.

James, after quickly suppressing a rebellion led by an illegitimate son of Charles, began to proceed with his intention of reconverting England forcibly to Catholicism. But even a Tory Parliament could not stomach this. When James persisted, refusing to disband the army which had suppressed the recent rebellion and trying to compel the Anglican Church to accept his religion, a number of important politicians of both parties went abroad to Holland to ask the Protestant William of Orange to become king. (William was married to Mary, a Protestant daughter of James I, born to his first wife before his conversion.) William accepted; James's army refused to obey him; and the Glorious Revolution was bloodlessly accomplished (1688).

William agreed to a Bill of Rights, passed by Parliament, and later to an Act of Settlement which excluded Catholics thereafter from the throne, however little hereditary claim the Protestant aspirant might have. (When Queen Anne, the second Protestant daughter of James, died in 1714, the crown passed to a German prince who could not even speak English.) Under the Bill of Rights William agreed that no standing army could be maintained without the consent of Parliament; that Parliament should be called frequently; that levying money without its consent was illegal; that election of members of Parliament should be free; that parliamentary debates should not be interfered with; that no excessive bail should be demanded; and that it was lawful to petition the king and to bear arms. (Many of these provisions reappeared in the United States Constitution and its first ten amendments.)

James II died in exile, and both his son and grandson unsuccessfully attempted with the aid of many of the Scots to overthrow the new Hanoverian dynasty (1715, 1745). Scotland and England, which had been ruled by the Stuarts in a personal union, were formally united in 1707 under Queen Anne.

FRANCE

When Louis XI of France died in 1483, he bequeathed a largely unified country to his son Charles VIII. Only Brittany in the northwest was still an independent duchy. The new monarch married Anne, the heiress of the duchy. When Charles himself died prematurely, leaving no heir, his successor, Louis XII of the the Orléans line, married his predecessor's widow in order to retain Brittany as part of the royal domain. Claudia, the sole progeny of this marriage, married Louis' successor, Francis I; thus Brittany finally became incorporated with France by the accession of their son Henry II in 1547, completing the consolidation of the realm.

Foreign Ambitions of the Valois Monarchy. Charles VIII (1483–1498) and his immediate successors were far from content with their French possessions. Charles himself made an expedition to Naples—the major result of which was the introduction of the Renaissance to France—but was compelled to relinquish its crown which he had briefly won. Louis XII reconquered the kingdom of Naples but was subsequently defeated by the Spaniards and forced to abandon his claims. He succeeded in taking Milan but was again driven out. Francis I (1515–1547) spent much of his reign warring with the emperor Charles V over their conflicting claims in northern and central Italy; but in spite of occasional successes and sporadic aid from the Turkish sultan, on the whole he had the worst of the engagements and nothing permanent was accomplished. The wars with the Hapsburgs, fought on both sides in pursuit of purely dynastic interests, were finally brought to an end in 1559 by the Peace of Cateau-Cambrésis, which left France with Calais, taken from the English in 1558,* and three imperial bishoprics to show for the more than sixty years of desultory warfare.

The Early Bourbon Monarchy. During the rest of the sixteenth century France was involved in the religious wars described in Chapter 11, which were settled only after the accession of Henry IV (Henry of Navarre, or Henry the Great, 1589–1610), who successfully faced the challenge of restoring order and prosperity to the long-divided kingdom. With the aid of a parsimonious Protestant finance minister, the Duke of Sully, and a program which called for "a chicken in every pot," Henry put his country back on the road to economic health, and provided a strong government until he was murdered by a religious fanatic in 1610. He left a nine-year old boy Louis XIII (1610–1643) as his heir and his incompetent wife Marie de Médicis as his regent.

A period of internal discord and further rebellions by the nobility followed until Louis in 1624 found a strong minister in Cardinal Richelieu, who for the rest of the reign dominated the country and was its virtual ruler. Richelieu pursued a policy of aggrandizement abroad while suppressing both the feudal nobility and the Huguenots at home. The most important domestic innovation of the reign was the establishment of *intendants,* royal ministers who supervised the various areas of the country in the name of the king. The system had the effect of strengthening royal power and putting an end to the independent power of the nobles, who thereafter accepted royal authority, contenting themselves with their lands and titles.

Abroad Richelieu intervened in the Thirty Years' War, as we have seen in Chapter 11; and his hand-picked successor Cardinal Mazarin managed to establish France as the greatest power in Europe at the Peace of Westphalia in 1648 and at the Peace of the Pyrenees in

* The English, through Mary's marriage to Philip of Spain had been drawn into the war on the side of the Spaniards in 1557 and lost Calais the following year. The Peace of Cateau-Cambrésis gave France only temporary possession of the city, but she gained permanent possession in 1564 in exchange for a large sum of money.

1659. By the first treaty the power of the imperial Hapsburgs and by the second treaty that of the Spanish Hapsburgs was considerably reduced. Both monarchs lost some territory to France, but the major consequence was the ending of the domination of the Hapsburgs in Central Europe and the gradual senescence of Spain, which soon sank to the rank of a minor power.

Reign of Louis XIV (1643–1715). For the rest of the century France was the unquestioned leader of Europe. She could not be defeated in war save by an alliance of several nations against her; and even when she fought almost alone, it was only with great difficulty that she could be worsted. French culture in both the seventeenth and eighteenth centuries was ascendant, and it was imitated everywhere save in England. French became the language of diplomacy and polite society, and Louis XIV himself in his new palace of Versailles, surrounded by his obsequious court, was by far the richest and most powerful monarch in Europe. He owed his wealth largely to the policies of Colbert, his finance minister, who greatly improved the tax-collecting system, cut down internal tariffs which prevented the free flow of commerce within France, set up new industries, and insisted on the maintenance of high quality in goods destined for export. He increased the use of French shipping by taxing foreign shipping and subsidizing his own. These measures, together with a protective tariff on imports, were a marked success and earned for Colbert the name of the "complete mercantilist."

During the regency of Louis' mother, Anne of Austria, and her favorite, Cardinal Mazarin, the nobles made their last attempt to resist the power of the monarchy. Mazarin, who was an Italian by birth, was universally unpopular and could not command the respect accorded to his predecessor Richelieu. The Parlement of Paris, the chief law court of France, which had the duty of registering the king's decrees before they became law, for a time refused to fulfill its functions and listened to complaints against the government. But neither Parlement nor nobles had any policy of their own, nor were their interests usually compatible. The result was that the small rebellions (*Frondes*) succeeded in driving Mazarin from Paris, but their leaders thereafter did not pursue a consistent policy and evolved no alternative program to absolute royal rule. When the loyal general Turenne—the other successful general Condé joined the conspiracy—defeated the rebels in 1653, Mazarin and his royal master returned. It was naturally realized by the king that it was thereafter safe to behave absolutely as he wished. When Mazarin died in

1661, Louis took personal charge of the government and ruled until his death without opposition except from religious dissidents.

Most of the wars of Louis XIV may reasonably be regarded as an attempt to acquire a defensible northern frontier for the country, rather than solely as an attempt at French aggrandizement. To the north were the Spanish Netherlands, a part of which had to be incorporated if France were to obtain the Rhine as her northern boundary. The independent Dutch Republic, which bordered the Spanish Netherlands, did not wish to have expansionist France as her southern neighbor. England did not wish to see France in control of both the Low Countries since this would threaten her security. The Holy Roman Empire, though primarily now a German power, still had some possessions to the east of France which were semi-independent. Alsace, Lorraine, and Burgundy were not yet in France.

The first three major wars fought by Louis XIV (War of Devolution, 1667–1668; Dutch War, 1672–1678; War of the League of Augsburg, 1688–1697) were all conducted against European alliances, in which the chief organizer was the Dutchman William of Orange (William III of England from 1689 to 1702). The Dutch suffered severely, at one time being forced to open the dikes to prevent a French conquest. But they held out, and though France in all the wars obtained some of her objectives, she never was permitted to keep all she conquered during the course of the wars.

The War of the Spanish Succession (1701–1714) was the most serious and prolonged of the wars. Charles II of Spain in the last years of the seventeenth century was slowly dying, leaving no obvious successor. The prize was a great one, even though Spain was no longer a major European power. It included the extensive Spanish colonial possessions and the Netherlands, as well as the kingdom of Naples and other Italian territories. There were three major claimants to the throne, each, in that age of dynastic marriages, having an almost equal legal title. England and Holland refused to countenance the possibility of the Spanish possessions falling into the hands of the French monarchy through Louis XIV's grandson, Philip of Anjou. They were hardly less averse to the Hapsburg claimant. On the whole they preferred the third claimant, a Bavarian prince who was only seven years old. Before the death of Charles II of Spain the powers agreed, in the interests of the balance of power in Europe, to a partition of the territories; but this was objected to by the ailing Spanish monarch. He bequeathed them first to the Bavarian prince, who suddenly died before himself. Then, still in the hopes of keeping his domain intact, Charles decided for Philip of Anjou, and died immediately afterward. Louis, though he knew it meant war, immediately abandoned all efforts at partition and had his grandson proclaimed king of Spain as Philip V.

The war which followed was fought bravely by the French but with success only for brief periods. The English Duke of Marlborough and Prince Eugene of Savoy, fighting for the emperor, had many notable victories against the French armies and almost won the war in 1708, when France was on the point of exhaustion. But Louis himself turned the tide by personal appeals to his people and the whole situation was changed by the death of Archduke Charles's elder brother, Emperor Joseph I, in 1711. The unexpected elevation of Charles to the imperial throne meant that if the war was won by the imperial alliance, the Empire would be enlarged by all the former Spanish possessions, as in the days of Charles V. Peace negotiations were soon begun, leading eventually to the Peace of Utrecht in 1713 and various subsidiary treaties which once more redrew the map of Europe. The former Spanish Netherlands (Austrian Netherlands) went to the emperor, together with most of the Spanish possessions in Italy. Philip V's title as king of Spain was recognized except by the Empire, which held out till 1720. It was agreed that the Spanish and French crowns should never be united in any one person. As major results of the War of the Spanish Succession, French expansionism was halted, and it was generally recognized that peace depended on the maintenance of the balance of power. All the participants in the recent war might thereafter be expected to intervene, as they had done on this occasion, if any single nation threatened to dominate Europe.

THE GERMANIES AND SWITZERLAND

The Holy Roman Empire in these centuries continued to be a basically German (Austrian) state with possessions beyond Germany which entitled it to be still called an empire. On the whole, these Hapsburg possessions were a source of weakness, rather than of strength, and they certainly prevented the unification of Germany as a truly national state comparable with England or France. The Turkish menace was ever present to the east, and the Hapsburg emperors performed a valuable service to the rest of Europe by keeping the Turks from encroaching further westward. In 1529 Charles V drove a besieging Turkish force from Vienna. In 1571 Don

John of Austria, commanding a Hapsburg and Venetian fleet, destroyed the Turkish navy at the Battle of Lepanto. Late in the seventeenth century a huge Turkish army again besieged Vienna, which was saved only by the arrival at the crucial moment of a Polish force under Jan Sobieski. A Christian counterataack then reconquered Hungary, adding it to the Hapsburg dominions together with Transylvania, Croatia, and Slavonia (Treaty of Karlowitz, 1699).

The varying fortunes of the Empire in the West have been largely discussed in earlier chapters. Though successful in the first years of the Thirty Years' War, the emperors were compelled to relinquish their ambitions at the Peace of Westphalia and failed in the War of the Spanish Succession to add the Spanish Hapsburg possessions to their own. Numerous German states, large and small, though nominally a part of the Empire, enjoyed practical independence. One, the former margravate of Brandenburg, to which Prussia—not a part of the Empire—was added in 1618, became an independent kingdom at the beginning of the eighteenth century. This achievement was mainly the work of Frederick William (the Great Elector), who ruled from 1640 to 1688. He organized a small but efficient professional army whose officers (Junkers) were drawn from the landowning class. This army enjoyed little success during the Thirty Years' War but gradually won the respect of the other powers in later years. When it was needed by the Hapsburg emperor in 1701, the price exacted was his recognition of the Great Elector's son as Frederick I, king of Prussia. This title was recognized by the other powers at the Peace of Utrecht in 1713.

The existence of a Swiss national state was given formal recognition at the Peace of Westphalia in 1648. The Confederation of Switzerland had its beginning with the union in the late thirteenth century of three forest cantons, to which other cantons were later added. The main purpose of the Confederation was to maintain independence from the Hapsburg rulers, and the means by which the Swiss won acceptance for their state was their astonishing ability at fighting. Mercenaries from Switzerland were in constant demand in European wars, including the Thirty Years' War, when Swiss Protestants fought on the Protestant side and Catholics on the Catholic side. To this day there are Protestant and Catholic cantons in Switzerland, the Protestant predominating, as they have done since the seventeenth century. Only with great difficulty was the

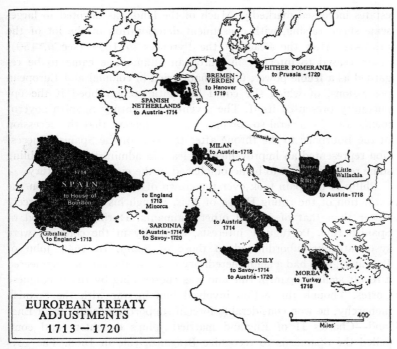

EUROPEAN TREATY
ADJUSTMENTS
1713 – 1720

Confederation preserved during the seventeenth and eighteenth centuries, and at times it was almost a dead letter. But the Swiss soldiers were too formidable to be taken on wantonly by foreign powers and it managed to survive. Though conquered by Napoleon, the Confederation was successfully revived in the nineteenth century and has remained independent as the longest-lived republic in the world.

THE IBERIAN PENINSULA

On the abdication of Charles V in 1556, his son Philip II became king of Spain. The treasure that continued to pour into the country from the Indies enabled Philip and his immediate successors to play a part in the European wars, which was in fact beyond the capacity of the relatively small and industrially undeveloped country. Within Spain the Church acquired ever more lands and greater power (especially under Philip III, 1598–1621), while the size of the nobles' estates increased markedly. Much of the land was devoted to large-scale sheep raising, with consequent deterioration in the lot of the peasants. After the Peace of the Pyrenees in 1659 (see p. 150), Spain ceased to interfere in European affairs. She came to be regarded as a feeble power, unjustifiably rich in colonial and European possessions, of which she could be legitimately robbed if the opportunity presented itself. The seventeenth-century Spanish governments were in general so corrupt and incompetent that the accession of the Bourbons to the throne after the War of the Spanish Succession represented an improvement at least in administration, enabling some reorganization to be accomplished in the eighteenth century.

Philip II of Spain took over the crown of Portugal in 1580 on the extinction of the ruling House of Avis, though his title was scarcely better than that of several other claimants. During the period of Spanish rule, Portuguese interests, especially in the colonies, were systematically subordinated to those of Spain. In 1640 John of Braganza, who had a slight hereditary claim to the throne, engineered a revolt against Spanish rule and was chosen king by the Portuguese Cortes. Though this action involved him in war with the Spanish monarchy, he won considerable foreign support, especially from England—Charles II of England married John's daughter—and compelled the Spaniards to recognize Braganza rule in 1668. The government, however, was scarcely modernized at all until the rule of Marquis de Pombal in the latter half of the eighteenth century.

SCANDINAVIA

The Lutheran revolt produced many political changes in northern Europe, out of which emerged two new monarchies, one of which, the Swedish, for a period became a great power with an extensive empire, though it was based on too few natural resources and too small a population to maintain its position for long. Norway and Finland, however, were unable to become independent and were subjected to rule by one or another of their more powerful neighbors.

Denmark. In 1397 Queen Margaret of Denmark united the thrones of Norway and Sweden, to which she had been elected by the magnates of these countries (Union of Kalmar), and her successors maintained this nominal unity until the early sixteenth century. But the Swedes, in particular, resented Danish supremacy in their country and seized the opportunity to throw off the yoke of the Catholic monarch of Denmark, Christian II in 1523. The Swedish leader, a noble named Gustavus Vasa, was proclaimed king and thereafter established a national Lutheran church in his country. Finland, originally conquered and converted to Christianity by Sweden in the twelfth century, followed Sweden in this secession. A civil war soon broke out in Denmark, resulting in the establishment of a Lutheran church in that country also by Christian III (1534–1559). Norway, which remained under Danish rule in the sixteenth and seventeenth centuries, likewise converted to Lutheranism.

During the long reign of Christian IV (1588–1648), who intervened unsuccessfully in the Thirty Years' War (see p. 149), both Norwegian and Danish provinces were lost to the powerful Swedes. At home, however, Christian made many reforms and converted his country into an effective national state by curbing the power of the nobility. His son Frederick III (1648–1670) made the monarchy hereditary.

Sweden. Both Gustavus and his successors put down many Catholic revolts in the early years of independence, succeeding in establishing a strong national state. They also expanded into Livonia and Estonia and intervened during the Russian interregnum which preceded the election of the first Romanov to the throne, winning sufficient land to cut the Russians off from the Baltic. Charles IX (1604–1611), youngest son of Gustavus Vasa, was made king of Sweden by his Lutheran countrymen's refusal to accept his Catholic nephew Sigismund (heir to the throne as the son of Charles' elder brother John III), who was also king of Poland. This action involved the country in wars with Poland which continued sporadically for sixty years.

Gustavus II, Adolphus (1611–1632), known as the Lion of the North, modernized the administration of Sweden while engaging in extensive intervention in the Thirty Years' War. After his death in battle his policy was carried on by his successor, Queen Christina, and her chancellor, Axel Oxenstierna; and Sweden made extensive territorial gains in Germany at the Peace of Westphalia in 1648. After the abdication (1654) of Christina, who converted to Catholicism, her successor, Charles X, engaged in the First Northern War, as the result of which Denmark lost some provinces and Poland acknowledged Swedish rule over Livonia (Treaty of Oliva, 1660). This time marked the apogee of Swedish success as a military power except for the brief period of ephemeral conquest under Charles XII (1697–1718), the greatest military genius of his age.

Unfortunately for him and for Sweden, Charles XII decided to take on the growing power of Russia under Peter the Great, who allied himself with both Poland and Denmark, Sweden's traditional enemies. Charles decisively defeated both Poland and Denmark and won a great victory over Peter at Narva (1700). But when after the defeat of Poland he penetrated too far into Russia, he himself was defeated by Peter (Battle of Poltava, 1709) and compelled to take refuge in Turkey. During his absence his empire fell apart and Sweden was soon confined within her old boundaries, though she kept most of Finland until the Napoleonic wars, when it passed to the Russian crown.

EASTERN EUROPE

In eastern Europe Russia after a brief period of strong rule under Ivan IV (the Terrible) relapsed into semianarchy until the rise of the Romanov dynasty, which gradually consolidated its position. Poland-Lithuania became ever weaker under its elected monarchs, almost all of whom were foreigners more interested in the affairs of their own family and homeland than in those of their adopted subjects.

Poland-Lithuania. The first century following the union of the Polish and Lithuanian crowns was marked by constant struggles between the monarchs and the nobility and gentry. The latter, whom the kings tried to exalt at the expense of the hereditary nobles, as in Russia, did not fulfill the task expected of them and became only with difficulty distinguishable from the older nobility. In 1505 they compelled the monarch to recognize the diet of the gentry (*Seym*) as the legislative body of the state. But every deputy was entitled to exercise a veto on legislation (*liberum veto*), making any legislative progress impossible. Thus the upper classes in effect obtained a free hand to do as they wished, which they used to reduce the peasants to serfdom and to prevent the burghers in the cities from having any say in the government. In 1569 Poland and Lithuania were definitively merged with common institutions (Union of Lublin). Desultory wars with Russia, Sweden, and Turkey occupied the sixteenth and seventeenth centuries, which, in spite of occasional advances, eventually lost them much of their territory, while at home, the Jesuits, usually supported by the Catholic king, reconverted the country (in which Protestantism initially had met with considerable success) to Catholicism.

Russia. Meanwhile the Russian monarchy was gradually consolidating its position and by the eighteenth century had established Russian predominance in Poland. Ivan IV (1533–1584), who became the first tsar of Russia in 1547, as already noted, used the gentry and an institution known as the *oprichnina,* a corps of elite guards, to destroy by force the power of the hereditary nobility (boyars). But in the reign of his son Theodore I (1584–1598) the boyars regained much of their power. Theodore's death was followed by the reign of Boris Godunov, a boyar chosen by the assembly, who could not establish himself effectively as ruler. His death was followed by a prolonged civil war (the "Time of Troubles"), during which both Poles and Swedes intervened, the former even penetrating as far as Moscow. At this juncture the national assembly elevated to the throne Michael Romonov (1613–1645), and gradually order was restored. During this reign Cossacks and other tribes penetrated Siberia to reach the Pacific, offering their conquests to the tsar, who thus assumed suzerainty over them, though he exercised little authority in the region.

During the reigns of the first two Romanovs, Michael and Alexis (1645–1676), the tsars increased their absolutism and put an end to the power of the boyars for good; whereas the gentry, whose fortunes were tied to those of the monarch, increased in influence. All the upper classes were united in degrading the status of the peasants, who were now formally made serfs with the approval of the national assembly (*Zemsky Sobor*). A great peasant revolt led by Stephen Razin and the Cossacks of the Don was ruthlessly put down in 1671, and the lot of the peasants became worse than ever. Some of the leading Russians realized, however, that their country was extremely backward in comparison with other European states; and Tsar Alexis in particular encouraged the immigration of western European technicians and merchants, who were paid substantial salaries when in royal employment and given privileges denied to native Russians when they set up in business for themselves. The majority of Russians greatly resented their presence, and antiforeign feeling reached its peak during the Westernizing reforms of Peter I, the Great.

Peter (1682–1725), the son of Alexis by his second wife, did not achieve full power until 1689, when he took over the reins from his half-sister, who had ruled in the name of her incompetent brother. In his early years as ruler Peter visited incognito most of the capitals of Europe, learning what foreign countries could teach him; then he set to work to reorganize his state and especially his army.

Everyone in the country was made liable to royal service in some capacity, and a senate was established to draft royal regulations as needed. Learning from his defeat by the Swedes at the Battle of Narva in 1700, he reorganized the army and invented a strategy to resist them which paid off in 1709 (Battle of Poltava). Peter built his new capital of St. Petersburg (Leningrad) as a "window on the Baltic." By the time of his death he had greatly enlarged his territory at the expense of Sweden and Poland, established himself as the undisputed ruler and autocrat of Russia, and in some measure succeeded in bringing his country within the framework of Western civilization. Russia from that time onward was a European power; her aid was solicited and her armies taken into account in all the European wars of the following centuries.

CULTURAL AND SCIENTIFIC DEVELOPMENTS

During these centuries science took on its modern orientation, primarily through the development of astronomy. Gothic architecture gave way to the baroque, which exhibited a characteristically Western exuberance far removed from classical restraint. In literature every nation developed its own vernacular tongue and the universal language of Latin virtually ceased to be used except in the Catholic Church. French literature was perhaps the most admired and imitated, but Spain enjoyed a cultural renaissance in the sixteenth century, while English literature continued to flourish, if not quite so luxuriantly as in the Elizabethan age. Dutch painting reached the height of its greatness in these centuries, especially in the baroque painting of Rembrandt, while in music Germany with the work of Johann Sebastian Bach for the first time rivaled Italy.

Science from Copernicus to Newton. It was the Pole Nicholas Copernicus (1473–1543) who initiated the revolution in astronomy leading to the Newtonian picture of the universe as a great machine, of which the earth was a comparatively insignificant part. As a mathematician Copernicus was dissatisfied with the rather untidy and inelegant picture of the universe inherited from the Hellenistic astronomers, which enabled its portrayers to predict cosmic phenomena well enough but required them to postulate many subsidiary planetary movements in order to explain how and why the phenomena appeared as they did to human observation. Finding that some Hellenistic astronomers had suggested that the earth moved around the sun in a circular orbit, he adopted the suggestion as a hypothesis and calculated its mathematical consequences. When he discovered that many of the difficulties of the Ptolemaic system thereby disappeared, he wrote his findings in a book titled *Concerning the Revolutions of the Heavenly Orbs* (dedicated to Pope Paul III), which was published in the year of his death.

The book caused relatively little concern in the Christian world at the time of its publication. Only a few mathematicians were inclined to accept it, the astronomers pointing out the difficulties involved in supposing that the earth was not stationary but rotated in space. Tycho Brahe (1546–1601), a Danish astronomer, spent his life observing the heavens with the aid of improved instruments, some of which he invented, leaving a mass of new observational data to his pupil the German Johannes Kepler (1571–1630). Unlike Brahe, Kepler was early converted to the Copernican hypothesis; but as a skilled mathematician as well as a skilled astronomer, he could not feel that it was proved until he discovered the three laws which bear his name, one of which states that the planets move in an elliptical, rather than in a circular, orbit around the sun. All the observations of Brahe now supported the hypothesis, and it was left to Galileo Galilei (1564–1642) only to confirm by observation through his recently invented telescope that Jupiter and Saturn indeed had their own satellites which revolved around them and not around the earth. Galileo's formulation of the laws of motion, which solved the problems that had troubled medieval physicists, together with Kepler's laws of planetary movement, provided the material for the great synthesis of the Englishman Sir Isaac Newton (1642–1727).

Newton, pondering on the problem of motion in the universe, conjectured that the same force which drew a falling apple to the ground might be active throughout the universe, and he calculated the mathematical consequences of such a hypothesis. At once it became clear to him that gravitation was universal and accounted for the elliptical movements of the planets observed by Kepler. Newton expressed this theory in mathematical form in his *Principia Mathematica*, published in 1687, using the calculus which he and the German Gottfried Leibniz (1646–1716) had recently separately invented.

This beautifully simple and elegant explanation of movement in the universe, and the precise means by which Newton arrived at his conclusions, had a profound effect on all scientific thought and practice thereafter and shook the foundations of religious belief. It helped to enthrone human reason as the tool which could solve all problems in the external world, and it gave rise to an optimism characteristic of the eighteenth century. Now that a method for discovering scientific truths had been devised and new discoveries could be fitted into a pre-existent framework, scientific research multiplied, and the medieval notion that all important knowledge had already been revealed to man and only needed to be assimilated was quickly abandoned.

Cartesianism and Baconianism. Meanwhile two scientific philosophers of very different bent had laid their impress on European thought. The Frenchman René Descartes (1596–1650) had come to the conclusion that the only method for discovering truth was by way of universal doubt, which led him to the famous remark "I think; therefore I am" as the only truth of which he could be certain. Hence he held that the only truths are what exist in the mind, or what he called "clear and distinct ideas," since the material world can be doubted away. Thus for him mathematics was the only true science—he was the inventor of analytical geometry—because the equations are eternally true even if they do not correspond to any real and observed data in the universe. Descartes thus formulated the problem of dualism which has ever since plagued philosophers: How can the nonmaterial mind know the material universe? The Englishman Thomas Hobbes (1588–1679) proposed to solve this problem by making the mind itself material, composed of "particles" of knowledge derived from sensation; in this theory to some degree he was followed by his fellow-countryman John Locke (1632–1704), who in his essay *Concerning Human Understanding* insisted that the mind at birth was a blank slate and became able to reason only on the basis of experience. (An important consequence of Locke's teaching was the notion so prevalent in the eighteenth century that education in itself was capable of creating geniuses, thus neglecting the still imperfectly understood role of heredity in the process.) The eighteenth-century German philosopher Immanuel Kant advanced a different interpretation (see p. 187).

Francis Bacon (1561–1626), lord chancellor of England under James I, was a scientific philosher at the opposite pole from Descartes but almost equally influential, especially in his own country. Far from denying the importance of observation, he insisted that too little attention was being paid to experiment. It was his view that the laws of nature would be discovered almost exclusively by observing a sufficient number of cases (induction) and that the making of hypotheses and deducing consequences from them was greatly overdone and should be avoided. Though Cartesianism held the field in most scientific circles in the seventeenth century, Bacon came into his own in the eighteenth and nineteenth centuries. Of course modern science combines both induction and deduction; the relevance of each varies with the particular field of inquiry.

Numerous other scientists were active in these centuries, notably William Harvey (1578–1657), who discovered the circulation of the blood, and a series of Italian anatomists who followed in his footsteps; Blaise Pascal (1623–1662), French mathematician, physicist, and religious philosopher—author also of a series of remarkable aphorisms called simply *Pensées* (Thoughts), who invented the theory of probability and measured atmospheric pressure; Christian Huyghens (1629–1695), who propounded a wave theory of light; and Robert Boyle (1627–1691), the precursor of modern chemistry, who in his *Scyptical Chymist* first distinguished elements from compounds, and in the law called after him described the relation between the pressure and volume of a gas. But scientific investigators were numerous during the seventeenth century, and few can even be named here. Whitehead has called the seventeenth century the "century of genius," and the title is not misplaced. Almost all the work in subsequent centuries has been based on the fundamental discoveries and theories of this era.

Art and Literature. The age may also be called the Age of the Baroque, a term difficult to define with precision but characterized by a reaction against the coldness of classicism—vital, exuberant, and experimental. Baroque architecture and art escaped from the bounds of older traditions. Though the trend began in Italy— much of St. Peter's at Rome is in the baroque style—it had its greatest successes elsewhere, especially in Germany and Austria. Spain developed her own baroque style, which was transferred to Mexico, where it became affected to some degree by the more ancient Aztec tradition. One of the major exponents of baroque painting in the sixteenth century was the Cretan El Greco, who did most of his work in Spain. Another was the Fleming Peter Paul Rubens, whose often fleshy but always vital portraits are masterpieces in genre. The Dutchman Rembrandt (1606–1669) succeeded in disciplining his art and achieving a greater profundity than almost any other painter of portraits, but he too in many of his aspects is a baroque painter. Baroque music is likewise a distinct form of music, developed in Italy with the oratorio and cantata, and perfected in Germany in the eighteenth century with the work of Handel and the fugues of John Sebastian Bach.

If we may transfer the baroque concept to literature, John Milton (1608–1674), the English epic poet, may be regarded as the baroque poet par excellence. His *Paradise Lost* though containing many allusions to antiquity, in which Milton was steeped, has nevertheless a tremendous vitality and is full of sonorous lines, while the conflict between good and evil becomes in Milton's hands a drama on a grand scale quite foreign to either classical antiquity or the age of the Renaissance.

The seventeenth-century classical age in France, still regarded by many as the epoch when French culture reached its apex, is marked by an effort to discipline the dynamism of the baroque. The painters Poussin and Gellée achieved a kind of calm amid stress, especially in their landscapes; the great masters of tragic drama Corneille and Racine chose noble themes, many of them from classical antiquity and tried to handle them in a heroic manner. Corneille is the more vigorous, Racine the better disciplined. Molière preferred to work within the framework of comedy with a serious undertone. His sense of character can be compared only with that of Shakespeare.

In the Palace of Versailles, built for Louis XIV, the baroque is to be seen in a purer and less disciplined form. This huge structure with its Hall of Mirrors and its immense formal gardens reflected the taste of the monarch himself for the grandiose, to which his architects and builders gave full scope. What they created may or may not be a masterpiece, but it is certainly different indeed from anything conceived during the Renaissance.

The baroque itself gave way in the eighteenth century to the florid rococo, as traditional Gothic gave way in the sixteenth century to flamboyant Gothic. Almost everything else in the eighteenth century, known as the Age of the Enlightenment, was likewise foreshadowed in the seventeenth as its almost predictable outcome. If the seventeenth century was "the century of genius" the eighteenth as surely was a period of consolidation, the last period of the "old regime" before the conflagration of the French Revolution.

13 THE EIGHTEENTH CENTURY —AGE OF ENLIGHTENMENT

Under the influence of the new scientific ideas of the Age of Reason, and in particular of a group of social and political thinkers known as the *philosophes,* the majority of whom were French, almost every European ruler in the eighteenth century attempted to modernize the institutions of his country. But this long-overdue reform was in the hands of the old regime and its absolutist rulers, who had to struggle against the traditional rights and vested interests of their subjects. Moreover, too much depended on the personal abilities of these rulers, who obtained their thrones by the chance of heredity; and neither they nor their privileged subjects had any interest in sharing power with the less privileged. Under them the eighteenth century, therefore, saw no growth in democracy, not even in England, where an entrenched oligarchy had replaced the monarchy as the effective ruler of the country. It remained for the American and French Revolutions, which began before the end of the century, to set in motion the forces that led to the growth of democracy in the last two centuries—and these revolutions themselves were made necessary by the inflexibility of the old regime both in England and France, the two countries which supplied most of the political and social thought of the era.

ENLIGHTENED DESPOTISM

By the middle of the eighteenth century, most European thrones were either occupied by reformers, or, as in France, the monarch was impelled forward by advisers who believed in the theory of enlightened despotism and were ready to engage in the inevitable struggle with the privileged classes. Only in England was there a different trend; but there, unlike on the Continent, the institution had already come into existence which could later be used to bring about popular government. In England therefore no more revolutions were necessary—only a slow and gradual evolution which culminated in the years just preceding the First World War.

Great Britain—Cabinet Government and the Whig Oligarchy. When the German-born George I (1714–1727) came to the throne of England and Scotland (Great Britain), he could speak no English, and throughout his reign he remained more interested in his electorate of Hanover than in his new kingdom. This situation gave his ministers an opportunity to consolidate their position. As early as the reign of William III (1689–1702), who was likewise a foreigner, it had become clear that if the monarch was to obtain funds and legislation that he needed, he could not appoint ministers to his Council who would be unable to persuade Parliament to do their master's will. Since Parliament already possessed elected members belonging to recognizably different factions, which gradually developed into true political parties, William and his successor Anne usually found it advisable to choose their ministers from the parties which could command a majority of the parliamentary votes. This tendency was accentuated in the reign of George I, who in 1721 chose Robert Walpole, the Whig leader, as the first true chief or prime minister. Walpole remained in office under George II (1727–1760) until 1742, virtually in command of governmental policy.

The theoretical powers of the king had not in any way been diminished except in so far as he was bound by the promises of his predecessors and by his acceptance of limitations on his power as embodied in Stuart legislation. He could still choose "his" ministers, but in fact he had to accept the ministers presented for his approval by his prime minister. He could choose the latter but could not expect to manage Parliament through a prime minister unacceptable to the majority. Walpole, on the other hand, could rule only as long as he could command a majority in Parliament. He therefore had to spend much effort ensuring the election of members of the Whig party. In large part he achieved this by using his influence with the king to satisfy those politicians who could deliver votes and who could control the numerous constituencies where election was decided by a tiny number of qualified voters (pocket and rotten boroughs). The patronage at the disposal of the king was still considerable, even though officers of the Crown could not also themselves sit as members of Parliament. Thus influential Tories might be persuaded to support even a Whig government if their patronage demands were satisfied. The rule of the Whigs in the first half of the eighteenth century has thus frequently been called the Whig Oligarchy. Many members of Parliament were virtually nominated by powerful magnates (notably the Duke of Newcastle) who controlled their constituents, sometimes by the simple method of purchasing them. Within the oligarchy, however, public opinion could make itself felt, and Walpole fell from power in 1742 when his policy ceased to command the support of his fellow Parliament members.

Though George II allowed his choice of prime minister to be dictated by the majority party, George III (1760–1820) was not content to see the remnants of royal power evaporate. What the Duke of Newcastle could do, the king, with the even greater resources at his disposal, could do better. By bribery and patronage he built up his own party, sympathetic to the Tories and usually known as the "King's Friends," which for many years was able on most issues to command a majority in Parliament. It was such a government (headed by Lord North) that failed in the War of American Independence, at the same time discrediting the whole system of government by the King's Friends. When a Parliament passed a resolution deploring royal interference in government, George gradually abandoned his by now futile efforts, and a moderate Tory party led by William Pitt the Younger, came to power in 1784 in free elections. Soon afterward George became intermittently insane. Since that time the power of the British monarchy has diminished almost to zero, to be replaced by occasional influence exercised behind the scenes, and its duties have become almost exclusively ceremonial.

France—The Death Throes of the Ancient Regime. The "Grand Monarque" Louis XIV reigned so long that his eldest son and grandson both predeceased him. He was therefore succeeded by his young great-grandson Louis XV (1715–1774). Louis grew up to become an amiable and pleasure-loving king, greatly influenced by his mistresses and generally lacking interest in the government, which he left to a series of often capable advisers—especially Cardinal Fleury, whose administration (1726–1743) paralleled that of Walpole in England. France for several decades remained prosperous; but in the later years of Louis' reign, excessive expenditures on wars and the luxuries of the court began to strain the fiscal resources of the country, which had a tax structure little modified from that of the later Middle Ages and a political and social system that had become increasingly rigid and incapable of evolutionary change. The ancient land tax (*taille*) was passed on by the noble landowners to the peasants, and its proceeds could not greatly be increased without inflicting further hardship—whereas the numerous indirect taxes were collected by private enterprise (the "farm") and remitted to the king after the deduction of commission. When the king grew short of money he borrowed on the security of future taxes, leaving himself increasingly in debt and with a necessarily lower income. The classes which could most afford to pay taxes, the nobles and the privileged upper bourgeoisie, too often enjoyed absolute immunity from direct taxation. Yet the country itself remained prosperous even up to the Revolution.

The king and his ministers were well aware of the need to collect money from the upper classes. Even if they themselves had known nothing of the matter, the deluge of advice they received from the *philosophes*, especially a group of economists known as the physiocrats, would have enlightened them. But whenever they tried to impose new taxes, they were faced by an obstinate refusal from their subjects and the opposition of the parlements, in which the upper bourgeoisie and the "nobility of the robe" (bourgeois who had won or purchased titles of nobility) were entrenched. The consent of the parlements had to be obtained to make the proposed new taxes legal. At last Louis and his chancellor Maupéou abolished the old parlements, replacing them with new courts staffed by their own nominees (1771). But the rage of the dispossessed was so great that Louis XVI, who came to the throne three years later, abolished the new system in the interests of his own popularity and peace of mind, thereby ensuring the bankruptcy of his government. These developments, however, will be considered in Chapter 14 as part of the background for the Revolution.

The wars of Louis XIV were continued by Louis XV with generally indifferent success. Lorraine and Corsica were added to France, but the greater part of the French colonial empire was lost to the British (see p. 185). Eighteenth-century wars were fought almost entirely by professional soldiers in the employ of the various governments, supposedly in the intersts of the balance of power, which became a dominant conception during the century. Alliances changed frequently, and there was relatively small loss of life in battle. Indeed, it was widely thought that the era of the great wars had come to an end, to be replaced by minor frontier adjustments with a minimum of actual fighting.

The first war (1733–1735) was fought over the succession of the Polish throne, the French backing Stanislaus, a Polish nobleman who had already been king in the early part of the century under

Swedish protection and whose daughter had recently married Louis XV. Austria and Prussia preferred the Elector of Saxony and took to arms when the majority in the Polish diet chose Stanislaus. At the end of the war Stanislaus renounced the throne in exchange for the duchy of Lorraine, ceded by the emperor on the condition that it should go to France after the death of its new duke.

In 1740 the male Hapsburg line became extinct. The last monarch, Charles VI, had tried to obtain the consent of the European powers to the Pragmatic Sanction, under which the Austrian lands should remain intact and go to his eldest daughter. Charles Albert, the elector of Bavaria, a collateral descendant of Charles V, also claimed the throne. The War of the Austrian Succession which followed concerned Germany more than France and will be dealt with later— though, since England backed Charles VI's daughter Maria Theresa, it led to war between England and France on the Continent and to the French and Indian War in America. During the course of the war the French conquered the Austrian Netherlands but restored them at the treaty of Aix-la-Chapelle (1748). Louis XV backed the elector Charles Albert, who was chosen emperor and nominally ruled for three years until Maria Theresa secured her throne and her husband became emperor as Francis I (1745).

The Seven Years' War (1756–1763) was a major European conflagration which resulted in France's loss of Canada to Britain. On the European continent French arms, used this time in support of Austria and against Prussia, were largely unsuccessful, and the Treaty of Paris (unfavorable to France) that followed increased the unpopularity of Louis XV at home, while it diminished still further the financial resources that remained to him.

Prussia. Much of the unrest on the Continent was the result of the ambitions of the new kingdom of Prussia and the military force that had been built up by Frederick William I, a disciplinarian and martinet, who organized a strong and well-trained professional army, which his son Frederick II, the Great (1740–1786), used to fulfill his ambitions. This new state could now challenge the Austrian Hapsburgs on equal terms, as had never previously been possible for any German ruler.

Frederick the Great at home was an "enlightened despot," the ideal king of the *philosophes,* who welcomed them to his court and for a time gave his hospitality to Voltaire, the most articulate of them. The Hohenzollerns of Prussia had always been autocrats whose word was law, and Frederick had inherited an efficient bureaucracy of dedicated royal officials unequaled in Europe. But at the same time he wished to enlarge his kingdom by the addition, in particular, of Silesia, which belonged to Austria. He took it from Maria Theresa, the Austrian queen, in the War of the Austrian Succession. With England as ally and paymaster who provided troops to defend the English king's possession of Hanover, Frederick began the Seven Years' War in 1756 by driving into Saxony toward Bohemia. But Austria, anxious to win back Silesia, in alliance with France, who was already fighting with England in America, held him. When this alliance was joined by Russia under the tsarina Elizabeth, daughter of Peter the Great, Frederick could only with great difficulty maintain himself, in spite of some British support mostly directed against France. At a crucial moment when he was facing imminent defeat Elizabeth died, to be succeeded by Peter III, an unbalanced young man who was a devoted admirer of Frederick and Prussia. Though Peter was soon overthrown in a palace revolution which brought his wife Catherine (the Great) to the throne, he had ruled long enough to take his troops out of the war (1762). By this time all the powers were war-weary and Frederick could make peace without loss, but without gains except Silesia, which was now finally ceded by Austria.

The next years were spent by Frederick in trying to restore his shattered armies and finances, codifying the law, and engaging in extensive public works. In 1772, while Russia was engaged in an eventually victorious war with Turkey, Frederick proposed to her and to Austria that Poland, which was in large measure dominated by Russia, should be partitioned among the three powers. Though his main desire was to add West Prussia to his domains, thus uniting several of the scattered Hohenzollern possessions, the move was also intended to prevent Austria and Russia from aggrandizing themselves unduly at the expense of Turkey. Presented with this diversion, the powers hastened to strip the feeble kingdom of Poland of its outlying territories. Further partitions were arranged in 1793 and 1795 under Frederick's successor. Thus Prussia by the last decade of the century was a great power with a much enlarged territory—though too weak, as it proved, to be able to stand against Napoleon.

Austria and the Empire. Maria Theresa (1740–1780), the first and last Hapsburg woman to sit on the Austrian throne, was in many respects Austria's greatest ruler. Forced by the European powers, especially by Frederick, to fight hard for her throne, she succeeded in arousing the latent chivalry in particular of her Hungarian subjects, who helped to restore her to her throne at the cost of Silesia, which had to be ceded to Frederick. During her reign the army and finances were greatly improved; though the army was now second to that of Prussia in the Germanies, it won many victories. She provided aids to agriculture and asserted her power over the numerous feudal principalities in the Austrian territory, thus in effect creating an Austrian national state within the still large Hapsburg Empire, made up of many nationalities. She herself, however, was not greatly influenced by the ideas of the *philosophes*, which by the time of her death had saturated Europe.

Her son, on the contrary, was probably the most doctrinaire of all enlightened despots. Joseph II, emperor from 1765 and sole ruler of Austria from 1780 to 1790, thus reigning at the moment when France was tottering toward her revolution, believed that he could create a revolution in Austria from above by despotic means. For all ten years of his reign streams of new laws issued from his palace, abolishing serfdom and feudalism, granting toleration to all religions, changing the tax and landholding system in the direction advocated by the physiocrats, founding hospitals and asylums, and attempting to impose the German language on all his subjects in the interest of efficiency. He reigned for too short a time to accomplish the majority of his aims, and he encountered opposition, even ridicule, from his ministers and his subjects. Leopold II, his brother who succeeded him in 1790 but ruled the Empire for only two years, had already achieved much in his Italian grand duchy of Tuscany by less arbitrary methods. He slowed the pace of reform in Austria and repealed some of Joseph's more radical measures. But he made no attempt to set back the clock. In the last year of his life he organized an alliance with Prussia to prevent the leaders of the French Revolution from undertaking an aggressive war outside their boundaries. His successor, Francis II (1792–1835, from 1806 emperor only of Austria), intervened in the French Revolution with disastrous results for Austria—and for Marie Antoinette, the sister of Joseph and Leopold, who as queen of France was guillotined during the Revolution.

The Iberian Peninsula. Bourbon rule in Spain, though not especially efficient by contemporary French standards, nevertheless breathed new life into the decadent Spanish monarchy. During the reign of Charles III (1759–1788) many administrative reforms were accomplished which helped to modernize the country, though all tended to exalt the rule of the monarch, a typical enlightened despot. The Church was assisted in so far as it remained subservient to the king, who ruled what was virtually a national Church (by the Concordat of 1754, arranged by Charles' predecessor Ferdinand VI). But Charles felt that the Jesuit Order was an impediment to his absolutism. He therefore deported some ten thousand Jesuits to the Papal States and sent his minister Floridablanca as ambassador to Rome to negotiate for the suppression of the whole order. The pope, besieged by similar requests from other Catholic monarchs, agreed to dissolve it in 1773. The Jesuits were not re-established until 1814.

In Portugal "enlightened despotism" triumphed in the reign of Joseph I (1750–1777), who allowed his minister the Marquis de Pombal to rule in his name. Pombal devoted himself to breaking the power of the Church and the nobles, while at the same time fostering technical education and improving the finances and industry of the country. After a serious earthquake in Lisbon in 1755 he energetically set to work to rebuild the city. He expelled the Jesuits from Portugal and Brazil (1759). Bitterly hated for his ruthlessness, he was put on trial, convicted, and sent into exile under the rule of Joseph's successor Maria I, who permitted the nobles to recover their old position.

Thus, neither in Spain nor in Portugal did the reform endure for long; but the administrative modernization, especially in the Spanish colonies, was effective and enabled Spain in the next century to resist the colonial independence movement longer than might otherwise have been possible.

Scandinavia. Sweden and Denmark both experienced periods of enlightened despotism in the eighteenth century. Gustavus III of Sweden (1771–1792) proclaimed religious toleration, attempted to improve the trade of his country, and assumed full authority over administration. After having arranged for a sham rebellion, which he put down with the aid of his army, he suppressed the privileges and rights of the nobility. He was eventually assassinated in the early years of the French Revolution by a hireling of the nobles. Denmark had a curious enlightened despot in the person of a German-born doctor who won the support of his weak-minded employer Christian VII (1766–1808). This man, John Frederick Struensee, ruled Denmark for less than two years, during which he attempted to modernize every phase of life in the country, while insisting on religious toleration and freedom of the press in accordance with the teachings of the *philosophes*. Like other enlightened despots he founded hospitals, provided care for foundlings, and attempted to improve trade. But he was not strong enough to take on the privileged officer caste also and was overthrown by a conspiracy and executed. After a decade of reaction the reform was resumed under another minister of German ancestry who virtually abolished serfdom in the country (1788).

Poland. Mention has already been made of the disintegration of the Polish state during the eighteenth century and the gradual ascendancy of Russia over the country. In 1768 the formation of an anti-Russian association, known as the Confederation of the Bar for Faith and Freedom, led to a violent civil war, which was suppressed by the Russians—supported at first by the modernizing Polish king Stanislaus II (1764–1795), who had been declared deposed by the Confederation. The Russian intervention and its attempted diversion by the Turks, who supported "Polish liberties," led to the First Partition of Poland in 1772. After the partition Stanislaus and his people tried desperately to strengthen and reform the state, and a new constitution, which abolished the *liberum veto* and created a hereditary monarchy, was accepted in 1791. But the Russians would not permit this and forced a second partition of the hapless country in 1793, in which Prussia but not Austria shared. This in turn led to a patriotic national uprising under the leadership, not of Stanislaus who abdicated, but of a patriot general, Thaddeus Kosciusko, who had fought on the American side in the War of Independence. This attempt to defeat the allied armies of Prussia and Russia was hopeless from the beginning, and the final partition of 1795 put an end to Polish independence for more than a century. Russia gained Lithuania and the Ukraine by the partitions; Prussia consolidated her territories as far as Warsaw; while Austria, who shared in the third partition, gained the territory to the south of Warsaw, including the ancient cultural center of Cracow.

Russia. After the death of Peter the Great in 1725, the throne passed first to Peter's second wife, then to several Romanovs of a collateral line. From 1730 to 1741 the government fell into the hands of German advisers until the accession of Elizabeth (1741–1762), younger daughter of Peter the Great. During her reign the Russian nobility asserted itself once more, winning various privileges from the tsarina. At the same time the Russians continued to encroach on Poland and took part of Finland from Sweden. If Elizabeth had lived a little longer, her armies would no doubt have crushed Frederick the Great and won major concessions in central Europe. But, as we have seen, Peter III withdrew from the war and was ousted by his wife, the minor German princess Sophia von Anhalt-Zerbst, who took the name of Catherine (1762–1796).

Catherine (the Great) attempted to be an enlightened despot and offered hospitality to several leading French *philosophes*. Faced with still powerful nobles entrenched in their various fiefs, each with its different laws and customs, she tried to bring some semblance of common law into the country through a commission which provided a tremendous amount of data—of which she made great use, even though she could not persuade and dared not coerce the nobles into abandoning their privileges. The serfs remained unemancipated until after the middle of the nineteenth century, and indeed serfdom was extended by the nobles during her reign. Her foreign policy was directed exclusively toward the aggrandizement of her country, and in this she was brilliantly successful, partitioning Poland, as has been described, and winning the Crimea by force of arms from the Turkish sultanate. She disapproved wholeheartedly, however, of the French Revolution and distrusted democratic institutions. By her industry and expansionary policy, she prepared the groundwork for the key role played by her grandson Alexander I (1801–1825) in defeating Napoleon, and her ideas were to bear further fruit in Alexander's comparative liberalism during the early years of his reign.

THE EXPANSION OF EUROPE TO THE FRENCH REVOLUTION

During the centuries following the discovery of America and the first efforts at colonization, all major European powers acquired colonies beyond the borders of Europe; and most of the European wars of the period were reflected in small-scale colonial wars, especially between the British and French in North America.

British Expansion. The earliest British North American settlements were founded at the beginning of the sixteenth century. In 1607 the Jamestown colony in Virginia was founded by Captain John Smith, who also explored the coast of New England but could not start a colony there. In 1620 the Pilgrims, in search of religious freedom, arrived at Cape Cod in New England; other coastal settlements quickly followed. Though most of them were self-governing at the beginning, by 1700 a majority were under royal governors appointed by the home country and all owed allegiance to the English monarch. By the end of the seventeenth century all European competitors had been driven from the eastern seaboard between Nova

Scotia and Spanish Florida, including the Dutch, whose settlement of New Amsterdam became New York in 1664. By 1733 when Georgia was founded, there were thirteen separate British colonies, each with a measure of self-government.

France in North America. In 1606 the French founded Port Royal in present-day Nova Scotia, and Champlain founded Quebec two years later, thus beginning the conquest of French Canada. In the late seventeenth century Père Marquette and La Salle explored extensively inland from the north, discovering the Mississippi River and sailing to its mouth. This expedition was followed by the founding of Mobile and New Orleans in the early eighteenth century. Cadillac founded Detroit in 1701.

These explorations and conquests brought France and Britain into frequent conflict, in which Spain was sometimes involved. During the War of the Spanish Succession, called in America Queen Anne's War, the British captured Acadia (Nova Scotia), deporting the French colonists to New Orleans, and were given secure possession of the disputed island of Newfoundland. But the French retained Cape Breton Island with its strong fortress of Louisburg. In King George's War (War of Austrian Succession) the British captured Louisburg but restored it by the subsequent peace treaty. Both French and British by this time were expanding rapidly in the interior, and the British colonists undertook the greater part of the defense operations. In 1755 the French and Indian War broke out (Seven Years' War in Europe), which William Pitt the Elder, the British war minister, recognized as a life-and-death struggle for the possession of North America. He provided enough reinforcements and supplies to win a complete victory in 1759 when Quebec fell to General Wolfe. After this war (Peace of Paris, 1763) France ceded all Canada to Britain and in return received back a number of West Indian Islands lost in the war. Spain ceded Florida to Britain. In 1774 the British passed the Quebec Act guaranteeing political and religious rights to the French settlers in Canada, who at this time considerably outnumbered the British.

Expansion to the East. When the Portuguese empire in the east began to decay at the end of the sixteenth century, it was the seafaring Dutch who first broke their monopoly. The Dutch East India Company chartered in 1602 at once became active in the Far East, founding Batavia on the island of Java in 1619, and driving the Portuguese from their major trading center of Malacca in 1641. In the 1620's, following a massacre of Englishmen in the area, the

Dutch established a trade monopoly in what is now Indonesia, which was not seriously disputed until the Napoleonic wars.

The British East India Company, founded in 1600 with a similar monopoly from the British crown, for a long time did not have much success in the Far East, where it was confronted with hostile governments little interested in its trade. But in India, where the Mogul Empire was gradually disintegrating, representatives of the Company established a foothold in the seventeenth century and improved their position by alliances with one Indian prince against another. In the early eighteenth century they met serious opposition from the French, who were engaged in the same pursuits. But the British company always received more reliable assistance from home than the French did. Though the Frenchman Dupleix was within measurable distance at one time of conquering all India and ousting the British, in 1757 Robert Clive, commander of the Company's army, decisively defeated the French and their native allies at the Battle of Plassey, and British rule over the whole country was gradually consolidated. The British government, however, could not tolerate the unfettered rule of the Company indefinitely when such a huge territory was at stake. In 1774 a governor-general appointed by the Crown, though he was still paid by the Company, took over the responsibility for the administration of the empire. This system of joint rule continued until 1858, when the Crown, following the revolt of natives in the Company's army (Sepoy Mutiny of 1857) annexed the entire country. Queen Victoria became "Empress of India" in 1877.

EIGHTEENTH-CENTURY SCIENCE AND THOUGHT

The entire atmosphere of European thought changed markedly as the result of a new view of the world derived from the scientific discoveries of the Age of Reason. The consequence drawn by most thinkers from the Newtonian laws was that the universe itself was like a machine, which might or might not have been set in motion by God, but at all events now was running smoothly without further interference. The notion that there were unbreakable laws in Nature was believed to be applicable in all fields of inquiry, from which there resulted a prolonged quest to discover such laws, deduce consequences from them, and apply them. It was not considered to be so important to observe the empirical phenomena, discover what actually happens in the world, and guide one's actions accordingly.

Science. The major achievements of the century came in the field of chemistry with the work of Henry Cavendish (1731–1810), who isolated hydrogen and discovered the composition of water, Joseph Priestley (1733–1804), who isolated oxygen, and Joseph Black (1728–1799), who discovered carbon dioxide. Throughout most of the century the erroneous theory that a heat substance called phlogiston existed prevented any great advance in the understanding of heat. This theory was discredited by the careful experiments of Antoine Lavoisier (1743–1794), who showed that heat is a product of oxidation. Botany was advanced by the work of classification accomplished by the Swede Carl von Linné (Linnaeus) (1707–1778), and the encyclopaedic work of the Frenchman George, comte de Buffon (1707–1788), prolific both in observations and theories. Toward the end of the century, Pierre Laplace (1749–1827) produced the hypothesis of the primal nebula to account for the origin of the earth. This hypothesis had already been advanced by one of the greatest philosophers of Western civilization, Immanuel Kant (1724–1804), who devoted most of his thought to the theory of knowledge (epistemology), and the question of how it is that the immaterial mind knows anything of the material world. He concluded that in all observation there is always the person observing, the representation in his mind of the thing observed, and the "thing-in-itself," which causally accounts for the nature of the representation but can never be truly known. George Berkeley, an Irish bishop (1685–1753), interested by the same problem, argued that since no observation is possible in the absence of an observer ("to be is to be perceived"), it cannot be shown that matter exists; in other words, all knowledge is subjective. David Hume (1711–1776), arguing along the same lines, came to the conclusion that the existence of a mind can no more be taken for granted than the existence of matter, and thus emerged in complete skepticism.

Scientific thought influenced religion in that men obsessed with the supremacy of reason came to believe that religion itself must be reasonable, and turned their criticism upon the hitherto accepted beliefs of Christianity, whose teachings of a savior, a God incarnated as man, who had sacrificed himself for humanity, appeared far from reasonable. Thus the tendency was toward regarding Jesus Christ as a good man who by his life and death had provided mankind with an excellent example and who had taught ethical principles which tended to elevate morality. Others argued that the universe showed the presence of a mastermind as creator, who could be regarded as a Supreme Being. These men were called deists, since they accepted at least an abstract notion of deity, whereas others like

Baron d'Holbach insisted that nature and the universe were simply facts to be accepted as such, with no need to postulate any being responsible for their existence. Such men went all the way to atheism.

As a reaction to this type of thought, religious leaders arose who claimed that the existence of God and the truths of Christianity were to be taken on faith, to which reason was even an impediment. These men, especially the brothers John and Charles Wesley (1703–1791, 1707–1788) preached salvation solely by faith in Christ, founding what came to be called Methodism, though the brothers themselves remained to the end within the Anglican Church. A different kind of reaction appears in the writings of Jean-Jacques Rousseau (1712–1778). Rousseau wished to escape from the aridity of eighteenth-century thought, and he held that there was a natural religion appealing to the human heart which all men could accept. He devoted his immensely influential educational treatise *Émile* to this theme. He believed that civilization tended to corrupt and that all education should be devoted toward developing the native faculties and natural goodness of man.

Political Thought. In political thought Rousseau gave his attention to the notion of a social contract advanced in the seventeenth century by Hobbes and Locke. Whereas Hobbes had imagined the origin of government to be in a contract entered into by primitive man according to which the ruler was required only to provide protection, Locke had supposed that the monarch under the social contract was bound to observe traditional rights of his subjects, who had the right to replace him if he failed in his task. Rousseau considered that sovereignty was vested in society as a whole, which had to agree to all laws imposed upon it; all citizens should try to ascertain the "general will" of the people. The general will in popular assemblies could be determined by majority vote by which any dissident minority should be bound. Hobbes's version of the social contract therefore favored efficient despotism, Locke's a limited constitutional monarchy, and Rousseau's democracy. Montesquieu (1689–1755), far more empirical than the other political thinkers of the century, wrote a collection of observations about the governments of his day and of antiquity in a book called the *Spirit of the Laws*, in which he drew conclusions as to which governments were best and set forth the principles on which their present actions should be based. Other thinkers, such as Voltaire (1694–1778) and the great majority of the *philosophes*, approved the enlightened despotism of the age but reserved for themselves the right to criticize the government on the ground that it was not, according to their views, sufficiently enlightened; and they poured forth numerous pamphlets during the century urging scientifically acceptable measures to improve the conditions of the people in the various European states.

Encyclopédie. The most important work of the century was undoubtedly the great twenty-eight volume French *Encyclopédie* edited by Denis Diderot (1713–1784), which made use of the talents of great writers and thinkers of the day, especially those whose political and scientific views were acceptable to the *philosophes*. The thread running through the whole is polite skepticism tinged with scientific determinism. The book therefore was found unacceptable by the still influential Jesuits and other religious thinkers, and had to be published clandestinely when the authorities took exception to it. Nevertheless, in due course the whole was published and very widely distributed, especially in France; and it influenced in some degree all the enlightened despots of the century.

Economic Science. Lastly mention should be made of the first body of serious economic thought since the Middle Ages. The physiocrats advocated a single land tax, absolute freedom from taxation of all manufactured and industrial goods, and the removal of all barriers to free trade—such as the dues imposed by feudal lords and monarchs which prevented the free movement of goods within a single country. Much influenced by the physiocrats was the Scotsman Adam Smith (1723–1790), the first major prophet of laissez faire, who launched in his *Wealth of Nations* an attack upon mercantilist policies. The economic thinkers based their proposed policies on the notion that there were three natural rights of man—life, liberty, and property—which should not be interfered with by governments. Enlightened self-interest and free competition would thereupon ensure the fair price of goods in the market. The English clergyman and economist Thomas Malthus (1766–1834), however, pointed out that population pressure would in time lead to poverty, since population increased by a higher ratio than production. Another English economist, David Ricardo (1772–1823), who lived in the early days of the Industrial Revolution, thought that the pressure for jobs by the working classes would tend to depress their wages (Iron Law of Wages) in the competitive struggle.

With these last two thinkers we enter the nineteenth century and the world of the Industrial Revolution, which will be discussed in Chapter 15.

14 THE AMERICAN AND FRENCH REVOLUTIONS AND THEIR CONSEQUENCES

The last quarter of the eighteenth century saw the first two great revolutions of the modern world. In the American colonies the successful rebellion against British rule was accompanied by enough changes in the form of government to justify the claim that it was a "revolutionary war" as well as a war for independence. The French Revolution was directed against the existing form of government and was thus a true revolution. It was followed by a military dictatorship whose ultimate defeat in battle resulted in a restoration of the monarchy shorn of its pre-Revolutionary absolutism.

THE FOUNDING OF THE UNITED STATES OF AMERICA

The British North American colonies had been founded in large measure by religious dissidents who wished to escape both from the pervasive established Church of England (and its hierarchy of clerics, which dominated English religious life) and from the oppressive laws against those who did not conform. Nevertheless, few wished to cut themselves off from the mother country, the major source of immigrants, whose culture and traditions were the colonists' own. Objection was raised only in a few quarters as the Crown gradually assumed complete responsibility for the settlements. By the eighteenth century the thirteen separate colonies all had their own legislative assemblies; but their duties and responsibilities were limited. The British Parliament passed major legislation binding on the colonies, while British governors controlled the executive and were in charge of law and order. As long as the colonists felt themselves endangered either by the French or by Indian tribes, they appreciated the aid they received from home and acquiesced in the limited freedom of decision which was its consequence. When the British won their resounding victory over the French in the Seven Years' War (1756–1763) and French Canada was ceded to them, the numerous grievances of the colonists against their British rulers could be given expression more safely. Now that they had no longer anything to fear from the French, they could more actively oppose British domination, especially those actions which adversely affected their growing mercantile interests.

The Colonial Conflict and the Declaration of Independence. The acquisition of Canada by the British did not reduce their expenses, and the decision was made early in the new reign of George III to compel the colonists to bear their share of the increased costs of the administration. The colonists, who had always objected to taxation imposed upon them without their consent, claimed the traditional rights of Englishmen and raised the cry of "No taxation without representation." For more than a century the articulate merchant class, especially in New England and Virginia, had objected to the British mercantilist view of the colonies as suppliers of raw materials and consumers of British manufactured goods and to the neglect of colonial interests under British tariff and navigation laws. When after 1763 the British attempted to tax the colonists (especially by the Stamp Act of 1765) and imposed what the latter regarded as discriminating duties on their products, the colonial legislatures began to pass resolutions against them. The demand for outright independence grew, advocated especially by such radicals as Samuel Adams of Massachusetts and the fiery orator Patrick Henry of Virginia. The Englishman Tom Paine was an unexpected recruit to the cause, stirring up colonial opposition by a series of powerful but well-reasoned pamphlets. In 1773 the British passed a particularly discriminatory duty on imported tea, which favored the interests of the British East India Company, whereupon colonists disguised as Indians dumped a shipload of tea in Boston harbor.

As the British refused to listen to their grievances, and indeed passed a new series of laws known as the Intolerable Acts, the colonists summoned a Continental Congress (September, 1774), which called for a boycott of British imports. The following year war broke out, and Congress authorized the enrollment of an army with George Washington as commander in chief. On July 4, 1776, Congress declared the independence of the colonies in a document drawn up by Thomas Jefferson which recounted acts of "tyranny" perpetrated by George III. The Declaration of Independence was solidly based upon the political thought of John Locke, who had held that when a monarch did not uphold the "natural rights" of men, the people had the right to depose him.

The War of Independence. In spite of many defeats at the hands of the more experienced British troops, the Continental army won the two decisive victories of the war. In 1777 the British army led by General Burgoyne was surrounded and compelled to surrender at Saratoga. As a result of this victory, the French, still smarting from their defeat in the Seven Years' War, entered into an alliance with the colonists (1778) and provided crucial aid. In 1779 Spain joined France in the hope of recovering Florida. In 1781 the colonists penned the British general Cornwallis into Yorktown in Virginia and forced him to surrender—whereupon negotiations began with the British, which were completed in 1783 (Treaty of Paris). The independence of the United States was recognized, and the boundaries between the new nation and the neighboring British territories were settled. The French gained almost nothing, but Britain ceded Florida back to Spain. (Florida, which had remained conspicuously loyal to Britain and had been an important base for the British armies during the war, was not acquired by the United States until 1819.)

The Federal Constitution of 1787. During the war Congress had continued to meet, agreeing in 1777 to the Articles of Confederation, under which the separate sovereign states entered into a confederation with the title of the United States of America. After the war the defects of this first constitution were soon recognized, especially the lack of sufficient cohesion between the states. A Constitutional Convention therefore met in 1787 at Philadelphia, which hammered out a federal constitution. This was ratified by the legislatures of the separate states and came into effect in 1788. The Constitution provided for a federal government with a Congress consisting of two legislative bodies, the House of Representatives and the Senate; an executive branch headed by a president; and a judicial branch headed by a supreme court. The House of Representatives was to be elected on a basis of population, but the Senate would comprise two members from each state. The president was to be chosen by an electoral college appointed by the states. George Washington was inaugurated as the first president in 1789. In 1789 also Congress passed the Judiciary Act establishing the Supreme Court, which was empowered to enforce the Constitution as the supreme law of the land (an authority which the Court in the case of *Marbury* v. *Madison* held to be above acts of Congress). Thus the federal government had the means for establishing some uniformity between state and national law and for preventing any law from violating constitutional provisions. The first ten amendments to the Constitution, which came into effect in 1791, incorporated most of the "traditional rights" of Englishmen (especially those embodied in the Bill of Rights of 1689) and established some areas in which Congress should not be permitted to legislate. This Constitution, with its authority strengthened by the "implied powers" theory developed by Chief Justice John Marshall and by broadening concepts of the rights that it provides, is still in effect; it has been amended only infrequently since 1789.

It only remains to be noted that between 1812 and 1814 the young United States again engaged in war with the British over the question of freedom for maritime trade. Some boundary adjustments followed at the conclusion of this war, which, among other results, ensured that Canada would remain a separate country from the United States.

THE FRENCH REVOLUTION

The effect of the American Revolution in Europe was considerable. Most impressive to European thinkers, especially in France, was the demonstration that ordinary citizens could overthrow a monarchy and establish a republic ruled by themselves through their representatives, and that such a government could survive. What British colonists in America, many of them simple farmers and merchants, could do, the long-civilized French could surely do as well. Men such as Thomas Paine, whose pamphlet *Common Sense* had greatly influenced the Americans, were prepared to support any French efforts in the same direction. In France, however, there was not only an absolutist monarchy but also privileged classes such as the clergy and the nobility, from which strong resistance might be expected. Nevertheless, revolutionary clubs were formed which gave serious thought as to how the government could be overthrown and what was to replace the monarchy when it fell. These clubs, especially the Jacobin, won ever greater influence as the Revolution progressed, even though they were responsible in a very small degree for its outbreak in 1789.

The Bankruptcy of the Government. Although there were many grievances against the old regime on the part of all classes of society, almost certainly none of these taken either together or in isolation would have led to a revolution if the government had not ceased to be able to govern for lack of the financial means to do so. For many decades the *philosophes* had complained of the unenlightened nature of the regime, and some, especially Voltaire, had criticized the superstition and intolerance of the Church. The peasants resented the continued dominance of their noble landlords and the fact that they still had to pay dues inherited from the Middle Ages. All classes resented government monopolies and the burden of excessive indirect taxation. The bourgeoisie, who felt themselves to be the only really productive class, objected to the tax immunities enjoyed by the nobles and the Church, and many of them wished for a share in the government. The city masses were hardest hit by the pre-Revolution price inflation; their grievances against the regime are reflected in the very active part they took in bringing it to an end.

The government, as described in Chapter 13, had tried without success to win the assent of the privileged classes to some diminution of their privileges. Louis XVI, who came to the throne in 1774, abandoned the efforts of his predecessor to subject the parlements to royal authority, preferring to authorize piecemeal reforms through a series of ministers, some of whom were both able and determined, but they were unable to accomplish much against the obstinate opposition of those affected. The king's government, unable to increase its income, heavily in debt, and unwilling to curtail its expenses, moved toward bankruptcy—even though the country for the most part remained as prosperous as ever. French participation in the American War for Independence increased the load of debt while achieving no worthwhile gains. In 1787 Louis called an assembly of notables which came up with no acceptable solution. In 1788, therefore, bowing to pressure from all sides, he summoned the States-General, which had not met since 1614, in the hope that it would approve of some reforms and be willing to consent to putting them into effect.

The States-General. The States-General was made up of three estates: the clergy, the nobility, and the so-called Third Estate, the bourgeoisie. Since no one knew in detail the composition of the seventeenth-century States-General, it was decided to allow the Third Estate to have six hundred representatives, as many as the other two estates combined. These were by far the most militant of the representatives, since they were fighting not to retain their privileges but to win reforms. Louis wished the representatives to vote by estates, with a built-in majority of two estates to one. Naturally the Third Estate would have none of this and insisted on converting the meeting into a National Assembly, in which demand the king acquiesced, since for the moment he lacked military strength to enforce his will. When he began to concentrate troops in the capital, the Parisian mob stormed the fortress and prison of the Bastille, this event marking the beginning of the violent phase of what had not yet become a revolution. A few days later great numbers of peasants began to take matters into their own hands (the "Great Fear") and dispossess the nobles by force. Thereupon the representatives of the latter in a grand gesture abolished their feudal rights over the peasants, who were thereafter satisfied and resisted the spread of the revolution.

The Constitutional Monarchy. In 1790 the National Assembly passed a Declaration of the Rights of Man, influenced by the American Declaration of Independence and probably the various bills of rights of some American states, as well as by the English Bill of Rights. It was also influenced by the ideas of the *philosophes,* notably Rousseau, as evidenced by the appearance of his famous formula in Article VI: "Law is the expression of the general will." Other articles affirmed such principles as that all sovereignty resides in the nation, that men are born and remain free and equal in rights, and that the natural rights of men are liberty, property, security, and resistance to oppression. The more specific paragraphs guarantee freedom of religion, speech, and publication, and forbid sequestration of property without compensation and *ex post facto* laws.

The National Assembly from the beginning proceeded to sequestrate lands belonging to the Church, in part for the purpose of obtaining funds. In 1790 it passed the Civil Constitution of the Clergy, which in effect placed the Church under the state and provided that all clergymen should be paid from state funds. By the end of 1790 it had also written a constitution which retained the monarchy, but gave the king only a suspensory veto. All legislation was reserved for a single-chamber legislative assembly. Louis accepted both constitutions only with reservations, but he was more seriously disturbed by the Civil Constitution of the Clergy, since he was a devout Catholic. When Pope Pius VI after long deliberation refused to accept it, Louis rescinded his own approval and, urged by emigré nobles and antirevolutionists, fled toward the frontier (June, 1791). He was captured and returned to Paris, and thereafter kept under close watch.

The National Convention and the Reign of Terror. Clearly a limited monarchy, such as was established by the National Assembly, needed the co-operation of the king. But Louis in fact was no longer interested in it. He had at first accepted it without conviction; now he was opposed to it, in which attitude he was backed not only by the emigrés but also by the other monarchs of Europe, who, trembling for their own thrones, issued threats to the Assembly which caused the downfall of the first government under the new regime. From the middle of 1791 the Assembly, and its successor, the National Convention, fell increasingly under the rule of two republican groups, the Girondists, who were the more moderate, and the Jacobins, whose leaders were Georges Danton and Maximilien Robespierre. (More extreme than the Jacobins were the Hébertists, who advocated a democratic republic under proletarian rule.)

Without having seriously prepared for war with foreign powers, the Girondist ministry in 1792 plunged the country into hostilities with Austria and Prussia, and France initially suffered several minor defeats. Thereupon the Girondist ministry fell, mobs attacked the royal palace, and the legislative assembly decided to abolish itself and called for a new republican constitution to be prepared by a national convention elected by manhood suffrage. A victory at Valmy (September 20, 1792) over the Prussians renewed French confidence in their ability to check foreign intervention, and the National Convention met. It abolished the monarchy on September 21, 1792, and executed Louis XVI in January, 1793.

War then began in earnest against a powerful alliance of European nations, and the executive power was entrusted by the Convention to a Committee of Public Safety, dominated by Jacobins. There ensued the so-called Reign of Terror, during which a revolutionary tribunal tried and executed all suspected counterrevolutionaries, including peasants and refractory priests who had risen in an insurrection against the regime. The government attempted to establish wage and price control, and ordered mass conscription (the first in modern history), which, in spite of resistance to it, eventually produced a French army able by virtue of its numbers, unmatched in any other country, to dominate Europe.

Meanwhile the Jacobin majority in the Convention brought its more moderate opponents, the Girondists, to trial and executed those of their leaders who did not escape to the provinces, abolished the traditional worship of God, and under the leadership of the deist Robespierre instituted a festival of the Supreme Being. Robespierre first isolated the Hébertists and executed their leaders and then turned on Danton, who was guillotined in April, 1794. By July Robespierre had created so many enemies within the Committee of

Public Safety and in the Convention that a coalition succeeded in ousting him and sending him to the guillotine. This event marked the end of the Reign of Terror. The remnant of the Girondists returned to the Convention; the Jacobins were discredited; and moderate elements resumed control (Thermidorean Reaction). The third Revolutionary constitution was then passed, which set up a directory of five members and a bicameral legislature. Opposition to the provision that two-thirds of the new legislative bodies should be made up of outgoing members of the Convention was thwarted by a Corsican artillery officer, Napoleon Bonaparte, who was rewarded by a grateful Directory with a military command in Italy.

The Directory and the Consulate. Meanwhile the war had been going favorably for France in Europe, and the French troops had been fairly widely accepted by foreign peoples as an army of liberation from their own absolutist governments. Prussia had been forced to make peace on the basis of the cession of the left bank of the Rhine to France; Holland had become the Batavian Republic under French protection; and Flanders (Austrian Netherlands) had been annexed, though Austria had not yet accepted the conquest. Britain was still at war with France, as she remained until 1801; but she played little part in the land warfare in these years, contenting herself with subsidizing anti-French alliances and strengthening her position at sea.

It was the army led by Napoleon in Italy that was conspicuously successful under the rule of the Directory. After a series of brilliant campaigns Napoleon compelled the Austrians to sign the Treaty of Campo Formio (1797), under which Austria ceded Flanders and accepted the loss of various Italian territories. Napoleon himself set up the Cisalpine and Ligurian republics in north Italy; other French armies organized the Helvetic Republic of Switzerland, the Parthenopean Republic of Naples, and the Roman Republic made up of the Papal States. All were client states of France, and their establishment marked the apogee of French revolutionary activity abroad.

At home the Directors, who were corrupt and unpopular even while their armies won victories, repudiated two-thirds of the national debt, and after one conspicuous failure eventually succeeded in restoring a sound currency. An election held halfway through their term was nullified when a royalist majority resulted. Thereafter it was more clear than ever that the Directory could survive only by the help of the military, and its authority as a government disintegrated. In 1798 Napoleon, its one conspicuous military find, was given at his own request a command in Egypt. But while he was away the other French armies in Europe had to submit to a number of humiliating defeats at the hands of the Second Coalition (Britain, Austria, and Russia), until the Russians withdrew from it in October, 1799. In the East Napoleon won some local battles against the Turks but failed in his other objectives, while his navy was routed by the British under Horatio Nelson at the Battle of the Nile (1798).

When Napoleon returned to France, the extent of his defeat was not as yet known, and he was able to sell himself to some of the Directors as the indispensable man. In November, 1799, a conspiracy of which he was the leader overthrew the Directory and replaced it by a Consulate of three. Napoleon himself became the first consul and thereafter was the unquestioned ruler of France. A constitution was drawn up and agreed to by plebiscite, enabling the First Consul to rule with the advice of two legislative bodies and an appointed council of state, and the administration and tax system were efficiently centralized. A Concordat was concluded in 1801 between France and the papacy which guaranteed the virtual independence of the French Catholic (Gallican) Church, whose clergy continued to be paid by the state. A uniform law code, based in part on Roman principles, was drawn up by distinguished jurists under the spur of Napoleon, and promulgated in 1804. Most of this *Code Napoléon* survives to this day. In 1808 Napoleon founded a state school system known as the imperial university, designed in part to fill the gap in education left by the closing of so many Catholic schools during the Revolution. His intention was to provide a corps of trained administrators, military men, and engineers to play their part in his empire. On the whole the scheme never functioned effectively in the primary grades, where Church schools continued to enroll most of the children. Its main success was in technical education, which was greatly improved during the Napoleonic regime. In 1804 Napoleon assumed the title Emperor of the French. This too was confirmed by plebiscite.

NAPOLEONIC WARS

Napoleon, now in full control of the destinies of France, extended his sway during the next decade over almost all of Europe. He did not put an end to the economic and social reforms of the Revolution; but in the political sphere he was at least as absolutist as any of the French monarchs. Political liberty was suppressed, but equality of opportunity remained, and the feudal survivals of the Middle Ages were abolished forever.

The Victorious Years. In 1800 the war was renewed against Austria, who was severely defeated both by Napoleon and by the revolutionary general Moreau (Battle of Hohenlinden). Thereafter Austria accepted an unfavorable peace (Treaty of Luneville, 1801), which virtually put an end to the Holy Roman Empire (formally abolished in 1806). In 1802 Britain agreed to the Treaty of Amiens, which left France in such a favorable position and the balance of power in Europe in such disrepair that the arrangement could not be expected to last long. It was in fact broken by both the British and the French before the end of 1802, and a Third Coalition against France was brought into being in 1805, again under British inspiration. Napoleon, who had been preparing for an invasion of England, promptly abandoned his plan and won the great victory of Austerlitz against the Austrians and Russians. Even the Battle of Trafalgar, won a few weeks previously by the British navy against the navies of France and Spain, did not greatly dim the luster of this victory, which forced the Austrians to make peace once again, with still more concessions to France. But the Battle of Trafalgar established British naval supremacy for an indefinite period and ultimately prevented the French from defeating England by blockade.

Prussia had prudently avoided entering the war on the side of Austria; but she objected to the formation of a new German confederation (Confederation of the Rhine) under Napoleonic auspices. Allied only with Russia among the great powers, she was no match for Napoleon and was severely defeated in 1806 at the Battle of Jena. Advancing eastward, Napoleon defeated the Russians at the Battle of Friedland in 1807. The following month the treaties of Tilsit were signed with Prussia and Russia, under which Napoleon's brother Joseph Bonaparte was recognized as king of Naples; another brother, Jerome Bonaparte, became king of a new Germanic kingdom called Westphalia; and Louis Bonaparte became king of Holland. Napoleon himself remained king of Italy north of Naples. Thus the structure of Napoleonic Europe was completed.

Continental Blockade. But the British were still undefeated. The only means immediately available to Napoleon to bring Britain to accept the new Europe was the strategy of a blockade. This plan, known as the Continental System, had been proclaimed in 1806 (Berlin Decrees), to which the British retaliated with a counterblockade (Orders in Council). But only after the treaties of Tilsit was

Napoleon strong enough to make a determined effort to enforce it. When Spain and Portugal, in expectation of British aid from the sea, refused to participate, Napoleon's armies conquered almost all Spain and a part of Portugal. Joseph Bonaparte was transferred to Spain as king, leaving Naples to Murat, one of Napoleon's marshals. The British contributed troops and supplies to prevent the French from reaching Lisbon, and, beginning in 1810, launched a strong counteroffensive, which after the defeat of Napoleon's Grand Army in Russia, liberated Spain and contributed to the final allied victory.

Following their defeats in 1805 and 1806, both Austria and Prussia, deeply humiliated, undertook programs of reform. In Prussia the German philosopher Fichte's *Address to the German Nation* was instrumental in arousing a new patriotism. Numerous administrative improvements were introduced, and conscription was applied for the first time in the country. But Austria struck prematurely at Napoleon and again was decisively defeated (Battle of Wagram, 1809). This time Austria lost much territory, agreed to become an ally of Napoleon, and the emperor gave his daughter Maria in marriage to Napoleon, who had divorced his first wife, Josephine.

In spite of his tremendous façade of power, Napoleon was unable, in large part for economic reasons, to enforce his Continental System. France simply could not produce enough to satisfy the needs of all Europe. Britain, who was already undergoing her Industrial Revolution, was outproducing every other country, and her cheaper goods were widely smuggled into Europe. This infuriated the emperor and drove him to quarrel with Alexander I of Russia, who had refused to adhere fully to the system and had other grievances against Napoleon. The emperor therefore decided that Russia too must be subjected to his suzerainty, and he set to work to organize his greatest army, to which Austria and Prussia sent contingents.

Abdication of Napoleon. This Grand Army of more than half a million troops invaded Russia in 1812. It fought one bloody battle at Borodino and captured Moscow, which had been deserted by the Russians. But as soon as Napoleon arrived in the city, fires broke out, and after a few weeks of fruitless negotiations with Tsar Alexander I, he and his army were compelled to retreat. Harassed ceaselessly by the Russians, the French suffered appalling losses, and their unwilling allies naturally deserted them. A Grand Alliance was quickly formed to exploit the French disaster, and Napoleon, in spite of some brilliant rear-guard actions, was decisively defeated late in 1813 at the Battle of Leipzig. The British armies in Spain

advanced into France, and Paris fell in March, 1814; whereupon
Napoleon abdicated and was exiled to the island of Elba off the coast
of Italy. The oldest surviving heir of the Bourbon family became king
under the title of Louis XVIII.

Treaty of Paris, 1814. A few weeks after the abdication, a treaty
was signed at Paris which was designed to make Louis more acceptable to the French people, now shorn of most of their conquests—
though not all, since the conquests of the first three years of the
Revolution were retained. This lenient peace was largely due to the
diplomatic finesse of Talleyrand, formerly foreign minister of Napoleon, who had deserted him in good time. Talleyrand laid the
entire blame for French expansion upon Napoleon, and convinced the
signatories that the best chance of obtaining a lasting peace in
Europe was to refrain from penalizing the French too harshly for
their part in the war, because if the peace were a mild one they
would accept Louis XVIII as a constitutional monarch, not associat-
ing him with a costly defeat. For his part Louis agreed to constitutional limitations on his rule and accepted a parliament on the
English model.

Congress of Vienna (1814–1815). Though the future of France
had been agreed to, the Napoleonic conquests in Europe had so completely altered its political structure that it was clear that a full
settlement would have to be worked out by negotiation. For this
purpose a Congress was called at Vienna, in which Tsar Alexander
and Prince Metternich, foreign minister of Austria, were the dominant
figures. So many difficulties arose during the negotiations, each power
demanding unacceptable compensation for its losses, that Talleyrand, even though he represented the defeated nation, could exercise
considerable influence. His solution was based on the principle of
legitimacy, namely that all the hereditary rulers should be restored
to their thrones and the victorious powers should see to it that they
were kept on them. Eventually this plan, together with the customary
compensation in the form of increased territories for the winners,
was accepted. Austria received the Italian provinces of Lombardy
and Venetia; Prussia increased her possessions in Germany and
received a part of Poland; the Netherlands (both Holland and the
former Austrian Netherlands) were constituted as a kingdom under
William I of Orange; and a Germanic Confederation of thirty-nine
independent German states took the place of Napoleon's Confederation of the Rhine. Sweden, ruled by a former marshal of Napoleon,
Jean-Baptiste Bernadotte, who had been accepted by the Swedish

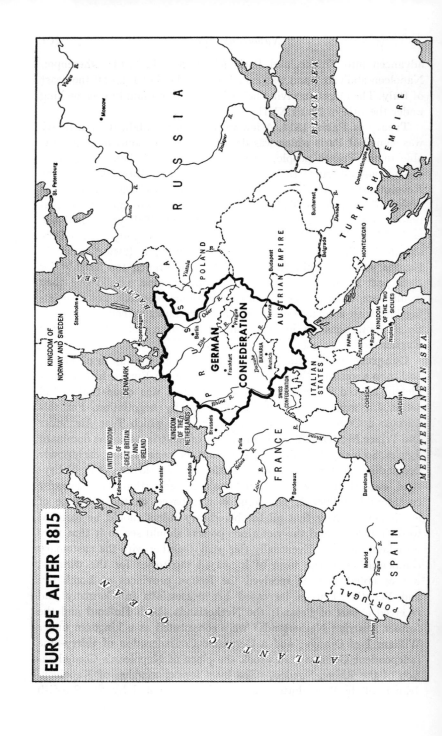

EUROPE AFTER 1815

ATLANTIC OCEAN

UNITED KINGDOM OF GREAT BRITAIN AND IRELAND

Edinburgh
Manchester
London

KINGDOM OF NORWAY AND SWEDEN
Stockholm

RUSSIA
St. Petersburg
Moscow
Volga R.
Dnieper R.
Dniester R.

BALTIC SEA

DENMARK
Copenhagen

KINGDOM OF THE NETHERLANDS
Brussels

GERMAN CONFEDERATION
PRUSSIA
Berlin
Elbe R.
Oder R.
Frankfurt
Prague
BAVARIA
Munich
Danube R.
Rhine R.
Vienna
SWISS CONFEDERATION

POLAND
Vistula R.

AUSTRIAN EMPIRE
Budapest

BLACK SEA

TURKISH EMPIRE
Constantinople
Bucharest
Danube R.
Belgrade
MONTENEGRO

FRANCE
Paris
Seine R.
Loire R.
Bordeaux
Rhone R.

ITALIAN STATES
PAPAL STATES
Rome
KINGDOM OF THE TWO SICILIES
Naples
CORSICA
SARDINIA

SPAIN
Madrid
Tagus R.
Barcelona

PORTUGAL
Lisbon

MEDITERRANEAN SEA

people as regent for Charles XIII (1809–1818), was enlarged by the addition of Norway. (Bernadotte became Charles XIV of Sweden in 1818.) Denmark was given compensation in northern Germany. The remainder of Poland, whose future proved to be the most difficult problem of all to decide at Vienna, became the personal fief of Alexander I of Russia, who assumed the title of king of Poland. Britain, desiring no Continental territory, retained Malta in the Mediterranean and some Dutch, French, and Spanish colonies captured during the war.

Before the Congress had completed its work Napoleon escaped from Elba and was welcomed by the French army and most of his surviving marshals. The Alliance sprang to arms against him and, under the Duke of Wellington, defeated him decisively at the Battle of Waterloo on June 18, 1815. Napoleon again abdicated and was exiled to the lonely Atlantic island of St. Helena, where he died in 1821.

This time the victorious powers were determined to punish France for her support of the discredited Napoleon. She had to pay an indemnity and restore the territories she had retained under the earlier Treaty of Paris. Even so, the second Treaty of Paris was far from being a really punitive peace, in this respect differing markedly from most of the peace efforts of more recent times. The Great Powers entered into an alliance to enforce the treaty (Quadruple Alliance) and agreed to hold regular international congresses to enforce the general peace settlement of Vienna. Tsar Alexander also obtained the signatures of all Christian monarchs, with the exception of the king of England, to a document which set up what he called a Holy Alliance, intended to uphold the Christian principles of charity and peace. This became later confused in the public mind with the Quadruple Alliance (Austria, Prussia, Russia, and England) and with the attempt to enforce the restoration of legitimate monarchs enshrined in the peace treaties. As such it became an object of derision on the part of European liberals, who regarded it as an instrument for the destruction of popular liberties and the suppression of national aspirations.

The Congress of Vienna as an exercise in old-style diplomacy cannot be considered a failure, and it is perhaps a measure of its success that there was no further major war during the century. But the French Revolution had given rise to so many hopes for a new and more liberal order and had given such a fillip to nationalism that these powerful forces could not be indefinitely held in leash. The manner in which the settlement was gradually destroyed and in which the new forces found their expression will be further considered in Chapter 16.

THE RISE OF ROMANTICISM

The French Revolution and the Napoleonic Wars, which brought the ages of Reason and Enlightenment to such a sudden end, greatly affected the cultural as well as the political life of Europe. Various tendencies may be noted, some apparently contradictory; but each may be considered as romantic, especially when romanticism is viewed as a reaction to the excessively rational and aristocratic eighteenth century. Romanticism stressed the primacy of human emotions over the reason. In this respect it is the offspring of Rousseau, the "natural man," who exalted his own feelings and intuitions and regarded them as suitable tools for understanding as well as for appreciating the world.

Romanticism as an Idealizing of the Past. Since the Renaissance every century had tended to despise the Middle Ages and to regard that period as barbaric. The present was assumed to be the greatest age thus far and the future anticipated with confidence. This assumption now ceased to be made, and there was a revival of interest in Gothic architecture, which was widely imitated; in early European literature; and in Christianity—inducing a respect for Catholic ritual which turned many back toward the old religion. Two of the greatest exponents of this point of view were the Frenchmen René de Chateaubriand (1768–1848) and Joseph de Maistre (*c.* 1754–1821). There was an astonishing vogue for the poetry attributed to Ossian, a supposed early Irish bard. Though the poems were in fact written by an eighteenth-century Scottish poet, James Macpherson, the belief in their authenticity and their popularity are significant. In political thought, the Anglo-Irish statesman, Edmund Burke (1729–1797) wrote movingly of the great British tradition of government, which he believed valuable simply because it had grown organically and was rooted in the past. In his *Reflections on the Revolution in France* he criticized the Revolution precisely because it broke with French tradition and attempted to overturn all that had been achieved in previous centuries—in method unlike the American Revolution, which was built on British traditions. Sir Walter Scott (1771–1832) initiated the tremendous vogue of the historical novel, beginning with *Waverley* in 1814. Almost all of his many novels and his verse ballads attempted imaginatively to re-create the past. Victor Hugo (1802–1885) outlived the era of Romanticism, but wrote in the romantic vein all his life, describing the past in his most imaginative manner in his late *Légende des Siècles*.

Romanticism as an Exaltation of Sentiment. Perhaps the most widely read of all the early romantic novels was the *Sorrows of Werther* (1774), by Johann Wolfgang von Goethe (1749–1832), in which a young man takes his life as the result of his unrequited passion for the wife of his best friend. In later years Goethe was ashamed of this work, having entirely outgrown his youthful romanticism. His tremendous poem *Faust,* on which he worked for the greatest part of his life presents a picture of a strong, restless, human being who is the prototype of Western civilization, eternally discontented and eternally seeking new fields to conquer. Though this concept too may be thought of as a romantic ideal, it is much more than this, and the self-pity of much of early romanticism, present so strongly in *Werther,* is absent. The *Adolphe* of Benjamin Constant (1767–1830, lover of Madame de Staël, herself an early romantic writer and publicist of German romanticism in France) is a work in the same genre as *Werther* though its psychology is more profound. Alphonse de Lamartine (1790–1869), French poet and novelist, introduced romantic poetry to France. His work is suffused with love of nature and religious sentiment. Love of nature, indeed, was typical of the romantics—not nature as found in the orderly French garden of the eighteenth century, but nature untamed. The English poets John Keats (1795–1821), Percy Bysshe Shelley (1792–1822), and William Wordsworth (1770–1850) followed in some measure the lead given by Rousseau, whose *Reveries* breathe the same spirit. Such painters as Constable and Turner attempted also to show nature in all her moods and mystery.

Romanticism and Nationalism. A direct result of the French Revolution and the Napoleonic Wars was the rise of romantic nationalism, which included love of freedom, hatred of tyranny, and the exaltation of the great virtue of a particular folk. The German Johann Herder (1744–1803) was the precursor of this form of romanticism. Lord Byron (1788–1824), who wrote the poem *Childe Harolde* and later lost his life in the struggle for Greek independence, was the typical figure of the knight errant crusading for freedom. Byron unquestionably encouraged the legend which painted him as a violent revolutionary melancholic personage, the idol of women, and the great lover. Shelley was a romantic revolutionary in the same tradition. The German philosopher Fichte (1762–1814) has already been mentioned as the great early figure in German nationalism who was deeply shocked by Napoleon's easy conquest of his country. George Wilhelm Hegel (1770–1831), professor at Berlin, created a metaphysics which aimed to show that the modern national state is the highest embodiment of the Idea manifesting itself in history.

Romanticism in Music. Lastly mention should be made of the influence of romanticism in Music. In the eighteenth century baroque music like baroque art, shaded over into the rococo; its greatest exponent was Wolfgang Mozart (1756–1791), whose flow of melody has rarely if ever been equaled. Ludwig van Beethoven (1770–1827), while retaining the melody of his predecessors, added depth to his music, especially in the later years of his life (after he had become deaf). He is usually regarded as much influenced by romanticism, later exponents of which included in particular Schubert, Schumann, and Frédéric Chopin (1810–1849), whose music was greatly affected by his Polish nationalism as well as by his romantic and melancholic temperament.

The Romantic Movement persisted throughout the first half of the nineteenth century, but gradually it gave way to "realism" and naturalism, the effort to portray life as it is in reality rather than through the distorted lens of the imagination. Nevertheless, romanticism in changed forms has persisted as a permanent ingredient of the amalgam of Western civilization.

15 THE EARLY INDUSTRIAL REVOLUTION

Toward the middle of the eighteenth century, the methods of production both in agriculture and in industry began to change. This change was marked by the introduction of new machinery and an ever increasing tempo of inventions; by improved organization for production; and by the application of science to practical life. Some historians distinguish two separate phases of the Industrial Revolution: the first marked by the improved use of wind, water, and steam for power, and the replacement of the old domestic or putting-out system by the factory system; the second involving the use of more sophisticated machines, methods of mass production, and planned scientific research. The two phases, however, are not easily distinguished, since one passed easily over into the other in certain industries and certain countries, and nowhere has there been any noticeable break between them. (The second phase will be reserved for discussion in the chapters which concern the twentieth century.)

THE AGRICULTURAL REVOLUTION

In order to make possible a truly urban civilization, it was necessary to increase the supply of food for the cities. The old medieval manorial system produced only relatively small surpluses for urban consumption. But once the serfs had been emancipated and smallholders, either owners or tenants, had taken their place, an incentive was provided to produce surpluses and sell them, using the money to buy manufactured goods from the towns. The movement to enclose the common lands (see p. 126) had resulted mainly in the increase of wool rather than of food. But it had the side effect of consolidating rural holdings into more efficient units, and in due course the landlords turned to raising livestock for food also. Robert Bakewell (1725–1795) made many experiments to improve breeds of livestock in England, and farmers everywhere began to follow his methods. A group of farmers in the county of Norfolk learned to make use of a more efficient rotation of crops which increased the productivity of the land; and by the end of the eighteenth century, several simple agricultural horse-drawn machines and improved tools had been invented. In 1840 Justus von Liebig made the first chemical analyses of plants and discovered much about their nutrition, thus doing the pioneer work necessary for the foundation of the chemical fertilizer industry, which has so greatly increased the productivity of the land. Since that time agriculture has indeed become revolutionized in almost all the industrial nations. In some even the horse is a rare phenomenon, having been replaced by diesel or gasoline-powered machines; and organic manure from farm animals has likewise been replaced by products of the chemical industry.

THE INDUSTRIAL REVOLUTION

Though citizens of other European nations made several of the crucial inventions, the greatest incentive to industrialize during the eighteenth century occurred in England. Population was rapidly increasing and there was too little land available for England to be able to feed herself from her own resources. This meant that food had to be purchased abroad, for which payment would have to be made in manufactured goods. Though the conscious decision to live by importing foods and raw materials and exporting manufactures was made only in the mid-nineteenth century (repeal of the Corn Laws, 1846), it had long been clear that such a course would ultimately be necessary, as it had been in ancient Athens. During the Napoleonic Wars, as was noted in Chapter 14, English goods, especially textiles, were already far cheaper than goods in the rest of Europe and no country wished to be without them. It was largely for this reason that the Continental System of Napoleon failed. Moreover, Britain subsidized all her Continental allies from the middle of the eighteenth century onward and largely paid the bill for the defeat of Napoleon. The money was available to her only because of her international trade. She was far less rich than France in resources and manpower, but because of her early industrialization and more efficient system of tax collecting, cash could be used as needed to support her foreign policy.

Improvements in Transportation. A steam engine that was inefficient because it wasted coal, had been invented by Thomas Newcomen and used from the early eighteenth century in the English mines, where its wastefulness was not a matter of great concern. In 1765 James Watt, a Scottish engineer called in to repair one of these machines, invented an improved engine which took only a quarter of the coal. Robert Fulton used the improved engine in 1807 to drive a river boat on the Hudson from New York to Albany, and George Stephenson in 1814 invented a steam locomotive. The screw propeller, invented in 1836 (by John Ericsson of Sweden), made possible a more efficient steamship than the paddle-wheeler that was now capable of making transatlantic crossings. The improvement in transportation made possible by the use of steam, combined with the eighteenth-century development of cheap canal routes, laid the foundation for the immense nineteenth-century growth in industry. It could now be located where the raw materials were available, or the raw materials themselves could be brought from anywhere in the world to the industrial centers at minimal cost. Manufactured goods and food could likewise be sent comparatively cheaply to their consumers.

The Textile Industry. The textile industry had been based in earlier centuries exclusively on hand spinning and weaving. Under the domestic system, handworkers at home had produced the cloth, using their own looms. The invention of the flying shuttle (by John Kay, 1733), the spinning jenny (by James Hargreaves, 1765), and a waterframe and carding machine (by Richard Arkwright, 1769, 1775), altogether changed the nature of this industry—as to a greater degree did the first power loom which could be used with horses, waterpower, or steam (invented by Edmund Cartwright, 1784). Cotton largely replaced wool in the nineteenth century, since it was much cheaper and its production could be rapidly expanded. The cotton gin, invented by the American Eli Whitney in 1793, which cleaned the cotton many times more quickly than had been possible by hand methods, provided the American South with what was virtually a new agricultural industry—in the process postponing the emancipation of Negro slaves for more than a half century.

Metallurgy. One of the more important series of discoveries led to the development of steel, the key material of modern civilization. Iron had of course been known for nearly four thousand years, but since it is full of impurities in its natural state, it had to be smelted (a process that removes some of the impurities, resulting in cast iron). However, if coal were used to smelt it, more impurities would ensue. The first crucial invention was therefore the reduction of coal to coke, which did not have the impurities. This was the work of Abraham Darby at the beginning of the eighteenth century, although in countries where wood was plentiful, charcoal was not replaced by coke for another century and a half. An efficient method for producing wrought iron was discovered at the end of the century, but not until the invention of the Bessemer process in 1856 was it possible to produce a heat blast capable of eliminating the major impurities and producing steel. The Siemens-Martin open-hearth method of smelting followed in 1866; this was useful to make large quantities of steel at one time. Two English chemists, Gilchrist and Thomas, invented a chemical process for removing impurities in 1878. By refinements of these techniques it later became possible to make steel of exactly the required composition, thus leading to the highly sophisticated steel industry of today. In more recent times, numerous other metals and alloys have come to be used for different specialized purposes, some of them in competition with steel, though for the foreseeable future steel is likely to maintain its primacy.

The Factory System. The growing use of a country's natural resources, especially coal, provided a new source of income to those men who owned them. The Duke of Newcastle, whom we have already noted as a political manipulator in eighteenth-century England, obtained much of his wealth from his possession of coal mines, as did the Duke of Bridgewater, pioneer in canal development. But large accumulations of capital were still scarce, and most of the new factories were built by relatively small operators who plowed back their profits into expansion. Even skilled workers in the late eighteenth and early nineteenth centuries might hope to set up in business for themselves. Thus the middle class was increased by the addition of manufacturers who had risen from the working class. By the early nineteenth century, there were a number of joint-stock companies, which enabled investors with relatively little money of their own to buy shares in the new industry.

The use of heavy machinery required both capital for its manufacture and purchase and the most efficient possible methods of production. Obviously this meant a decline of the putting-out system, since such machines could not be installed profitably in private homes. It was gradually replaced by the system under which employees of the manufacturer who owned the machinery worked in a factory, where the machines were kept in operation for as many hours of the day as was feasible. Workers who had formerly lived in rural areas now went to live in towns, usually in houses provided by the manufacturer. Thus arose the characteristic mill town of northern England which has not yet quite disappeared.

THE BRITISH WORKERS AND THE INDUSTRIAL REVOLUTION

Clearly the Industrial Revolution presented numerous new problems to be solved either within the existing political framework of the industrial nations or by revolutionary changes in the governmental structure. In England there was a constant duel between the working classes and the classes which controlled the government, but parliamentary institutions proved adequate to the task of reconciling them.

The Chartists. For a long time in the Industrial Revolution the workers were at the mercy of their employers. Too many employees wished to work in the factory and earn steady wages. Ricardo derived his Iron Law of Wages (see p. 189) from the observations of conditions in the early factories. Wages were fixed on the basis of the absolute minimum for maintaining life and on the assumption that every member of the family worked. Working conditions in the mines were worse even than in the factories.

Yet the workers in England were forbidden to combine to win an increased wage. Combination acts had been passed in 1799 and 1800, when England, at war with France, was in deadly fear of being infected by the bacillus of Jacobinism. In 1824 these acts were repealed, but the repeal was followed by an immediate wave of sometimes violent strikes. In 1855 a new law was passed, prohibiting violence and threats, although it permitted combinations to seek improved wages. Strikes, however, continued to be put down by state power, since violence usually resulted from them. The working classes therefore decided to try to win influence in Parliament, from whose ranks they were still excluded. In 1838 a Workingmen's Association presented a Charter demanding radical political reforms that would permit working-class members to sit in Parliament (including manhood suffrage, pay for members of Parliament, and equal electoral districts). Though the agitation was carried on for nine years, with "monster petitions," Parliament steadily rejected all demands, and in spite of riots the movement petered out after 1848, when the last petition, containing many obviously fictitious names, was rejected.

Parliamentary Action. Meanwhile Parliament itself had taken steps to redress some of the worker's grievances. Reports of parliamentary committees on conditions in textile factories (1830) and mines (1842) resulted in legislation regulating hours and conditions of work (1833, 1847). Factory owners fought the legislation but were outnumbered in Parliament by radical humanitarians and Tory landlords, who were not involved. All parties in Parliament, except some of the Radicals, objected to the dilution of their membership by the working class and to the implied threats of violence behind the Chartists.

Rise of Labor Unions. In 1859 the law against trade (labor) unions was again modified in favor of the workers, but strikes still came under the ancient laws of conspiracy. Not until the early 1870's were unions finally legalized and peaceful picketing permitted. By this time a considerable number of skilled workers had won the right to vote and used it to win reforms for their class (1867; see p. 253). In 1884 the franchise qualifications were lowered to take in almost the entire working class in the cities, and union officials at last began to organize the unskilled workers, resulting in a huge dockers' strike in 1889. Though the House of Lords (the supreme court of Britain) in its Taff Vale decision nullified some of the gains won by the unionists in 1901, a Labor party dominated by organized labor now had twenty-nine of its members sitting in Parliament, and a Trade Disputes bill was passed in 1906 which in return nullified the Taff Vale decision. Thus Britain demonstrated how it was possible for the workers to obtain redress for their grievances through their own direct efforts and how through the use of the vote and working through Parliament they could prevent the power of the state from being employed against them.

SOCIAL AND ECONOMIC THOUGHT

There was little theory behind the British unions, which were organized to meet existing conditions. The Industrial Revolution, however, did excite the interest of many theorists, who realized that a revolution was indeed taking place which would transform Western society. Institutions that had slowly evolved to meet totally different conditions might well prove unable to change to meet the new challenges. Most of the thinkers of the Age of Enlightenment had expended their ingenuity in devising theoretical structures based on abstractions like natural rights. The nineteenth-century thinkers, even those, like Karl Marx, who gave birth to important theories, based them more on the empirical facts they observed and on their study of history than on abstract ideas.

Utilitarianism. Jeremy Bentham (1748–1832) was a pioneer student of English institutions, which he regarded as thoroughly illogical and antiquated. He thus as a practical matter advocated numerous reforms, suggesting at the same time a general principle by which their desirability could be gauged: A "calculus of pain and pleasure" should be drawn up in the light of which each measure should be examined. If it provided more pleasure to many than it gave pain to a few, then it was a desirable measure. An ideal bill should provide the "greatest good for the greatest number" of people. Utilitarianism, as this system was called, was therefore not especially tender to the rights of minorities, but when put into practice by Bentham and his numerous followers (notable among whom was the philosopher John Stuart Mill [1806–1873], himself a civil libertarian), and by the group of parliamentary Radicals, it led to much legislation that benefited the workers.

Utopian Socialism. Bentham's contemporary the Comte de Saint-Simon (1760–1825), a French nobleman, had relatively little influence in his own time and was regarded as a "utopian" (after Sir Thomas More's sixteenth-century fantasy). Though an aristocrat, he sympathized with the Revolution and recognized that the workers would be subjected to ever increasing exploitation in the coming industrial age. He advocated state interference for their benefit and state, as well as private, co-operatives. Moreover, private inheritance, in his view, should be forbidden. All of an individual's money and property at his death should go to the state, which would use the proceeds to establish co-operatives. Some of Saint-Simon's ideas were adopted by subsequent thinkers revolted by industrial society. Charles Fourier (1772–1837) founded several small co-operative communities, none of which succeeded for long. Robert Owen (1771–1858), a British industrialist, greatly improved conditions in his own factory in Scotland but failed when he attempted to set up self-contained communistic colonies in England and America. The great co-operative success was a consumers' co-operative set up in Rochdale, England, by twenty-eight Lancashire weavers (Rochdale Society of Equitable Pioneers), from which the whole co-operative movement has spread. It still exists in England as a gigantic chain of wholesale and retail establishments, and there are few countries in the Western world which do not possess co-operative movements of varying size and strength—even though they sometimes make but a minor contribution to the problems they were designed to solve.

Marxism. Saint-Simonians were often known as utopian social-ists. It was for this reason that Karl Marx (1818–1883) spoke of his system as "scientific socialism" (also in this diverging from humanitarian reformers such as Charles Kingsley who advocated "Christian Socialism"). Marx was an indefatigable researcher, polemi-cist, and theorist who was probably more familiar than any of his contemporaries with economic realities of his day. It is unfortunate for his reputation that he has also been regarded as an infallible prophet whose theories and predictions are eternal verities rather than brillant conclusions derived from the data available to him in the mid-nineteenth century.

All history, Marx decided, is the history of class struggle—in ancient Rome a struggle between patrician and plebeian, in the Middle Ages a struggle between landlord and peasant, in the nine-teenth century a struggle between employer and worker. Each of these struggles results in a new equilibrium in society, according to the regular formula for change postulated by the German philosopher Hegel. Marx himself began as a student of Hegelianism but claimed in later life that he had stood the idealist philosopher right-side-up through his perception that it was economic forces, not the Idea trying to manifest itself, that determined history. Hegel had called his system *dialectical idealism.* Marx called his own system *dialecti-cal materialism,* the "dialectic" consisting in the phases of the class struggle, namely the *thesis, antithesis,* and *synthesis* of Hegel. The bourgeoisie (antithesis) had in the course of history destroyed the ancient feudal structure (thesis) and substituted the economic method of capitalism (synthesis). In the process it necessarily pro-duced its antithesis, the proletariat, and was thus "its own grave-digger." The proletariat would as a historical necessity destroy the bourgeoisie and establish its own synthesis, which would bring the process to an end.

Marx and his friend and constant supporter, Friedrich Engels, filled with their insight, produced in 1848 a revolutionary document which they called the Communist Manifesto. The Manifesto ends with the stirring words: "The proletariat have nothing to lose but their chains. They have a world to win. Workingmen of all countries unite!" Marx and Engels, though they believed in the inevitability of the proletarian revolution, nevertheless, like their followers since, were not content to allow history to take its course. They preferred to help it along by organizing the working classes to play their future role as revolutionary destroyers of bourgeois capitalism, and in 1867 Marx published the first volume of his monumental work *Das Kapital* as a contribution to the education of the workers. He continued to write on the subject for the remainder of his life, the last two volumes being published by Engels after his death. The huge and difficult work became the bible of the international communist movement. The more moderate Marxist socialists, who did not believe in trying to foment immediate revolutions, all accepted the greater part of Marx's analysis, especially the theory of surplus value, according to which the workers were forever doomed under capitalism to receive far less than their labor deserved. This condition was attributed to the fact that the bourgeoisie owned the "means of production." When society itself owned these means then the class struggle would be over, but the bourgeoisie would fight to retain them in its own hands and would ultimately have to be dispossessed, by force if necessary but if possible by ordinary parliamentary means through the action of working-class representatives.

The first necessity for the followers of Marx would therefore be to make the working class aware of its future role. Since the working class was distributed throughout all industrial nations, the Marxist movement must be international. Though Marxian socialism for a long time attempted to organize "Internationals" they soon came up against national prejudices and rivalry and were not very successful. Indeed, the most conspicuous failure of Marx as a prophet was his underestimation of the force of nationalism. He also, as was to some degree justified in his own time, underestimated the flexibility of the capitalist system, which in fact during the next century underwent many changes in the direction of improving the income of the working classes, thus making the system itself more acceptable to them. In particular, the perception of the American manufacturer Henry Ford that high wages tended to increase profits by permitting the workers to buy more of the products of industry, went far to disprove the theories of Marx. The fundamental changes in capitalism that resulted have gone far to reconcile the working classes to their position in all the industrial countries. In fact, no Marxist-inspired revolution has ever succeeded except as the result of either the breakdown in government, a civil war, or a losing international war; and the communist system in all cases had to be imposed by force by a minority of dedicated Communists rather than as Marx had predicted, by an uprising of the working class.

Socialist Parties. Marxism gradually absorbed the various socialist movements in nineteenth-century Europe, with the exception of the

English movement, which preferred to work for moderate reforms through the machinery of the parliamentary system. The Fabian Society in England was a gradualist group of thinkers who continually put forward programs of reform, most of which were adopted by the Labor party. Social Democratic parties in other countries have maintained a theoretical Marxist base; but when they won office they preferred, like the British Labor party, to work for social reforms, including the establishment of state industries and the nationalization, or state control, of various key enterprises formerly in private hands.

Anarchism and Syndicalism. Other revolutionary movements in the nineteenth century were anarchism and syndicalism. Anarchists were against all governments but differed among themselves as to what was to replace them. Pierre Proudhon (1809–1865) attacked the system of private property and favored co-operative associations. Michael Bakunin (1814–1876) wished to replace the state with mutual protective associations and to replace religion with atheism. The followers of Bakunin, who regarded all governments as necessarily tyrannical and destroyers of individual freedom, frequently resorted to symbolic acts of violence, especially the assassination of government leaders, including King Humbert I of Italy; Empress Elizabeth, wife of Francis Joseph, emperor of Austria; and Presidents Carnot of France and McKinley of the United States.

Syndicalism arose as a reaction against the socialist parties, which tended to become moderate when in office. The working class, according to syndicalists, ought to take direct action to destroy the capitalist system, using the strike as their major weapon—preferably a general strike which would paralyze the capitalists and their bourgeois governments. The industrial union, which organized all workers, skilled and unskilled, in a particular industry, was a favorite concept of syndicalists. The great *Confédération Générale du Travail* (CGT), the French association of labor unions, was at first under syndicalist control, and it called many major strikes during the period of its ascendancy, the end of the nineteenth and the early twentieth centuries. It still has many syndicalist tendencies. Syndicalism was strong also in Spain, and the larger Spanish unions continued to be in great measure syndicalist. The industrial unions in the United States, combined as the Committee for Industrial Organization (CIO) were syndicalist in inspiration, but under American conditions have never engaged in the political action advocated by the nineteenth-century founders of the movement.

Conclusion. All the movements described in this chapter were founded for the purpose of improving the lot of the working classes, who were being exploited unmercifully during the early phases of the Industrial Revolution. By the First World War the lot of the workers had already been greatly improved in most industrial countries, and the revolutionary tendency of the early movements had begun to subside. The changes in capitalism and the advances in productive methods which reconciled most workers to the regimes under which they lived will be dealt with in later chapters since they belong more to the twentieth century than to the nineteenth. But it is essential to bear the changing economic structure in mind if the political events now to be described are to be fully understood.

16   REACTION, REFORM, AND REVOLUTION, 1815–1850

As a consequence of the French Revolution and the subsequent wars, two major trends became apparent in Western civilization: a trend toward liberalism and through liberalism to democracy and a trend toward ever increasing nationalism. Only Russia held aloof under its absolutist monarchy. An attempt by a group known as the Decembrists to put a less autocratic monarch on the throne was suppressed in 1825 by Tsar Nicholas I; and the tsars remained for the entire century opposed to all diminution of their powers, refusing to grant a constitution.

NATIONALISM

Nationalism may be defined as the emotional identification of the individual with his nation and his fellow nationals. Today it is widely regarded as a natural emotion. But it is worth noting that in the days before the existence of the nation-state it did not exist. In the Middle Ages loyalty was given to Christendom rather than to any particular nation, and even in early modern times it was not considered at all unreasonable for a territory to be transferred from one ruler to another—as, for example, the Spanish Netherlands were transferred to Austria by the Peace of Utrecht. Belgium did not as yet exist and could command no loyalty from Belgians. Austria was a ramshackle empire ruled by the Hapsburgs; it was held together by the monarchy in Vienna and by its centralized institutions. Prussia's territories were not even contiguous; it had come into existence as a country as the result of the work of its Hohenzollern rulers but had no other unity. Germany was a congeries of nearly forty states under different rulers.

The Revolutionary and Napoleonic Wars succeeded in arousing the latent antiforeign feeling that lies behind all nationalism. Napoleon, in placing his relatives on so many European thrones, had demonstrated clearly that Europe was his by right of conquest; all his nominees were regarded as aliens and resented accordingly. A true national uprising by the Spaniards drove Joseph Bonaparte from his throne. Prussians were aroused by Fichte and others to drive out the foreigner and assert themselves as true Germans. Both the revolutionaries and Napoleon himself roused French national feeling. As soon as the foreigners invaded France the National Convention found it possible for the first time to institute conscription, thus involving the whole people, not professional soldiers only, in the war. Thereafter the war was a national one. Throughout the nineteenth century there were frequent wars for national independence. Latin America threw off the Spanish yoke; and the Turkish empire in Europe was divided into independent national states, leaving only the city of Constantinople and a small hinterland in Turkish hands. The Slavic and Magyar provinces of Austria attempted without success to win their independence. Poland struggled against Russian domination. Catholic Belgium became separated from Calvinist Holland. Germany and Italy were unified as national states. Thus the nineteenth century may be regarded above all as a century of nationalism. In the twentieth century nationhood was achieved by those who had been unsuccessful in the nineteenth, and the overseas possessions of the European powers, which had barely begun the march to independence by the turn of the century, with few exceptions had followed the same path and won it by 1964.

LIBERALISM AND DEMOCRACY

Though liberal ideas were spread beyond their country of origin by the French armies, the American and French Revolutions destroyed or changed many traditional institutions and thus exercised a greater influence than the wars themselves in the dissemination of liberal ideas. Liberalism in the nineteenth century was essentially a middle-class movement which sought to bring eighteenth-century absolutism to an end and to replace it by middle-class rule. The Americans had curbed the "tyranny" of George III and established a republic with a propertied franchise that ensured the predominance of the rural and urban propertied classes in most states. The charter granted by the restored Bourbon monarchy in France likewise provided for a franchise based on a property qualification similar to that which had prevailed in England for centuries. To the liberals either a constitutional monarchy or a republic was acceptable. What was important was that no hereditary monarch nor aristocracy, nor even an absolutist usurper like Napoleon, should be permitted to rule. A parliament, following the English example, was the best available institution for the establishment of middle-class rule; but it was thought that the parliament should be composed of those solid citizens who had a stake in the country and could thus be expected to rule responsibly.

Democracy, on the contrary, was associated with Rousseau and Jacobinism, and it was widely regarded as having been discredited by the excesses of the French Revolution. Clearly if universal franchise were conceded, the majority would rule; this would mean rule by the poor who had little stake in the country and might be expected to "dispossess the possessors." It was in the United States and in the British overseas dominions that universal manhood suffrage was first put into effect and remained in operation. Only after a long rear-guard action by the privileged classes did the British government concede it; and the French, who had initiated it during the Revolution, were granted it only to see it made useless during the Second Empire, when the country was run according to the wishes of Napoleon III. Democracy did not make rapid headway until the last decades of the century.

SUCCESSFUL INDEPENDENCE MOVEMENTS

In the first half of the nineteenth century, as a direct result of the French Revolution, the Spanish colonies in Latin America won their independence as republics; Portuguese Brazil became independent of the mother country as a constitutional monarchy under a scion of the Portuguese royal House; Haiti became an independent Negro republic; and Greece escaped from a Turkish rule that had lasted nearly four hundred years, thus beginning the breakup of the whole Ottoman Empire.

Spanish Colonies. The French Revolution had relatively little influence on the thinking of the mestizos (persons of mixed native and European origin) and the American-born descendants of Spanish immigrants in South America, who constituted the upper and middle classes in the colonies. These classes had long resented the domination of the Spaniards from Spain (*Gachupines*), who occupied all the important positions in the colonial governments. Since they regarded themselves as the natural equals of the Spaniards in all respects, it was only a matter of time and opportunity before they asserted themselves. This opportunity was provided when

Ferdinand VII of Spain was driven from his throne by Napoleon in 1808. In 1813 Simon Bolívar, a Venezuelan soldier and revolutionary, was proclaimed by the Venezuelans as "Liberator," but he was unable at first to make good his title and was driven into exile. Ferdinand was restored to his throne by the Congress of Vienna before Bolívar could return. By that time the restored monarchy had shown itself as determined to keep the colonies by force. Its repressions excited a stronger national spirit within the Americas and this time the rebellion was successful. From his base in Venezuela and Colombia, Bolívar marched over the Andes to Ecuador and Peru and created the state named for him (Bolivia). In Peru he met Jośe de San Martin, an Argentinian with experience in the Spanish armies, who had already liberated his own country and aided in the liberation of Chile. The Spaniards resisted for as long as they could but were compelled in 1824 to recognize the independence of all the new states. Uruguay and Paraguay experienced difficulties from the Portuguese in Brazil and from the Argentinians before they could establish themselves as independent states, separate from the other new states in South America.

In Mexico, where a stronger native Indian culture had survived the centuries of Spanish rule, liberal ideals were more in evidence in the initial rebellion against Spain, begun by Miguel Hidalgo, a priest who had long crusaded for social justice. A motley army made up mostly of Indians followed him after his proclamation of independence in 1810; the Spanish troops defeated it without any difficulty. Though two successive priestly leaders were vanquished and executed, the rebellion continued. It was successful when Agustín de Iturbide, a Spanish general, turned against his own country and allowed himself to be proclaimed emperor (1821). Although his rule was recognized by the Spaniards, it soon came to an end when he lost his support in Mexico. Again the Spaniards took up arms but this time were defeated and accepted the inevitable (1829). Iturbide's empire had included the present-day Central American republics. After his expulsion they formed a confederation which soon fell apart, leaving the separate independent states.

Brazil. When the Portuguese royal family was driven out of their kingdom in Portugal by Napoleon, they took refuge in Brazil, which thus for a time was the center of the Portuguese Empire. But King John VI returned to Portugal in 1821, leaving a son Pedro as regent. In 1822 Pedro was proclaimed emperor (Pedro I, 1822–1831), and he promulgated a constitution the following year. When he inherited the Portuguese throne in 1826, he refused to move from Brazil and had his seven-year-old daughter Maria proclaimed queen of Portugal. Thus the two countries were separated with very little discord, and Pedro's son who came to the throne as a child in 1831 (Pedro II, 1831–1889) devoted himself exclusively to Brazil, which under his rule enjoyed a long period of material progress and prosperity.

Haiti. The fall of the Bastille in 1789 was the signal for the outbreak of a mulatto rebellion in Haiti. The French, who ruled the western half of the island, quickly suppressed this first rebellion, but the French Revolutionary governments were unwilling to send enough troops to put down a new rebellion led by a former Negro slave, Toussaint l'Ouverture, especially when he agreed to drive the Spaniards from the eastern half of the island (Santo Domingo) and to rule jointly with the French. Santo Domingo was then cleared of Spaniards, and Toussaint became ruler of the whole island. Napoleon, however, reversed the policy of the Directory, captured Toussaint by treachery, and tried to win back the island. The rebellion continued until the island became independent in 1804. It has since remained independent under Negro rule. In 1844 the Haitian Negroes finally quit Santo Domingo, which then became the Dominican Republic.

War for Greek Independence. Turkish rule over Greece had been faltering for many years before the outbreak of rebellion in 1831. Greek officials in Turkish employ had long held major positions in the Turkish provinces in the Balkans, and the eighteenth-century wars between Russia and Turkey had greatly weakened the latter. A rebellion in a Rumanian province encouraged the Greeks to revolt. Although this initial revolt failed, the Greeks in Morea (Peloponnesus) took matters into their own hands and massacred the Turkish minority in that province. Turkish retaliation was severe, and though the Greeks declared their independence in 1822, Turkish forces, aided by armies and a fleet from Egypt, won back almost all they had lost. At this point the greater powers intervened and attempted to arrange an armistice and the concession of autonomy to the Greeks under Turkish suzerainty. When all efforts failed, the British, French, and Russians blockaded the Greek mainland and destroyed the Egyptian fleet at the Battle of Navarino (1827). The Russians then invaded Turkey by land and came close to taking Constantinople in 1829. In 1830 Turkey conceded the independence of mainland Greece, which accepted a Bavarian prince as king (Otto I, 1832–1862). The island of Crete was not joined with the mainland of Greece until 1908. Turkey recognized Serbia as an autonomous state under her suzerainty in 1829, leaving only a few Turks in the country in garrison towns (Treaty of Adrianople, 1829). These troops finally left in 1867 and the country became officially independent in 1878. By the same treaty the Russians won the mouth of the Danube and the eastern coast of the Black Sea.

THE VIENNA SETTLEMENT AND ITS AFTERMATH

The Quadruple Alliance which resulted from the Congress of Vienna was expected to police the Vienna settlement (see p. 203). But the British soon left the alliance, since they had no desire to interfere whenever there was a revolution in any European state, and the whole system was irretrievably damaged by a series of revolutions in 1830, initiated by France.

Concert of Europe. It had been decided at Vienna that the Congress should meet at regular intervals to discuss matters of common interest and the operation of the peace treaties. The first such Congress, held at Aix-la-Chapelle in 1818, accepted France as a member since she had paid the indemnities imposed upon her. The Quadruple thus became a Quintuple Alliance (Britain, Prussia, Austria, Russia, France). The Congress of Troppau, held in 1820, was forced to consider a revolution that had broken out in Spain, where Ferdinand VII had suspended the constitution and unmercifully suppressed the liberals. An army revolt had driven him temporarily from his throne. The kingdom of Naples was meanwhile captured in a revolution led by a secret society (the Carbonari) against the restored Bourbon monarch Ferdinand I. The Congress passed, over the dissent of the British foreign minister, Lord Castlereagh, a protocol which bound the powers to take action when internal disturbances endangered European peace. It otherwise took no immediate action. The Congress of Laibach, held in 1821, authorized the use of force to suppress the rebellion in Naples. The Congress of Verona (1822) gave France permission to suppress the continuing revolution in Spain. The new British foreign minister, George Canning, refused to countenance the intervention and soon thereafter withdrew from the Alliance. The French succeeded in restoring Ferdinand VII, but he refused to accept French advice to grant a constitution and ruthlessly suppressed revolutionary and liberal elements. Austria, who had succeeded in restoring Ferdinand I to the throne of Naples in 1821—thereafter the monarch grandiloquently renamed his realm the Kingdom of the Two Sicilies—intervened soon afterward to suppress a rebellion in Piedmont in northern Italy. In 1831 she intervened in the papal states and in the duchies of Parma and Modena, earning thereby the derisive title of the "fire-brigade of Europe."

Revolutions of 1830. The year 1830 saw a new revolution in France. Louis XVIII had been succeeded in 1824 by his brother Charles X, who adopted a policy of trying to restore the monarchy to its pre-Revolution position. Such an effort was bound to fail in the changed conditions of the 1820's. The elected Chamber, even though chosen by a propertied franchise, was resolutely opposed to the restoration of absolutism, which would have deprived it of all power, and successive elections returned liberal majorities. The king, finding it impossible to govern through cabinets which lacked a majority in the Chamber, issued in July, 1830, a series of ordinances designed to change the electoral system to give him an ultraconservative majority. At this the Parisian populace rebelled, backed by the liberal majority in the Chamber; Charles fled to England; and the liberal deputies invited Louis Philippe of the Orléans House, son of a revolutionary prince descended from Louis XIII, to be king of the French. Most Parisians would have preferred a republic and accepted him reluctantly, but the new monarch held his position for seventeen years.

This "July Revolution" was followed in August by an uprising in Belgium against the rule of William I of Holland, who had been imposed on the Belgians by the Congress of Vienna. The Calvinist king was extremely unpopular among his Belgian subjects, who were mostly Catholics. Moreover, William had tried to impose Dutch officials and the Dutch language on most of Belgium—in spite of the fact that Belgium was more populous than Holland. Though Nicholas I of Russia wished to intervene in the interests of the principle of legitimacy, Austria—busy in Italy—and Prussia were persuaded by the British and French to agree to Belgian independence. But Holland refused to accept the terms offered and invaded the country, from which she had to be expelled by the French. William did not recognize Belgian independence and the frontiers agreed to by the powers until 1839. Belgium accepted a German prince, Leopold of Saxe-Coburg, as her king (Leopold I, 1831–1865).

Tsar Nicholas was prevented from intervening in Belgium by a serious rebellion which broke out in Poland (now under the personal rule of the tsar), whose army Nicholas proposed to use in Belgium and France. Poland had been granted a constitution by Alexander I, but as the erstwhile liberal monarch grew older, he had not troubled to invoke it, preferring to rule almost as absolutely in Poland as in Russia. In 1830 the Polish nationalists declared Tsar Nicholas deposed and took to arms. The Poles, far from united among themselves, were helpless to resist for long the substantial forces brought against them by the tsar, who took Warsaw in September, 1831. Alexander's constitution was abrogated; all political rights were abolished; and Poland thereafter was treated as a virtual province of Russia.

The Concert of Europe had been seriously damaged by these revolutions. Though Austria, having no uprising at home, had played her due part in suppressing rebellions in foreign lands, the other powers had been prevented from or been unwilling to interfere abroad. But the Congress system had not as yet totally disintegrated, and, in spite of the changes in the Low Countries and in France, Europe was much the same as before.

THE REVOLUTIONS OF 1848

It was far different when a new series of revolutions broke out in 1848 and continued for almost two years. Prince Metternich, foreign minister of Austria, who had been largely responsible for the Vienna settlement, was this time himself forced into exile by an insurrection in Austria. Though reaction for the moment triumphed in these revolutions, when the dust had cleared it was evident that the Metternich system had collapsed and that Europe would never again be the same.

France. The government of Louis Philippe had proved disappointing to the majority of Frenchmen. Throughout the reign there were several minor insurrections by workers in Paris and Lyons, which a conservative government mercilessly suppressed. The government itself was controlled by the propertied and industrial middle class; and the Industrial Revolution, now making rapid progress in France, brought few benefits to the workers, who became increasingly revolutionary. Even some conservatives began to desert the monarch, who by the 1840's was interfering constantly in the government and dictating policy to the Chamber, whose members were elected with the aid of every resource available to a corrupt group of ministers. Secret societies abounded, which were too numerous to be suppressed. A severe economic depression in 1847 was the decisive factor in the determination of the workers to take direct action.

In February, 1848, the Parisian workers began to throw up barricades, and fighting began. In two days they had taken control of Paris, whereupon Louis Philippe abdicated. The workers then demanded a republic, which was agreed to by the liberal deputies in the Chamber. These deputies then formed an uneasy coalition government with socialist Louis Blanc and workers' representatives, who persuaded the new provisional government to accept a scheme for National Workshops to relieve unemployment. When elections to a National Assembly resulted in the victory of the moderate republicans, led by the poet Alphonse de Lamartine, the Parisian mob refused to allow the Assembly to function. The government then abolished the National Workshops and a violent insurrection broke out, to which the government responded by conferring full powers on General de Cavaignac, who put down the revolt with great loss of life. The Assembly then wrote a new constitution calling for a presidential regime. In the elections which followed, the moderate republicans were decisively defeated by Louis Napoleon Bonaparte (a nephew of the great emperor), who had been a radical opponent of Louis Philippe but was relatively little known in France —except for his illustrious name.

As president Louis Napoleon showed himself a master politician and discredited so many of his opponents that a coup d'état organized shortly before his period of office was due to expire was successful (December, 1851). A plebiscite was held in the best Napoleonic manner, and the following year Napoleon was proclaimed emperor (1852–1870). Thus the Second Empire succeeded the short-lived Second Republic.

Austria. Within the great Hapsburg Empire there were many nationalities, including, in addition to the German ruling class, the Magyars in Hungary and the Czechs in Bohemia. Each minority group desired a measure of self-government. The Hungarians were the most vociferous, since they regarded themselves as in all respects equal to the Germans and superior to the many Slavic minorities. Following the news of the revolution in France, rebellions broke out in all parts of the Empire, the Austrian middle class demanding national reforms, the Czechs calling for full autonomy within the Empire, and the Hungarians divided as to whether to demand full independence or to content themselves with autonomy within the Empire. The Czech revolutionaries, led by the moderate Francis Palacky, were quickly suppressed by the Austrian army; but the rebellion led by Louis Kossuth, champion of Hungarian independence, was much more serious. For a time Hungary became actually independent, with Kossuth as president. When Austrian revolutionaries captured Vienna itself, the emperor, Ferdinand I (1835–1848) abdicated in favor of his eighteen-year-old son Francis Joseph. But help was at hand. Tsar Nicholas of Russia offered his armies to aid in suppressing the Hungarians, and the revolution was ended by August, 1849.

Meanwhile Austria had been experiencing considerable difficulty in her Italian provinces acquired at the Congress of Vienna. In March, 1848, a great rebellion broke out in Milan, which won support from the single independent monarchy of northern Italy, a union of Piedmont and Sardinia ruled by Charles Albert of the House of Savoy. Venetia also declared her independence, and Rome proclaimed a republic. Naples also experienced a swift but totally unsuccessful revolution. President Napoleon of France, in pursuit of a pro-Catholic policy, sent forces to Rome to protect the papacy against the Italian patriot Garibaldi.

Though Charles Albert for a time was in possession of the Austrian province of Lombardy, he was decisively defeated in March, 1849 (Battle of Novara) and abdicated in favor of his son Victor Emmanuel II. Venice was captured from the revolutionaries in August and the rebellions were at an end. The only gain made by the liberal forces was in Piedmont-Sardinia, where Victor Emmanuel (1849–1878) refused to abrogate the relatively liberal constitution granted by Charles Albert. This state, though it lost its first war for the unification of Italy, thus became the leader in subsequent efforts, which were crowned with success in 1870 (see p. 236).

Germany. The German Confederation set up by the Congress of Vienna was for a long time dominated by Austria, still the most powerful Germanic state by virtue of her possession of a non-German empire. In 1834, however, Prussia organized a customs union of a number of German states (*Zollverein*), from which Austria was excluded, thus laying the groundwork for the later unification by Prussia under Bismarck. In March, 1848, an uprising occurred in Berlin, which King Frederick William IV of Prussia brought to an end by promising reforms and setting up a Prussian constituent assembly. Minor rebellions broke out in other German states. To many German intellectuals it seemed that the time had come to unify Germany, with or without Austria. More than eight hundred notables, chosen from all parts of Germany, therefore assembled in Frankfurt for this purpose. But after Austria had suppressed her revolutions in her own territories and granted a new imperial constitution which included all Hapsburg lands, the Frankfurt delegates abandoned the idea of an all-German union, and offered the crown of Germany to Frederick William IV. He, however, refused the offer on the grounds that it could be made only by the German princes, not by an elected assembly. Whatever his pretext, there is no doubt that he feared the reaction of Austria—a fear that proved to be well justified when the Austrians late in 1849 refused to countenance even a limited Prussian union approved by the monarch ("Humiliation of Olmütz"). The failure of these efforts to bring the German states together through peaceful negotiations convinced Otto von Bismarck that Germany could be unified only by "blood and iron."

PROGRESS IN BRITAIN AND NORTH AMERICA

Though revolutions did not take place in Britain or the United States in the first half of the nineteenth century, Britain in particular was affected to some degree by the revolutions on the Continent, and the tempo of reform was probably speeded up in part because of the demonstration of what might happen if reform were refused. The United States Constitution was so interpreted during these years and Congress legislated in such a manner as to hasten reform and consolidation within the country.

England to the Reform Bill of 1832. In the years after the Battle of Waterloo, when military procurement dropped catastrophically, a severe economic depression occurred in Britain, which was aggravated by the demobilization of close to half a million soldiers. The Tory government of Lord Liverpool did little to remedy the situation and forcibly suppressed the agitation that followed. This policy increased the demand among all classes except the privileged few for parliamentary reform and the repeal of the protective tariff on imported grain, which kept the cost of living excessively high. In the 1820's the Tory government was strengthened by the accession of a number of liberal ministers who introduced some social and economic reforms, including the drastic overhaul of the antiquated penal system. Some import duties were lowered or abolished, but the landlords were not prepared to forego the protection of their own high-cost agricultural products. It was in 1824 that the laws against trade unions were for the first time lifted (see p. 211). Lastly, the seventeenth-century Test Act (see p. 158), which placed political disabilities on Catholics and Protestant dissenters, was repealed, and a Catholic Emancipation Act was passed in 1828 by the

Tory Parliament, now led by the military hero of Waterloo, the Duke of Wellington.

This Act was made necessary in part by Irish agitation. In 1800 Ireland and Great Britain had been united in a union under which the Irish sent representatives to the British Parliament. But this solution of the Irish question was never accepted by the Irish people, especially the overwhelmingly Catholic population of southern Ireland, whose representatives exercised little power in a Parliament that was foreign to them. The problem of what to do with this oppressed colony so near to home that it was of strategic importance plagued British governments throughout the century, as will be discussed further in Chapter 17.

The late 1820's and the early 1830's were dominated by the question of parliamentary reform. The reform movement, led by the Radicals and later by the Whig party, which was out of office during most of the period, had two major objectives: first, the relaxation of property qualifications for the vote to enable at least all members of the well-to-do middle class to exercise it and, second, the equalization of the electoral districts. The second was, in the eyes of the Whigs, far more important. There were numerous rotten and pocket boroughs,* surviving from earlier centuries, where there were few, if any, voters. One of the districts, indeed, had long before the nineteenth century sunk beneath the waves, but its owner still nominated members to Parliament. Several large manufacturing centers that had grown up in the eighteenth century returned no members at all. When the Whig party, led by Earl Grey, came into office in 1830, soon after the successful July Revolution in France, the new government was determined to pass a Reform Bill.

Moderate though the bill was, it failed at first even in the House of Commons in 1831. An election was then fought on the issue. Many even of the men who nominated members for the rotten and pocket boroughs voted for reform, and the Whigs won the election handsomely. A new bill passed the House of Commons but was twice rejected by the House of Lords. The king (William IV, 1830–1837) reluctantly agreed to create new hereditary peers to swamp the Tory majority, and the Lords at last gave way. The bill became law in 1832. Under its provisions fifty-six boroughs were abolished and another thirty lost one member apiece. The franchise was granted to

---

* Rotten boroughs were constituencies with so few electors that they could easily be controlled by the wealthy and influential. In pocket boroughs a single owner could actually nominate the representative.

more property holders than before, but the total electorate remained very small. About half the property holders but none of the working classes now had the vote.

Repeal of the "Corn Laws." The next years were filled with agitation by the Chartists (see p. 211), who were disappointed with the bill because it favored the middle classes and not themselves. At the same time a demand for the repeal of protective duties on grain was put forward vociferously by an Anti-Corn Law League formed for the purpose. Some legislation favorable to the workers was passed (for example, the Factory Acts of 1833 and 1847, regulating child labor and woman labor). Following a series of disastrous harvests and a great potato famine in Ireland, Sir Robert Peel, at the head of a Tory government, united with the Whigs to pass the repeal of the Corn Laws in 1846, thereby calamitously splitting his party but ensuring cheap grain for an indefinite future. This action was favored by the Whig industrialists, whom it spared the necessity of raising wages, but fought bitterly by the Tory landlords, who foresaw catastrophe for themselves. In fact they lost relatively little by it since they improved their efficiency and found themselves usually able to compete with foreign imports. But the repeal meant that Britain from this time onward committed herself to virtually free trade. For a long time she profited by this system, advocated as long ago as 1776 by Adam Smith (see p. 189), since she exported ever increasing quantities of manufactured goods, paid for by the import of food from her customers. For a while other countries followed her lead and reduced their own tariffs. But they soon reverted to protectionism, being in most cases unable to withstand competition from British goods, which had obtained a commanding lead in world trade during the previous century.

The United States. Much of the early history of the United States is concerned with the major constitutional problems arising in a federal system. Although the separate states of the union were powerful entities, their sovereignty was limited by the federal power as spelled out in the Constitution and interpreted by the Supreme Court. Especially under Chief Justice Marshall (1801–1835), the Court exercised its authority to nullify acts of Congress and of the states which it deemed contrary to the Constitution. At the same time it consistently enhanced federal power by interpreting in a broad manner the rights of the federal government in particular over interstate commerce. In this view the Court was at one with the Federal party, which included many of the nation's ablest statesmen. Marshall's work in strengthening the young national government was greatly influential in keeping the country together and preventing the separate states from imposing their will on the whole—even though it took a bloody civil war to maintain the Union in mid-century.

The first half of the nineteenth century saw the gradual acceptance of manhood suffrage, which had formerly been confined to only a few states. The last property qualification for the exercise of the franchise disappeared in the 1850's. General Andrew Jackson, elected in 1829, was the first president to come from the lower ranks in society. His election and his re-election for a second term were widely regarded as a triumph for the "common men," who chose him and kept him in power, and for "frontier democracy."

Meanwhile the United States was increasing rapidly in population and power and extent of territory. In 1803 President Jefferson purchased the enormous territory of Louisiana from Napoleon, to whom it had recently been ceded by Spain. Millions of Americans trekked westward in the following years, to reach the Pacific Oregon coast, where British and American interests conflicted until a treaty was signed in 1846. This treaty established the 49th parallel as the division between Canada and the United States. A network of canals pierced the Middle West, to be followed by the great transcontinental railroads. Following the pattern established by the Northwest Ordinance (1787), each new territory settled was eventually admitted as a fully equal state by act of the United States, which thus became ever more of a national government and less influenced by the local interests of the smaller, long-settled states of the Eastern seaboard. But the conflict between what were virtually two distinct civilizations of North and South continued to grow during these years, with the main question at issue being whether Negro slavery, which was a settled custom in the South and responsible, so the Southerners believed, for the success of their economy, should be extended into the new states. Compromise after compromise was briefly accepted, only to be questioned and resisted by one side or the other until the outbreak of the Civil War (see p. 256).

The United States expanded also southwestward, at the expense of Mexico. Texas had been partly settled by United States immigrants with the permission of the Mexican regime. But the Americans greatly resented their subservience to the Mexicans, and in 1836 they declared Texas independent. Santa Anna, president of Mexico, sent an army against the rebels, which massacred the besieged Americans at the Alamo fortress. General Sam Houston, with a new force of Americans avenged the defeat (Battle of San Jacinto), and Texas for nine years was an independent state. In 1845 the United States annexed it, thereby bringing on a war with Mexico, which ended with the capture of Mexico City and the cession to the United States not only of Texas but also of California and New Mexico. United States territories were rounded off by the purchase in 1853 from Mexico of part of New Mexico and Arizona. In 1867 Alaska was purchased from Russia, who had been settling the territory from the middle of the eighteenth century.

In 1822 the United States government, in the Doctrine proclaimed by President Monroe, defined the relations which it believed should obtain between Europe and the Americas. The United States, Monroe declared in his annual message to Congress, would regard the future colonization of any part of the Americas by a European power as an unfriendly act. In return the United States proposed thereafter to take no part in the wars of Europe. This unilateral declaration, which was of course not binding on European powers, thereafter became a fixed element in United States policy and is still quoted approvingly— in spite of United States participation in two major European wars within the memory of living man.

Canada. After passing the Quebec Act of 1774, under which the French inhabitants of Canada were guaranteed the free use of their language and the free observance of their Catholic religion, the British planned to confer a measure of self-government upon their colony. The American War of Independence postponed this advance until 1791, when Upper and Lower Canada were each given an elected assembly, while the British-appointed governor carried on governmental business with the aid of a council chosen by himself. The system of granting the right to discuss without executive responsibility worked extremely badly. The elected assemblies were constantly at loggerheads with the governors and their councils and were used mainly as a forum for expressing grievances and agitating for reform. In Lower Canada especially, where the population was mostly French, the English councils were a target of attack.

In 1837 rebellions broke out, one in each province, which were easily suppressed. But the British dispatched a Radical peer, Lord Durham, on the basis of whose report the two provinces were reunited (1840); and a subsequent governor, who continued to appoint councils until 1856, began to treat the elected assembly as a parliament whose advice should be taken, thus moving in the direction of responsible government. In 1867 Canada became a self-governing federal state, under a constitution drawn up by the Canadians themselves (British North America Act). The Maritime Provinces, hitherto under a separate administration, joined with Ontario and Quebec provinces (Upper and Lower Canada), and the western provinces joined in due course. Newfoundland remained an independent self-governing colony until 1949, when it was joined to the now entirely independent Dominion of Canada.

17 NATIONALISM, REFORM, AND STEPS TOWARD WAR, 1850-1914

During the six decades which preceded the First World War, Western civilization reached the apogee of its self-confidence and optimism. Most nations were on the way to achieving unity, and all governments, even that of absolutist Russia, were slowly becoming more responsible to public opinion. The remaining problems seemed capable of solution along the paths already laid out by the pioneers. The natural world was yielding up its secrets, and material resources could in the future be used for the increasing benefit of mankind. Western civilization was expanding over the whole globe, and soon, it was hoped, even the "lesser breeds without the Law" would be brought within its fold, and the world could look forward with pleasurable anticipation to eras of unending progress. Some writers, it is true, seemed doubtful of the future and inclined toward pessimism; but they were a minority, and many of them attacked their society only because they wished to improve it. They did not despair of it, as many were to despair later in the twentieth century. Such confidence and optimism, however, rested upon unstable foundations and were shattered in 1914 by the outbreak of the First World War.

UNIFICATION OF ITALY

Italy for centuries had been little but a geographical expression, with a common language and a common literature and art, but no political unity. Northwest Italy had come under the rule of the House of Savoy, with a base in Piedmont, to which was joined the undeveloped island of Sardinia (which in this chapter will be called simply Piedmont). This was one of the two monarchies in Italy. The other monarchy was the Kingdom of the Two Sicilies, which included Naples and Sicily under the unenlightened rule of the Spanish Bourbons. The rest of Italy was made up of various duchies ruled mostly by princes of foreign ancestry, Papal States ruled by the pope, and the Austrian provinces of Lombardy and Venetia in the north.

Early Independence Movements (Risorgimento). The Carbonari, already mentioned, was only one of many secret and semi-secret societies, looking toward the unification of Italy. An important group was known as Young Italy, led, usually from exile, by Giuseppe Mazzini, an inspired publicist and writer, who devoted his life (1805–1872) to the movement for unification known as the *Risorgimento*. The most spectacular leader was the free-lance soldier Giuseppe Garibaldi (1807–1882), who was from the beginning a member of Young Italy, fought for a time in South America, and returned to Italy in the 1840's. Thereafter he and whatever troops he could muster fought almost continuously until the achievement of independence and unity in 1870.

The Wars Against Austria. The failures of 1848 and 1849 have already been described in Chapter 16. Though Piedmont had ultimately been defeated by the Austrians, it won much prestige among the Italians for its efforts and for its refusal to follow the example of the other European states which abrogated the reforms granted under pressure during the revolutions. In 1852 Count Camillo di Cavour, a moderate Italian nationalist, became prime minister of Piedmont and thereafter devoted his single-minded efforts toward unification—which in his view should be carried out under the aegis of his master Victor Emmanuel II. He recognized that little could be achieved without foreign support and set himself to win the aid of Napoleon III of France, who had in his youth been a member of the Carbonari. After playing a small part in the Crimean War (see p. 243) to attract attention to Italy and her aspirations, Cavour signed an agreement with Napoleon for a joint invasion of Austrian territories in Italy. This war began in 1859, but the battles with the Austrians proved to be so bloody that Napoleon made a separate peace, under which only Lombardy was ceded to Piedmont, leaving Venetia still in Austrian hands. During the war several central Italian duchies initiated their own revolutions and after the war voted in plebiscites to join Piedmont. In the south Garibaldi with his small army of devoted Red Shirts captured Sicily from the Bourbon monarch Francis II and drove him from his capital of Naples. The complete and unexpected success of this adventure Cavour regarded as dangerous—though he gave his approval to the expedition—since Napoleon still had an army in Rome to protect the papacy, and was opposed to the annexation of the Papal States. Nevertheless, when Naples and Sicily voted in plebiscites to join Piedmont, Cavour had Victor Emmanuel proclaimed as king of Italy (March, 1861), in spite of the fact that Rome was still in papal hands and Venetia under Austrian control. A few months later Cavour died. During the so-called First Italian War for Independence, Nice and Savoy had been ceded to France, as had been agreed to in the initial negotiations for the aid of the French. These provinces have remained in French hands to the present.

Unification Completed. It was obvious to all that the existing situation could not exist for long, but it was not so clear how the militarily weaker Italians could oust Napoleon from Rome and the Austrians from Venetia. Garibaldi, chafing at the delays imposed by royal diplomacy, invaded Italy with the intention of taking Rome by force, but he was defeated and captured by the Piedmontese army and forced into temporary exile. In 1864 Napoleon III agreed to evacuate his army from Rome. But, far more important, in 1866 Victor Emmanuel's government entered into an alliance with distant Prussia, whose chancellor Bismarck was engaged in maneuvers to draw Austria into war. The Austrian defeat by Prussia in the Seven Weeks' War (see p. 238) resulted in the cession of Venetia to Piedmont, in spite of Italian defeats at the hands of the Austrians.

Meanwhile Garibaldi, taking advantage of the withdrawal of French troops from Rome, marched on the Papal States (1867). Napoleon III at once sent an army and defeated him, thus postponing complete unification for a further three years. During the Franco-Prussian War, however, Napoleon was compelled to withdraw his troops; whereupon the Italian armies stormed the city of Rome and annexed the Papal States. Pope Pius IX refused to recognize the annexation in spite of numerous guarantees proffered by the Italians, and he and his successors chose to regard themselves as "the prisoners of the Vatican" until 1929.

Democratic Regimes in Italy, 1870–1914. Italy during the Risorgimento had battled for unity and drawn on reserves of enthusiasm and idealism for the struggle. Now that union had been achieved, the new government had to be made to function, and it quickly became clear that the several sections of the country had reached very different stages of economic and social development. The south was poor in soil, overpopulated in relation to its resources, illiterate and backward; and it lacked industry. Northern Italy was capable of industrial expansion, its workers were skilled, its rural areas productive. No government could hope to solve such a problem overnight, and it continues to plague modern Italy. Without experience of democratic government, numerous parties arose, each representing sectional and special interests, and most of the governments were weak and corrupt. The property and literacy qualifications for voting were lowered steadily until the achievement of universal male suffrage in 1912.

Agitation continued for further expansion in the northern areas still ruled by Austria but largely populated by Italians (the *Trentino*), and Italy wished to engage in colonial expansion in spite of her relative poverty. She was seriously defeated in Abyssinia in 1896 at the Battle of Adowa and compelled to relinquish her ambitions for a period. However, she was able to take Tripolitania and Cyrenaica from helpless Turkey just before the First World War. But the government during these years achieved relatively little in comparison with the hopes entertained during the Risorgimento, and it enjoyed little international prestige. Just before the war there was an epidemic of strikes, led by socialists, anarchists, and others; and it is not impossible that there would have been a serious revolution if the war had not broken out and circumstances had not brought Italy into it in 1915.

CENTRAL EUROPE

Germany in 1871 at last achieved unification under the leadership of Prussia after two successful wars with her neighbors. The first war excluded the Austrian Empire from the future Germany and forced the recalcitrant non-Prussian states into a reluctant acquiescence in Prussian ambitions. The second war brought all the German states except Austria together in a military contest with a national enemy in the person of Napoleon III of France. This struggle cemented German unity, and the Prussian king became ruler of a new German empire in 1871.

The Seven Weeks' (Austro-Prussian) War. After the Humiliation of Olmütz (see p. 228), the Prussian monarchy was faced with the realization that Austria could never be persuaded to leave the leadership of Germany to Prussia. Moreover, it was clear that Austria could command the support in the All-German Diet of several important German states, which were opposed to Prussian ambitions—especially the Catholic states of Bavaria and Württemberg, which felt a greater affinity for Catholic Austria than for Calvinist Prussia. The one diplomatic trump card possessed by Prussia was the fact that Austria was not a wholly German power and that the non-German Austrian possessions would be welcomed by few Germans as part of a united Germany. It therefore became the policy of Bismarck, Prussian chancellor from 1862 to 1890, to play this card for all it was worth and to back it up by strengthening the army against the probability of future war with Austria. The Prussian parliament set up during the revolutions of 1848, controlled by liberals, did not wish to grant credits for the expansion of the army. Bismarck, sure of the backing of his king, William I (1861–1888), went ahead with the reorganization in spite of the opposition, and the parliament was powerless to prevent it. After the success of the army in the war with Austria, it agreed retroactively to what Bismarck had done.

Bismarck shrewdly inveigled the Diet into authorizing an Austro-Prussian intervention in Denmark over the question of two provinces (Schleswig and Holstein) which were ruled by the Danish monarch but peopled largely by Germans. The resulting war with Denmark was won without difficulty. But in the peace which followed Bismarck persuaded Austria to undertake the administration of Holstein, to which she had access only through Prussia. Angling for the opportunity to make war on Austria, Bismarck carefully made this access as difficult as possible. With a few vague promises he won the benevolent neutrality of Napoleon III—who made a similar agreement with the Austrians—and he signed a full-fledged alliance with Italy.

Thus fortified, Bismarck played his recently acquired trumps in Holstein. Denouncing Austrian actions in the province, he moved Prussian troops in, thereby compelling Austria to denounce Prussia in the All-German Diet. Several of the larger German states, which were not in the Zollverein and had not become reconciled to Prussian leadership, joined Austria in the anti-Prussian vote, and thus, with Austria, became Prussia's victims in the war that followed. The well-prepared Prussian armies crushed Austrian and dissident German resistance in seven weeks. By the peace treaty that followed, Austria was forever excluded from Germany, several North German states were annexed by Prussia, and others were brought together into a political and economic North German Confederation (1867). The South German states were required to join in a military alliance against the possibility of a French attack, and all joined the Zollverein.

The Franco-Prussian War. At this point a German parliament existed in the form of an assembly dealing with economic matters, and the greater part of Germany was completely dominated by Prussia. Napoleon III, who was able to win nothing from his neutrality and from his tortuous negotiations for the enlargement of France, was gradually isolated in Europe by the diplomacy of Bismarck, who did not scruple to expose Napoleon's expectations to England. It remained only to arrange for the opportunity for war with France in such a manner that Napoleon would seem to European, and especially to South German, opinion, to be the aggressor. This aim was soon achieved when the Spanish throne became vacant and Leopold, a young Hohenzollern prince, was approached to accept the crown. Bismarck encouraged the candidacy, knowing that it would greatly offend the French. The latter reacted as expected, and the French Chamber adopted a bellicose tone toward the Prussians, who the deputies believed could easily be defeated by the recently reorganized French army. When Leopold's father instructed his son not to accept the offer, the French believed they had won a great diplomatic victory, and the French ambassador to Germany demanded assurances from William I that the candidacy of his kinsman would never be renewed. The old king had no intention of giving any such assurances; and Bismarck issued his own version of the interview making it appear that William had treated the ambassador with disdain (Ems Telegram, July, 1869). The French clamored for war and Napoleon III with reluctance agreed and set an invasion in motion.

The Prussians, with a far more effective war machine and aided by the South German states, drove into France. Without allies, France was no match for the perfectly prepared Prussian army. Napoleon was defeated and taken prisoner at the Battle of Sedan, six weeks after the outbreak of war, and the victorious army marched on Paris, which yielded after a three-months' siege. The independent German princes then requested the Prussian monarch to assume the title of kaiser of a new German empire, within which they themselves would retain their old titles and estates. William accepted, and in January, 1871, the German Empire was proclaimed at Versailles in the Hall of Mirrors. France was made to pay a heavy indemnity and to cede Alsace and Lorraine to Germany.

Imperial Germany to 1914. Though the new German Empire was a semifederal state, it remained to a large degree dominated by Prussia, which held an effective veto through the king of Prussia, who was also the German kaiser. Bismarck became imperial chancellor, a position he held until 1890 when he was dismissed by the young kaiser William II (1888–1918), who wished in all essential respects to be his own chancellor. The new constitution, however, made for efficiency; and during the rest of the century Germany made rapid progress in many fields. Bismarck initiated a campaign against Catholic influence in the country (*Kulturkampf*), including the dissolution of religious orders, the dispossession of numerous bishops, and other measures. But discovering later that the program lost him much valuable political support from the conservative Catholics, he quietly dropped it. He also tried to suppress the growing power of the socialists by legislation. Though this effort succeeded only in driving them underground, a series of important measures to help the lot of the workers (thereby stealing the socialists' thunder) was outstandingly successful, and later imitated in almost every country in Europe (though not in the United States, where a comparatively few similar reforms came into effect in the 1930's under the New Deal). The new laws (1883–1889) provided for sickness and accident insurance and for old-age pensions on a contributory basis, part of the cost being paid by the workers, part by the state, and part by employers. After the fall of Bismarck, more laws were passed providing for arbitration in labor disputes, inspection of factories, and an up-to-date uniform law code. The various laws on social security were consolidated in 1911. Education made very rapid progress, and for a few decades graduate study in Germany was regarded as the model for the civilized world.

Nevertheless, the German socialists were far from defeated. From 1892 onward the Social Democratic party made gains in most elections for the Reichstag, the lower house of the German imperial parliament. In the elections of 1912 it was the largest party in the state. Though the German constitution did not give full power to the Reichstag, this body proved an invaluable forum for debate on foreign issues, especially the arms race, which increased its pace in the twenty years before the war. But when war approached even the Social Democrats, who had resisted the arms race as far as possible during the earlier years, finally voted for the military appropriations in 1913.

During the period of Empire, the Germans turned decisively against free trade, still favored by the British. Behind strong tariff walls they built up their heavy industry, and they surpassed Britain and France in steel production, taking second place only to the United States. With the aid of their aggressive salesmanship and governmental support, they were making severe inroads into British supremacy in international trade before the outbreak of the First World War. They were even selling goods in the British market itself.

The Dual Monarchy in Austria. Following the revolutions of 1848 and the suppression of the Hungarian rebellion, the Austrian government made a serious attempt to Germanize all the territories in the Empire. The policy was naturally bitterly opposed by the subject nationalities, especially the Hungarians. After the loss of the province of Lombardy in the war with Napoleon III and Piedmont, this policy was reversed and a half-hearted effort was made to convert the Empire into a federal state. This too failed, since the Austrians were not yet prepared to risk the possible combination of their subject nationalities against them. After their defeat in the Austro-Prussian War, they decided to share power with the Hungarians, who could be trusted to maintain their own dominance over the non-Magyar population in Hungary. The emperor of Austria then became the king of Hungary, and both Austria and Hungary were granted constitutions which established two separate parliaments. Thus began the Dual Monarchy of Austria, with a common currency and a common foreign policy, which lasted until 1918.

The Czechs in the Austrian province of Bohemia, and to a lesser degree the Croats and others in Hungary, were deeply disturbed by their failure to win even local autonomy and consistently agitated for more rights, the Czechs at times using the new parliamentary institutions in pursuit of their "national" ends. Their greatest triumph was the achievement of universal manhood suffrage (1907). This success, however, merely made parliamentary government impossible, since very few interests were shared by all the deputies. Thereafter most legislation was promulgated simply by imperial decree.

Hungary experienced less difficulty with her subject nationalities, who formed an actual majority in the state, since she yielded little to their demands and suppressed agitation with a firm hand. Moreover, the position of Croatia as neighbor to the aggressive Serbs (who were regarded largely as barbarians and who belonged to a different branch of Christianity) aided Hungary, whom the Croats often regarded with less aversion than they did the Serbs. The new state of Rumania, carved from the Turkish dominions, continually demanded Transylvania from the Hungarians, causing the latter to keep their Rumanian minority under firm control. But at the same time Austria and Hungary were often at loggerheads, especially over the Germanization of the army; and the movement for full independence was still powerful under Louis Kossuth and his son. But Hungarian intransigence was always neatly overcome by the king-emperor, who threatened to introduce universal suffrage into the Hungarian parliament, which would have left the Magyars at the mercy of their minority peoples.

Austria-Hungary pursued an aggressive policy in the Balkans, which were in a state of constant turmoil, while new independent states were in the process of being formed. She was in perpetual enmity with the Serbs, who looked to tsarist Russia as their protector, since Russia proclaimed herself friend of all the Slavs and adhered to the same religion as the Serbs. The annexation by Austria-Hungary of Bosnia and Herzegovina in 1908 brought her close to war with both Russia and Serbia, in which she could look for help only to Germany—and even that help was far from certain if she went to war over the Balkans, which were of relatively little concern to her ally. In June 1914, the murder of the Austrian heir to the throne, Archduke Francis Ferdinand, by a Serb in the Bosnian city of Sarajevo was the culminating event which brought on the First World War.

RUSSIA—THE REAR GUARD OF EUROPEAN ABSOLUTISM

In Russia by mid-century there had been little internal change. The movement for the settlement of Siberia had been progressing rapidly, but there had been no change of importance in the social structure; the serfs had not yet been emancipated; and Tsar Nicholas I, as absolutist as ever, had just intervened to help his fellow monarch in Austria to suppress the Hungarian revolution.

The Crimean War. Austria did not show herself particularly grateful to Nicholas when he became involved in the increasing decay of the Ottoman Empire, much of which he hoped to inherit— at a very minimum the Danubian principalities of Moldavia and Wallachia. Several times the tsar had suggested to Britain that they divide the bulk of Turkey's European possessions between them; but the balance of power in eastern Europe was too precarious for any one nation to be able to move safely in the area without arousing the opposition of the others. A ridiculous quarrel between the tsar and the French emperor, over whether Russians (Greek Orthodox) or French (Catholics) should have the right to protect Christian monks in Turkish-ruled Palestine, led to a series of demands by the Russians on the Turks. These were opposed by the French and by the Turkish sultan. The Russians, who had previously been invited into Moldavia-Wallachia to suppress a nationalist revolt, reoccupied the provinces in 1853, whereupon Austria, who was greatly interested in the area herself, attempted to mediate. The Turks preferred to declare war and invaded Russia, but were decisively defeated in a naval battle in the Black Sea.

At once Britain and France declared war on Russia and went to the aid of Turkey. Thus began the Crimean War (1854–1856). Britain entered in large part because of British dislike for Russian autocracy and high-handedness, which was whipped up by the popular press. Austria demanded of Russia that she evacuate Moldavia and Wallachia. When this was agreed to, she occupied them herself, but she did not enter the war. This was regarded as an act of gross ingratitude by all. Britain and France then attacked Russia in the Crimea; and after appalling losses through their outdated methods of warfare, general unpreparedness, and hopeless arrangements for the sick and wounded—later partly remedied by the work of the English nurse Florence Nightingale—finally took the Russian fortress of Sebastopol. The Russians then agreed to make peace on the basis of the abandonment of their previous claims; pressure by Britain and France on Turkey led to a new and more liberal policy toward Christians in the Turkish Empire; and Austria at last in 1857 evacuated Moldavia and Wallachia, which then received autonomy, later to form the independent state of Rumania.

Reforms of Alexander II. The Russians did not make peace while Nicholas lived. Alexander II, a much more moderate man, who succeeded in 1855, was at first interested not only in peace with the European powers but also in internal reforms and in more freedom for the oppressed Poles. In 1861 he emancipated the serfs, who were granted an allotment of land of their own to be paid for over several decades. But his efforts to moderate Russian oppression in Poland led to an uprising by discontented groups of Poles, who demanded more than he offered. The uprising was suppressed and the old policy of Russification was resumed. Alexander made many domestic reforms in Russia. Local government under a propertied franchise was introduced, and an improved judiciary system based on the French model was put into effect. However, liberals demanded real constitutional government, while radical secret groups which hoped to overthrow the government altogether began to be organized.

Tsar Alexander, who had meant well by his reforms, became increasingly embittered, and he retaliated by strengthening his police force.

Russo-Turkish War and the Congress of Berlin. In 1877 Russia again went to war with Turkey, this time in the interests of the Pan-Slavic movement, represented by Serbia, who had provoked a war with the Turks in the hope of winning some more territory at Turkish expense. The Russians were able to rescue Serbia from the consequences of her folly, but the peace they imposed on the Turks (Treaty of San Stefano, March, 1878) after their speedy victory was not found acceptable by the other European powers, since it created a large Bulgaria, which would have been dominated by Russia, and left Turkey with only Constantinople and a small hinterland in Europe together with a few semiautonomous provinces to which she had no access by land. The British objected to the increase of Russian influence and the dismemberment of Turkey; and the Austrians complained that the Russians were proposing to take part in the control of Bosnia and Herzegovina. Under heavy pressure the Russians agreed to attend a Congress held at Berlin in June, 1878, and to accept an altogether different Balkan plan devised by the other European powers. Austria was granted sole control of Bosnia and Herzegovina, and "Greater Bulgaria" was divided into three sections. The smaller European Turkish provinces were granted virtual or outright independence, and Britain was rewarded with the island of Cyprus, leased to her by the sultan for an indefinite period.

Formation of Revolutionary Parties. In 1881 Alexander II was murdered by terrorists, to be succeeded by Alexander III (1881–1894), who repressed all opposition ruthlessly and permitted no further reforms—though industrialization, with the aid of foreign, especially French, capital proceeded rapidly. Nicholas II (1894–1917) was faced by numerous political parties, which, unable to operate openly in Russia, were forced to meet and plot abroad. The most important were the Social Democratic party, divided into Bolsheviks and Mensheviks in 1903, and the Social Revolutionary party, mostly peasant, organized in 1901. In 1904 the Russians, who had been engaged in expansion in the East at the expense of China (to be discussed in Chapter 18), were brought face to face with the Japanese engaged in the same quest. When they refused to negotiate seriously with an upstart Oriental people, the Japanese attacked Port Arthur and in a series of battles by land and sea routed the Russians (1904–1905).

Revolution of 1905. The Russian government, which had shown itself so feeble in war with a despised enemy, was hopelessly discredited at home. A group of workers calling upon the tsar to petition for reforms was fired on by the troops. This action led to a series of strikes and widespread violence, which at last induced the tsar to promise a liberal constitution. But when the constitution was finally promulgated in 1906, it left little power to the elected representatives in the Duma, all of whom continued to criticize the government appointed by the tsar. The tsar then modified the electoral system until at last he had a group of conservative deputies ready to co-operate with him in suppressing the radical groups and in passing some moderate agrarian reforms sponsored by the prime minister, Peter Stolypin. When Stolypin was assassinated in 1911, the reforms came to an end. The repression continued, driving the revolutionaries who were still free abroad, where they plotted to take power later when the times might become more propitious.

THE DISMEMBERMENT OF EUROPEAN TURKEY

Turkey throughout the nineteenth century was compelled to relinquish one after another of her European provinces in the Balkan Peninsula. Russia and Austria were the two major powers who hoped to profit by Turkish losses; but Britain, as the leading naval power, was anxious to keep the seas open and in particular to prevent the Russians from taking Constantinople—a feat well within their capabilities if they were not stopped by the other powers. France and Germany were both interested in trade concessions in Turkey, including Asiatic Turkey. After the unification of Germany, German financial interests were especially active in projecting a Berlin-Bagdad railroad, a plan which conflicted with British imperial interests in the Middle East.

The Ottoman Empire. To western Europeans Turkey appeared as a totally unenlightened despotism in a progressive age, though Russia in the mind of most was scarcely any better. The entire Turkish governmental system, in the Western view, needed to be reformed, especially if Turkey was to become a profitable field for investment, as the Westerners wished. After the Crimean War the Turks, under pressure from their allies, especially Britain and France, agreed to many reforms, including increased toleration for Christian minorities. These reforms however, were not greatly welcomed by the minorities themselves, which would have preferred to escape from Turkish rule altogether and become independent national states—like Greece, who had blazed the trail in the 1820's. There was also disagreement among the European powers on whether Turkey should be partitioned or reformed. Britain and France, who lacked territorial ambitions in the Balkans, favored reform and increased opportunity for investment, whereas Austria wished to extend her empire into the Balkans. Russia as a Slavic nation regarded herself as the natural protector of the Slavic peoples in the Balkans and therefore wished to keep all the new Balkan nations which might result from the breakup of Turkey within her own sphere of influence.

Within Turkey herself there were many Europeanized reformers who tried to put pressure on the sultan, determined to make their country into a modern nation. These Young Turks, as they came to be called, were thrown into disarray by the actions of Sultan Abdul Hamid II (1876–1909), who granted a constitution on his accession but withdrew it after a year, preferring to suppress the reformers by force. Those who escaped the repression plotted abroad and infiltrated the ranks of the army. An army revolution sponsored by the Young Turks in 1908 forced, first the restoration of the constitution of 1876, and then the deposition of Abdul Hamid the following year. Thereafter the Young Turks became responsible for the government of the country.

The Ottoman Successor States. It was, of course, by mid-century totally unclear what new states would emerge from the loss of Turkish control in the Balkans and whether Turkey could hold on to any of her possessions indefinitely. It has already been noted that the Danubian principalities of Moldavia and Wallachia first fell under Russian control, then until 1857 were occupied by the Austrians. In 1862 Turkey permitted the union of the two principalities as Rumania, under the rule of an elected Rumanian prince, Colonel Alexander Cuza. When the Rumanian Assembly found his rule unsatisfactory they attempted to choose a substitute, but were compelled instead to accept the nominee of the French and Prussians, a Hohenzollern prince named Charles (Carol I). The new state, still under Turkish suzerainty, joined Russia in the Russo-Turkish war of 1876–1877 and was rewarded by having its independence recognized by Turkey and the other powers at the Congress of Berlin in 1878. Carol was proclaimed king in 1881.

The Bulgarians, who had been a powerful people in the Balkans centuries before the first Ottoman Turk had entered Europe, began an important nationalist movement in the mid-nineteenth century, which led to insurrections against Turkey in 1875 and 1876. The Turks suppressed the Bulgarians with unexampled severity. These "Bulgarian Horrors" shocked all Europe, especially William Ewart Gladstone, the English opposition leader, who personally wrote a pamphlet on the subject which sold over 200,000 copies. Russian intervention followed, and the treaty of San Stefano provided for a new Bulgarian state, which included much of Macedonia, under Turkish suzerainty. The Congress of Berlin (see p. 244) modified this treaty and provided for a smaller Bulgaria without Macedonia. Bosnia and Herzegovina, which had likewise rebelled against Turkey, were recognized as within the Austrian sphere of influence.

Russia continued to dominate Bulgaria, which became self-governing under a German prince, Alexander of Battenberg. But Alexander soon fell foul of the Russians and was made to abdicate (1886). The Bulgarian assembly then chose another German prince, Ferdinand of Saxe-Coburg, who in the course of the next years reconciled himself with Russia. He declared the independence of his country in 1908 and assumed the title of tsar. Turkey recognized Bulgarian independence the following year.

Meanwhile one little state had been virtually independent throughout the whole century. Montenegro, a country of hardy mountaineers, had not been completely subdued at any time by the Turks, who usually left it alone to be ruled by its native princes. After a revolt in Herzegovina aided by the Montenegrins, the Turks asserted their supremacy. The longer rebellion of Bosnia and Herzegovina in 1875–1876 was used by the Montenegrins as the occasion to drive out the Turks; and the country was recognized as an independent nation at the Congress of Berlin.

Serbia, which had become fully independent at the same conference, was unable to assert itself as an effective power, lacking a government which commanded wide support in the country. For most of the nineteenth century Serbia was a prey to feuding families; only in 1903 with the accession of Peter I Karageorgevitch (1903–1921) did she obtain a competent ruler—though even he could do little to control the vociferous nationalism of his countrymen and the terrorist Serbian organizations whose activities finally brought about the First World War.

The Balkan Prelude to War. The Balkan cauldron finally exploded dangerously in 1912 and 1913 with two Balkan wars which gave great concern to the powers. The annexation of Bosnia and Herzegovina by Austria in 1908 infuriated Serbia and Montenegro, who looked upon the territories as a natural field for their expansion, and Turkey, who was still their nominal suzerain. Russia was hardly less excited, though her foreign minister had known of the plan. Eventually Russia and Turkey were pacified and accepted the inevitable, while the Serbs and Montenegrins were prevented by pressure from the other powers from taking matters into their own hands. In 1912 the Serbs and Bulgarians entered into an agreement to despoil Turkey a little more for their own benefit, to which alliance Greece later adhered. In October, 1912, the three states began a joint invasion of the dying empire. Turkey, already at war with Italy, quickly made peace with her to meet the new threat but was unable to face the allied armies, which reached the Adriatic in the west and approached Constantinople in the east of the peninsula. Pressure from the powers again compelled the abandonment of the war and the cession of more territory by the Turks. Bulgaria profited most from the treaty, since the Austrians refused to let the Serbs have access to the Adriatic. Greece and Serbia then turned on Bulgaria, beginning the Second Balkan War (June–July, 1913). They were joined by Rumania and by Turkey, who hoped to recover some territories lost by the recent treaty. After the swift defeat of Bulgaria by the coalition, further territorial adjustments were made at the expense of Bulgaria.

This was the situation in the Balkans when, on June 28, 1914, Archduke Francis Ferdinand was murdered at Sarajevo in Bosnia by a Serbian terrorist, precipitating the First World War. No permanent boundaries had yet been accepted by the small nations of the peninsula; Austria and Russia were deeply embroiled in Balkan politics, almost always on opposite sides; while Turkey, who had just begun her new constitutional rule, remained a formidable military power with an army in the process of being reorganized with German advice—which the British and Russians, in particular, did not believe was totally disinterested.

DEMOCRACIES, OLD AND NEW

In the 1850's Napoleon III, an enigmatic character with a revolutionary past and the desire for French aggrandizement characteristic of his family, was ruling France and keeping Europe in a state of tension because of his unpredictability. Britain, with a powerful navy and a people that believed in their mission to maintain what they fondly thought of as a *Pax Britannica,* was moving rapidly ahead with social and political reforms at home. The United States was on

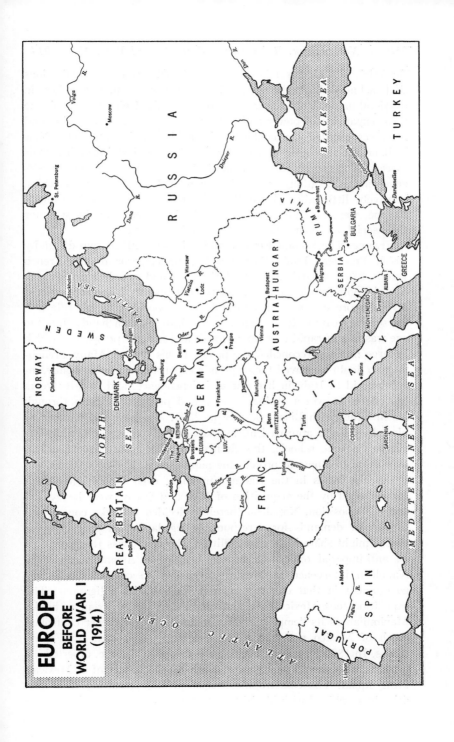

EUROPE
BEFORE
WORLD WAR I
(1914)

the brink of a civil war between two virtually separate civilizations that acknowledged the same flag and were bound together in a federal union. Until the war was over and the Union preserved, the great expansion of power and influence to which her population and resources entitled her could not be achieved. Australia and New Zealand, at the other end of the world, were just beginning their careers as the torchbearers of political and social reform under self-governing institutions; while in northern Europe the monarchies, relatively little affected by the revolutionary changes in Central Europe, were becoming constitutional, thus preparing the way for their social achievements of the twentieth century.

France. The Second Empire, which began with a coup d'état by which President Louis Napoleon became emperor of the French (see p. 226), started as an absolutist state and ended as a relatively liberal regime under a much-chastened emperor. Napoleon enacted several repressive measures to stifle the opposition to his rule and for several years took ever more power into his own hands. But the age was one of rapid economic growth and general prosperity, which in large measure reconciled the people to his regime. Many Frenchmen no doubt approved the emperor's expansionist foreign policy, involving aid to Italy in her war of independence, and in later years the efforts to win a Rhine frontier and perhaps Belgium through his intrigues with Bismarck (see p. 239). A substantial number of his subjects also approved his support of Catholicism, especially his aid to Catholic schools, though many doubted the wisdom of his expedition to Rome to protect the pope (see p. 236).

But the losses in the Italian campaign, even though they were compensated by the acquisition of Nice and Savoy, were heavy and excited opposition. Napoleon therefore decided to make concessions to popular demands for a responsible legislature, in part in order that it might share his responsibilities. The result was the growth of an anti-imperial opposition in the Legislative Assembly. In 1861 Napoleon intervened in Mexico, ostensibly to compel the Juárez government in that country to meet its financial obligations. The expedition took Mexico City and established the Austrian archduke Maximilian as its "emperor." Maximilian, however, never controlled much of Mexico and had to be constantly supported by French troops. In 1866 Napoleon, needing the troops in Europe, deserted his protégé, who stayed on to meet death at the hands of a Mexican firing squad. The catastrophic loss of prestige resulting from this debacle, combined with his failure to prevent or profit by the Austro-

Prussian War, persuaded the emperor to make further concessions at home. During the last years of his reign the constitution was several times modified. By 1870 Napoleon was almost a constitutional monarch with a prime minister (Émile Ollivier) in charge of the government.

The Franco-Prussian War (see p. 239) brought the Second Empire to an end. When Paris surrendered to the Germans, Adolf Thiers, a journalist and former minister under Louis Philippe, was chosen as head of state by a hastily elected assembly and given the task of negotiating terms with the enemy. The Assembly was made up mostly of royalists elected from rural constituencies, from whom the Parisian republicans expected nothing but a return of the hated monarchy. When the peace terms, which included the cession of Alsace and Lorraine, were made known, a furious insurrection broke out known as the Paris Commune. After two weeks of bloody fighting, it was suppressed by regular troops sent against it by the Assembly. These troops visited further reprisals on the revolutionaries after their defeat. The indemnity was paid and the Germans withdrew as a result of the efforts by Thiers, who was then deposed by the Assembly, since its monarchist majority desired to restore either the last male heir of the Bourbon line (Comte de Chambord, grandson of Charles X) or the Orléanist heir (grandson of Louis Philippe). The Comte de Chambord refused to accept the throne if the tricolor flag of the Revolution were maintained, whereas the "legitimists" would not accept the Orléanist heir while Chambord lived. The Assembly therefore chose a monarchist president, Marshal MacMahon, as a temporary measure, with the understanding that he would resign on the death of Chambord. But meanwhile Léon Gambetta and other convinced republicans were successfully organizing the electorate, and republicans were winning almost all the by-elections held for vacant seats in the Assembly. The result was that by the time Chambord died in 1883, the Third Republic was solidly established. President MacMahon attempted in 1877 to appoint a prime minister who lacked the confidence of the Chamber. When the Chamber censured the new minister and a successor, chosen after an intervening election, MacMahon gave way. Thereafter full ministerial responsibility was ensured. The president gradually became little but a figurehead, and never again during the Third Republic did a president attempt to dissolve the Chamber. To do so under the constitution he would have needed the consent of the Senate which, like the Chamber, became increasingly republican.

Nevertheless, there were so many parties in the Chamber that it was difficult—as it was also under the Fourth Republic—to obtain a stable government. In 1889 a popular military leader, General Georges Boulanger might have seized power, but at the last moment he lost his nerve in face of determined opposition from the government, which proposed to try him for treason. A scandal over the misuse of money subscribed for the building of the Panama Canal involved many deputies and senators (1892–1893). Finally the famous Dreyfus affair, which began in 1894 and was not settled until 1906, not only deeply divided France but also shook the foundations of the Republic. Captain Alfred Dreyfus, a Jewish officer in the French army, was condemned by court martial for treason on the basis of documents later shown to have been fabricated. But for a long time the unfortunate officer languished in the penal settlement of Devil's Island while the Dreyfusards (led by the novelist Émile Zola) and anti-Dreyfusards (mostly Catholics, monarchists, and conservative army officers) traded insults and pamphlets. Dreyfus was again tried by court martial in 1899 and once more found guilty. He was then pardoned by President Loubet. Not until 1906 was the conviction reversed by the Board of Appeals, and Dreyfus reinstated and promoted.

The Dreyfus case persuaded many republicans that the power of the Church should be reduced. They therefore pushed through the Chamber in 1905 a bill providing for the separation of church and state (thus abrogating the Concordat of 1801) and guaranteeing full liberty of conscience. Religious schools run by the Catholic orders (believed to be hotbeds of royalists and antirepublicans) were closed down and public education became the norm in France. The republican government at the turn of the century gave attention also to the provision of social security, including factory laws (1892), workmen's compensation (1896), and contributory old-age pensions (1910). Serious strikes were endemic for a few years while the CGT, the congress of trade unions, was controlled by syndicalists. But the state took strong action and broke them, thereby demonstrating the strength of the French republican governments, which, though the ministries changed frequently, adopted a consistent policy of moderate reform until the outbreak of the war.

Britain. After the fall of Sir Robert Peel, the Tory (Conservative) leader, in 1846 (see p. 230), England was ruled for a couple of decades mostly by the Whigs (Liberals). But neither party possessed a secure majority in the House of Commons during these years, and almost all the governments were coalitions. Meanwhile Disraeli was rebuilding the Conservative party and providing it with a program distinct from that of the Liberals, emphasizing in particular the role of the country in international affairs and the extension of the British Empire overseas. In the 1860's a strong demand arose for further franchise reform, advocated initially by the Liberals—who disagreed, however, among themselves on the amount of reform to be offered. Gladstone, originally a Tory, had by this time become the leading Liberal. In the midst of the agitation for electoral reform the Conservatives decided that they would, as the prime minister Lord Derby put it, "dish the Whigs" and introduce a bill of their own. Though the Liberals declared that it did not go far enough, they voted for it, and the Second (1867) Reform Bill became law. The great majority of the working class was now enfranchised, but it did not in the ensuing elections endorse the Conservative party. The Liberals, promising reforms for Ireland as well as domestic changes, were returned with a handsome majority, and Gladstone for the first time became prime minister (1868).

From this time onward Gladstone fought hard for reforms, and ultimately for self-government, in Ireland. He achieved much in the way of alleviation of the major Irish grievances; but the opposition to Irish self-government (Home Rule) was so great, even within his own party, that he never succeeded in his self-imposed task.

During Gladstone's first administration a major education bill was passed (1870), under which local authorities were required to maintain schools where private schools were insufficient. In 1880 education was made compulsory and free up to the age of ten. In 1891 most school fees were abolished, but not until 1918 were all fees abolished in elementary schools, and compulsory attendance required up to the age of fourteen. The civil service was reformed and opened to competitive examination, and the courts were reorganized. When Disraeli succeeded Gladstone in 1874, he too was impelled to produce measures of reform, especially in the field of public health. Since his party was less averse to the growth of labor unions than were the Liberals, he assisted them by legislation. He also forced through further regulation of the conditions in factories.

But the Disraeli administration (1874–1880) was on the whole more interested in foreign affairs, and the prime minister was in large part responsible for the Congress of Berlin in 1878 (see p. 244) from which he brought back, as he said, "peace with honor" and the island of Cyprus. It was he who made Queen Victoria the Empress of India, and he who bought Suez Canal shares on his own responsibility and with borrowed money, until Parliament approved the purchase—thus setting the stage for British intervention in Egypt, which had to be carried out in 1882 by a reluctant Gladstone. In Gladstone's second ministry (1880–1885) another Reform Bill was passed (1884), giving the franchise to the rural classes and to the remainder of the workers, and an extensive redistricting was accomplished. By this time almost all the male population had the right to vote.

Gladstone, unlike Disraeli, was opposed to the expansion of the British Empire. When he was forced to take action, as he frequently was, this action was likely to fail since it was half-hearted. His government fell when a relief expedition to rescue General Gordon, besieged in Khartoum in the Sudan by a Muslim imperialist known as the Mahdi, arrived too late to save him. But he was back in office the following year and this time introduced a measure for Home Rule (1886). The Liberal party split on the issue and it was defeated, in spite of support from the Irish Nationalists who sat in the British Parliament. Again in 1892 Gladstone campaigned for Home Rule, and he was enabled to take office only by the aid of the Irish Nationalists. The bill this time was passed in the House of Commons but overwhelmingly defeated in the House of Lords. Gladstone, who was now eighty-five years old, finally retired (1894), and for the next decade Conservative governments led by Lord Salisbury and Arthur Balfour held office. These years saw the high tide of British imperialism, to be discussed in Chapter 18. In 1902 a major education bill was passed setting up a national system of secondary education; but other reforms were held up until the great electoral victory of the Liberals (under the leadership of Campbell-Bannerman and Herbert Asquith) in 1905.

In 1906 labor unions were at last left fully free to strike and picket, and a Workman's Compensation Act was passed. In 1909 a system of noncontributory old-age pensions was introduced. But the major reforms—and the major struggle—were the result of the budget of Chancellor of the Exchequer David Lloyd George in 1909.

The government, faced with the necessity of greatly increased tax revenues to pay for naval expansion and the social security program, decided to tax property owners far more severely than hitherto. Inheritance taxes were also greatly increased. A surtax was levied on large incomes, and heavy capital-gains taxes were placed on increased land values. Such a budget was designed to redistribute income in a manner never contemplated before. The House of Lords felt itself to be the sole bastion defending the rights of property against the workingmen's vote. But by tradition it could not amend money bills—though it could amend or prevent the passage of other bills for an indefinite period and had in fact recently rejected or emasculated much Liberal legislation. Constitutionally it might be possible for the Lords to change the budget altogether if they were prepared to face the consequences. By a vote of almost three to one they decided to reject the 1909 budget.

Prime Minister Asquith, denouncing the rejection as a breach of the constitution, called for a general election, in which his party lost votes but was still able to govern with the aid of the Irish Nationalists. Their price was the introduction of a new Home Rule bill and the reform of the House of Lords so that it could never again reject a Home Rule bill passed by the Commons. The budget was therefore reintroduced and this time was passed by the Lords. Thereupon Asquith introduced a bill to modify the powers of the Lords by preventing them from vetoing money bills (budgets) and converting their absolute veto on other legislation to a suspensory veto with a limit of three years. When the House of Lords rejected this bill, Asquith, like Earl Grey before him (see p. 229), obtained a promise from the new king George V (1910–1936) to create new peers to the number necessary to pass the bill. The House of Lords gave way and the Parliament Bill of 1911 became law.

In 1912 the Home Rule bill promised for Ireland was introduced. This time Protestant Ulster (Northern Ireland) raised furious objections. The bill was twice passed by the Commons and rejected for two years by the Lords. The third year a somewhat different bill was passed and the House of Lords no longer had the power to reject it. But the act was not to come into force until different arrangements had been brought into effect for Ulster. By the date of the royal assent to the bill (September 18, 1914), Britain was already at war, and its promulgation was postponed for the duration. During the course of this long struggle over the changes in the constitution and Home Rule for Ireland, an even more epoch-making measure had been passed into law in 1911. By the National Insurance Act, British workers under a certain wage obtained compulsory health insurance, and over two million workers in certain industries were compulsorily insured against unemployment. Though the first provision was already in operation in imperial Germany, the second was new in 1911. It has since been imitated in every industrial country of the Western world.

In spite of these reforms, the workers remained dissatisfied. The last prewar years were filled with strikes for a "living wage." A great general strike had been called for September, 1914. But on the outbreak of war in August almost all the workers, like those elsewhere, rallied behind the government and thereby without doubt prolonged its life. The last years of the peace were also filled with agitation by women for the vote. The suffragette movement was marked by sporadic violence, designed to dramatize the issue, which met with a negative response from the government until after the war (women received limited suffrage in 1918).

The United States. United States politics in the 1850's was dominated by the question of the extension of slavery, which raised in an acute form also the problem of states' rights. The territory of Kansas, which had not yet won statehood, became briefly (1854–1858) the battleground between free-soilers, who were determined to permit no slavery there when it became a state, and the proslavery forces. The Supreme Court in 1857 laid down the principle that slaves were not citizens but property and thus that slaveowners could not be deprived of them by law (Dred Scott decision). In the presidential election of 1860 Abraham Lincoln was nominated by the Republican party on a program opposing extension of slavery. He was elected president in spite of receiving no electoral votes from any slaveholding state. Seven states of the lower South then seceded from the Union, believing that without the extension of slavery to new states, their own position as slaveholders and their agricultural economy were doomed. They chose their own president, Jefferson Davis, and proceeded to seize federal property. The war began with an attack by the Southerners on Fort Sumter, South Carolina (April 12, 1861). Lincoln then appealed for 75,000 militia, and the four border slave states thereupon joined the Confederacy. The Civil War which followed at first favored the militarily better prepared South, but the weight of numbers was eventually decisive and the war came to an end with the surrender of the Confederate general Robert E. Lee at Appomattox, Virginia, on April 9, 1865. During the course of the war, Lincoln by presidential proclamation emancipated the slaves in areas held by the Confederates (January 1, 1863), an act that was later ratified and extended to all slaves by constitutional amendment (1865). A few days after Appomattox, soon after he had entered on his second term as president, Lincoln was assassinated.

In the era of Reconstruction that followed, the South was frequently treated as a conquered territory, and it was slow to recover. The old economic and social system based on slavery was gone, but in due time it was replaced by social and economic discrimination against the Negroes, backed by local state law. The seceding states were readmitted one by one to the Union after ratifying amendments intended to protect the Negro. But economically the region remained depressed until very recent times, and it has never caught up with the North, whose industries continued to prosper, in large part because of their expansion to meet the needs of the war.

During and after the war expansion westward, always at the expense of the Indians, continued, and the various mainland territories were admitted as states to the Union, concluding with Arizona and New Mexico in 1912. The United States became the world leader in steel production, and her population, by immigration and its natural increase, surpassed that of every European country except Russia. Labor unions of various types grew up after the Civil War; all of them met with hostility from both state and federal governments and from business. Most strikes therefore resulted in violence on both sides; but concessions were won from employers and from some state governments. A law intended to curb industrial monopolies (Sherman Antitrust Act of 1890) was frequently used to suppress combinations of workers, until 1914, when the Clayton Antitrust Act exempted labor unions from antitrust provisions. Farmers also organized to protect their interests and worked for agrarian reform. When neither of the established parties (Democratic and Republican) seemed to offer much help to farmers and urban workers, a new party was formed in 1892 (Populist party); but though it was the most successful of the United States third parties, it did not come close to winning the election. The Democrats eventually took over most of the Populist program, but they themselves did not come to power until the election of Woodrow Wilson as president in 1912. Meanwhile President Theodore Roosevelt (1901–1909) tilted against "malefactors of great wealth" and succeeded in having some of the major monopolies dissolved. But in general little was accomplished comparable to the social reforms enacted in Europe during these years. The philosophy of the United States, except in the matter of tariffs, which were kept high to protect business, remained that of the laissez-faire economists of the eighteenth century, notably Adam Smith. Her problems were different from those of Europe. She absorbed many millions of imigrants, educated them, and allowed them to fend for themselves in the same way as other Americans. It was not yet believed that it was a vital concern of government to legislate for the social welfare of American citizens. Equality of opportunity was provided, except for the Negroes; it was for each man to take advantage of that opportunity and enjoy the fruits of his enterprise.

The Smaller European Countries. In Spain monarchical misrule resulted in a short-lived revolution in the 1870's, which established a republic. When Alfonso XII was restored in 1875 he granted a constitution and became a constitutional monarch. But the political parties that governed during the next decades were more interested in holding office than in reforms and were far too weak to make headway against the opposition of the entrenched Church and nobility. Portugal had a constitution from 1852, but the parties behaved much as in Spain. Only when Carlos I suppressed his ineffective parliament in 1906 did the people react, and after the king had been murdered in 1908, a republic was established (1910). The succeeding governments proved to be no more effective.

Holland and Belgium were constitutional monarchies during the period. William II of Holland granted a constitution after the revolutions of 1848, with a restricted franchise under which the middle class ruled. Reform bills were passed in 1887 and 1896, which greatly increased the electorate, but universal suffrage was not granted until 1917. Little social legislation was passed until after the First World War. In Belgium the major division between the parties in the parliament, which was elected by a restricted franchise until 1919, concerned—then as now—the religious schools, which were approved by most of the French-speaking Catholics (Walloons) and opposed by most of the Flemish population. The Labor party, which rose to prominence and provided the parliamentary opposition to the ruling Clericals, was socialist in its beliefs and used the weapon of the strike, often with great effect, to force reforms until universal suffrage was achieved.

Norway, united with Sweden after the Congress of Vienna, had her own constitution and parliament (the Storting), but for a long time the Swedish monarch used his veto freely. Norway was granted independence in 1905 and chose a king from the Danish royal family. Responsible government in Sweden was likewise thwarted by the monarchs until 1909, when she won universal manhood suffrage. In Denmark the monarch granted a constitution giving power to the middle class after the revolutions of 1848. Health insurance and old-age pension laws were passed in 1891 and 1892, and the rural co-operative movement, a present characteristic of the country, grew rapidly. Fully responsible government under a truly constitutional monarchy was not achieved until 1915. The Confederation of Switzerland almost disintegrated in 1847, when some Catholic cantons seceded. But the rebellion was quickly put down and a new constitution closer to a federal union was proclaimed in 1848. Federal power increased for the rest of the century, but cantonal governments still control most aspects of life, and some of these are of the ancient town-meeting type.

Australia and New Zealand. Australia, discovered by the Dutch in the early seventeenth century and rediscovered for the English by Captain James Cook in the second half of the eighteenth, was then used as a British settlement for convicts, including political deportees. The first free settlers in the parts of the continent where the convicts were housed (New South Wales and Tasmania) used them as a source of cheap labor. But elsewhere the convicts were few, and in time all were freed and mingled with the rest of the population. The discovery of gold in the 1850's led to a great increase of immigration, especially from England, including many of the working class, some of them Chartists, who were dissatisfied with English labor conditions. Largely because of this element the Australian colonists, as soon as Britain granted responsible government to the then separate colonies (1852), voted for universal manhood suffrage (1860) and the first secret ballot in the world (1856). Australia early had a Labor party devoted to the improvement of social welfare by governmental action and had free and compulsory secular education as early as the 1870's. From 1894 women were granted the vote in each of the states in succession. In 1900 the colonies were federated as the Commonwealth of Australia with fully responsible government subject—until 1931—to certain constitutional safeguards which were retained in British hands. From 1902 women had the vote in all federal elections. The Labor party, which had been dominant in several previous governments won an over-all majority of seats in the House of Representatives in 1910 and remained in power during the First World War—enacting as much social legislation as was compatible with Australia's active participation in the war.

New Zealand, though she took no convicts, was peopled almost entirely by immigrants from Britain, among whom were very few from the upper classes. The social composition of the country was thus similar to that of Australia. Settlement was held up to some degree by the presence of a Polynesian people (the Maoris), who were in possession of much of the land. The settlers deprived them of a large part of this territory over the first half of the nineteenth century. After several Maori wars, which the British were unable to prevent, the New Zealanders accepted their presence and later granted them some political and social rights in the government, which was a responsible one from 1856, subject to the same limitations as Australia. New Zealand early used the power of the state to further social welfare, and the Labor government of Richard Seddon (1893–1906) was the world pioneer in much social legislation, including free compulsory primary education (1877), a vast series of laws protecting the workers, noncontributory old-age pensions (1898), an infant welfare program (1907), a graduated income tax, and similar measures. With the exception of the small American state of Wyoming (1869), New Zealand was the first to grant women suffrage (1893). This program was greatly enlarged during the 1930's, eventually (1941) becoming the first complete national health program.

INTERNATIONAL DISCORD AND THE OUTBREAK OF WAR

The balance of power in Europe had been drastically changed by the unification of Germany, which was a far stronger military power than Prussia had ever been and was ruled from 1888 by a kaiser who was determined to make his country, if not supreme, at least one whose interest should always be taken into consideration in world affairs and a major colonial power. No equilibrium among the powers was established in the period between the unification of Germany and the First World War, and the various chancelleries of the great powers were always insufficiently informed on the real intentions of the others. Aside from the strict secrecy observed on most of the interstate treaties, it was never quite certain whether the powers would honor the treaties of the moment in the event of war. Moreover, since most countries had conscription and, fortified by the national feeling that had been increasing throughout the nineteenth century, could bring to bear all their manpower and resources, war was likely to be far more destructive than in the past.

The Alliance System. Bismarck, the German chancellor after 1871, was well aware that his actions had disturbed the balance of power and that France was not likely ever to accept with equanimity the loss of Alsace and Lorraine, ceded to Germany after the Franco-Prussian War. He therefore made it his chief task to try to isolate France, and for some time he encouraged her to expand in Africa and elsewhere in preference to seeking revenge and redress in Europe. This policy had also the advantage of keeping Britain and France from allying themselves, since the two countries were everywhere abroad in competition with one another. Though for a time Bismarck attempted to win the friendship of both Austria and Russia, this was difficult to achieve since the interests of the two countries clashed and were likely to continue to clash in the Balkans. He therefore decided to choose Austria, with whom Germany entered into a binding alliance in 1879, which Italy joined in 1882. This Triple Alliance lasted until 1915, when Italy abandoned it. Nevertheless, Bismarck continued to make overtures to Russia, and in 1887 re-negotiated a treaty (Reinsurance Treaty) that had had a shadowy existence since 1872 and formal existence since 1881 (Three Emperors' League, between Germany, Austria, and Russia). In 1890 Germany signed an agreement with England under which she abandoned her claims in Africa in exchange for the island of Helgoland in the North Sea, which she planned to use for a naval base.

But when Bismarck fell from power in 1890, his system was quickly abandoned by Kaiser William II. Immediately after his dismissal the kaiser and his new ministers decided not to renew the Reinsurance Treaty, which expired that year. Since this left Russia isolated, she was thrown into the arms of France, who had been seeking an alliance ever since 1871 but had hitherto been rebuffed. In 1892 and 1893 the tentative negotiations bore fruit in an alliance between the two countries, whose interests in fact did not clash so seriously as did those of Austria and Russia in the Balkans. The kaiser also offended Britain deeply by giving verbal, and occasionally diplomatic, support to President Kruger of the Transvaal in his quarrel with the British in South Africa; and he decided that Germany must be a naval as well as a land power (1898 onward), thus seriously alarming Britain and setting into motion a naval arms race. After a very serious colonial dispute in Africa in which the British compelled the French to retreat from Fashoda in the Sudan (1898–1899) and the loss of prestige by Britain in the Boer War (see Chapter 18), both powers moved closer together for the first time in centuries. Britain, content for a century to adopt a policy of "splendid isolation" backed by her navy, realized that German naval power might come to threaten her and that it was no longer so certain that she could remain aloof from the Continent. After negotiating a treaty of alliance with Japan in 1902, she finally came to an understanding with France (*Entente Cordiale* of 1904), which did not amount to a firm alliance but settled many outstanding problems between the two countries and assured each of diplomatic support from the other in case of need. This agreement was supplemented by a similar understanding with Russia negotiated in 1907 (Triple Entente).

Moroccan Crisis. This agreement was soon put to a test by the expansion westward by France from her long-held colony of Algeria in North Africa. The kaiser, who had not been consulted and was determined to assert German rights, decided to support the sultan of Morocco against French designs. He paid him a personal visit in 1905, as a result of which France was compelled to agree to an international conference, held at Algeciras in 1906. At the conference the kaiser was supported only by Austria. Though an agreement was patched up, France continued with her policy in Morocco and sent an army there—whereupon the kaiser despatched a German warship to Agadir to "protect German interests" (1911). But, again finding himself almost isolated, he agreed to accept considerable French territory in Africa in exchange for consenting to French hegemony in Morocco.

Balkan Crisis. The background of the Balkan crisis which actually brought on the war has already been described (see p. 248). Austria was determined to teach Serbia a lesson and was prepared to risk the hostility of Russia. She harbored indeed serious doubts as to the efficacy of the Russian army after its defeat in the Russo-Japanese war and believed she could rely on the help of Germany in spite of the fact that the Triple Alliance did not cover the exact situation that arose in the Balkans after the murder of the Austrian heir presumptive at Sarajevo on June 18, 1914. Before taking any irrevocable steps after the murder Austria requested and received full assurances of support from the German chancellor, Bethmann-Hollweg, and the kaiser (the "blank check"). On July 23, she sent an ultimatum to Serbia, most of which the little country accepted. But Serbia refused to accept every point, since to do so would have violated her sovereignty beyond repair. On July 28 Austria declared war on Serbia. In spite of frantic last-minute efforts, the machinery of the alliances then came into operation. The Russian tsar was persuaded to order general mobilization. When the kaiser urged him to rescind the order in favor of negotiations with Austria, he found it impossible to halt the mobilization—whereupon Germany sent an ultimatum to Russia. A German inquiry to France as to whether she proposed to support Russia was met by French mobilization. Germany then (August 1) declared war on Russia and two days later on France. When Germany invaded Belgium, contrary to an international agreement guaranteeing Belgian neutrality that had been in existence since Belgian independence, Britain declared war on Germany (August 4). Austria declared war on Russia and Serbia on Germany on August 6.

18 THE GROWTH OF IMPERIALISM IN THE NINETEENTH CENTURY

At no time in the history of Western civilization have the European nations lacked the desire to expand and extend their rule over non-Europeans. The first such venture was the Crusades, carried out in the name of religion but with the desire for material gain and new lands not far below the surface. In the fifteenth century, America was rediscovered and the East was dotted with Portuguese outposts to protect the trade that was being opened up. In the sixteenth century, Latin America was subjected to Spain. In the seventeenth century North America was peopled by English and French, while the Dutch built an empire in the Far East. In the eighteenth century, the conquest of India was begun by the British, to be completed in the nineteenth. But none of these ventures could equal the tremendous expansion that took place in the second half of the nineteenth century, so that by the outbreak of war in 1914 there was scarcely an area in the world that had not been subjected either to some European nation or to the United States; and those lands that retained nominal independence were all (with the exception of Japan, who had become imperialist herself) to some degree controlled by the West and their freedom of action seriously circumscribed.

MOTIVES FOR THE GROWTH OF IMPERIALISM

The motives behind this resurgence of imperialism were varied and seldom, if ever, unmixed. The primary motive behind the forcible opening of China and Japan was undoubtedly economic; and nowhere was the economic motive totally absent. But much of Africa was certainly taken for reasons of prestige and to win a "place in the sun" in competition with other European powers.

Economic Motives. During the Industrial Revolution all the manufacturing countries needed new markets for their products and new sources of raw materials required for manufacturing. The Oriental countries, which had long been civilized, could be expected to provide the Europeans with a good new market; and many Oriental products, especially tea, could be bought in return. The undeveloped countries could not be expected to buy much; but they possessed certain raw materials, notably cocoa and palm oil, that were in increasing demand in a Europe having a sweet tooth and learning to wash regularly. In these countries the supply was irregular until it was organized by expatriate Europeans. Lastly, there was a considerable surplus of European money available for investment, which could be lent with profit to countries that could afford to pay interest on it. Since most non-European rulers were not accustomed to paying interest promptly and regularly, a number of imperialist ventures were initiated for the purpose of ensuring the payment of interest on loans, many of which had been squandered by the borrowers on personal expenditures. In other cases an industrial nation invested money in the transportation or communication system of an undeveloped country for the primary purpose of ensuring the flow of raw materials to the coast. Railroads could hardly be managed by the natives of these countries, certainly not in such a manner as to show a profit to the investor. The investment was used to buy heavy equipment from the mother country, thus creating a new export market even when ordinary consumer goods could be sold only to the few Europeans in the country.

Missionary Ventures. In the nineteenth century, almost all the branches of Christianity believed it to be a part of their task to convert pagans. From quite early in the century, missionary enterprises were active in the Far East and in Africa. In Africa they became especially interested in stamping out the remnants of the slave trade, which had been abolished in British territories as early as 1807. Though some European nations were slow to follow this example, and the Arabs in Africa continued the trade until almost the end of the century, most European governments aided the missionaries in their self-imposed task. Missionaries were sometimes murdered by the Africans, and in the East they were frequently persecuted as agents of foreign powers. It was damaging to the prestige of a powerful European nation if it left such actions unpunished. In the East African territory of Uganda, Catholic and Protestant missionaries were in direct competition with one another, and their respective converts adopted a similarly hostile attitude. This conflict was partly responsible for British intervention.

Nationalism. Once a colony had been acquired it was necessary to protect the lines of communication between it and the home country. Thus some small colonies, for example Aden in the Red Sea, were acquired for strategic reasons and as refueling stations. But it is unlikely that the partition of the non-European world would have been as nearly complete as it was if the climate of European opinion in the late nineteenth century had not been so favorable to the enterprise. Britain, who possessed the largest overseas empire in 1815, was inclined to regard it for the next fifty years as an economic liability and there were many influential "Little Englanders" who favored the abandonment of the colonies, even including India—although India was not yet even fully conquered. But it was much easier to hold on to the colonies in which many Englishmen had acquired a vested interest than to give them up— even if there had been any native rulers to whom the English could have yielded their sovereignty.

Once the European countries began seriously to compete with one another for colonies, national prestige became involved. No country could allow itself to lose face by giving up a colony to another without equivalent compensation. Moreover, a relatively small European nation could feel more powerful if it possessed an extensive empire overseas. When Germany became unified, Bismarck at once recognized that his country became in fact more powerful only by industrial development at home. He regarded overseas colonies as likely to be more of a drain than an addition to the national wealth. But he encouraged France to seek colonies, believing that they would both sap her strength and divert her from seeking revenge in Europe. Eventually even he was compelled to recognize the strength of national feeling, and he realized that he could not afford to refuse diplomatic help to free-lance Germans engaged in colonial enterprise. Kaiser William II, who shared the prevailing view that every nation should demonstrate its superiority and prowess by assuming its share of the "white man's burden," actively sought colonies for Germany and insisted that he should be consulted and if possible compensated whenever new territories were to be subjected to European rule.

EXPANSION IN THE FAR EAST

By the second half of the nineteenth century, Britain had subjected the whole of India and Ceylon and had been brought into contact with Burma. The European powers had begun to take military action against China to force trade concessions, and the Dutch were busily engaged in making their Indonesian empire profitable through a contract system for the cultivation of export crops.

The Opening of China and Japan. The British East India Company throughout the eighteenth century had been importing tea into England from China through a trading reserve, or "factory," which they had been permitted to open in Canton. But the Chinese emperors regarded their country as in all respects superior to the West, whose rulers they thought of as barbarians. Having no wish to import anything from England in return, they insisted on being paid in silver coin. In 1773 the Company first shipped opium (grown in its Indian territories) to China, and the drug made rapid headway in the country in spite of imperial prohibitions. In 1839 the emperor sent to Canton an official named Lin as his personal commissioner to enforce the prohibition. Lin destroyed some 2,000,000 pounds' worth of opium and imprisoned the British in their own factory. This incident led to the First Opium War (1841–1842), which demonstrated clearly that Chinese arms and military technique were so inferior to those of the Europeans that China would have to grant concessions. The Treaty of Nanking, dictated by the British, provided for the opening of certain "treaty ports" to European trade, a uniform import tariff, and the cession of the then uninhabited island of Hong Kong. At once the other European nations demanded the same treatment which was soon conceded. This treaty was followed— at the insistence of the United States, whose missionaries had been active in China since 1830—by the grant of "extraterritoriality" to foreigners, placing them under the jurisdiction of their own courts.

Objections to these concessions, combined with widespread agrarian unrest in the country, culminated in a huge rebellion (Taiping Rebellion, 1850–1864) by the Chinese against the Manchu (Mongolian) Dynasty, which occupied the imperial throne. The emperor was able to suppress this rebellion only with European assistance, notably that of General Charles (Chinese) Gordon (see p. 274). Meanwhile, before the rebellion was brought under control, friction in the new treaty ports led to the Second Opium War, in which the British and French co-operated, first to capture Canton and then to march on Peking. The emperor agreed to a series of treaties (Treaties of Tientsin, 1858) legalizing the import of opium, opening further treaty ports, and setting up a customs service staffed by Europeans. On the way to the capital of Peking to ratify the treaties, some Europeans were attacked by Chinese troops, whom they repelled without difficulty. Determined to teach the Chinese a lesson, a new Anglo-French expedition stormed Peking and burned the imperial Summer Palace. The treaty was then extended to include a larger indemnity to be paid by the emperor. In this war the Russians, who were already well-entrenched north of Manchuria, persuaded the emperor that they alone could keep the western Europeans in check, and were rewarded by the cession of a large strip of land reaching to the Pacific, on which they built the ice-free port of Vladivostok.

China was now virtually helpless against European exactions, and Europeans did more or less what they wished there for the rest of the century, each nation winning for itself "spheres of influence," fortifying territories leased by the emperors, controlling the numerous "treaty ports," and managing the customs service on the emperors' behalf. But the competition among the different powers was strong enough to prevent any one from taking too much, and the nominal integrity of China was thus maintained.

This renunciation did not, however, apply to the tributary provinces of the Chinese Empire. France, who had been appointed by the pope as protector of Catholics in the Far East, experienced many difficulties with the Vietnamese emperor, who ruled Annam, Tonkin, and Cochin-China. In 1862 this emperor ceded three provinces of Cochin-China, from which base French forces moved into the rest of Cochin-China and into Cambodia (1887). In the 1880's France pursued a more definitely imperialistic policy, compelling the Vietnamese to accept a French protectorate over Annam and Tonkin (1883). The Chinese emperor meanwhile had been unable to protect his vassal, and Siam, which tried to protect its vassal, the small kingdom of Laos, had to allow the French to establish a protectorate there also. A French expedition to Bangkok in 1893 forced the Siamese to give way, but Siam (Thailand) retained a precarious independence and even added some Laotian territory to her own by permission of the French. The French created an administrative federation of all their possessions in Indo-China in 1907. The Chinese had no option but to recognize French conquests in the area.

The gentleman's agreement, under which European powers would not annex outright the parts of China they controlled, was broken by the Japanese. Opened to European trade by United States Commodore Perry in 1853, Japan had altered her form of government and decided that she could maintain her independence only by imitating Western techniques and by establishing a government based on institutions similar to those of the West. In the process the Japanese had come to realize that their future rested on the exploitation of the Chinese market and on the winning of extensive concessions for themselves. Thus they began to imitate the methods of the Western imperialists, and they looked with disfavor on the modernization of China, which the emperors, with European assistance, attempted to put into effect in the last decades of the century. In particular, Japan began to interfere in Korea, a Chinese vassal state. This situation resulted in the Sino-Japanese War of 1894–1895, in which the Japanese destroyed the Chinese army and navy while the European powers vainly tried to mediate. In the Treaty of Shimonoseki (1895), China was compelled to recognize the "independence" of Korea and to cede Formosa and the whole Liaotung Peninsula to the Japanese, at the same time paying a large indemnity. Such extensive concessions could not, however, be permitted by the European powers, and they compelled Japan to relinquish the peninsula in exchange for an increased indemnity.

The European powers then proceeded to make their own further demands on China. The American secretary of state, John Hay, felt impelled to warn the Chinese that the United States desired an Open Door policy of equal economic concessions to all. The emperor speeded up the process of modernization with a series of reform edicts. These, together with the loss of face entailed by such extensive foreign intervention, proved to be too much for the regime. The dowager empress Tzu-Hsi, who had backed the Chinese reforms in previous years, took full control of the government in 1898. She was then willing to co-operate with the ultraconservative Chinese secret societies, which in 1900 began a rebellion (Boxer Rebellion), directed primarily against foreigners. Many were murdered, while others were besieged in their legations. An international army, in which Americans and Japanese took part, marched on Peking and took it without difficulty from the rebels who had captured it. Though it was agreed that the rebellion should not be regarded as a war against the West, an indemnity was nevertheless imposed. After the failure of the rebellion, Chinese reforms were resumed at an increased pace, including even some political changes in the direction of democracy. But the effort came too late to save the regime, which was overthrown in 1911. Meanwhile the Russians, who had established a virtual protectorate in Manchuria, had been defeated by the Japanese in

1904–1905 and ceased their expansion, returning Manchuria, at the insistence of the European powers, to China. Korea became a Japanese protectorate and was annexed in 1910.

British Annexation of Burma. In the early nineteenth century, the British in India clashed with the kingdom of Burma, which was itself an imperial power in the Far East, having expanded for more than a century at the expense of her neighbors. The Burmese in the 1820's began to interfere in Assam, which the British regarded as their own preserve, and they actually invaded India in 1824. The British thereupon sent an expedition to the Burmese seaport of Rangoon and compelled the Burmese monarch to cede Assam to British India and to pay an indemnity. The Burmese monarchs, still unwilling to accept their military inferiority, continued to make difficulties for the British, who provoked a war in 1852. As a result of this war the kingdom was partitioned, and the British this time kept Rangoon. After a period of improved relations under a new Burmese king, his successor, Thibaw, decided to play off the British against the French and to grant concessions to the latter in exchange for arms. The French, busy in Indo-China, were in no position to interfere in a territory so clearly within the sphere of British influence. But Britain took advantage of Thibaw's hostility to invade his country in 1885 and conquer him. Burma was then made into a province of India.

Changes in India. India herself, after the Sepoy Mutiny of 1857 (see p. 186), was under the complete control of the British, who had invested large sums of money in the country and ruled it autocratically through viceroys and an efficient civil service. The India National Congress was founded in 1885, and at the turn of the century there were sporadic local uprisings against British rule. In 1909 the British granted some political concessions, permitting Indians to be chosen by "communal" (separate Muslim and Hindu) electorates to fill positions in provincial legislative councils, which were given the right to discuss the budget and other matters. In 1906, since the Indian National Congress was in large measure dominated by Hindus, the All-India Muslim League was founded, to which most of the politically-minded Muslims gravitated. A new series of political reforms were granted after the war (see p. 335).

Malaya. The British East India Company, during its period of monopoly in the East, had obtained the trading post of Penang (1796) from a local sultan; by 1824 it had won from the Dutch the island of Singapore and the old Portuguese outpost of Malacca. These became the colony of the Straits Settlements. From these outposts the British began to penetrate inland, especially after the demise of the Company in 1858. The Malay sultans were gradually required to accept British Residents as advisers. A group of four states was made into a federation, with the sultans still as nominal rulers but under British control (Federated Malay States, 1895). The other sultans in the peninsula were left free from direct control but accepted Residents to guide their policies (Unfederated Malay States).

Borneo. North Borneo on the island of Borneo, adjoining the Dutch possessions, was granted to a British company to develop in 1882 by agreement with the sultan. In 1888 the British established a protectorate in the territory. The sultanate of Brunei, where oil was later discovered, became a protected state with a Resident in 1906. The sultan of Brunei, nominal ruler of Sarawak, had granted this territory to an Englishman, James Brooke, as early as 1841. From that time it continued to be governed by Brooke's descendants (the White Rajahs), though Britain was its formal protector from the 1880's.

The Philippine Islands. The Philippine Islands, which had been a Spanish possession since the sixteenth century, were the scene of a major insurrection against the Spaniards in 1896, led by Emilio Aguinaldo. When the United States went to war with Spain, mainly over Cuba, Filipinos, although they made an agreement with the Spaniards under which reforms were to be introduced, renewed the rebellion and co-operated with the Americans, expecting to be granted independence after the war. But Spain ceded the islands to the United States in 1898, and President McKinley decided they were as yet unfit for self-government. After a period of guerrilla warfare, in 1901 Aguinaldo bowed to the inevitable and agreed to accept temporary United States sovereignty. In 1907 the islands obtained representative institutions under a severely restricted franchise; but independence was postponed and they remained a United States colony until 1946.

Other Pacific Islands. To the east of Indonesia was the large island of New Guinea, to which the Dutch had some claim, which would ordinarily have been acknowledged by Australia, who had become accustomed to the Dutch Empire as her neighbor. But in the 1880's Germany began to expand into the Far East, greatly alarming the Australian colonies, especially Queensland, which was nearest to the island. Queensland herself annexed eastern New Guinea in 1883, but the Gladstone government in Britain disallowed this action, whereupon Bismarck claimed the northeastern section on behalf of Germany. Though Britain established a protectorate over southeastern New Guinea—which was handed over to the Common-wealth of Australia in 1905—Germany was permitted to annex her sector, known thereafter as Kaiser Wilhelmsland (1886). Soon afterward an agreement was made among Britain, Holland, and Germany granting the Dutch the western half of the island and delimiting the boundaries between the British and the German sectors.

The British, French, Germans, and Americans soon picked up the various islands in the western Pacific, including Samoa, which for a time was a bone of contention among the British, Germans, and Americans. It was finally divided between Germany and the United States. The United States also annexed the Hawaiian Islands (1898), in which she had considerable commercial interests. When the native monarchy interfered with these interests, resident Amer-icans staged a coup d'état, which was in due course made official by an act of annexation.

THE CARIBBEAN

In addition to the Hawaiian Islands, the United States acquired some possessions in the Caribbean during the course of the late nineteenth and early twentieth centuries. Cuba, under Spanish rule, had been in a turmoil for much of the century. There had been several rebellions by the Cubans against the Spaniards; and Amer-ican economic interests, which had begun to invest in the islands, despaired of the ability of the Spaniards to maintain law and order effectively enough to enable these enterprises to prosper. When the United States battleship *Maine* was blown up in Havana harbor in 1898, a pretext was given for direct military intervention. There followed the swift and one-sided Spanish-American War, as a result of which the Philippines, Guam, and Puerto Rico were ceded outright to the United States; and Cuba was granted her independence sub-ject to the right of the United States to intervene in case of neces-sity (Platt Amendment). The United States in fact used this right fairly freely during the next twenty years.

Elsewhere in the Caribbean the United States intervened to ensure interest payments on loans contracted not only in her own territory but abroad. Since the United States refused under the Monroe Doc-trine to permit foreign powers to intervene themselves, she acted on behalf of all. At different times, Haiti, the Dominican Republic, and Nicaragua were occupied by United States marines for periods of several years. The United States also acquired the Panama Canal Zone on a perpetual lease from the new republic of Panama. The republic of Colombia, which had hitherto exercised sovereignty over the Isthmus of Panama, had delayed ratification of an agreement with the United States permitting the construction of the Canal. President Theodore Roosevelt therefore encouraged and helped a number of Colombian rebels to secede and create a new republic, which promptly agreed to allow the Canal to be built on American terms.

EXPANSION IN NORTH AFRICA

Most of the North African littoral in the mid-nineteenth century was still a part of the Turkish Empire, though under native rulers. The sultan of Morocco was independent and acknowledged no Turkish claims. Algeria was gradually conquered by the French from 1830 onward and administered as a part of France; the Tunisian beys had been virtually independent for centuries. Turkey still administered Tripolitania and Cyrenaica until these provinces were taken from her by Italy in the early twentieth century.

British Protectorate over Egypt. In the early nineteenth century the Turkish governor over Egypt, an Albanian Muslim named Mehemet Ali, made himself virtually independent of Turkish suzerainty. It was as a separate power that he gave aid to the Turks in the Greek War of Independence (see p. 222). Indeed, he captured Syria from his overlord and could only with great difficulty be persuaded to relinquish it. Mehemet Ali also conquered the Sudan to the south of Egypt.

But Mehemet's successors fell into the toils of European financiers and by the 1870's were so heavily in debt that the foreign bondholders were pressing them hard. By agreement with Khedive Ismail the French constructed the Suez Canal, which was opened in 1869; but the khedive retained only a minority interest. Loans to him were almost all spent for personal extravagances and not for income-bearing investments in his country. After the purchase of the Suez Canal shares by British Prime Minister Disraeli, British interest in Egypt increased; it was clear that the Canal would be highly important to Britain as part of her communication system with India. The French, who were the largest creditors of Egypt, regarded the country as being within their own sphere of influence but were prepared to work with the British to achieve financial stability in the country and ensure service on its external debt. When Khedive Ismail refused to make arrangements satisfactory to Britain and France, the latter requested the Turkish sultan to "depose" his nominal vassal. The sultan readily agreed and Ismail decided to go into exile with what he could take with him. He handed over the bankrupt country to his son Tewfik, who agreed to the appointment of European financial controllers. At the same time, following an insurrection of army officers and anti-European nationalists, he appointed a ministry of Egyptians to share in his responsibilities.

As the nationalist movement continued to grow, the British and French sent a joint expedition to compel the dismissal of the new ministers, whereupon riots broke out and British ships bombarded Alexandria. Shortly afterward the British began to land troops and swiftly occupied Cairo (1882). The French, who had taken Tunis only the year before, refused to extend their commitments and withdrew their forces from Egypt. The British then established a protectorate in the country under the rule of their consul-general, Sir Evelyn Baring (Lord Cromer), who provided an efficient administration and soon brought the country to solvency.

The following year, Mohammed Ahmad (the Mahdi), a Muslim warrior-prophet, began to encroach on the Sudan, nominally a dependent state of Egypt. He was so successful that the Gladstone government decided that the territory was not worth keeping and that it should be left to the Mahdi. But first the Egyptian garrisons had to be evacuated. For this purpose General Gordon was sent to negotiate with the Mahdi. When he could make no headway he decided to fight; but he was besieged in Khartoum and killed when the Mahdi captured the city. The expedition which Gladstone had been compelled by public opinion to send to his relief found itself unable to achieve anything and returned. The country remained in the hands of the Mahdi and his successor until General Kitchener in command of a large army forced his way into the Sudan from 1896 to 1898, and decisively defeated the enemy at the Battle of Omdurman (1898). Thereafter Sudan was restored to "Egypt" and administered by the British with the same efficiency as they ruled Egypt.

Tunisia. In Tunisia, as in Egypt, the French were the most important foreign creditor of the ruler (the bey of Tunis). When the bey could not meet his payments, an international commission on which both British and Italian creditors were represented was forced upon him (1869). The British and Germans agreed at the Congress of Berlin in 1878 that the French should have a free hand in the country. The Italians who formed the majority of European inhabitants, objected very strongly; but the French, using the pretext of border raids from Algeria into Tunisia, sent an expedition to the country in 1881 and forced the bey to accept a protectorate.

Tripoli. The Italians, who for many years refused to accept the accomplished fact in Tunisia, nevertheless could do little except enter the Triple Alliance with Germany and Austria (see p. 261). In the early 1900's their eyes turned toward Tripoli (present-day Libya), which they believed they could take from enfeebled Turkey if the other powers would permit it. France, busy in Morocco, was willing to allow the proposed conquest, and the other powers were quite content for Italy to have some compensation for her losses elsewhere. With barely a shadow of a pretext Italy declared war on Turkey in 1911 and annexed Tripoli. Though the war with Turkey did not prove as easy as the Italians expected, they were ultimately successful; and in spite of great difficulties during the war from Turkish and Arab guerrilla fighting, the country was kept under control without trouble when the war was over.

Morocco. France and Spain were both interested in Morocco, nominally ruled by an independent sultan, but in fact usually a prey to numerous warring tribes. Spain had long held a foothold in the country, namely, the city of Ceuta across the Straits of Gibraltar. The sultan, like his fellow-rulers in Tunisia and Egypt, owed a great deal of money to the French, who had obtained the consent of Britain to intervention. Italy also consented, in exchange for a free hand in Tripoli, while Spain expected to share in the spoils and was likewise agreeable. But France had not seen fit to consult Germany. When therefore in 1905 the French began to intervene seriously, the kaiser appeared in person at Tangier. This incident was followed by the Algeciras Conference of 1906 and a further international incident at Agadir (Morocco) (see p. 262). The French were allowed to establish a protectorate over the country in 1912, but required almost twenty years of fighting with the Berber tribes before it could be entirely subdued.

Italy in Northeast Africa. Before discussing the partition of Sub-Saharan Africa, we should briefly mention Italian efforts in the Horn of Africa. Without too great difficulty, Italy in the 1880's took possession by purchase and conquest of the two desert territories of Eritrea and Benadir (Italian Somaliland), while the French purchased Djibouti (French Somaliland) and began to build a railroad to the capital of the ancient independent state of Abyssinia (Ethi-

opia). The British established a small protectorate (British Somaliland) in 1884 south of the Gulf of Aden. The Italians tried hard
to win the consent of the Abyssinian monarch, Menelik II, to an
Italian protectorate for his country. But Menelik, backed by French
technical aid and military training, refused to be "protected" and
decisively defeated a big Italian army at the Battle of Adowa in
1896. This, the only important victory of a non-European army
over a European, proved decisive and ensured the independence of
Abyssinia until 1935 (see p. 295).

PARTITION OF SUB-SAHARAN AFRICA

The interior of Africa in the mid-nineteenth century was an almost unknown land to Europeans. The Portuguese had been ensconced in Mozambique and Angola in southeast and southwest
Africa for centuries, but they had not penetrated far inland, preferring
to use their coastal cities as entrepôts for the slave trade. Some trans-
African voyages had been made from one colony to the other, but
nothing of permanence had been achieved. Only in South Africa,
where a long-established Dutch colony had been ceded to the British
after the Napoleonic Wars, was there any substantial European
settlement.

South Africa to the Union. South Africa, as a land suitable for
permanent European settlement, had become peopled over the years
mostly by farmers of Dutch descent, the Boers (Afrikaners), who
had subdued and often enslaved the earlier Bushmen and Hottentot
inhabitants. When the British tried to establish a strong colony in
their new territory (Cape Colony), brought in British immigrants,
and emancipated the slaves, the Boers greatly resented their interference with their old customs and their relatively liberal native
policy. In 1836 a considerable number decided to "trek" inland in
search of new territory where they could be free of British control.
This, however, meant that they would be compelled to dispute their
lands with the African Bantu, who had been entering the country
from the north for many years and were in the process of establishing themselves. The British had already been compelled to fight
several small wars with the Bantu (known as Kaffir Wars); and the
Boer trek involved them in several more. In the process they annexed Natal, from which most of the Boers then withdrew; but the
latter were finally permitted to keep two territories of their own
(Transvaal and Orange Free State) on condition that they abolish
slavery in them.

When in 1867 diamonds were discovered a little to the west of the Boer states, the British annexed the territory, thus infuriating the Boers. Soon afterward Transvaal became so financially weakened and in such danger from the Bantu that she requested annexation. When the British had subdued the Bantu, the Boers repented of their decision. In 1881 Paul Kruger, leader of Transvaal, proclaimed its independence again. This was recognized by Gladstone, after the British had lost the small skirmish of Majuba Hill. In 1886 gold was discovered in the new South African Republic, as it was now called, and thereafter the precious metal dominated the politics of South Africa. Miners, mainly British, flocked into the territory, soon outnumbering the original Boers in most of the country.

Cape Colony, whose settlers had been granted a measure of self-government by the British in 1853, now had its own prime minister, the empire builder Cecil Rhodes. Having become a millionaire through his investments in gold and diamonds and dreaming of an all-British Africa from the Cape to Cairo, Rhodes began negotiating for concessions in the lands to the north of the Transvaal. His British South Africa Company (formed in 1889 to exploit some mining concessions granted him by an African chief named Lobengula) soon was able to drive the chief himself from his lands, thus adding Rhodesia to the British possessions in Africa. Meanwhile Kruger was making the lot of the immigrants as difficult as possible and trying to win diplomatic support from Germany, who had in 1883 proclaimed a protectorate over South West Africa and thus had extensive interests in the area. At the same time he tried to obtain a concession from Portugal to win an outlet to the sea for his landlocked republic. But the British themselves came to an agreement with Portugal and shut off the Transvaal from the sea by another annexation. Germany tried to give diplomatic support to Kruger for a time, but such aid could not prove effective in face of local British military superiority and the kaiser's unwillingness to risk a war in southern Africa with a major power.

In 1895 Rhodes backed a movement intended to undermine the position of Kruger, which, if successful, might have overturned his government; but the raid into Transvaal (Jameson Raid) was set in motion too soon and was easily repelled by Kruger. Then Kruger began to import arms and drill troops and it was clear that a showdown was imminent. The South African Republic, joined by the Orange Free State, began the war in 1899. At first the Boers were successful, but British military superiority, once it had been brought

to bear, was too great for them. The Boers were fighting the war
without allies against troops from all parts of the British Empire.
In the Treaty of Vereeniging (1902) the Boer republics were annexed
but promised representative government as soon as feasible. The
British also gave the Boers (Afrikaners) a considerable sum of
money for reconstruction. In 1906 and 1907 Transvaal and the
Orange River Colony (as it was called from 1902 onward) received
constitutions; and soon afterwards a convention of all the separate
colonies agreed to form the Union of South Africa, with responsible government. Louis Botha, a Boer general who had distinguished himself in the recent war, became the first prime minister.

   Congo Independent State. In the early 1850's the Scottish
explorer-missionary David Livingstone began his journeys through
central Africa. Though others were exploring at the same time, it was
his journeys that caught the imagination of the Western world. On
his last journey he was "found" by an Anglo-American journalist,
Henry Morton Stanley, who publicized this event and was accepted
himself as an explorer of the first rank. Stanley was financed in a later
journey of exploration (1874–1877), which took him across Africa
from east to west, until he finally emerged near the mouth of the
Congo. On his return to Europe, he was approached by an emissary
of King Leopold II of Belgium, who had recently organized an association for "the exploration and civilization of Africa." After failing to interest the British government in a new expedition, Stanley
entered Leopold's employment and obtained the signatures of numerous African chiefs to treaties ceding their land to Leopold. Simultaneously Savorgnan de Brazza, an Italian nobleman in French
service, was engaged in the same occupation on behalf of his masters.

   In 1885 a grand conference to discuss African colonial problems
was convened by Bismarck at Berlin, where the powers agreed that
Leopold's association—which by this time was controlled entirely by
himself—should be granted sovereignty in a new Congo Independent
State. Brazza's explorations won for France most of what later became French Equatorial Africa. The Congo Independent State for
a long time was financially unsuccessful until a new system of forced
labor was introduced, under the control of ruthless concessionaires
and officials. In the mid-1900's the system, adopted also on a lesser
scale by the French, created an international scandal, which persuaded Leopold to hand his state over to the Belgian government
in 1908.

West and East Africa. The French had long possessed a colony near the Senegal River, bordered by the small British settlement of the Gambia to the south. The colony, not greatly valued by them, had been briefly conquered by the British in the Napoleonic Wars. During the governorship of General Faidherbe (1854–1865), the French had penetrated far up the Senegal; and they gradually made their way in the following years into the interior of Africa, eventually reaching other territories, bordering Lake Tchad, which were in the process of being conquered from the south (French Equatorial Africa). Most of the French expeditions were made by African soldiers led by French officers, and few of the territories they won were of value. The British took most of the richer areas, which were opened up first by trading companies.

In West Africa the French by the early twentieth century possessed the colonies of Mauritania, Senegal, French Guinea, Ivory Coast, and Dahomey, all of which bordered on the ocean, and the Soudan, Upper Volta, and Niger, which were carved out of the hinterland. The conquest of Dahomey presented the greatest difficulty, since the powerful native kingdom, with its army of Amazons, had first to be subdued. A Guinean chief named Samoury fought for many years (1885–1898) before the French took him prisoner and exiled him. In 1904 the French West African territories were combined in an administrative federation known as French West Africa.

The British settled Sierra Leone from 1787 onward as a haven for freed slaves. After experiencing great initial difficulties, it became a colony in 1808. In the Gold Coast, where the Portuguese had founded a major settlement in the sixteenth century, the British were faced with competition from the Dutch and the Danes, but bought out the Danes in 1850 and eventually persuaded the Dutch to leave in exchange for concessions in the Far East. They had to fight several wars with the powerful Ashanti people before they completed their conquest. In Nigeria, by far the most populous of African colonies, the British and the Royal Niger Company competed with the French for several decades before an agreement was finally worked out in 1898. The British took over the country from the Company in 1900 and made all except the ancient colony of Lagos into a protectorate. The most widely adopted system of government in all British territories, called "indirect rule," consisted in allowing the major African chiefs to retain their power under British suzerainty on condition that they accept British advice. The French also largely used the same system, but customarily took the chiefs formally into French service and gave them salaries.

In 1896 the French decided to send an expedition under Captain Marchand from their Congo territories right across Africa in the hope of reaching the Red Sea, thus cutting a swath of French territory through the continent. After great hardships the expedition reached Fashoda on the Nile, to learn that the British General Kitchener was himself on the way south through the Sudan. Kitchener, hearing of Marchand's presence, pushed quickly southward with a much superior force, arriving at Fashoda late in 1898. This encounter led to a grave crisis in Franco-British relations, since Marchand refused to leave without instructions from home. Eventually the French government backed down and ordered evacuation, thus bringing the French dream to an end.

Meanwhile Germany had decided to join in the scramble for colonies. In 1884 a German explorer with a small naval expedition proclaimed a protectorate over Togoland, and a week later a similar protectorate was announced over the coast of the Cameroons (Kamerun). Though Togo was small and hemmed in by the colonies of other powers, Kamerun faced onto an unexplored hinterland. The Germans pushed quickly inland, ultimately reaching Lake Tchad. It was to enlarge this colony that the French ceded extensive territories in exchange for German agreement to their protectorate in Morocco (see p. 262).

Madagascar off the east coast of Africa was taken by the French after they had been influential in the island for more than a century and had ousted a powerful native dynasty. On the mainland of East Africa the British and Germans were the chief European contestants. British missionaries had long been active, especially in Nyasaland and in Uganda, in which country there was a strong African kingdom (Buganda), considered too powerful and well governed to be subverted and overcome by the usual means. An extensive slave trade was carried on until the 1870's by Arab traders working out of the Arab-ruled island of Zanzibar, which was under a sultan. This sultan claimed to be the ruler also of extensive mainland territories and maintained an open slavemart in his capital until 1873. The Europeans, especially the British, who were determined to wipe out the slave trade, thus had a convenient pretext for intervention; and the sultan was not averse to granting concessions to both British and Germans in his nominal dominions. Carl Peters, a free-lance German agent, obtained wide concessions in

East Africa, ultimately including even Buganda, where there were several political factions ready to play off one European power against the other. Eventually the British settled for a protectorate of Uganda, to which was soon added the colony of British East Africa (Kenya), part of which continued to be leased from the sultan (until

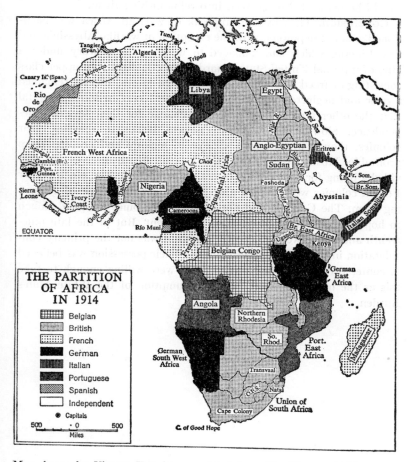

Map drawn by Vincent Kotschar, reprinted from *The Western Heritage,* by Stewart C. Easton. Copyright © 1961, Holt, Rinehart and Winston, Inc. All rights reserved.

1963) in exchange for an annual payment. The Germans took the large colony of German East Africa, which after the First World War became the mandated territory of Tanganyika. Zanzibar became a protected state under the sultan, who accepted a British Resident as adviser. The British and Germans acknowledged Portuguese rule over a Mozambique which was much smaller than the territory the Portuguese had claimed; but they nevertheless entered into an agreement to partition the Portuguese territories between them if Portugal should be persuaded or coerced into relinquishing them.

Conclusion. Thus by the outbreak of war, all Africa was partitioned among the powers, with the exception of warlike Abyssinia and tiny Liberia, which had managed to weather the century under a kind of informal United States guardianship. Ruled by an upper class consisting of freed Negroes from the United States, Liberia remained a poor and neglected republic, without the access to foreign capital that the other territories gained in exchange for their loss of independence. Slowly the European powers began to develop their colonies, though always with an eye to making and keeping them profitable. Most of the British colonies paid for themselves and provided a living for the administrators who ran them. The much poorer French colonies were seldom able to pay for the expense of governing them. The Germans did not keep their colonies for long enough to hope to make a profit on their investment. But in the late nineteenth and early twentieth centuries, profit was not the primary consideration in the ownership of colonies. Their possession was believed to confer prestige on their owners, who were willing enough to take this as the major payment for the assumption of the White Man's Burden.

19 THE FIRST WORLD WAR AND THE PEACE TREATIES

The First World War, as we now call the war of 1914 to 1918, which in its own time was known as the Great War, was more lethal than any war until that time, and the number of human beings actually killed in action surpassed the numbers killed in the Second World War.

THE WAR

The war itself, though it was fought in many parts of the world, was actually decided on the Western Front. The Central Powers won many victories in other regions, and they even succeeded in knocking Russia out of the war altogether and dictating a peace to her. But as soon as the Allies achieved victory on the Western Front, the German armies were compelled by the terms of the Armistice to withdraw from all the territories they had gained.

The Western Front. The Germans, better prepared than the Allies for the war, began it with a drive on Paris which was stopped at the Marne River in September, 1914. This was followed by a German offensive on the Channel ports opposite England. Though the Germans succeeded in capturing a few of the Belgian ports, they were unable to take Dunkirk, Calais, or Boulogne. During the latter part of 1915 the Allies counterattacked but made no significant gains and the front remained relatively stable. Most of 1916 was occupied by a prolonged German effort to take the fortress of Verdun, which was stubbornly defended by the French. The British, who had not been able previously to provide massive armies for use on the Continent, launched a tremendous counterattack on the Somme, in July 1916; but in spite of enormous casualties they advanced in total only about seven miles. With the entry of the United States into the war in 1917, it became the Allied plan to await the arrival of reinforcements from across the Atlantic who might serve to turn the tide of battle. Even so, several major offensives were launched, but with the same general lack of success. In 1918 the Germans, with the Russians now out of the war, decided that they should strike with all their power in the hope of winning the decision before the Americans were ready. The greatest German offensive since 1914 began in March, 1918 and penetrated to within forty miles of Paris. But the Allies, with a unified command under Marshal Foch, held the advance and counterattacked in July with the aid of American divisions. They forced the Germans to retreat, slowly at first and then with rapidity. When the German commanders realized that defeat was inevitable, they sued for peace and an armistice was concluded on November 11, 1918. Two days before the armistice Kaiser William II abdicated. The victorious Allies dictated the peace signed at Versailles on June 28, 1919.

The War in the Balkans. In Serbia, where the war had begun (see p. 262), the Austrians were several times defeated by the Serbs before they could take the Serbian capital of Belgrade (December, 1914), and even so were driven out a few days later. Meanwhile, Turkey, strengthened by the arrival of some German warships, entered the war on the side of the Central Powers in November, 1914; after long negotiations Bulgaria joined her in October, 1915. Greece remained officially neutral until 1917 in spite of the wish of Venizelos, her prime minister, to enter on the Allied side. A great offensive by Germany and Austria in October, 1915, in which they were joined by Bulgaria, proved too much for the Serbs to resist in spite of the aid of British and French troops who had landed in Greece. In August, 1916, long diplomatic efforts, especially by the Russians, to win Rumania as an ally, met with success. Though the Rumanians were decisively defeated in a few months by the Germans, Austrians, and Bulgarians, most of the promises made to the Rumanian government as inducements to enter the war were honored by the Allies when the war was over. Not until the last year of the war did the Allies have any troops to spare for a major offensive, in spite of the fact that they had kept an army for several years in the Greek city of Salonika. In two weeks following the offensive, Bulgaria was forced to make peace (September, 1915), and the Serbs triumphantly took their own capital back on November 1.

The Fall of the Ottoman Empire. Immediately after entering the war, the Turks begain an offensive against Russia, and the Allies reluctantly agreed that if they won the War Russia could have Constantinople as a free port. The British then (April, 1915) sent an expedition, made up mostly of British and Australian troops, to the Straits of the Dardanelles (Hellespont), for which the Turks were at first unprepared. But after the expedition had failed to fight its way through the Straits, the Turks recovered from their surprise and reinforced their defenders. The expedition withdrew, after considerable casualties and loss of prestige, in December, 1915. In the Near East the Turks held their own. In 1916 they compelled an Anglo-Indian force to surrender at Kut in Mesopotamia, and they drove the Russians back into their own country in the same year. What proved eventually decisive was an Arab revolt in 1917 and 1918—assisted by the British adventurer Colonel T. E. Lawrence—which tied down a considerable number of Turkish troops during these years. From Egypt General Allenby led a British offensive on Palestine, which took Jerusalem in December, 1917, and late in 1918 he pushed forward until the Turkish lines were broken. Turkey sued for an armistice in October; the Allied navy entered Constantinople, set up a military government in Turkey, and began preparations to dismember the country, including its Asiatic provinces.

But the Allied plan was foiled by a nationalist movement led by Mustapha Kemal. Between 1918 and 1922 Kemal organized enough resistance to the Greeks and Italians, who proposed to partition his country with the approval of the other Allies, to make the scheme impossible. In 1922 he compelled the last sultan, Mohammed VI, to abdicate, and a national state of Turkey was recognized by the Treaty of Lausanne in 1923. Turkey lost her non-Turkish provinces but retained Constantinople (renamed Istanbul), a small hinterland in Europe, and all Anatolia. Turkey became a republic in October, 1923, with Kemal as president. (Kemal later took the name of Atatürk, "Father of the Turks.")

The Eastern Front. The Germans bore the brunt of the first years' attacks on Russia, winning two major battles (Tannenberg and Masurian Lakes) in August and September, 1914. But they were unable to take Warsaw since both they and the Austrians lacked sufficient troops for a major offensive into Russia. In April of the following year the Germans and the Austrians began a huge offensive in the south, followed by another in Poland. Both were spectacularly successful, and the Russians were pushed out of Poland and deep into their own country. In 1916 the Russians counterattacked in a later offensive led by General Brusilov, but after winning some successes, the offensive was stalled by the arrival of German reinforcements. At the end of the year the Russian armies were dispirited and defeatist. In March, 1917, an army mutiny led to the abdication of Tsar Nicholas II and the formation of a Provisional Government, which tried to continue the war against the opposition of the working class and the vast majority of the conscript troops.

These circumstances gave the Germans and Austrians the opportunity to renew their offensive and conquer Latvia. When the Bolshevik Revolution (to be discussed in Chapter 20), whose leaders wished for peace at almost any price, broke out in November, 1917, the Central Powers took advantage of the situation to impose the Peace of Brest-Litovsk (March, 1918). Under this treaty the Russians ceded Poland, Lithuania, the Ukraine, the Baltic provinces, Finland, and various territories beyond the Caucasus. These territories, after brief fighting, were occupied by the Central Powers.

Italy in the War. Italy, who had been a member of the Triple Alliance since 1882, declared as early as July, 1914, that she was not bound by the alliance since Austria had declared war on Serbia, thus starting the war. The Italians then negotiated with both sides to see which would make the best offer. The result was the secret Treaty of London (1915), as a consequence of which Italy declared war on Austria-Hungary a month later. The Italian offensive made little progress but held down Austrian troops until late in 1917, when the Germans and Austrians together launched a major attack (Caporetto campaign), which drove the Italians far back into Italy and broke their morale. The Italian army had recovered enough by October, 1918, however, to win the Battle of Vittorio Veneto against the by now demoralized Austrian army. This victory was followed by an armistice on November 3. Charles I, the Austrian emperor, abdicated on November 12.

The War at Sea. In the war at sea the great fleets of Britain and Germany did relatively little damage to one another. It was the German policy to avoid any but local action and occasional raiding around the world, carried out by strongly armed warships. This policy, in the German view, was forced upon her by the inferior size of her navy, but the existence of this navy prevented the British from having full command of the sea. The sole important naval battle of the war was fought at Jutland in 1916 between the British and German high-seas fleets. The battle was indecisive, but it had the effect of preventing the German fleet from risking its destruction again against superior odds. The Japanese entered the war on the

Allied side in August, 1914, but confined their operations to the capture of German-held islands and German possessions in China.

Far more important than the operations of the surface navy was the activity of the German submarines (U-boats), since they could be used to sink merchant shipping and were the only means available to Germany to drive Britain out of the war. In 1915 the Germans turned their attention to passenger ships and sank the British liner *Lusitania* by torpedo, exciting a furious protest from United States President Woodrow Wilson. Before the end of 1915 Germany gave assurance that passenger liners would not be sunk without warning. But in early 1917 the German government came to the conclusion that only by unrestricted submarine warfare could it hope to win the war, and Wilson was so informed. During the next months the Allies lost unprecedented numbers of ships and several United States merchant ships were also sunk. The United States entered the war in April, 1917, but the sinkings continued. At last an effective system of convoying merchant ships was developed, and the Germans began to lose more U-boats than they could replace. Before the end of the war the convoys had gained the mastery over the submarines.

THE PEACE

President Wilson had several times attempted to mediate between the belligerents on a basis unfavorable to German aspirations, including in his proposals the return of Alsace and Lorraine to France. But at no time could he win the approval of all the powers involved for the "peace without victory" that he desired. After the entry of the United States into the war his proposed terms naturally changed; but he never ceased to be interested in the conditions of peace which he formulated at the beginning of 1918 in his Fourteen Points.

The Fourteen Points. This program included a number of general points; among them were the abolition of secret treaties, freedom of the seas in peace and war, disarmament, and the removal of economic barriers to international trade. It also contained specific and enforceable provisions such as the establishment of an independent Poland and the evacuation of Belgium. Wilson enunciated also the general principle of self-determination for subject nationalities, to be applied to Austria-Hungary and Turkey, and a specific proposal for a League of Nations to guarantee the political independence and territorial integrity of all states, old and new, big and small. The Central Powers when on the verge of defeat (October, 1918) requested an armistice on the basis of the Fourteen Points; and though no guarantees were given under the terms of the armistice itself, Wilson's program naturally came up for discussion at the Paris Peace Conference.

The Peace Treaties. It was soon clear that the Allied ministers —Prime Minister Lloyd George of Britain, Premier Clemenceau of France, and Premier Orlando of Italy—had differing views as to what they wanted. Wilson got his League of Nations accepted by all, and the Covenant of the League became a part of the ensuing treaties; but in other respects the European powers, for the most part, had their way. Germany was made to admit her guilt for the war, and was compelled to agree to the payment of an astronomical sum as reparations. Alsace and Lorraine were returned to France. The industrial area of the Saar was to be detached from Germany and kept under international supervision while France used the mines. The German army was to be reduced to 100,000 men with limited armaments, the left bank of the Rhine was to be demilitarized, and an Allied army was to occupy the Rhineland. The Treaty of Versailles, which incorporated these provisions, was ratified under protest by Germany, still blockaded by the European powers. The United States Senate, in spite of Wilson's efforts, did not ratify it, because of fears that the nation's sovereignty would be impaired by membership in the League; and thus the United States did not become a member of the organization which her president had done so much to promote.

Other treaties (of St. Germain and Trianon) arranged for the dismemberment of Austria and Hungary. Czechoslovakia, Yugoslavia, and Poland became independent states, and much of the territory demanded by Italy was duly ceded. In Hungary, where a Bolshevik regime under Bela Kun had briefly held power, a new war broke out and the Rumanians invaded the country. After taking the capital they were rewarded with Transylvania, while other territories were granted to newborn Czechoslovakia and Yugoslavia. What was left of the old empire became the two small states of Austria and Hungary, the former with a population almost half of which was concentrated in Vienna. Finland, Lithuania, Latvia, and Estonia, formerly part of tsarist Russia, became independent states, though much trouble and a minor war occurred before a new boundary between Poland and Lithuania was accepted.

Thus the war was over and nationalism had won new victories. All the larger new nations had strong minorities within their bound-

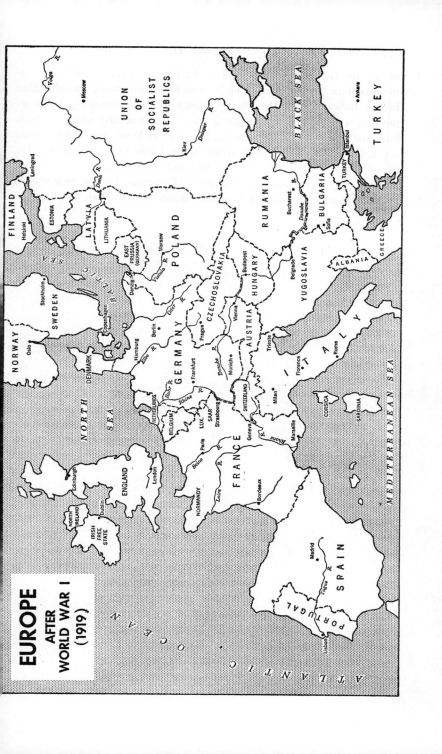

EUROPE
AFTER
WORLD WAR I
(1919)

aries; but the independent nations in Europe were much more numerous than before, even though there was some slight consolidation in the Balkans with the disappearance of tiny Montenegro, incorporated with Yugoslavia. Since it was the democratic nations which had won the war, all the new nations had at least democratic forms for a time, with or without constitutional monarchs. With the rise of totalitarianism in the 1930's, however, democracy began to disappear. Only Czechoslovakia, the most Westernized of the new states, retained it until the outbreak of the Second World War.

20 THE LONG ARMISTICE

The period between 1918 and 1939 is often known as the Long Armistice. Until 1929, though the peace was an uneasy one, broken by sporadic local conflicts, many people thought that the League of Nations might preserve it and that the dissatisfied and dispossessed nations might in time come to accept it and content themselves with the pursuit of prosperity. When the Great Depression showed that such prosperity could not be expected in the existing condition of Europe, Germany, under the leadership of Adolf Hitler, decided that she would try to recover her power lost under the Treaty of Versailles. Meanwhile post-Revolutionary Russia held apart from the rest of Europe until she thought herself threatened by Germany. Then she decided to join the League of Nations and try to use the new peace-keeping institutions she had played no part in founding. When this hope proved illusory, she made her own alliance with resurgent Germany and thus helped to precipitate the Second World War.

THE RISE OF TOTALITARIANISM

The Russian revolutionaries who seized power in 1917 remodeled their state by force and never showed an inclination to adopt any features of democracy, beyond the forms. The Weimar Constitution of postwar Germany was the product of democratic theorists who made limited provision for ruling by decree (to be applied in unusual circumstances); it could not survive in the chaotic years that followed. Italy, as one of the winners, did not change her constitution after the war, but it proved to be no more effective than it had been before the war and was overthrown by Mussolini in 1922.

The Russian Revolution and the Regime of Stalin. The Russian Revolution of March, 1917, brought to power a Provisional

Government—pending the election of a constituent assembly to decide on a new republican constitution. The government's most substantial leader was the socialist Kerensky. In spite of the obvious unpopularity of the war, the government decided to make a further effort to win it. Even Kerensky, who became prime minister in July, continued to plan a military offensive. But from March until July the government never succeeded in taking full control of either the country or the army, since the various parties which wished to foment an all-out revolution were organizing themselves into "soviets" of soldiers and workers and encouraging the seizure of the land by the peasants. In mid-July, the Bolsheviks, led by Lenin and Trotsky, attempted to seize power; but the government was strong enough to force Lenin into exile and to imprison Trotsky. The Bolsheviks were not backed either by the Social Revolutionaries or by the more moderate Mensheviks. In September Kornilov, a military general who distrusted not only the revolutionary parties but Kerensky himself, attempted to unseat the latter by an attack on the capital. This plan was frustrated by his own troops and by the workers, who refused to transport them.

Lenin, who had by this time returned from Finland, and Trotsky, who had been released from prison by Kerensky, thereupon decided that the time was ripe to stage their own revolution. The other revolutionary parties, which showed themselves indecisive in the crisis, were unable to command a majority in the Congress of Soviets, leaving the Bolsheviks to take matters into their own hands. With the aid of dissident soldiers they attacked the government offices and drove Kerensky into exile ("October Revolution"). A few weeks later elections were held for the constituent assembly. When the Bolsheviks found that they were heavily outnumbered by the Social Revolutionaries (most of whom were peasants), they dispersed the assembly and thereafter ruled by force. Though peace was made with Germany the following year (March 3, 1918), the Bolsheviks were forced to engage in prolonged civil war against several different armies led by tsarist generals, who at times controlled the Ukraine, the Baltic areas, much of southern Russia, the Caucasus, and Siberia. In addition the French sent troops to the Black Sea and an Anglo-French force, to which was later added an American contingent, took Archangel, while another British force occupied Murmansk in the north. The Germans also controlled much of Russia until the Armistice. Eventually the Red Army organized by Trotsky as minister of war defeated all the tsarist armies, and the Allied troops withdrew.

Meanwhile, the Bolsheviks tried to establish an outright Communist system known as "War Communism," under which all land and industry were to be nationalized. This was met by widespread opposition, especially from peasants and farmers, to which the Bolsheviks replied with systematic terror. Though the army was triumphant, there was widespread famine throughout most of Russia in 1920 and 1921, particularly in the fertile Ukraine. As a result of this experience Lenin decided in 1921 to modify the communist system and instituted a New Economic Policy (NEP), permitting a modified form of private enterprise and even the organization of small-scale private farms. The economy recovered partially during the next years, and NEP lasted until after the death of Lenin in 1924. As long as he lived Lenin was the undisputed dictator of the country, though in form it was a "dictatorship of the proletariat" as advocated by Marx. In fact the Communist party was supreme in the state and was the only party permitted. The party itself was ruled by its Central Committee and the Political Bureau. It was through this bureau that Lenin and later Stalin exercised their dictatorship. In 1922 the name of the state was changed to the Union of Soviet Socialist Republics (USSR).

After the death of Lenin a struggle for power ensued between Josef Stalin, secretary of the party, and Trotsky. Stalin advocated the return to "socialism" in Russia, even if there were to be no "socialist" revolutions elsewhere—whereas Trotsky wished to extend the revolution abroad by all means available. Stalin won the contest. Trotsky was exiled and later murdered, and in 1928 Stalin instituted the first Five Year Plan, which involved the total liquidation of NEP, at whatever cost. The private farmers (kulaks) were now dispossessed; state farms and collective farms were set up to replace them; and the government took charge of all industry. The kulaks desperately resisted, and as a class they were wiped out by force and terror. Famine followed, especially in 1932 and 1933; but the government stubbornly persisted in its course. Stalin gradually liquidated all opposition from within the ranks of the Communist party, and gradually the program began to make headway. When the First Five Year Plan had almost run its course, a new program of economic targets to be attained was proclaimed; such plans have followed regularly to the present day. Another constitution was promulgated in 1936, but the functioning of the government was little changed by it. The Communist party continued to be the only one permitted in the state and its "presidium" as before constituted the ruling oligarchy. Stalin controlled the Communist apparatus until his death in 1953.

Fascist Dictatorship in Italy. The Italians were greatly disappointed with the results of the Peace Conference, which had granted them little of what they had been promised when they entered the war. The democratic governments that followed the war found themselves unable to effect any major social reforms, in part because of their general unpopularity and lack of authority and prestige. They could not stem a series of strikes, many of them political in nature and some managed by syndicalists. It was in such circumstances that Benito Mussolini, once a socialist, organized his Fascist party devoted to direct action, extralegal if necessary, against Communists—who were not in fact very numerous—and other opponents. In 1922 the Fascists staged a March on Rome (so-called although most of the Fascists converged on Rome by train!), and demanded that King Victor Emmanuel III appoint Mussolini prime minister. The king agreed to do so, in spite of the fact that the Fascist party had only thirty-five deputies in the Chamber. Mussolini then proceeded to govern without the participation of the elected parties, and before long made the Fascist party the only legal one in the state. Thereafter he ruled as a personal dictator (Il Duce), backed by the Fascist party. A façade of government by "corporations" was eventually constructed, but it continued to be Mussolini's will that determined the policy of the state. In some respects Fascist Italy was an improvement on the democratic governments that had preceded it. Law and order were established; "the trains ran on time"; and for almost a decade Mussolini was widely admired in much of Europe. Some spectacular public works were inaugurated, a concordat was signed with the Vatican in 1929, under which Vatican City was recognized as an independent state, and Italy paid compensation to the papacy for its lost territories. Italy in general co-operated with the other European powers in international affairs until 1935. But no opposition to Il Duce was tolerated and enemies of the regime were treated harshly, if not so harshly as in Nazi Germany.

The Great Depression revealed the hollowness of the government's claim that it had solved Italy's economic problems. New efforts were made which gave the government far more complete control of industry than before, but little was achieved. The major "cure" for unemployment was a plan to enroll more soldiers in the army and attack Ethiopia, thus revenging the Battle of Adowa (see p. 276) and making Italy a great imperial power—as befitted the legatee of imperial Rome (a favorite theme of Mussolini). The invasion of Ethiopia and the efforts made by the League of Nations to prevent it threw Mussolini into the arms of Adolf Hitler, his fellow-dictator in Germany, who was as isolated in Europe as himself.

The Rise of Hitler to Power in Germany. The Weimar Constitution in Germany was a generally liberal instrument, though it gave the president the right to rule by decree in case of emergency. The government for several years was in the hands of the relatively moderate socialists of the Social Democratic party, but it could never obtain a sufficient majority in the Reichstag to rule without support from other parties. This government had to rule a Germany which was far from reconciled to the peace terms virtually dictated at Versailles. It had to attempt to pay the huge sums required for reparations, while Germany was trying to recover her peacetime markets in a competitive world where the terms of trade were not in her favor. In 1923 it had to sustain an invasion of the Ruhr industrial area by French and Belgians to compel Germany to pay reparations. This was followed by a ruinous inflation which wiped out the savings of the middle class and predisposed great numbers of Germans toward a strong-man government, which would reassert the latent power of the German people and restore the economy.

As an outcast and demilitarized power, Germany made a treaty with the Bolsheviks in 1922 (Treaty of Rapallo), which provided for the training of some German officers on Russian soil. Nevertheless, for several years the Germans attempted to live up to their agreements. Germany entered the League of Nations in 1925, and, under her foreign minister Gustav Stresemann, was willing to cooperate with Europe (Treaties of Locarno, 1925) provided that the reparations were scaled down to such a sum as she could pay (Dawes Plan, 1924; Young Plan, 1930). Under the Locarno treaties Germany agreed to accept arbitration in eventual disputes with France and accepted the boundaries with France and Belgium imposed on her in 1919, subject to guarantees by Britain and Italy. Her reparation payments were made possible largely because of substantial foreign investments in the country, especially by the United States.

But under the surface, German discontent was seething, and the ephemeral prosperity of the late 1920's was obviously a precarious one. Adolf Hitler, who had a program for tearing up the Treaty of Versailles and establishing systematic anti-Semitism, attempted with the support of Field Marshall Ludendorff, one of the most success-ful generals during the war, to stage a coup d'état (*Putsch*) in 1923. The German government had no difficulty in suppressing it and im-prisoned Hitler for a few years—during which he occupied himself with writing his autobiography, *Mein Kampf,* in which he explained his whole program and methods for attaining it. When the Great Depression struck Europe in the early 1930's, it became impossible for any German government to rule effectively. Heinrich Bruening, the last prime minister who had any substantial support in the Reichstag, was dismissed by President Hindenburg in May, 1932; thereafter Germany was governed by Franz von Papen, and then, briefly, by General Kurt von Schleicher. Both of these men ruled by decree, with the support of the aged president. Meanwhile, Hitler, released from prison, had organized his National Socialist party and enrolled a body of Storm Troopers, who engaged in street fights, especially with Communists, making orderly government almost impossible. The National Socialist (Nazi) party contested each of the many elections for the Reichstag, and became the largest single party, though far from large enough to rule without support from others.

At last Hitler entered into an alliance with the small Nationalist party, made up mostly of industrialists, and Hindenburg was per-suaded that Hitler should be appointed chancellor. In January, 1933, Hitler took office, and almost immediately afterward a spectacular fire was staged. The responsibility for it is still disputed. The Reichs-tag building was burned down, whereupon the Communists, blamed for it by Hitler, were outlawed as a party. Having disposed of his major opposition, much as Mussolini had done in Italy, in 1934 he turned against many of his companions among the Storm Troopers who were unwilling to abandon their old habits of trying to intimidate the government by extralegal means, and made himself supreme in the government. When Hindenburg died in 1934 Hitler became presi-dent as well as chancellor.

In 1934 the Germans attempted a *Putsch* in Austria through a Nazi party in that country. But after the clerical Austrian chancellor Dollfuss had been murdered, the effort was foiled by a show of force by Mussolini, who had his own totalitarian party in Austria, which was not yet ready to take second place to the Nazis. In the same year Germany left the League of Nations, and Hitler began systematically to defy the Allied Powers by unilaterally abrogating the Treaty of

Versailles. In 1935 he instituted conscription and in 1936 he marched his troops into the Rhineland, which had been evacuated by the Allies a few years before. The Allies protested but took no direct action, having turned to the policy of "appeasement" as the best way of dealing with Germany (see p. 307). Meanwhile Hitler in pursuit of his program of anti-Semitism instituted numerous discriminatory measures against the Jews, excluding them from any form of governmental service and making it virtually impossible for them even to make a living. He "solved" the unemployment problem largely by his armament program; and by purchasing the surplus export crops of several depression-ridden smaller countries in exchange for "blocked marks," which could be spent only for German goods, he gradually won a commanding economic position in these countries, and helped overcome the food shortages in Germany.

Austria. Prior to the signing of the Treaty of St. Germain (see p. 288), Austria petitioned to be allowed to be incorporated with Germany. When this union was forbidden by the treaty, the Austrians did not totally abandon hope of being united with their fellow-Germans. The economy of the country was unviable without the union, and the Allies had to grant considerable sums to enable the process of reconstruction to be carried out. Even so, during the 1920's Austria experienced great difficulty in paying her way, and there was constant struggle between the Christian Socialist federal government and the municipality of Vienna, which was ruled by Socialists determined to put their program into effect in the capital. The Christian Socialists maintained a close relationship at all times with Fascist Italy, and both Christian Socialists and Socialists organized private armies even as early as the 1920's. The former received the support of Mussolini, and the *Heimwehr* was organized along the lines of Italy's Black Shirts. When the Depression came in Austria, the only possible solution seemed to lie in a customs union with Germany, but this, too, was forbidden by the Allies. In March, 1931, the leading Austrian bank, the Credit-Anstalt failed, paving the way for similar failures elsewhere, and in May, 1932, the Christian Socialist Engelbert Dollfuss became chancellor. In February, 1934, Dollfuss attempted with the aid of the *Heimwehr* to destroy the other parties in the state, including both the National Socialist party backed by Germany and the party of the Socialists in Vienna. The latter resisted dissolution, and the government destroyed socialist housing units in Vienna and imprisoned all the Socialist leaders. When Hitler staged his coup a few months later, he was stopped by the threats not only of Italy but also of Yugoslavia, then under the authoritarian rule of King Alexander I.

Kurt Schuschnigg, who replaced Dollfuss as Austrian chancellor, spent the next years trying to defend the precarious independence of his country without changing the authoritarian policies of his predecessor. He ousted the fascist-backed leader of the Heimwehr and incorporated his militia into that of his own party (Fatherland Front). But Mussolini could not support him much longer against Hitler, whose power was increasing rapidly, and in 1938 Schuschnigg was ousted by Hitler, and Germany and Austria were united under the Nazi regime.

Hungary. Hungary, ruled by a conservative government after signing the Treaty of Trianon (see p. 288), likewise maintained close relations with Fascist Italy. For much of the interwar period the main issue was whether or not the Hapsburgs should be restored. The head of state (Admiral Horthy) was still a regent for the absent Hapsburg heir, but since a restoration could not be countenanced by the new nations carved out of the Hapsburg Empire, Horthy remained regent until the Nazi occupation during the war. Hungary, a largely agricultural state, therefore not so hopelessly unviable in the economic sphere as Austria, continued to be in many respects feudal. Its leaders kept agitating for the return of the territories lost after the war. The Nazi party in the country grew rapidly during the 1930's; but, aside from agitation, the Nazis made no overt moves against the country. Hungary shared in the partition of Czechoslovakia in 1938 and 1939 and collaborated with Germany during the war.

Yugoslavia. The immediate postwar years in this new state were filled with quarrels between the Catholic Croats and the Orthodox Serbs. The Serbs refused to grant a federal state, as the Croats demanded. In 1929 King Alexander I, himself a Serb, suspended the constitution and proclaimed himself dictator, thereafter suppressing Croat agitation by force. Though he granted a constitution a few years later, he was murdered in 1934; then the government of his son Peter II, who was still a child, continued to rule by dictatorial means until the eve of the war. In August, 1939, the Croats and Serbs formally settled their differences, and the Croat leader became vice-premier.

Albania. The little state of Albania, which had come into existence in 1912, survived the First World War but never achieved more than the form of a democratic government after the war. The premier Ahmed Zogu, who took office in 1925, became King Zog I in 1928 and ruled the country dictatorially. During the 1930's, Albania was in a state of constant friction with Italy, culminating in the taking over of the country by Mussolini in April, 1939. Victor Emmanuel then replaced Zog as king in a personal union between the two countries.

Rumania. In 1921 Rumania entered into an alliance with Czechoslovakia and Yugoslavia to help preserve their gains (Little Entente). Carol II, who was king for most of the interwar period, attempted to rule in an authoritarian manner and was generally successful in his manipulations, thus keeping the country from embarking on any significant reforms as many of its democratic leaders wished. For a period during the 1930's Carol backed the pro-Nazi, anti-Semitic Iron Guard and persecuted the Jews in spite of the fact that he had a Jewish mistress. In 1938 Carol assumed full control of the country through his own party, the Front of National Rebirth; suspended the constitution; and thereafter suppressed the Iron Guard and had its leaders killed. But during the war, with Nazi help the Iron Guard under General Ion Antonescu seized power and drove Carol from the country (1940).

Greece. In 1924, following the failure of Greek intervention in Turkey, a military junta briefly ruled the country, forcing King George II into exile. Under the republic that followed, some social reforms were carried out, especially under the premiership of Venizelos. But during the worldwide economic depression of the 1930's, when a number of anti-Venizelos leaders began to call for the restoration of the monarchy, Venizelos ceased to win elections. In 1935, George II was restored, and the following year a military dictatorship on the Italian model was established by General John Metaxas, who retained his position until the occupation of Greece by the Germans during the war.

Poland. After the First World War, the new state of Poland engaged in aggression to enlarge the country so that it would, so far as possible, include all its eighteenth-century territories. Some additions were made at the expense of Lithuania and Bolshevik Russia, with whom the Treaty of Riga was signed (1921), which defined the boundaries of the two countries. The dominant figure in Poland for many years was Marshal Pilsudski, who overthrew the parliamentary government by force in 1926 and twice revised the constitution to enable him to rule as a virtual dictator through a president of his

choice. After he died in 1935, the government was administered by a
military junta. In 1934 a nonaggression pact was signed with Nazi
Germany; and in 1938 Poland took part in the dismemberment of
Czechoslovakia. But thereafter she herself was subjected to extensive demands from Germany. When these were refused, the Germans
invaded Poland on September 1, 1939, thus beginning the Second
World War.

The Baltic States. All the new Baltic states—Latvia, Estonia,
and Lithuania—experienced some difficulty in establishing and maintaining their positions against the Soviet Union and, in the case of
Lithuania, against Poland also. The Lithuanian constitution was
suspended early in 1926, following a coup d'état by Antanas Smetona,
who remained dictator until the war. Latvia was taken over by Karlis
Ulmanis in 1934 and Estonia by Konstantin Paets in the same year.
Though constitutional government was restored in Estonia in 1937,
the Paets government controlled the subsequent elections so that
until the outbreak of the Second World War in 1939, Paets continued as president. All three countries fell to the Russians in the
first year of the war, by agreement with Germany.

The Iberian Peninsula. Spain remained neutral during the First
World War, but the postwar government was faced by rebellions in
Catalonia, which had prospered during the war, and by continued
fighting in Morocco, culminating in a severe defeat in 1921. In 1923
General Primo de Rivera, a former governor of the Philippines,
ousted the civilian government with the support of King Alfonso
XIII and ruled as dictator until 1930. The following year a republic
was established and Alphonso was driven into exile. The republic
lived a precarious existence until 1936, unable to unite the country
against the opposition of conservative forces. In 1936 a civil war
broke out which lasted until 1939, when General Francisco Franco,
having defeated the republicans with German and Italian help (see
p. 306), became dictator and head of state. He has remained in
office to this day.

Portugal played a small part in the First World War but made no
gains from it. The war was followed by numerous uprisings until
1926, when one under General Carmona succeeded. In 1928 Carmona, having been made president, appointed the economist Antonio
de Oliveira Salazar as minister of finance. Salazar, with the approval
of the army, became prime minister in 1932, a position he has
retained ever since, as virtual dictator under a series of military
presidents. The army ceased to take much part in politics and was

gradually reformed in such a way that all its substantial leaders were appointees of Salazar.

THE DEMOCRACIES DURING THE LONG ARMISTICE

By the 1930's few democracies remained in Europe. Only Czechoslovakia of all the new states had survived without succumbing to dictatorship. Even Czechoslovakia had her problems, especially with the Germans within her borders (Sudeten-Germans), who with the support of Hitler organized a movement that persistently called for union with Germany. The Slovaks also had a strong secessionist movement in the 1930's. But under presidents Tomás Masaryk and Eduard Benes democratic government was retained until the pressure by Germany which led to the partition of the country in 1938.

Great Britain. Britain, though victorious in the war, was never able to recover her position as the world's leading economic power. Not only had the United States won a commanding lead, but also much of Britain's machinery was obsolescent; she lacked a secure home market since for another decade she was a free-trade country; and her labor was restive. A serious depression overtook her in 1921; not even in the late 1920's, when the United States was enjoying a booming economy, did Britain really recover. Moreover, she had lost in battle many of her potential leaders, since her system of voluntary enlistment, maintained until 1917, tended to favor the less responsible and adventurous and was particularly hard on the class from which most of her prewar leaders had been drawn. In 1921, following a sharp civil war in Ireland, the Irish question was at last settled by the Lloyd George government, which had survived the First World War and won the first postwar elections. Ireland was partitioned between Ulster (Northern Ireland), which had dominion status, and the remaining counties, which became the Irish Free State. In subsequent elections Northern Ireland continued to reject union with the south.

In 1923 the first British Labor government, under Ramsay MacDonald took office with the support of the Liberals. When the Liberals deserted it in 1924, a general election brought Stanley Baldwin to power at the head of a Conservative government which had to deal with a general strike in 1926, followed by a prolonged miners' strike. In 1929 the Labor party won more seats than the Conservatives and, again supported by the Liberal party (now quite reduced in numbers), continued in control of the government. The

Depression struck Britain in 1930 and unemployment rose rapidly, exhausting the reserves in the Unemployment Insurance Fund. The government then decided to make direct grants to persons who had exhausted their insurance benefits; thus it inaugurated the "dole" in spite of the fact that this device necessitated an unbalanced budget. In the financial crisis that followed, a majority of the Labor ministers refused to impose a "means test" for the dole, and Ramsay Mac-Donald resigned. The next day he formed a coalition government with the Conservatives, which after the next election became a National Government, still under Ramsay MacDonald as prime minister. This government left the gold standard and instituted a protective tariff, thus abandoning free trade, and in 1932 it entered into an agreement with the Commonwealth nations providing for reciprocal tariff preferences. The economy then slowly recovered; but unemployment continued high until it was reduced considerably in the 1930's by a program of rearmament to meet the German threat.

Baldwin, prime minister from 1935, and Neville Chamberlain, who succeeded him in 1937, adopted a foreign policy which became known as appeasement. This involved trying to work with Italy and Germany, recognizing their demands that the British leaders considered just, and acquiescing in Hitler's policy of circumventing the Treaty of Versailles. Britain even signed an agreement with Hitler in 1935 limiting the tonnage of German warships to 35 per cent of Britain's —in spite of the fact that Germany was not permitted any warships under the Treaty. Though Britain was compelled by public opinion to oppose Italy's imperial ambitions in Ethiopia and eventually took the lead in imposing sanctions on Italy, as soon as this crisis was over, new "friendly" Anglo-Italian agreements were formulated. How this policy helped to bring on the Second World War will be discussed in a later section (see p. 307).

France. France, on whose soil most of the First World War had been fought and who had suffered the most casualties on the Allied side, was determined to prevent the rise of German power again and used the League of Nations as much as she could as an instrument for her own security. This policy was bolstered by a series of alliances with the new nations and ultimately with the Soviet Union. France was likewise determined to make Germany pay for the recent war and for the reconstruction of northern France; especially during the premiership of Raymond Poincaré (1922–1924), she tried to compel payment. The invasion of the Ruhr in 1923 was, however, a costly failure, since the Germans adopted a policy of passive resistance. The effort resulted in an uncontrollable inflation in Germany which the German government made little attempt to stop. Under a later government led by Poincaré (1926–1929), the franc was stabilized and the country given a stable financial structure, though at the expense of French exports (deflation). When the Depression struck France, she weathered the immediate storm far better than Britain, but she did not recover from it since, unlike Britain, she refused to devalue her currency again. French governments in the 1930's were unstable and racked by accusations of corruption; and riots had to be put down by military action. In 1936 a Popular Front government made up of left-wing parties and supported by the Communists, came to power under the Socialist Léon Blum. Though this government enacted numerous overdue social reforms, the country could not afford to pay for them, and the financial and economic crisis continued. In such circumstances France was unable to carry out an independent foreign policy and followed the British lead in appeasing Germany. It was not Britain but France, however, who had a binding military alliance with Czechoslovakia and Russia; therefore France was more seriously discredited by abandoning Czechoslovakia to Germany in 1938 and 1939.

The United States. In the postwar period, the United States, after failing to ratify the Treaty of Versailles, gradually relapsed into isolation, concentrating on domestic affairs except for occasional efforts to spur the League of Nations into action—notably in the case of Japan's aggression in China from 1931 onward. In addition Secretary of State Kellogg took the lead in winning European signatures to a paper peace pact—including no sanctions—which outlawed war as an instrument of national policy. Relations with Britain and France were strained by the failure of these countries to honor their war debt to the United States when they ceased to receive reparations from Germany. In part as a response to this feeling, Congress passed several Neutrality Acts (1935, 1936, 1937), prohibiting the sale of arms to foreign combatants and restricting other sales during the time of war to what could be paid for in cash. The United States, although she was the major creditor nation of the world, continued to increase her tariffs, culminating in the Hawley-Smoot Tariff of 1930—thereby making it almost impossible for the war debts to be paid and reducing purchases of United States products by foreigners to a minimum, since they lacked the dollars to pay for them.

Nevertheless, with a huge home market to be satisfied, the United

States, especially during the presidency of the Republican Calvin Coolidge (1923–1929), enjoyed a period of unprecedented prosperity, and prices in the stock market reached unheard-of heights. The stock market crashed in October, 1929, while Herbert Hoover was president, thus marking the onset of the Great Depression in the United States. By the end of this presidency in 1933, unemployment had reached appalling levels; and most of the banks in the country, unable to meet payments, had closed down when Democratic President Franklin Roosevelt took over the administration on March 4, 1933.

There followed several years of legislation prepared by Roosevelt's advisers and passed by a Congress which was overwhelmingly Democratic. This legislation, collectively known as the New Deal, attempted to master the Depression by as many laws as could be pushed through Congress and upheld by the Supreme Court as constitutional. Unemployment insurance, social security and old-age pensions, federal subsidies to farmers, numerous relief acts, and public works were all passed and upheld. The rights of labor unions were acknowledged and supported by law. Some of the acts, however, were declared unconstitutional, including the National Recovery Act of 1933, a basic law which granted considerable powers to the federal government in the control of the economy. Others were upheld after the composition of the Supreme Court had changed in the late 1930's. It remains a matter of dispute whether the New Deal in fact helped the United States to recover from the Depression; but it certainly breathed new confidence into citizens of the country who believed in taking positive action rather than in merely ending the deprivations of the Depression—though the majority of the laws passed during the era were such as were already in successful operation in European countries. The New Deal therefore brought the United States more closely into line with practices in other Western countries, even though at the end she still lacked most of the benefits for individual citizens that were more easily provided by the unitary governments of Europe.

Canada. In the 1930's Canada passed much legislation similar to that of the New Deal. Most of this was accomplished by the Conservative government of Richard Bennett in the hopes of staving off defeat in the next election—a hope that was not fulfilled. The Supreme Court of Canada invalidated most of these laws on the ground that such legislation was reserved to the provinces. They were subsequently repassed by the Mackenzie King government after agreement had been reached with the provinces to abate their powers in the interest of the country as a whole. Canada provided for family allowances during the war and instituted a National Health program in 1957.

Smaller Democratic Nations. The democratic states of Scandinavia (Norway, Sweden, and Denmark) all remained neutral during the First World War and all engaged in considerable social reform under the auspices of the state. Denmark recovered from the Depression by the use of strict controls over agriculture imposed by socialist governments. In Holland a National Socialist party was formed and gained ground during the Depression but soon lost its support when the economy began to recover. In Belgium a fascist party whose members were known as Rexists was founded in the 1930's and won several seats in the parliament in 1936. The Rexists fomented disorder for a couple of years, but their strength had evaporated by the outbreak of war. In none of these countries did any fascist or other totalitarian group come within measurable distance of taking over the state.

THE PRELUDE TO WAR

The League of Nations, established under the Treaty of Versailles (see p. 288), had been gradually joined by almost all the independent nations of the world—though Russia and Germany were never members at the same time. For many years it was widely thought of as the best guarantee for peace, and "collective security" became a major slogan in the interwar years. But the League was never given an international police force, as France in particular urged, and it proved unable to take really effective action when the great powers were involved. Several issues, however, were settled by the League in its early years, though such successes were dependent on the willingness of national governments to let it make decisions—which, needless to say, were those that did not affect their own vital interests.

The Versailles System. The peace treaties after the First World War imposed harsh terms on the losers—though not so harsh as those imposed by Germany on Russia at Brest-Litovsk in 1918— and created at least as many new problems as they solved. The governments in the new nations were almost invariably unstable, and the minorities, included against their wish in their territories, agitated constantly for more rights, or for "return" to a different nation. Hitler thus won some support in other countries than his own. But in

Germany he used the Treaty as a means of arousing passions in his countrymen, winning more support on each occasion that he tore up a new clause, always with impunity.

The Formation of the Axis. But Hitler could not win the support of any major ally until Mussolini, hitherto a rival, found himself isolated during the Ethiopian War, which he waged against the opposition of all the powers then in the League. When Mussolini drove into Ethiopia in 1935, the British and French were willing to make a deal with him in the best nineteenth-century manner. Under the Hoare-Laval Agreement, Ethiopia would have lost some territory but maintained her independence. However, when the details of this pact became known in England, it had to be abandoned because of outraged public opinion. Britain then called for economic sanctions to be taken by the League, as required under its Charter. Though some sanctions were voted, they were insufficient to prevent the Italian conquest. No embargo was placed on oil, lack of which might have been enough to halt the Italians. Thus the League had been shown to be without the will to coerce a major power.

Hitler took the opportunity in March, 1936, while the Ethiopian War was in progress, to march into the Rhineland. France seriously considered sending in her own army, which was at the time far superior to that of Germany; but she could not win the assent of Baldwin's government in Britain. It is now known that Hitler would have been overthrown by his own army if the French had marched. The occupation of the Rhineland was therefore the crucial moment of the interwar years, little though this fact was understood at the time. The German army command thereby gained confidence in Hitler's "intuition," which it had hitherto doubted. In October, 1936, Hitler and Mussolini entered into an alliance, known as the Rome-Berlin Axis. The next month Japan, likewise an isolated and aggressive power, signed a treaty of alliance with Germany, ostensibly directed against the Communist International. The Axis functioned effectively enough during the Spanish Civil War (1936–1939), in which both Germany and Italy intervened. The Soviet Union intervened on the opposite side. But since Britain and France refused to intervene actively and indeed organized a nonintervention pact to which all the European powers and the United States adhered, Germany and Italy were left free to give the Spanish rebels enough aid to win the war. Russia was too far away to provide effective assistance to the Loyalists, though she helped raise an International Brigade and sent such supplies as she could.

The Austrian and Czechoslovakian Crises. Early in 1938 Hitler changed the personnel of the German high command, making the army thereafter a subservient tool of the Nazi party. In March of that year Germany occupied Austria; Italy now dependent on German aid, acquiesced and contented herself with occupying Albania in the following year. Hitler's next victim was intended to be Czechoslovakia, where a local minority of Germans (formerly inhabitants of the Austrian Empire but never of Germany) demanded to be made part of Hitler's Third Reich. The British, deep in their policy of appeasement, sent a special emissary to see if there were any way of reaching an accommodation in the country. Though the British and the French stoutly proclaimed their intention of standing by their alliances and by the Covenant of the League, and though the Czechs made it known that they would fight to defend their independence, Lord Runciman's mission greatly disturbed the Czechs, who believed the British were preparing to abandon them.

In September, 1938, the Sudeten-German minority began to foment riots and appealed to Germany for aid. Hitler gave them his full backing and demanded "self-determination" for them. At this point Prime Minister Neville Chamberlain paid a visit to Hitler at Berchtesgaden, as a result of which he put great pressure on the Czechs to cede the Sudetenland. When they reluctantly agreed, Chamberlain returned to Germany to see Hitler again (at Godesberg), only to find that he had raised his terms so high that even Chamberlain could not accept them. The Russians, who had urged from the beginning that no concessions be made, now won support from the French for their viewpoint, and all the Allied powers began to make preparations for war. But Chamberlain had not yet despaired of peace. He and President Roosevelt appealed to Mussolini to use his influence, and Hitler agreed to meet the Allied leaders. There followed a conference at Munich on September 29, 1938, at which most of Hitler's demands were met. The Czechs, who were not represented, were then compelled by their allies to acquiesce in the arrangements, under which they lost their one defensible frontier in exchange for an international guarantee. Chamberlain, returning from Munich, declared he had won "peace in our time." Both the British and French peoples were inclined to believe him and rejoiced in the triumph of appeasement.

In March, 1939, the Germans marched into the now indefensible Czechoslovakia and occupied what remained of it. No opposition was offered by the international guarantors. The British and French governments were now, too late, thoroughly aroused, and offered a guarantee to Poland, which seemed likely to be the next on Hitler's list. They also entered into serious discussions with the Soviet Union, who after Munich was more deeply suspicious than ever of British and French intentions and doubted their willingness to keep any promises they made. Moreover, the Poles themselves were unwilling to let Russian armies through their country in the event of war with Germany. In these circumstances, Stalin preferred to sign an agreement with Germany under which each side promised not to wage war on the other (August, 1939). Immediately afterward Hitler stepped up his demands on Poland and on the city of Danzig (which had been made a free city within the Polish customs union by the Versailles Treaty); and he despatched an ultimatum to Poland on August 31. The following day Germany invaded Poland. Two days later (September 3) Britain and France declared war on Germany. Italy for a time remained neutral, though ready to enter on the German side if the conditions warranted it.

Thus began the Second World War.

21 A CENTURY OF MATERIAL PROGRESS AND ITS CULTURAL CONSEQUENCES

In the second half of the nineteenth century, what may be thought of as a second Industrial Revolution began to follow hard on the heels of the first, which had been dominated by Great Britain. During the next century all the Western nations, as well as Japan in the Far East, became industrialized. The process has continued and there is no end in sight.

CHARACTERISTICS OF THE SECOND INDUSTRIAL REVOLUTION

This second phase of the Industrial Revolution was characterized not only by the spread of industry throughout the Western world but also by at least three major changes in the industrial process itself. First, new sources of energy, such as gas, electricity, and oil, gradually began to take the place of coal. Second, science was applied more directly to industry, not only in the creation of new man-made materials such as the plastics but also in research for the purpose of improving the quality and usefulness of manufactured products. Third, there was great improvement in production methods, including the use of machines to make ever more complex tools and interchangeable parts (mass production) and the more efficient use of labor. All these changes tended to freeze the small man out of industry, since he did not have access to the quantities of capital necessary to finance research, nor could he buy the machines or hire the labor required for mass production.

Inventions. The key inventions of the period were the dynamo (by Michael Faraday, 1791–1867), which made practicable the production of electricity on a large scale; the incandescent lamp (by Thomas Edison, 1847–1931); the telephone (by Alexander Graham Bell, 1847–1923 and Edison); radio (by Guglielmo Marconi,

1874–1937); television (mainly by John Baird, 1888–1946); the internal combustion engine (by Nikolas Otto, 1832–1891, and Gottlieb Daimler, 1834–1900); the diesel engine (by Rudolf Diesel, 1858–1913). Numerous scientists worked on the problem of the utilization of atomic energy, which may prove to be the most revolutionary of all, not only for the production of explosives, on which it has already had a tremendous effect but also in industry. The Italian Enrico Fermi was the first to achieve a nuclear chain reaction (1942). In the field of industrial organization and scientific management the great pioneer was the American Frederick Winslow Taylor (1856–1915), but it was the automobile manufacturer Henry Ford (1863–1947) who was the first to visualize the possibilities of mass production in industry.

Economic Consequences. The major consequence of the new phase of the Industrial Revolution has been the transfer of industrial leadership to those countries where there is an assured home market for manufactured products and where there are sufficient raw materials available for use in industry. It is possible for countries where materials are in short supply to purchase them abroad, and such countries as Britain and Japan have not ceased to be industrial nations. But they are at a disadvantage in comparison with, say, the United States, in that they have to make sales abroad before they can buy the raw material they need, and such sales have to be made in a world market where prices are kept low because of competition. This disadvantage is partly offset, however, by the low price of the raw materials when they are in large supply.

The assured domestic market, usually protected from foreign competition by tariffs, means that the manufacturer can sell most of his products at home at profitable prices and is not dependent on export sales, which to him are a bonus rather than a necessity. The home market, if it is large enough, will enable him to use the technique of mass production with the consequent lowering of unit costs.

Nevertheless, the capital requirements are tremendous; and if there is a drop in consumer demand, the manufacturer is compelled to reduce expenses by laying off large numbers of workers, leading to mass unemployment. Many of his expenses continue, including payment for his machines, whether or not they are in use. He is put to continuous expense in trying to develop his home market by means of advertising and the expansion of his force of salesmen. Thus the economy has become far more precarious than it was in early centuries, when there was a limited but regular demand which a relatively small number of manufacturers were able to meet.

Social Consequences. The primary social consequence of this revolution has been the degrading of the status of the worker, who is now himself an almost "interchangeable part" in the industrial process. Neither he nor his employer is a truly free agent, both being dependent to a large degree on the vagaries of the market. Nevertheless, all members of modern industrial societies have seen their standard of living raised (as well as their expectations). Modern industry is dependent on an ever increasing demand from consumers, and all efforts have been concentrated on how to put industrial products into their hands—by increasing wages (in which goal the labor unions have played their part), by extending credit, by artificially stimulating the desires of potential buyers, and similar means. The result of all this has been, above everything else, the concentration of human energies in the production of ever more material goods and the equating of the possession of such goods with the achievement of the "good life"—a quest that in various guises has been man's aim since the beginning of recorded history.

Parallel with the drive for the possession of material goods has been the quest for comfort and pleasure, both of which ordinarily require good health. Thus the last century has seen the tremendous development of medical science: first, in the avoidance, treatment, and cure of physical diseases; and, second, in a newer branch of medicine, the treatment of diseases and maladjustments affecting the human psyche and preventing the achievement of joy and satisfaction. To minister to man's pleasure there has been an equally massive increase in the provision of all kinds of entertainment, including movies, radio, television, and the means for rapid movement from one place to another in search of new and different environments and experiences.

RESULTS OF THE REVOLUTION

It is not surprising that these tremendous changes have been reflected in literature, art, and thought. At the same time man's own picture of his place in the universe has been influenced by ideas that first gained currency in the nineteenth century.

The Theory of Evolution. Man in the seventeenth and eighteenth centuries came to be regarded by many advanced thinkers as an insignificant being alone in an enormous universe which, like himself, was subject to mechanical laws. But it was left to Charles Darwin (1809–1882) and his successors to demonstrate that man was the product of chance genetic mutations and was in all essential respects an animal—having, however, a mind developed over countless millennia by the process of "natural selection." This theory, which Darwin put forward in two major books *The Origin of Species* and *The Descent of Man* was seized upon by thinkers in many other fields. Herbert Spencer (1820–1903), who had already coined the phrase "the survival of the fittest" before the appearance of Darwin's books, looked upon all life as a struggle for existence in which those organisms, including man, which were best fitted to survive, did so. This principle accounted for progressive evolution from primitive to more advanced forms and from primitive society to advanced civilization.

The first proponents of Darwinism were ridiculed and attacked, especially by churchmen who believed that man has a "soul," which indeed distinguishes him from the animals. Thomas Huxley, an articulate early disciple of Darwin, was accused of believing that his not very remote ancestors were apes. Eventually, as more scientific evidence became available—especially the work of the monk Gregor Mendel (1822–1884) in the field of genetics, a work which was not rediscovered until after his death—it was generally accepted that acquired characteristics are not inherited but that genetic mutations, most of them harmful, occur and that the most useful characteristics do indeed survive by a process of natural selection. Many churchmen, conceding that the doctrine of progressive evolution was true, said that it was the method used by God to enable mankind to progress. Men tended therefore in the nineteenth century to talk more of "mind," that is the capacity to think, and less of "soul," which they felt was too mysterious and unverifiable an entity to be acceptable to science.

The New Science of Psychology. One result of the belief in the animalic nature of man was the increased interest shown in the behavior of animals, from which, it was believed, much could be learned about man. The pioneer in this work was the Russian Ivan Pavlov (1849–1936), who discovered that animals could be trained to perform certain acts instinctively by what he called the "conditioned reflex." From his work has stemmed the "behaviorist" school of psychology, founded by the American John B. Watson (1878–1958). Sigmund Freud (1856–1939), a Viennese psychologist, chose a different method of investigating the "mind" of man. Realizing from his early study of hysterical patients that human beings are sometimes ruled by irrational emotions, he postulated the existence of a "subconscious" or unconscious as the depository of repressed emotions which do not reach the surface of consciousness and yet influence man's supposedly conscious acts. Freud developed a technique known as psychoanalysis to bring the repressed feelings to the surface. Numerous other schools of psychology sprang up to investigate human behavior and to try to help human beings to live normal "happy" lives. Some of them were founded by pupils of Freud (for example, Alfred Adler, Karl Jung), who accepted his fundamental discovery of the subconscious but deviated from his views in other important respects. The theories of Freud and his disciples greatly influenced novelists, biographers, and literary critics, who endeavored to find the subconscious motivations in great men of the past and in the literary masterpieces of long-dead writers.

Medical Advances. In medicine many of the great discoveries that lie behind twentieth-century achievements stem from the work of Louis Pasteur (1822–1895) and Robert Koch (1843–1910), who demonstrated the bacterial origin of many diseases, leading to their treatment by antisepsis (pioneered by Joseph Lister, 1827–1912). In the twentieth century the virus, a smaller entity than the bacterium, was discovered. Though the virus is known to be responsible for numerous diseases, its nature is still imperfectly understood. However, viruses can be controlled by the process of immunization, a technique originally invented at the end of the eighteenth century by Edward Jenner (1749–1823), who used his process to immunize against smallpox. In the twentieth century, research into drugs has led to the development of antibiotics, which have met with remarkable successes in the treatment of diseases that in the past led to a swift death. The earliest and still one of the most effective of these is penicillin, discovered in 1939 by Alexander Fleming. The development of anesthesia and antisepsis led to great advances in surgery. The progress in medicine, the improvement in sanitation, and the destruction of micro-organisms by various forms of poison have increased the life span of human beings all over the globe. This achievement has led on the one hand to the proportionately increased incidence of the degenerative diseases and on the other to the revival of Malthusianism (see p. 189), which held that the production of food would not keep pace with the increase of population. The maintenance of adequate living space is also seen as a problem.

Physics. Pure science has continued to flourish, especially in the

twentieth century, when governments, universities, and private industry have made huge sums and extensive facilities available for
the use of scientists. Nevertheless, the greatest advance in physical
theory was made by Albert Einstein (1879–1955), who was employed
at the Swiss Patent Office at the time he propounded his Special
Theory of Relativity (1905). This theory, together with his General
Theory of Relativity (1915), by demonstrating the equivalence of
mass and electrical energy and explaining gravitation as a field rather
than a force, not only added to Newton's fundamental laws (now
seen to be applicable only to ordinary terrestrial phenomena), but
also opened up to later investigators the realm of the subatomic
world. The Quantum Theory of Max Planck (1858–1947) was the
other major achievement in theoretical physics which led to the
modern concept of matter. This discovery was, of course, supplemented by research into the nature of the atom, especially associated
with the name of Ernest Rutherford (1871–1937), and into the
phenomenon of radioactivity, discovered by Pierre and Marie Curie
at the turn of the twentieth century.

The Realistic and Experimental Novel. The serious literature
of the past century has been marked by a tendency toward realistic
or naturalistic description. Of course, there have been novels of all
kinds, including many which have experimented with new modes
of expression and new techniques. The tendency toward naturalism
had already appeared in the mid-nineteenth century with Gustave
Flaubert's *Madame Bovary,* and to a lesser degree with Honoré de
Balzac in a long series of novels which he called collectively *The
Human Comedy.* These novelists were reacting against the excesses
of romanticism and were not yet enough freed from it merely to write
descriptions of life (especially its seamier side), as did Émile Zola
and the American Theodore Dreiser at the turn of the century. The
Victorian Charles Dickens also wrote of this side of life, but to him
the characters were of greater importance and a vein of whimsicality
runs through his descriptions. In this century realistic novels such as
Erich Remarque's *All Quiet on the Western Front* and Ernest Hem-
ingway's *A Farewell to Arms* emerged from the First World War. The
tradition has been carried on, especially by American writers, such as
James Farrell (*Studs Lonigan*) and John O'Hara. The Second World
War likewise had its spate of realistic novels, including Norman
Mailer's *The Naked and the Dead* and James Jones's *From Here to
Eternity.* In this vein realistic Russian writers such as Mikhail Shol-
okhov wrote on the early Bolshevik Revolution (*And Quiet Flows*

the Don)—diverging from the nineteenth-century Russians Leo
Tolstoi and Fëdor Dostoevski, whose novels, though realistic, even
at times pessimistic, are deeply concerned with ultimate values and
meanings, a concern missing in Sholokhov.

Experimental novelists include James Joyce with his *Ulysses* and
Finnegans Wake, which use a stream-of-consciousness technique to
describe a day and a night in the life of the heroes, and Marcel
Proust, whose *Remembrance of Things Past* tries to recapture lost or
fleeting memories in such a way as to make them into a meaningful
pattern. Franz Kafka in his novels *The Trial* and *The Castle* attempts to create an atmosphere in which man's feelings of guilt and
oppression are symbolically portrayed. Thomas Mann in *The Magic
Mountain* presents a haunting picture of a Swiss sanitarium which
the hero cannot escape because of the contradictions of his nature.
Albert Camus in *The Stranger* presents a man who commits a
murder unintentionally, but being totally without conscience and
without ability to come to any relation with his fellow-men, is unable to defend himself and is meaninglessly executed. Such works
as these by the finest imaginative artists of the twentieth century
suggest the failure of modern industrial society to offer any purpose or meaning to life acceptable to the artist.

The Other Arts. The realistic drama, best represented by the
Norwegian Henrik Ibsen, the Swede August Strindberg, and the
American Eugene O'Neill is hardly less pessimistic. Poetry, in the
nineteenth century led by Charles Baudelaire and his followers in
the French school (Arthur Rimbaud, Paul Verlaine, Stephen Mal-
larmé), moved into symbolism—as did painting, represented by the
schools of impressionism (Cézanne), postimpressionism (Van Gogh),
and surrealism (Salvador Dali), which eventually with abstract and
nonobjective art (Picasso, Matisse, Kandinsky) left the observed
world altogether. Much modern poetry (for example, Ezra Pound's)
has obscure allusions comprehensible only to a few. Experimental
architecture, on the other hand, has flourished in the modern industrial world, which has provided new materials and new techniques,
making possible the functionalism of Frank Lloyd Wright and Le
Corbusier. Though the romantic and classical traditions in music
were carried on in the nineteenth century by Brahms, Tchaikovsky,
Bruckner, and others, and by the great operatic innovator Richard
Wagner, modern music, noted for its atonality and experimentalism
—best represented in the works of Schönberg, Alban Berg, Paul
Hindemith, and the earlier Stravinsky—has moved far from the

music of the past. It has been assisted in this departure by the great increases in the musical resources available to orchestras. Though modern music of this kind has never become really popular, jazz music with its syncopated beat has strongly appealed to many.

Philosophy. Philosophy has tended to travel in the same direction as literature. The pessimist German Arthur Schopenhauer, who saw the cosmos as an aimlessly striving Will, led the way in the nineteenth century. Another German, Frederich Nietzsche, likewise glorified the will but preached the Superman and the "courage to strive." In answer to Darwin, Nietzsche passionately asserted that man must now take in hand his own evolution. The Dane Sören Kierkegaard (1813–1855) insisted on man's free will as the only source of ethical deeds, in which emphasis he has been followed by the twentieth-century existentialists, notably the French Jean-Paul Sartre and the Germans Heidegger and Jaspers—though only Jaspers among this group followed Kierkegaard in retaining the belief in God as a philosophical necessity. Other philosophers, such as the American William James (1842–1910) and his distant disciple and younger contemporary John Dewey denied ethical absolutes with their pragmatism and instrumentalism, holding that propositions are to be considered true only if they work in practice—in this approach providing a satisfactory philosophy for modern science with its mixture of induction and deduction. Logical empiricists have devoted themselves to the analysis of meaning, denying that any propositions incapable of verification are meaningful. One of the most important modern philosophers, Henri Bergson (1859–1941), took issue with Darwin, insisting that a "vital force" (*élan vital*) is the creative element in evolution and that the intellect, however competent it may be to understand the inorganic world, cannot apprehend the organic but that higher faculties, not yet fully developed in present-day man, are necessary for such a grasp. (Religions, according to Bergson, have been created by the imagination and intuition and can no more be disproved by the intellect than they can be created by it.)

Religion. Religion has not been content to allow popular Darwinism and scientific materialism to take possession of the field. The Catholic religion has reasserted its ancient doctrines, and Pope Leo XIII in the nineteenth century encouraged the revival of medieval scholasticism, which has resulted in the reinterpretation of the teachings of St. Thomas Aquinas known as Neo-Thomism (whose best representatives are Jacques Maritain and Étienne Gilson). Moreover, the same pope and two of his successors, Pius XI and John XXIII, have emphasized the duty of employers toward their employees and the concept of a truly Christian society; and Pope John XXIII devoted himself during his short pontificate (1958–1963) to attempts to bring all the Christian churches together. Partly for this purpose he summoned an Ecumenical Council to discuss Church problems and explore the possibilities of greater unity. After his death, the Council was reconvened by his successor Paul VI. Protestantism has produced outstanding theologians such as Karl Barth, Reinhold Niebuhr, and Paul Tillich. Religious sects have been prolific since the early nineteenth century, led by the Church of Jesus Christ of Latter Day Saints (Mormon), the Seventh Day Adventists, and Jehovah's Witnesses, all of which rely on new prophetic inspirations given by their founders. There have also been reactions to the common overemphasis of interest in the material world—as, for example, in Christian Science, founded by Mary Baker Eddy, which insists that matter and disease are illusion and the only reality is Divine Mind.

The culture of the late nineteenth and twentieth centuries may therefore be viewed as in large measure a reflection of the changing life of man in society, a change far deeper and more pervasive than any that have taken place in all the other periods of history considered in this book. Change in earlier centuries was gradual, almost imperceptible for those who experienced it; whereas in the past hundred years Western civilization appears to have speeded up its tempo. We are now deep in the atomic age, but it is not a century since Faraday invented his dynamo. The fact that man has yet to adjust to the new world in which he lives is reflected in his philosophies, his literature, and his art. This condition after all can scarcely be a matter for surprise though it may provide food for thought.

22 THE SECOND WORLD WAR AND ITS AFTERMATH

German conquests were far more extensive in the Second World War than they had been in the First, and they were retained for a longer period. For a time Germany seemed within measurable distance of winning the war, and, apart from a few neutrals, only Britain and Russia on the continent of Europe remained outside the new German empire. But the German invasion of Russia, followed within a few months by the entry of the United States into the war, made the odds too great for Germany to sustain—especially since her control of Europe was based almost exclusively on force. From the end of 1942 to 1945, her victories were few and her armies were worn down by gradual attrition. Japan, who entered the war on the side of the Axis in December, 1941, made extensive conquests during the first few months thereafter but was then on the defensive throughout the rest of the war, while she, too, was worn down by the superior resources and manpower of the United States. Allied victory was followed by growing tensions between the Soviet Union and the Western powers.

ASCENDANCY OF THE AXIS POWERS, 1939–1942

During the first weeks of the war Poland was conquered and divided between Germany and the Soviet Union. For the rest of the winter the war with Germany relapsed into quiescence, while the Soviet Union, who had compelled the small Baltic states (Lithuania, Latvia, and Estonia) to provide her with military bases, began a war with Finland, who had refused to follow their example. In spite of a heroic defense by the Finns, the Russians (in March, 1940) compelled them to sue for peace, under which Russia was granted the bases she required. Most of the territory, however, was ceded outright. In April the Second World War began in earnest.

The Norwegian and French Campaigns. Unexpectedly, since the Germans did not command the sea, they began their attack on the Western powers by sea and air invasion of Norway and occupation of Denmark, who offered no resistance. The British and French, unprepared for this eventuality, sent reinforcements and occupied the Norwegian city of Narvik. But the Germans were able to reinforce their units quickly and effectively. By the end of April they had put an end to resistance except in Narvik, which the Allies evacuated six weeks later.

On May 10 the Germans invaded the Low Countries in a lightning attack, forcing the Netherlands government to surrender in four days. On May 17 they invaded France and then drove quickly to the French and Belgian seaports. Belgium surrendered on May 26, enabling the Germans to surround the Franco-British expeditionary force at Dunkirk. In one of the most remarkable feats of the war this force was evacuated to England (June 4) but lost all its equipment. Italy entered the war and invaded southern France, but this force made little difference to the campaign. The German mechanized forces rolled up all northern France and drove on Paris, where the government of Paul Reynaud fell. Reynaud was replaced by a hero of the First World War, Henri Pétain, who requested and was granted an armistice (June 22). Under the armistice, three-fifths of the country was to be occupied by Germany, leaving the remainder to be governed by Pétain and his vice-premier Pierre Laval from the new French capital, the former spa of Vichy. Meanwhile, an acting brigadier general, Charles de Gaulle, one of the few French commanders who had enhanced his reputation during the recent debacle, escaped to England and proclaimed his intention of continuing the war together with any Frenchmen who would join him. His French National Committee was supported by the British government, now under the control of Winston Churchill, who had replaced Neville Chamberlain as prime minister on May 10, the day of the French invasion of Belgium.

The Battle of Britain. It seems evident that the sweeping nature and speed of the German victory surprised Hitler, who was not yet ready to undertake the invasion of Britain that would be necessary to win the war. Churchill refused to even consider any negotiations with him and with his matchless eloquence encouraged the people to resist to the end. The British navy and small but efficient air force easily broke up such tentative efforts as Hitler made to assemble an invasion force. But German bombing planes launched an all-out attack in an attempt to force Britain's surrender without invasion. The United States, whose President Roosevelt was scarcely less anti-German than was Churchill, quickly concluded an agreement to reinforce the British navy with fifty over-age destroyers in exchange for the lease of British bases in the Western Hemisphere. The Germans, in spite of inflicting immense damage on Britain, soon found themselves losing too many bombing planes at the hands of the British fighters, and they were compelled to relax the assault by the end of 1940. The United States Congress in March, 1941, passed a Lend-Lease Act, which replaced the Neutrality Acts of the 1930's. Under this Act food, of which the British were becoming critically short, and arms were made available to "any country whose defense the President deems vital to the defense of the United States" without immediate payment. Lend-Lease shipments were crucial to Britain's defense, enabling her to fight on until the Germans began to turn their arms against Russia.

Axis Conquest of the Balkans. Mussolini, whose armies had done little in the conquest of France, made extensive demands on Greece in October, 1940. When they were refused, the Italians invaded Greece but were unsuccessful and were driven back into Albania, from which they had launched the attack. British planes also destroyed most of the Italian navy in its home base of Taranto. From this situation the Germans rescued their allies by invading Yugoslavia and Greece the following spring. The Yugoslav government surrendered, leaving the struggle to be carried on by guerrillas. Athens was captured in spite of the presence of a British expeditionary force, and the island of Crete was taken by German parachute troops, which however suffered very severe losses in the process. The eastern Mediterranean with the exception of Cyprus thus fell into Axis hands.

North African Campaigns. Meanwhile the Italians, who had invaded Egypt from Libya in August, 1940, were driven out by a vigorous British counteroffensive under General Wavell, which swept on to Benghazi in Cyrenaica. Italian Somaliland and Ethiopia were likewise taken from the Italians, who lost all their East African empire by the end of 1941. But Wavell was compelled by the Nazi advance in Greece to send reinforcements to that country, thus leaving North Africa open to a drive by the Italians, now reinforced by Germans trained for desert fighting, led by General Rommel. This drive expelled the British from Cyrenaica except for the fortress of Tobruk (April, 1941). But the Germans in turn had to release troops for the

Russian campaign in mid-1941, enabling the British to fight their way once more across the desert to Benghazi (December, 1941). In May, 1942, Rommel counterattacked, this time driving as far as El Alamein, less than a hundred miles from Alexandria, and capturing Tobruk without difficulty. But German losses in the Russian campaign prevented any further advance; and the Germans were driven back for the last time by Field Marshal Montgomery and a greatly superior British army—to meet in due course with the Anglo-American troops who had invaded Morocco and Algeria late in 1942. By May, 1943, all North Africa was in Allied hands.

German Advances in Russia. In June, 1941, the Germans without warning launched an attack on the Soviet Union, who was thus compelled to defend herself against a power with whom she appeared to have been co-operating. Britain at once promised Stalin every assistance, while the United States extended the Lend-Lease Act to Russia. For several months the Russians were driven back, scorching the earth as far as possible in their retreat. But they successfully defended Leningrad (St. Petersburg) and Moscow. They moved behind the Urals all industrial equipment capable of being transferred, and they continued to manufacture enough armaments with which to continue the war. During the winter they were even able to mount an offensive and recapture a few important cities, all the time taking severe toll of the Axis forces, which were insufficiently prepared for a Russian winter.

The following year the Germans staged a new drive, advancing to the Caucasus and the important city of Stalingrad, which held out for five months against repeated attacks. In January and February, 1943, Leningrad and Stalingrad were relieved; the Russians captured the remainder of the besieging German army at the latter city; and thereafter initiative rested with them until they drove the Germans back into their own country.

The Japanese Attack. Japan, who had been engaged in trying to conquer China ever since 1931 but had never succeeded in putting an end to Chinese resistance, entered into an alliance with Germany and Italy in September, 1940, under which it was understood that Japan would co-operate with her allies when she deemed the time to be propitious. The following year she signed a neutrality treaty with Russia, which gave her a free hand to do as she wished in the East without fear of a two-front war. The treaty was not denounced by the Russians until April, 1945. On the other hand, the United States gave consistent support to the Chinese Nationalist government under

Chiang Kai-shek and in 1941 placed an embargo on strategic trade with Japan. The Japanese war party, whose leader was General Tojo, concluded that war with the United States was inevitable if Japanese aspirations for a "Co-Prosperity Sphere" in the East were to be fulfilled. Japan therefore moved slowly but inexorably toward the war, making arrangements with the Vichy government of France to use French Indo-China as a military base and compelling Thailand (Siam) to submit to Japanese occupation.

In December, 1941, while her diplomats were engaged in desultory conversations with the United States, she struck at the American navy and air force as far west as the naval base of Pearl Harbor in Hawaii, inflicting great damage, which could not be quickly repaired. She simultaneously attacked in the Far East according to a well-prepared plan. The United States was unable to reinforce her troops in the Philippines after the Pearl Harbor disaster, and the islands fell to the Japanese. A tremendous series of victories netted Japan all of British Malaya, including Singapore, the colony of Hong Kong, Burma, the entire Dutch empire in Indonesia, and numerous Pacific islands. In due course the United States recovered, and Anglo-American troops fought some rear-guard actions on the mainland, especially in Burma, with some success. But by the end of March, 1942, Japan was everywhere triumphant and busily engaged in organizing her new empire. Meanwhile, Germany and Italy had declared war on the United States, on December 11, 1941, thus bringing in as their open enemy the power which had hitherto co-operated with the Allies but had not yet committed her own armed forces to the struggle.

DECLINE AND FALL OF FORTRESS EUROPE— THE WAR OF ATTRITION

The Axis powers by the end of 1942 were greatly overextended and were compelled to defend what they called Fortress Europe from a coalition which, in spite of serious depredations by German submarines, possessed overwhelming superiority at sea. Moreover, all the countries occupied by the Germans, though in some cases ruled by native puppet rulers (for example, Quisling in Norway) backed by German troops, were only waiting for the relaxation of German vigilance and the weakening of German power to rebel against the Nazi tyranny. The Germans engaged in the systematic destruction of the Jews, and their treatment of the Slavic peoples (whom they regarded as racial inferiors) under their domination was only slightly worse than their treatment of the French, who were requisitioned as laborers to make up for the attrition of Germany manpower. Spain, whose dictator, Franco, had been helped to power by German air support during the Civil War (see p. 306), greatly disappointed Hitler by refusing to join the Axis powers, though Spanish volunteer troops fought on the Russian front. It was therefore clear by the end of 1942 that Germany, and her ally Japan, could no longer hope to win the war and moreover that the type of war the Germans had waged made impossible a negotiated peace which would have left them any of their gains. It became necessary for the Allies to fight it out to the bitter end and to accept the losses that would be inevitable when they eventually made the attempt to land on the continent of Europe.

The Landings in North Africa and Southern Italy. In August, 1942, a small force made up mainly of Canadians raided the coastal city of Dieppe and tested the defenses of the Continent. Losses were so severe that it was generally recognized that as yet Europe was impregnable. On November 8 of the same year a landing was made in North Africa by an Anglo-American force, which quickly put an end to the Vichy government in Algeria and eventually chased the Germans and Italians out of Africa. The Germans retaliated by taking over unoccupied France. At Casablanca in January, 1943, in a conference between Roosevelt, Churchill, and the Free French, the Allied leaders agreed upon war strategy. Stalin meanwhile called ever more urgently for a "second front" in Europe to relieve pressure on his armies and refused to recognize the African invasion as a suitable alternative.

In July, 1943, the Allies, now under the command of General Dwight D. Eisenhower, invaded Sicily, which was captured in six weeks. Mussolini was forced out of office by Marshal Badoglio, who concluded an armistice with the Allies on behalf of Italy. Further Allied operations on the mainland were held up by the arrival of considerable German reinforcements, and for a further nine months the Allies were contained south of Rome. Mussolini, who had been placed under arrest by Badoglio, was rescued by German paratroopers and continued in authority under the Germans in northern Italy. Two days before the invasion of Normandy the Allied forces captured Rome.

Invasion of France and Belgium. On June 6, 1944, an Anglo-American force, with the aid of Commonwealth and other troops, invaded Normandy and pushed into France against crumbling German resistance. Paris and Brussels were recaptured, and, with the aid of a force landed near Marseilles in southern France, the Germans were cleared out of France and most of Belgium. But the Allies were held up until the following year by the great fortifications of the Siegfried Line. Their air forces, however, were so superior in numbers that they could make raids deep into Germany almost at will and absorb whatever losses they sustained without impairing their essential strength. Not only were numerous German military installations destroyed, especially from early 1944, but almost every important German city suffered incessant air raids, in which bombs far larger and more destructive than had been available in the first years of the war were used. A number of German officers, seeing the end approaching, attempted in 1944 to kill Hitler, who was determined to fight on even though it involved the destruction of Germany. The attempt failed and the conspirators were executed.

The Collapse of German Resistance. Throughout the later part of 1943 and all of 1944 the Russians were on the offensive and before the end of 1944 drove into the Balkans, crushing German-controlled Rumania, Bulgaria, and Yugoslavia (where they had considerable aid from the native "Partisans," led by Marshal Tito, the assumed name of Josip Broz). Other armies invaded Poland and the Baltic provinces. Warsaw fell in January, 1945, and Budapest the following month. In February, 1945, Roosevelt, Churchill, and Stalin held a conference at Yalta in the Crimea to make final plans for the defeat and occupation of Germany; and Stalin there agreed to make war on Japan, from which he had hitherto refrained.

On February 8, the assault on Germany, which had been held up by the fortifications of the Siegfried Line and by a German counteroffensive, was renewed, and the Allied armies fought their way across the Rhine while Russian troops advanced on Berlin from the east. The Russians began their assault on Berlin on April 19 and met with the Americans at the Elbe on April 25. On May 1, as resistance in Berlin collapsed, it was announced that Hitler had committed suicide in his chancellery. Four days earlier resistance in Italy had been brought to an end. Mussolini, captured by Italian partisans while trying to escape to Switzerland, was executed. On May 7 Admiral Doenitz, Hitler's successor, signed an armistice and the United States president Harry Truman (who had taken office following the death of Roosevelt on April 12) proclaimed the end of the war in Europe (V-E Day, May 8), as did Stalin the following day. An Allied Control Committee became responsible for the German government at the beginning of June.

The Fall of Japan. From August, 1942, the United States had been making slow progress in the Pacific, capturing one island after another, always against stubborn Japanese resistance. From mid-1944 these attacks had been supplemented by destructive air raids on the Japanese homeland. The Philippine Islands were recaptured by United States' troops under General Douglas MacArthur, beginning in October, 1944. In April, 1945, the island of Okinawa, only a little over three hundred miles from Japan, was invaded, enabling the Americans to attack at will. However, when German resistance was brought to an end and Japan stood alone, it was still estimated that perhaps millions of land troops would be necessary to force her surrender. It was not known how seriously morale had been collapsing in Japan and how close the Japanese were to the end.

In July and August, 1945, the Big Three again met, at Potsdam, Germany (Clement Attlee replacing Winston Churchill for the end of the conference, since the Labor party had just won the elections in Britain) to decide on future plans, including strategy for the as yet unfinished war with Japan. At this conference Stalin was informed of the existence of a new superweapon, the atomic bomb, recently tested in the United States. The demand was sent to the Japanese to lay down their arms, but without mentioning the bomb, which was then dropped on the city of Hiroshima with devastating effect on August 6, 1945. The Soviet Union thereupon invaded Manchuria to drive the Japanese out of that section of China. On August 9, while the Japanese were still unable to formulate a decision to surrender, an even more destructive atomic bomb was dropped on Nagasaki. On August 14, the Japanese surrendered, a decision that was made formal on September 2. Under the terms of the surrender the United States provided an army of occupation for the reorganization of Japan, though the emperor Hirohito was permitted to retain his throne, stripped of all but ceremonial functions. In due course the army of occupation withdrew, leaving the Japanese with a country that had been changed in a revolutionary manner by the American troops and civilian experts, and with new democratic institutions. A peace treaty was signed in 1951.

POSTWAR ALLIED TENSIONS

Throughout the war there had been far from perfect harmony between the Soviet government and the governments of its allies from the West. The nations, indeed, were rather cobelligerents than true allies. There was too long a history of distrust to be overcome merely by fighting a common war against a universally detested enemy. The Allies could not be oblivious to the fact that the Soviet Union was a communist state which had always expressed its intention of fomenting revolution throughout the world—even though during the course of the war the Third International, its agency for the spread of revolution, had been dissolved. Nor could they forget that the Soviet Union had co-operated with Germany and refused to ally herself with the West until she had been actually invaded. The Soviet Union, for her part, could not forget that the Western powers had intervened in the Bolshevik Revolution and that they had a long history of attempts to thwart the revolution, which they had consistently opposed. Worst of all, from the Soviet point of view, the Russians had been shouldered aside at Munich, in spite of their alliance with France, and the future of Czechoslovakia had been decided without them. They were far from convinced that it had not been the intention of the Western powers to divert Hitler's aggressiveness from themselves and direct it against the Soviet Union —in the hope that Germany and Russia would destroy each other for the benefit of the "capitalist" world. Thus the alliance was always an uneasy one, and Stalin during the last period of the war concentrated his attention on gaining the utmost from his victories for the future security of his country—as well as installing communist regimes wherever opportunity presented itself.

The Wartime Conferences. The disagreements became clear at all the wartime conferences attended by Stalin. A conference held at sea between President Roosevelt, whose country was then not yet in the war, and Winston Churchill (August, 1941) showed that the two leading democracies were in substantial agreement. The Atlantic Charter, signed at this conference, contained a declaration on the part of the democratic powers to seek no territorial aggrandizement from the war, and statements that they wished to see independence restored to the nations enslaved by Hitler, to promote equality of economic opportunity for all, and similar sentiments. Aims far different were exposed at the conferences of Teheran (1943–1944), Yalta (February, 1945), and Potsdam (July–August, 1945). At Teheran the Soviet Union was granted the right to annex East Prussia after the war. At Yalta the Russians were already in possession of Poland and were determined to keep at least that part of the country they had taken in 1939. As some compensation Stalin was prepared to see Poland annex much of eastern Germany. Churchill during the war had favored some territorial concessions from Poland to Russia, but the Polish government in exile established in London remained consistently anti-Soviet and would not yield. Partly for this reason the Russians never recognized this government in exile, and when the time came for them to recapture Warsaw, they delayed for several weeks while the Germans massacred the Jews and Polish supporters of the London government. Stalin thereupon set up a Polish Provisional Government of his own. At Yalta Stalin did not make clear the extent of his demands in Poland, and the leaders contented themselves with a joint statement that free elections would be permitted in the country. At Potsdam Stalin did make his aims clear, and there was nothing to do but accept them, with the understanding that the boundaries of the new Poland should be "provisional." Agreements were also reached with regard to various occupation zones controlled by each power (including France, who was granted a zone detached from the British and American zones).

The Question of Reparations. Endless discussions centered on the question of reparations, revealing fundamentally different viewpoints. Russia, of course, had suffered most from Nazi depredations and was the one power that could actually make good use of capital equipment from the more developed countries that had now fallen under her control. Western Russia, whose industries had been destroyed during the Nazi advance, was still far from reconstructed. Britain and the United States were more concerned with the question of whether Germany would ever be reconstructed both politically and economically—a question of less interest to the Soviet Union. If vast reparations were extracted from Germany it would be they who would be required eventually to compensate for them in order to enable Germany to survive in the postwar world. In fact Stalin, in spite of assurances to the Allies, took almost whatever he could use from all the countries occupied by the Soviet Union, including the zones which she was supposed to be administering as a part of a concert of powers. On the other hand all the Allied powers cooperated in bringing "war criminals" to justice in a series of trials held at Nürnberg and elsewhere, as a result of which several of the Nazi leaders were convicted and hanged.

The Satellite System. In southeastern Europe Yugoslavia alone was allowed to govern herself with little Soviet interference since she was already ruled by a Communist, determined to impose a communist system on the country. Rumania, from which Bessarabia was permanently detached, and Bulgaria were impelled into the communist orbit. Albania had already under Enver Hoxha set up a communist regime on her own. Hungary was allowed some choice in the establishment of a provisional regime until a peace treaty was signed. A coup d'état by the Communists in 1948 converted this government to a single-party communist regime. Czechoslovakia, some of whose former territories were annexed outright by the Soviet Union, was also permitted a left-wing government with Communist ministers in key positions. In 1948 this government, too, was taken over by the Communists, led by Clement Gottwald, who had become prime minister after the elections of 1946. In Poland one of the London leaders was taken into the government as vice-premier. The communist-dominated government won the (no doubt controlled) elections of 1947 by a landslide and a one-party communist government was soon established.

All these changes were made by the Soviet Union in accordance with her policy of setting up communist governments, dependent upon herself and therefore reliable, and constructing buffer states on her western frontiers as security against any attack from the West. The Allied powers had no effective means of preventing the arrangements since it was the Soviet Union with her enormous armies who was in physical control of the areas. Only Finland, which had a reasonably reliable government from the Soviet point of view, was left alone in exchange for the promise to pay reparations and the cession of some territory. In Greece, however, where a civil war had broken out as early as the end of 1944, the Soviet Union did not continue to back the communist group for long, but left the country within the British sphere of influence. When Britain felt she was no longer able to afford the cost of maintaining order against guerrillas backed by Yugoslavia the United States took over the task. The Truman Doctrine, stated by the president in 1947 and approved by Congress in subsequent legislation, held that "totalitarian regimes imposed on free peoples undermine the foundations of international peace and hence the security of the United States," and that therefore military and economic aid should be sent to the victims to enable them to retain their independence.

Four-Power Control of Germany and Austria. In Germany and Austria, where control was divided among the four powers, and in the former capital of Berlin, likewise controlled by the four powers, irreconcilable differences soon appeared between the three Western powers on the one side and the Soviet Union on the other. The Soviet Union demanded ten billion dollars of reparations from current German production, whereas the Western powers, anxious for

Germany to recover as quickly as possible, were not prepared to permit any reparations from current production. When the Western powers, after holding several provincial elections, united their zones and issued a common currency, the Russians retorted by doing the same thing in their zone, and soon afterward instituted a blockade of Berlin, which was wholly within their zone. The Allies were able to nullify the blockade by their ability to make shipments by air. In May, 1949, the Federal Republic of Germany was created by the joint action of the Western powers, to which the Russians replied by creating the German Democratic Republic in their zone in October of the same year. These maneuvers obviously made impossible the reunification of Germany except by the abandonment of its policy by one side or the other. The governing of Berlin caused similar difficulties, which have continued. The Russians have hitherto been unwilling to break altogether with the Western powers and to risk nuclear war by taking over all sectors of the city.

Austria was freed from Nazi domination by both Russian and Allied armies, each approaching from different directions. Each retained control of its own zone, the Russians stripping theirs of great quantities of materials for reparations. An all-Austrian elected government was not controlled by the Communists. In 1955 the Russians agreed to a peace treaty which granted the country full independence.

By 1947 it was clear to all that few bases existed for co-operation between the Allied powers, especially the superpower, the United States of America, and the Soviet Union. The premises on which their policies were based seemed incapable of reconciliation, and have remained so during the years which followed. To this period of uneasy peace, the Cold War, the next and final chapter of this Outline will in part be devoted.

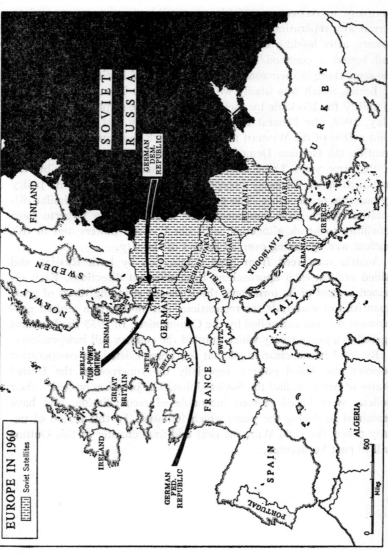

Map drawn by Vincent Kotschar, reprinted from *The Western Heritage*, by Steward C. Easton. Copyright ©
1961. Holt, Rinehart and Winston, Inc. All rights reserved.

23 *THE POSTWAR WORLD*

There are two major subjects for consideration in this final chapter: the retreat from colonialism and the confrontation between the Communist and non-Communist worlds (the Cold War). Each of these situations has had its effects on the work of the United Nations, as this new international organization took over the role of the defunct League of Nations; the United Nations therefore will be considered first as the one body that has so far been able to accommodate (with one notable exception—Communist China) the nations of both East and West under one roof and provide both forces with a continuing forum for discussion.

THE UNITED NATIONS AND ITS INFLUENCE

The United Nations (to which some powers attach the word "Organization") came into being as the result of a conference held at San Francisco during 1945, when the armies of the Axis were crumbling and victory for the Allies was expected at any moment. It was intended that the United Nations should be a more effective body than the old League of Nations, based on a more realistic assessment of the power structure of the modern world.

The Security Council and the General Assembly. Two major organs of the United Nations were therefore created: the Security Council, which was given the task of maintaining peace, and the General Assembly, in which all nations should be able to make themselves heard. In the Security Council the principle of unanimity among the great powers was the key provision. These powers—held at that time to be the United States, Great Britain, France, the Soviet Union, and China (then under the government of the Nationalist regime of Chiang Kai-shek)—all had to be in agreement on measures to preserve peace. If any of these cast a veto no action

331

could be taken. The General Assembly could discuss any subject it wished; but since in it all nations, great and small, had one vote each, the Assembly was not given the right to initiate action to preserve peace. Its actions were confined to discussing and recommending action to the Security Council. When it was found that the Soviet Union and the other powers lined up so frequently on opposite sides, and the Soviet Union therefore vetoed all action, the General Assembly, on the proposal of United States Secretary of State Dean Acheson, voted by a large majority (1950) that when action in the Security Council was prevented by the veto it should itself recommend action to all the members of the United Nations directly. Though unlike the Security Council, the Assembly had no legal power of coercion, it was hoped that members would obey this mandate voluntarily. The Soviet Union, of course, regarded such action as both illegal and contrary to what had been agreed to in San Francisco, on the basis of which she had joined the United Nations. However, she was powerless to prevent it, though in recent years she has begun to refuse to pay assessments for actions taken by the United Nations contrary to her wishes.

Steps to Preserve Peace. The United Nations has taken positive steps to preserve the peace on several occasions. In 1947, when the British served notice that they would no longer maintain their mandate in Palestine in face of the hostility between Arabs and Jews, the United Nations General Assembly recommended the partition of the country and the establishment of a new state of Israel. When this course of action resulted in a war between Israel and the Arab nations, the United Nations succeeded in arranging an armistice and sent an international police force to enforce it until peace had been agreed to. The force is still engaged in the same task. In 1956 President Nasser of Egypt nationalized the Suez Canal, and the British, French, and the Israelis, whose borders were being violated by the Egyptians, attacked the country. The United Nations General Assembly persuaded them to cease hostilities, and sent another truce mission to enforce the peace. In 1947 and 1949 the Dutch were instructed by the Security Council, in which, of course, the Netherlands had no veto, to come to terms with the Indonesians, who were fighting for their independence. On the first occasion, a cease fire resulted, which was soon violated by both parties; on the second occasion, a Round Table Conference was summoned at the Hague and independence was granted soon afterward.

In 1950 the United Nations Security Council, from which the

Russians were temporarily absent, authorized the enrollment of a United Nations force to drive back the North Koreans, who had invaded South Korea (see p. 349). After the Russians returned to the Council, the Assembly authorized subsequent actions and an armistice commission to police the eventual settlement. In 1956 when the Soviet Union subdued by force the revolt of her Hungarian satellite, the General Assembly condemned her action; but since, unlike the case of Korea, where the United States supplied most of the troops, no power was willing to undertake to prevent it, the resolution had no effect on the Soviet intervention. In 1960 the Security Council authorized intervention in the Congo, where the army of the recently independent state had mutinied and Belgium, the former colonial power, had sent troops to restore order. Belgium, as a nation without a veto, could not prevent a United Nations force from being sent to the country with instructions to see that the Belgians withdrew. Subsequent decisions were objected to by France and the Soviet Union, but no veto was imposed and the new state, one of whose provinces (Katanga) had seceded, was finally in 1962 reunited by United Nations' action, under the original authorization of the Security Council.

The United Nations and the Colonial Problem. The United Nations' membership has greatly increased since 1945 as each former colony achieved its independence. In the case of the United Nations trust territories—the former League of Nations mandated territories, plus Italian Somaliland—the General Assembly was required to authorize the conditions under which they received their independence. A Trusteeship Council set up by the United Nations Charter, on which administering and nonadministering powers were equally represented, discussed reports from the territories and took whatever action seemed necessary. A Committee of the General Assembly (Fourth Committee) recommended action both to the Trusteeship Council and to the General Assembly when the time for independence had come. The Assembly also set up a Committee on Information on Non-self-governing Territories, which receives reports from colonial powers on their colonies which are not trust territories. In view of the admittance of so many former colonies to United Nations membership, colonial problems formed an ever greater proportion of business before the Assembly, with the result that considerable moral pressure was put on the colonial powers. Although the actual record of performance by the United Nations Security Council and General Assembly may not be outstanding, the fact that the United Nations exists, with the power to exercise international supervision over armistices and with its services always available as a mediator in international disputes, has made it of far more importance in world affairs than the League of Nations ever was. In addition to the work of its major organs, the international cooperation involved in its numerous councils and agencies has accustomed nationals of all countries to working together; and much noteworthy work has been done in many fields, most remarkably perhaps in the field of health, in which the advances in Western countries have been diffused throughout the world.

RETREAT FROM COLONIALISM

Since the end of World War I only one colony has been added to the possessions of the Western powers—Ethiopia, taken by Italy in 1936 over the opposition of the League of Nations (see p. 306). Though no colony became fully independent during the interwar period, the struggle for independence had begun, especially in India; and the Philippine Islands had been promised independence by the United States to take effect after the war. Since the Second World War almost all the colonies have achieved their independence. At present few that are capable of independent existence remain colonies, and most of those few are well advanced on the path. Only the Portuguese colonies have seen no change, with the exception of Goa and a few tiny enclaves within other countries which have been taken over bloodlessly by the latter.

The United Nations and the Anticolonial Movement. The League of Nations had done little to alleviate the colonial problem. The former German colonies and some Turkish provinces had come within its purview through the Permanent Mandates Commission. Of the Turkish provinces only Iraq became independent in the interwar period, leaving the remainder to do so during the Second World War or immediately afterward. The United Nations Trust Territories (see p. 333) were given independence when the colonial powers felt they were ready for it, in exactly the same manner as non-Trust territories. The United Nations General Assembly in a few instances supervised plebiscites in territories whose future was open to doubt, and United Nations visiting missions often criticized the pace of advance and perhaps exercised some influence. A special committee was set up in 1960 with the task of implementing an Assembly resolution calling for an end to the colonial system. This committee has probably exercised some moral pressure, though as yet without noticeable results, on the Portuguese system, the primary target of its attack.

The Far Eastern Colonies. Britain conferred some representative institutions on India at the end of the First World War. But Indians, under the leadership of Mohandas Gandhi and the Congress party, preferred to agitate and demonstrate for immediate self-government and independence making use of a technique of non-violence (*Satyagraha*), later used also in Africa by nationalists. A Royal Commission (Simon Commission) took a great deal of evidence in the 1920's and proposed that the huge country should become a federal state. Several Round Table Conferences followed, none of which led to any agreement between the Muslims and the Hindu majority. Moreover, the independent Indian princes, whose authority the British had respected, wished to retain at least a measure of independence in their own lands. The Hindus continued to object to communal electorates (elections by Hindus and Muslims voting separately), and for some time the Congress party refused to participate in the provincial governments set up by the British in the mid-'30's and continued their agitation for full independence at once. Congress party leaders spent many years in prison. By the outbreak of war, in which India was involved by British action on her behalf, no solution was in sight. When Japan entered the war, many of the Congress party leaders were even willing to sabotage the war effort rather than accept the proposals put forward by the British. They were again jailed. After the war, when the Muslims continued to insist on a separate state, the Hindus gave way rather than attempt to coerce them, and Britain granted independence to Pakistan and India as separate nations, leaving the Indian princes to deal with one or the other as they wished. Only in Kashmir did any major difficulties arise on this score. The Maharajah of Kashmir, a Hindu, chose to join his predominantly Muslim state to India, whereupon each of the two new countries took a part of the state by force. No solution has yet been achieved for Kashmir. Many of the millions of Indians who were left at independence as a minority under the rule of Muslims or Hindus tried to escape into the country ruled by their own coreligionists. Untold numbers were killed or became refugees in the process. Meanwhile the two parts of Pakistan are separated by thousands of miles of Indian territory and have difficulty in agreeing even with one another.

Burma, which had been governed by the British as a part of India since annexation, was separated from her in 1937. But Britain would not set a definite timetable for independence, and the first popularly elected Burmese governments under British rule in the late 1930's were unstable. Many Burmese leaders in the circumstances decided to collaborate with Japan. When the Japanese invaded Burma in 1942, these men returned with armies from Japan and were entrusted by the Japanese with many of the tasks of government. Japan indeed granted formal independence to Burma during her occupation. When it was clear that the Japanese would lose the war, these Burmese leaders switched their allegiance and helped to drive them out. The British had no choice but to accept their help, nor could they oust them after the war, since there was no alternative party available. They accepted the inevitable and granted independence in 1948.

Ceylon won her independence more peacefully in the same year, since there was no reason for it to be withheld once a party leader arose who commanded a sufficient majority to rule. The Philippines, which had been promised independence by the United States before the war, received it on the appointed date in 1946, in spite of the fact that the islands had been overrun by the Japanese during the war. The reconquest by United States forces put an end to a puppet regime, instituted by the Japanese.

The Netherlands East Indies were likewise granted a substantial measure of self-government by the Japanese during the war, thus giving the present Indonesian president Sukarno some taste of power. When the war was over, Sukarno proclaimed the independence of Indonesia. The Dutch, however, with initial aid from the British, returned and reconquered most of the country. But they could not consolidate their position against continued Indonesian opposition and the hostility of the United Nations. The Dutch granted independence in 1949.

French rule in Indo-China had persisted throughout the war, since the Vichy government agreed to collaborate with the Japanese. In March, 1945, however, the Japanese decided that they could no longer rely on this collaboration and occupied the whole country. At the end of the war a Communist revolutionary, Ho Chi Minh, took over the government in the north, while the French with British aid were returning in the south. Though the French for a time recognized the Ho Chi Minh government, they soon decided to restore the whole country to their rule and drove this government from the northern capital of Hanoi. But the Communists countered with guerrilla warfare and greatly increased their strength when the Communists under Mao Tse-tung took over China in 1949. In 1954, in spite of stubborn French resistance, the Communist Viet Minh inflicted a decisive defeat on the French at the Battle of Dien Bien Phu, whereupon a conference held at Geneva agreed to the partitioning of the country. Thereafter the United States undertook to bolster the government set up in the south by a reliable anticommunist, Ngo Dinh Diem, who held power until late in 1963 when his government was overthrown by a military junta, which was opposed to his nepotism, authoritarianism, and persecution of Buddhists. During his entire period of rule, Diem was faced by ever increasing opposition from the Communist Viet Cong, which engaged in guerrilla warfare with the aim of joining South Vietnam to the Communist north. The independence of Laos and Cambodia was recognized by the Geneva Conference of 1954.

The British made a successful return to Malaya and to their part of the island of Borneo after the war. Following an attempt to set back the clock in Malaya and restore full colonial rule, they devolved power on a coalition party made up of Malays, Chinese, and Indians, which showed itself competent to deal with a smouldering communist insurrection that had been trying to overthrow the government since shortly after the war. After a period of responsible rule by this coalition (the Alliance party) the British granted independence to mainland Malaya in August, 1957. The port of Singapore, however, with its military base and its dominant Chinese population, was excluded from these arrangements. Instead, a State of Singapore was created, with internal self-government but lacking full responsibility for defense. The Borneo colonies developed slowly, receiving a measure of self-government only in very recent times. In 1962 a plan was projected for the union of these colonies with Malaya and Singapore, to be called the Federation of Malaysia. Both the Philippines and Indonesia interposed objections to this federation, and in the protected state of Brunei a small rebellion led by an anti-Malaysian party with the support of Indonesia had to be suppressed in December, 1962. Nevertheless, the new Federation was duly proclaimed in September, 1963, though up to the time of writing it has been recognized neither by Indonesia nor by the Philippine Republic.

The western half of the island of New Guinea was returned by the Dutch after the independence of Indonesia until 1962. Then, under pressure from Indonesia, the United States, and the United Nations, the Dutch transferred it to Indonesia to administer for ten years, with a plebiscite to be held at the end of that time. After a six-months' interim administration by the United Nations, it was turned over to Indonesia in 1963. The United Nations trust territory of North Eastern New Guinea (administered by Australia) and the Australian section of Papua remain under Australian rule. Most of the Pacific Islands are too small to expect independence. An exception is West Samoa, formerly a United Nations trust territory under New Zealand administration. This tiny territory became independent on the last day of 1961.

North Africa. Egypt was granted an autonomous status under a king in 1922 but remained under British control. A treaty was signed in 1936 which gave the country formal independence, subject only to the presence of British troops in the Suez Canal zone. Egypt then entered the League of Nations. From 1922 onward the Egyptians constantly demanded the "restoration" of Sudan. The British paid no attention to this demand until the 1950's, when they gave the Sudanese the opportunity to decide for themselves whether or not to join Egypt. When the vote went against the union, the Egyptian government refused to accept the decision. At last General Naguib, who had replaced King Farouk by a coup d'état in 1952, agreed to the British plan for independence for Sudan under its own government. The country became independent in 1953. Naguib was ousted by Colonel Gamal Nasser the following year.

Tunisia and Morocco both agitated continually against the rule of the French Union imposed upon them after the war. After long efforts to suppress the agitation and sporadic rebellions, the French granted independence to both in 1956. Algeria, long regarded as a part of France, was a different proposition. A rebellion which broke out in 1954 developed into a full-scale war, complicated by the intransigence of the French and other European colonists, supported by French army leaders. These men for years refused to admit even the possibility of independence under Muslim rule. The weak postwar governments in France could neither finish the war nor impose a political solution. In 1958 the French settlers rebelled against their metropolitan government and were instrumental in bringing General de Gaulle to power. De Gaulle, however, eventually recognized the necessity for granting independence. By careful shuffling of commands he placed in power a different group of officers, who supported him through another rebellion by the colonists. A series of agreements looking toward continued close association between the two countries was negotiated in March, 1962. A violent last-ditch effort by the settlers to sabotage the agreements collapsed, and Algeria became independent in July, 1962.

Libya, taken from Italy after the war, was at first administered by the British, who had conquered it, while the United Nations struggled with the problem of what to do with it and with the other Italian colonies. Libya became an independent federal state under a monarchy in December, 1951. Eritrea was given to Ethiopia as an associated state, and Italian Somaliland became a trust territory for a period of ten years under Italian administration. It became independent, in July 1960, as the new state of Somalia, joined shortly afterward by the former British protectorate of Somaliland.

The Mediterranean. Cyprus, an island populated by a Greek majority and a Turkish minority, was torn by dissension after the war. The Greeks were passionately desirous of becoming united with Greece (*Enosis*), to which the Turks were adamantly opposed. The Greeks organized terrorism against the British rulers which was never fully brought under control. Eventually, in the winter of 1959, the Turkish and Greek governments thrashed out a solution between them, to which the British agreed. Cyprus became independent in July, 1960, under a joint government of the two communities, each of which was autonomous in its own affairs. The British were permitted to keep a military base on the island.

Malta, which had been subjected to severe devastation during the war at the hands of Axis bombers, was restored with the aid of the British after the war. But a plan for its self-government could not be agreed upon by the British and the various Maltese political parties. The British naval base, which had been the mainstay of the Maltese economy, was no longer required, and the economic future of the small island was therefore uncertain. It now appears that the island will become independent, and the British have informed the Maltese that they will leave by the end of May, 1964, whether or not the parties have agreed on a constitution for independence. Gibraltar, which is internally self-governing, remains in British hands.

Sub-Saharan Africa. Following the example of colonial peoples in the Far East, the Africans began to agitate after the war for some share in their government and for ultimate independence. The way was blazed for the British colonies by Kwame Nkrumah, who emerged from jail in early 1951 to become "Leader of Government Business" (the British designation for a man who commands a majority of votes in a colonial parliament, but whose power is restricted by various built-in safeguards) in the Gold Coast. The British gradually devolved more power and responsibilities on his government until in March, 1957, the colony was granted full independence under the name of Ghana. In Nigeria a similar process took place, but it was complicated by the very different cultural and political development of the component Regions. The British were willing to grant independence as soon as these problems were settled. But this settlement did not evolve until October, 1960, when the whole country became independent under a federal system which left considerable power to the three Regions.

Sierra Leone, originally settled as a colony for freed slaves, was likewise plagued by cultural differences between the Creoles (descendants of the slaves) and the less well-educated Africans in the hinterland. In 1957 the colony was granted a considerable measure of self-government, and a doctor from the hinterland (Sir Milton Margai) became its leader. Independence was granted in April, 1961. In East Africa, Tanganyika, a United Nations trust territory with a considerable number of European and Indian settlers, was for many years regarded by the British as too backward and too short of educated leaders to be capable of independence. But Julius Nyerere, a schoolteacher, organized an effective national party which was supported by the leading members of minority groups, thus demonstrating the possibility of granting independence to a multiracial government. After this party had shown its strength in several elections, the British granted independence in December, 1961.

Uganda, including Buganda as a state within a state, presented almost insuperable problems to the British, since the king and people of Buganda did not wish to be ruled by a government in which they would form only a minority. After many years of conflict, during which the king (Kabaka) of Buganda was deported, only to be restored two years later, a semifederal state was set up, which gave Buganda almost complete autonomy. The country became independent in October, 1962. Zanzibar, a British protected state with a substantial minority of Arabs who have ruled the country for generations, became independent in December, 1963. In elections held in June, 1963, an electoral coalition made up of a predominantly Arab party and a splinter African party, won a comfortable majority to form the first independent government. Negotiations for the formation of an East Africa Federation made up of Kenya, Tanganyika, Uganda, and Zanzibar, have so far failed.

Kenya, with its considerable minority of European settlers who dominate most of the economy of the country, has presented problems which made the granting of independence difficult. A rebellion broke out in 1953, as a result of which the chief African political leader, Jomo Kenyatta, received a prison sentence. The British could not make up their minds to confer any substantial autonomy on the Africans until 1960. Since then Kenyatta has been liberated and has taken over the leadership of a party the majority of whose members belong to one tribe (the Kikuyu). Most of the members of the other tribes joined an opposition party, which has been strong enough to win substantial autonomy for the various provinces of the country. In the elections held in May, 1963, Kenyatta's party emerged victorious, and he himself became prime minister. The country became independent in December, 1963. Many Europeans who refuse to live under Kenyatta's rule have emigrated, finding it impossible to reconcile themselves to the loss of their political ascendancy, which they exercised during almost the entire period of British rule.

The greatest difficulties of all in British Africa are to be found in the Federation of Rhodesia and Nyasaland, composed of three territories, one of which (Southern Rhodesia) is a British colony which has been ruled by the settlers since 1923. Neither Northern Rhodesia nor Nyasaland (both protectorates) was ever ruled by the settlers, and the British have held complete responsibility for their governments. In 1953 the three territories, over the dissent of the African majority in each, were brought together in a federation which was controlled by the settlers rather than by the Africans. In 1959 serious riots in Nyasaland led to the imprisonment of its African leader, Dr. Hastings Banda. But the British, finding it impossible to settle the problems of his territory without his co-operation, eventually released him, and he became prime minister of his territory. Soon afterward Nyasaland won full internal self-government, and will become independent in July, 1964. In late 1962, Northern Rhodesia, an area rich in copper, was granted a large measure of self-government under a coalition of two African parties. It, too, has been granted the right to secede. In Southern Rhodesia, however, the government is in the hands of a right-wing settler party, and African voting is severely restricted. The Federation was dissolved on December 31, 1963, but the British refused to promise independence to Southern Rhodesia, as they promised it to Northern Rhodesia and Nyasaland, feeling that they cannot grant it to a settler-dominated government unless it gives substantial assurances for widening the franchise to enable the Africans to win a majority.

For some years after the war the French contented themselves with granting their Sub-Saharan colonies local assemblies having limited power and a restricted franchise, while permitting their representatives to sit in the French Chamber and French Senate in Paris. The Africans, dissatisfied with this arrangement, agitated for more rights and formed strong political parties to press for their aims in France. In 1956 the French parliament at last passed an enabling act (*loi-cadre*) which split the two federations of French West and French Equatorial Africa into separate territories and granted semiresponsible governments in each, under French presidents supported by African vice-presidents. The same arrangements applied to the island of Madagascar. Soon after de Gaulle came to power in 1958, he retired the French presidents, leaving African-controlled governments. His plan was for them all to associate themselves with France in a new Community, which would obviate the necessity for a totally independent status. In September, 1958, the colonies were given the opportunity to vote for or against this system. If they voted against it, they could become independent at once. Guinea alone made this choice—and in spite of the ensuing hostility from their former masters, the Guineans were able to preserve their independence. This example suggested to the other colonies that they could do the same. First a new federation between Senegal and Soudan was formed under the name of The Federation of Mali, and the Federation requested independence. Madagascar followed suit. This train of events proved to be too much for the other colonies, which all asked for formal independence, too. In the course of 1960 all became independent republics, and the Community institutions, so recently set up, collapsed. But all, including even Guinea, have very close economic ties with France, who supplies most of their capital and technical needs.

The former German colonies of Togoland and the Cameroons, mandated by the League of Nations to Britain and France, which administered separate segments of unequal size, became United Nations trust territories under the same administrations. British Togoland voted in a plebiscite held in 1956 to join Ghana when the latter became independent. French Togoland became independent in April, 1960, after a two-year period of semiautonomous government. Considerable difficulty was experienced in French Cameroun owing to the existence of a radical left-wing party which fomented sporadic rebellions but which was favored by the Communists and most African nations in the United Nations. Eventually the French persuaded the United Nations to grant independence without prior elections, in spite of the fact that a moderate coalition government was in power, and the country became independent on January 1, 1960. British-administered Cameroons voted in two separate plebiscites held to ascertain its wishes. The northern Muslim sector voted to join Nigeria, and the southern to join the independent state of (French) Cameroun.

The Belgian Congo, the richest in resources of any African country, has presented the greatest difficulties for the world in general and the United Nations in particular. The Belgians during their period of rule concentrated on economic development to the almost complete exclusion of political advancement. Not until 1957 were the first elections held, and then only for assistant mayors. The Belgians then drew up a detailed timetable for constitutional advances but were not prepared to maintain it in face of African opposition and disorders, which began in January, 1959 and continued in some degree until independence. In early 1960 the Belgians decided to take the risk of conferring independence on the country, in spite of its lack of well-organized political parties and educated leaders. Elections were held, contested by numerous local parties and electoral coalitions, as a result of which a deal was engineered under which Patrice Lumumba became prime minister and Joseph Kasavubu head of state. Neither had more than minority support.

Immediately after independence a mutiny broke out in the Congolese army and Belgian parachutists returned to the country to restore order. The United Nations Security Council, appealed to by Lumumba, decreed that the Belgians must leave and authorized the dispatch of a United Nations force to restore order in the country. Meanwhile Katanga, the richest province, seceded under the leadership of Moise Tshombe, and declared itself independent. Three years later Katanga was at last compelled to submit to the authority of the central government, now headed by Cyril Adoula, whose parliamentary support is even more precarious than was that of Lumumba. Lumumba himself was murdered in Katanga in February, 1961. The United Nations force played a decisive part in the restoration of Katanga. United Nations experts have tried to set the Congolese economy in order. Belgians have returned in considerable numbers, and there is a semblance of order in the country as a whole. But it still has no agreed constitution; tribal secessionism is rampant, only partly assuaged by the creation of several new provinces; and there is a budgetary deficit far beyond the capacity of the govern-

ment to meet in the foreseeable future. The Congo remains the outstanding example of the dangers of granting independence when no
adequate preparation has been made and no government exists which
has had at least a modicum of experience—as it is also an example of
the danger of precipitantly driving out the colonial power which alone
had the knowledge of the country and the experience to set it on its
own feet after independence.

Belgium was not much more fortunate in her small trust territory known as Ruanda-Urundi, a mountainous area with few resources, ruled by two kings under Belgian guidance. These kingdoms
were still far from independence when the Congo was freed. But
with the catastrophic loss of prestige suffered when they left the
Congo, the Belgians could not afford to delay long. Even so, they
tried to set up governments likely to be favorable to them after independence, but this the United Nations would not permit. Belgium
was also unable to hold the two territories together in a single
country. They became the two new independent nations of Rwanda
and Burundi (Rwanda a republic and Burundi still a constitutional
monarchy) on July 1, 1962.

The Portuguese, who regard Angola, Mozambique, and Portuguese
Guinea as overseas provinces of Portugal, have refused to promise
self-government to the Africans, and no lawful means of compelling
them to do so has been discovered. In Portuguese Angola a large-scale
rebellion led by Angolese living in the Congo broke out in 1961,
which is still not entirely suppressed. In 1963 a similar rebellion
broke out in Portuguese Guinea, backed by the neighboring independent states of Senegal and Guinea.

Lastly, South West Africa, a former German colony mandated to
the Union of South Africa after the First World War has since been
controlled by the Union, which has governed it against the will of
its African majority and established the same system of segregation
and legal coercion as exists in South Africa. The United Nations
has never persuaded the Union government to give it the status of a
trust territory, and it cannot be compelled to do so without the use
of force.

Thus almost all Sub-Saharan Africa has now achieved independence. To the few exceptions enumerated above should be added only
the sparsely settled British protectorate of Bechuanaland and Ba-
sutoland and Swaziland, two enclaves within the Union of South
Africa. All are coveted by South Africa, but the British have thus far

refused to yield them up to the mercies of a system so manifestly abhorred by their African inhabitants.

The Union of South Africa itself, was not, of course, a colony, but in view of its importance as a bastion of continuing white supremacy, it deserves some mention. Here a Nationalist government has held power since 1948, which has gradually whittled away the few rights that the Africans previously possessed. Its proclaimed policy is *apartheid,* or separateness, under which the Africans (who outnumber inhabitants of European ancestry by more than four to one) are to be confined to reserves, known as Bantustans, where they can have a limited self-rule under governmental supervision. The Africans who live in the European sectors of the country are kept under strict supervision enforced by severe laws and can look forward to no participation in the government of the country. There have been several minor revolts by the Africans but all have been put down with ease, and the United Nations has been able to do little. Faced by opposition in the British Commonwealth from many of its members, the South Africans withdrew from it in 1961 and after a referendum declared the country to be a republic.

THE COLD WAR

The history of the postwar period has been dominated by the almost unbroken hostility between the "Free World" (the United States and her allies) and the Soviet Union. It is impossible to determine to what degree the Soviet Union has been backed by her own allies since, as Soviet satellites, they have never been free agents. The People's Republic of China, formed in 1949 after the expulsion of Chiang Kai-shek has been at least as hostile to the Western nations as the Soviet Union has been. In recent times Communist China has appeared to be influencing the latter to more intransigent policies toward the West than the Soviet leader, Nikita Khrushchev, would have adopted of his own accord.

The Armaments Race. In 1946 the United States, after having brought the war to an end by the use of the atomic bomb, proposed that all development of atomic energy be placed under international control through a specially constituted International Control Agency (Baruch Plan). The Soviet Union, who as yet had no atomic bomb, proposed that all atomic weapons should be outlawed and existing ones destroyed and that the proposed agency should be required to work through the United Nations Security Council, in which she has a veto. By 1949 she was able to explode her first atomic bomb. The United States continued research into the possibility of a much more deadly weapon, the hydrogen (fusion) bomb. In March, 1950, President Truman gave instructions that this bomb should be made. In November, 1952, the United States exploded the first hydrogen bomb in the Pacific. The Russians continued their own research and in due course exploded their first hydrogen bombs. Both nations now possess enough bombs to destroy every building on earth and to kill the world's population many times over provided the bombs can be delivered on their targets.

The attention of the powers has therefore in recent times been directed to improved methods of delivery. The United States and her allies have continued to rely to some degree on manned bombers. The United States has also developed nuclear-powered submarines, notably the Polaris submarine, which can deliver rocket bombs with nuclear warheads from any part of the world's oceans. Two types of long-distance rockets (intermediate and intercontinental) have also been developed, a feat imitated, like the others, by the Russians, usually after an interval of two or three years. But when the Russians sent their first man-made satellite known as a *sputnik* into orbit (1957) it became clear that they had stolen a march on the United States by developing rockets with a superior thrust. In all other fields the United States retained her supremacy. Defense budgets increased every year, as further efforts to develop a defense against Soviet missiles were undertaken (antimissile missiles), and early warning systems were improved. The United States has undertaken a crash program to reach the moon before the Soviet Union does so. Both sides have sent numerous satellites (including manned ones) into space. Considerable information has been obtained on such matters as the temperature and atmosphere of the planets, while some satellites are used for the improvement of earthly communications and weather information.

The armaments race in 1963 received its first significant check, with the signing of a treaty between United States, Britain, and the Soviet Union, to which numerous other nations have adhered (with the notable exception of France and Communist China). Under this treaty atmospheric nuclear testing will be suspended indefinitely by the signatory nations. Previously there had been only an informal agreement which lasted for a few years, at the end of which time the Soviet Union resumed the testing of bombs with an enormous explosive potential. The United States followed suit, to the relief of several leading scientists and military men, who continued to oppose the test ban treaty and tried to prevent its ratification.

Efforts to win agreement on disarmament have hitherto failed as the result of irreconcilable differences on the kind and extent of disarmament that should be envisaged. The United States has favored disarmament by stages, whereas the Soviet Union has called for complete disarmament immediately—a plan regarded as unrealistic by the United States. In the absence of any trust between the two super-powers, it is clear that each side is compelled to demand adequate safeguards for the behavior of the other, and these it has been impossible to obtain by negotiation. The United States still regards the Soviet Union as a nation determined to impose its rule and its communist ideology on the world by whatever means are available to it; and the Soviet Union regards the United States as an imperialist power determined to destroy "socialism" in the interests of its profit-seeking capitalists. No reconciliation appears possible between these two extremes, and thus no basis for trust is visible. The temporary alternative is therefore "coexistence," a stalemate in which neither power is willing to use its nuclear weapons since destruction would be mutual; but thrust and counterthrust are still permissible as long as neither side places the other in a position from which there is no escape but by thermonuclear war.

The Alliance System. The United States in 1947 put into effect a remarkable plan (the Marshall Plan), under which its resources were made available for the economic recovery of Europe. The Soviet Union and her satellites refused to take advantage of it, in spite of the initial wish of some of the satellites to do so. Recovery in these countries was therefore much slower, dependent as it was on the use of their own resources and those of the Soviet Union. The Western countries made an astoundingly quick comeback, and by 1953 all, including the Federal Republic of Germany, were headed for a new prosperity. In 1949 the United States took the initiative in forming a new defense organization for the Western allies, known as the North Atlantic Treaty Organization (NATO), with a common army composed of units contributed by each member. The Council of NATO, composed of representatives from the member states, meets at regular intervals. Since 1954 atomic weapons have been placed at its disposal, though these remain the property of the United States, who retains the right to order their use. The most important question for the West for many years was whether the Federal Republic of Germany should be admitted to the organization. An effort to form a European army, with the participation of West Germany, collapsed in 1954 when the French parliament failed to ratify the treaty. A new approach was then tried, under which Germany was required to forego the manufacture of nuclear arms, but provided twelve divisions for mutual defense. These terms were approved by all the NATO powers, and the Federal Republic was admitted to NATO in 1955. NATO thus became an alliance of all the Western nations except Sweden and Switzerland, who preferred to remain neutral, and Spain, whose dictatorial government was still regarded with disapproval by most of the European nations. Spain, however, entered into separate agreements with the United States under which she provides bases for NATO use.

The Russians could retaliate to this alliance only by making a formal pact with Communist China (1950) and—subsequent to the entry of West Germany into NATO—with her satellite nations (Warsaw Treaty, 1955).

After the return of de Gaulle to power in France in 1958, considerable efforts were made by France to acquire a "nuclear deterrent" of her own. These efforts had been set in motion by previous French governments, but de Gaulle stepped up production, and in due course French devices were exploded in the Sahara. The United States, unalterably opposed to the proliferation of atomic weapons, although her atomic secrets had long been shared with Britain, was unable to prevent this effort by a major ally, but refused to assist her with technical information. In 1962 President de Gaulle began to express public doubts as to whether it was in the interests of Europe that the sole authority over the use of nuclear bombs should be in American hands, which might not release them in the event of an attack upon Europe alone. Since he gave this fear as his major reason for pursuing the separate French deterrent, some people began to believe that NATO was in danger of disintegration—especially when a separate treaty of friendship between Germany and France was negotiated and ratified early in 1963. The United States began to put forth suggestions on sharing responsibility for the use of nuclear devices. But at the time of writing no fully acceptable alternatives have been agreed to by all.

International Tensions. During the interwar period while there has been a stalemate in Europe, tensions have been concentrated in the less stable areas of the world. The one major exception has been Berlin, where the existence of the Soviet-sponsored German Democratic Republic, whose territories surround the former capital, has been a constant irritation to the West. This Republic is not recognized by any Western power, since it is Western policy to regard the Federal Republic as the nucleus of some future all-German state to which East Germany will some day be reunited. To recognize the German Democratic Republic would mean the acceptance of a divided Germany for an indefinite period. The Soviet Union would, of course, like to put an end to the division of Berlin and to win the withdrawal of Allied troops—the more so since West Berlin is far more prosperous than the Soviet-controlled sector. Premier Khrushchev has frequently asserted his intention of signing a peace treaty with East Germany and relinquishing Soviet rights of occupation to her satellite, thus compelling the Western powers to deal with a regime they do not recognize. Since late 1958, when Khrushchev threatened to sign such a treaty and devolved more power on his satellite, West Berlin has been in a virtual state of siege. A wall was built to keep refugees from the eastern sector from escaping to the west. The Allied powers in return have reiterated their intention to fight if there is any attempt to drive them out by force or coercion, and Khrushchev up to the time of writing has not pushed matters to extremes.

The Nationalist regime of Chiang Kai-shek was unable in the postwar years to establish its full authority over the whole of China. In spite of receiving considerable military supplies from the United States, the Nationalist government was unable from its own resources to resist a growing Communist rebellion led by Mao Tse-tung. In 1949 Chiang was driven out of mainland China to the island of Formosa (Taiwan), where he established his regime, which was recognized and protected by the United States. He also retained a group of islands off the Chinese coast (Pescadores), which have been sporadically shelled by the Chinese Communists. But Chiang's hold on the islands has not been loosed, and the United States' navy has effectively prevented them from being invaded. The Chinese Communist government has been aggressively anti-Western from the beginning, and consistently hostile in particular to the United States, who has refused to recognize it and used her influence to exclude it from the United Nations.

In 1950 the North Koreans invaded South Korea, which was in the United States' sphere of influence, and the United States persuaded the United Nations to defend it. This necessitated the provision by the United States, as well as by a few other nations which sent token forces, of considerable reinforcements for the outnum-

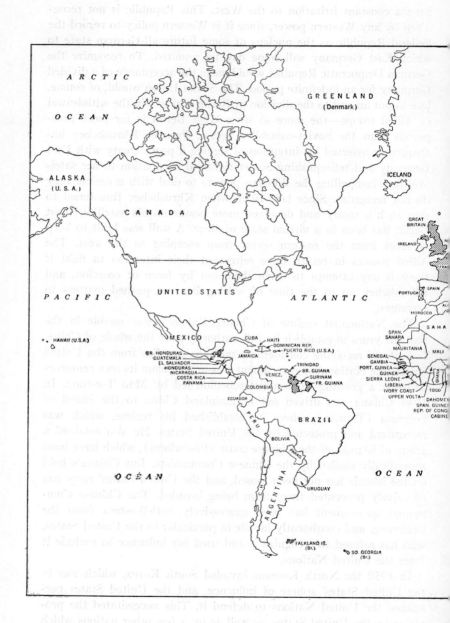

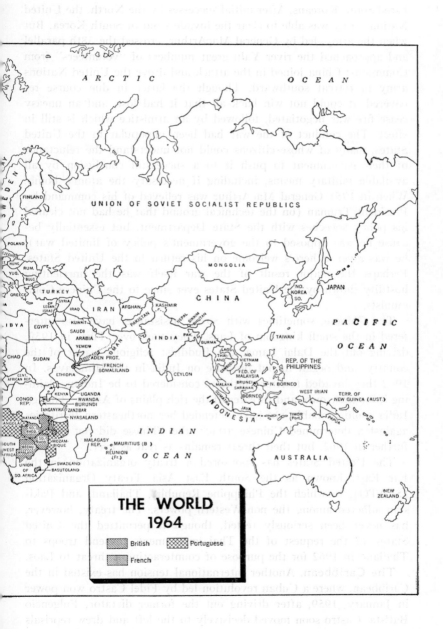

bered South Koreans. After initial successes by the North, the United Nations army was able to clear the invaders out of South Korea. But when the army, led by General MacArthur, crossed the 38th parallel and approached the river Yalu great numbers of "volunteers" from Communist China joined in the attack and drove the United Nations army in retreat southward. Though the latter in due course recovered, it could not win back all that it had lost, and an uneasy cease fire was negotiated, followed by an armistice which is still in effect. The conduct of the war had been unpopular in the United States, many of whose citizens could not understand the reluctance of their government to push it to a successful conclusion by all available military means, including if necessary the atomic bomb. When in 1951 General MacArthur was relieved of his command by President Truman (on the technical ground that he had not cleared his policy speeches with the State Department, but essentially because he was opposed to the government's policy of limited war), he was given a hero's welcome on his return to the United States. Perhaps the major result of the war itself was the unrelenting hostility shown by the United States ever since to the Chinese Communists.

The Chinese, sometimes with Soviet assistance, have also interfered in the small kingdom of Laos. They took over Tibet in 1959, driving out the Dalai Lama, the Buddhist religious leader of the country, and began to put pressure on India in the Himalayas. In 1962 they invaded territory hitherto considered to be Indian, claiming it for their own, and threatened the rich plains of Assam. Though India could probably not have defended her northeastern territories against a determined Chinese attack, the Chinese did not press it further in 1962, but their threat remains as real as ever.

The United States has sponsored a treaty organization in the Far East, known as the South East Asia Treaty Organization (SEATO), to which the Philippine Republi , Thailand, and Pakistan adhered among the non-Western powers. The treaty, however, has never been seriously tested, though it permitted the United States, at the request of the Thai government, to send troops to Thailand in 1962 for the purpose of counteracting a threat to Laos.

The Caribbean. Another international tension has existed in the Caribbean, where a Cuban revolution led by Fidel Castro won power in January, 1959, after driving out the former dictator, Fulgencio Batista. Castro soon moved decisively to the left and drew reprisals upon himself when he nationalized the major industries (foreign as well as native) in his country. Faced by economic sanctions from the United States, he turned to the Soviet Union for help. This was given, with the result that in due course the island became a full-fledged communist state. The United States in 1961 sponsored an abortive invasion of the island by Cuban exiles, whereupon Castro requested military aid from the Soviet Union. This was provided at first in the form of extensive arms shipments and technical and military experts, who began to train the Cuban army. Late in 1962, when news was confirmed that nuclear missiles were being installed in the island, President Kennedy demanded that they be removed and instituted a naval "quarantine" of the island. Premier Khrushchev, faced with this demand, agreed to dismantle the missile bases and remove the missiles. But the situation remained dangerous.

EFFORTS TO UNIFY EUROPE

Europe remains a group of national states, each with its own policy and hesitant to abandon its sovereignty except in limited areas. Though a number have agreed on a unified defense through NATO, none of these has been willing to work only through NATO—a course which leaves them in almost total dependence on the United States. But European democracies have attempted in the postwar years a limited co-operation, especially in the development of a unified economy. The United States has encouraged these efforts to the maximum of her ability, even on occasions pushing so hard as to disturb European nationalists, with results that were far from her intentions.

In 1949 a Council of Europe was established with headquarters in Strasbourg in Alsace; its Council of Ministers is composed of the foreign ministers of the various European powers. The Council has served as a forum for the presentation of ideas, but it has never achieved much influence. A Coal and Steel Community was inaugurated in 1952, made up of six industrial nations, with its own international government. This was enlarged in 1957 under the Treaty of Rome signed in that year. This treaty brought into operation the European Economic Community, usually known as the Common Market, which is composed of three small nations, Belgium, the Netherlands, and Luxembourg (which had previously enjoyed a customs union among themselves, known as Benelux), together with the three large nations of France, West Germany, and Italy. The aim of EEC is to have a complete customs union between the component countries and a tariff against outside nations.

Frequent negotiations in the years since 1957 have brought this objective close to realization. The British, excluded from the Common Market, formed the European Free Trade Association (Britain, Norway, Sweden, Denmark, Austria, Switzerland, Portugal), commonly known as the Outer Seven, which was a looser union and never came close to rivaling EEC. In 1961 Britain opened negotiations with EEC with a view to her acceptance as a full member, but it soon became clear that France was opposed to her entry. De Gaulle's government expressed the view that Britain was too insular and that, as head of a Commonwealth of independent nations with which she already had a system of tariff preferences, she could not be expected to become a wholehearted member of a European "community." Nevertheless the negotiations continued through 1962, while Britain agreed to abandon many of the Commonwealth preferences at once and to effect the reduction of others in definite stages. It was widely believed, especially in the United States, that Britain and most of her fellow EFTA nations would eventually be admitted. In this expectation President Kennedy obtained from Congress in 1962 a law authorizing him to negotiate for the reduction of EEC tariffs and to reduce United States tariffs accordingly.

Behind de Gaulle's stand was his opposition to a political union of Europe, including Britain, for which the economic groundwork was being prepared—a union desired by most of the non-French European leaders as well as by President Kennedy and his advisers. All de Gaulle would agree to was a limited confederation of European sovereign nations and associate status in EEC for Britain. But Britain would not accept this, in which position she was backed by the United States, who wished Britain to form a counterweight to France and Germany in the counsels of Europe. A conference on nuclear arms between Britain and the United States held in December, 1962, gave de Gaulle the opportunity to denounce the "special relationship" between Britain and the United States, and to cite it as evidence that Britain preferred not to become a truly integrated member of a European Community. He then cast his veto on British entry into EEC for the present and possibly for an indefinite future. Since, under the Treaty of Rome, unanimity is required for the admission of a new member, Britain is for the time effectively blocked. It is not yet clear whether the application will be renewed later under more favorable circumstances, or whether the veto marks the end of any attempt at European integration along the lines hitherto considered.

Thus the world of the 1960's remains unstable. Stalin has been replaced by Khrushchev in the Soviet Union (since 1953), but Soviet foreign policy continues, with no fundamental change apparent—though there is some relaxation within the country and Russia has now far more to lose by military action than she had during the Long Armistice. The Western powers have been on the defensive since the war with the initiative usually held by their more aggressive Communist opponent. Major initiatives from the West calculated to kindle the imagination of the world have been conspicuously lacking since the Marshall Plan. Communist China, with by far the largest population of any country in the world, has shown no particular signs of wishing to live at peace with other countries, even though she is engaged in a tremendous revolution at home. The new states of Africa, together with other small powers, dominate the voting in the United Nations, but lack the power to do more than exercise moral pressure on the larger nations who control the military might of the world. The Arab nations, united in an Arab League, constantly threaten Israel, whose destruction remains almost the only policy on which they are agreed.

DOMESTIC ADVANCES IN THE POSTWAR DEMOCRACIES

Internally the United States has made considerable progress, though her rate of economic growth has in recent years lagged behind that of the Common Market countries. The United States under its presidents Truman (1945–1953), Eisenhower (1953–1961), and Kennedy (1961–1963), has been reasonably stable with conservative Congresses controlled, except for two brief periods, by nominally Democratic majorities—though in fact by an informal alliance between Republicans and Southern Democrats. This situation has been reflected in the paucity of social legislation, in which the United States has fallen decades behind European countries, where national health insurance, family allowances, and similar measures have long been regarded as a proper field for national legislation. After the assassination of President Kennedy on November 22, 1963, Vice-President Lyndon B. Johnson became President and pledged himself to continue his predecessor's foreign and domestic policies—the latter far more forward-looking than Congress has as yet shown any signs of approving.

Britain under a Labor government led by Clement Attlee (1945–1951) enacted a major series of measures establishing a national health service and numerous other social programs, including the nationalization of the British railways. But the austerity program of this government, its high taxation and price control in the interests of a stable currency, were unpopular, and a Conservative government was voted to power in 1951 under Winston Churchill. Since Churchill's retirement in 1955, the Conservatives have remained in power under prime ministers Sir Anthony Eden, Harold Macmillan, and Sir Alec Douglas-Home. British economic growth has been far less than that of the Common Market countries.

French governments for many years were so unstable that they could accomplish relatively little, though social security was extended —beyond, indeed, the capacity of the country to pay for it. France was also plagued by expensive colonial wars and by a serious balance of payments problem which lasted until the economic recovery of the late 1950's, sparked by the success of the Common Market. The constitutional changes of 1958 which followed the restoration of Charles de Gaulle to power in May of that year, gave France for the first time the possibility of a strong stable government, largely directed by the president, who since 1962 has been backed by an over-all majority of his own party in the Chamber. Italy, on the other hand, enjoyed a stable government from 1945 to 1953 under Prime Minister Alcide de Gasperi, leader of the Christian Democratic party. But Italy made little economic recovery until the recent successes of the Common Market. Italian governments since 1953 have been coalitions, but all have maintained a fairly consistent policy, and the Christian Democratic party has remained the largest party in the coalitions. However, industrialization, though spectacularly successful in north and central Italy, has brought few benefits to Sicily and the south which continue to present a serious problem that as yet is far from solution.

West Germany remained under its first chancellor, Konrad Adenauer, until 1963, though after 1961 his Christian Democratic party lacked an over-all majority in parliament, and he ruled only with the aid of the Free Democrats, another conservative party. Adenauer agreed to retire before the end of the tenure of office of his government, and was succeeded by Ludwig Erhard in October, 1963. West Germany (though lacking Prussia and Saxony, lost to the East) nevertheless under Adenauer's rule again became the greatest industrial nation in Europe, and has had a surplus available for investment in foreign countries, including the former colonies of all the colonial powers.

CONCLUSION

The Western nations today enjoy on the whole by far the greatest domestic prosperity they have ever known, and all provide some economic aid to the less developed nations. The world is economically interdependent, but its institutions, based as they are on the separateness of the national state, do not reflect this truth. Whether the antagonisms of national states will lead to a worldwide holocaust or whether a recognition of present dangers will lead to a general realization of mankind's basic unity, with a consequent change in outmoded political institutions, is a question that may well be decided in the remaining decades of the twentieth century.

KEY DATES IN WESTERN HISTORY

B.C.

THE PREHISTORIC AGE

ca. 500,000	Java Man and Peking Man
ca. 150,000	Neanderthal Man
ca. 50,000	*Homo sapiens* (Cro-Magnon Man, etc.)
ca. 8000–5500	Mesolithic Age
ca. 5500	**Neolithic Revolution in Near East**

THE ANCIENT NEAR EAST

ca. 3000–2200	Old Kingdom of Egypt
ca. 3000	Bronze Age in Sumer and Crete
ca. 2000–1792	Middle Kingdom of Egypt
ca. 1800	Hammurabi Code
ca. 1800	Hyksos invasions of Egypt
ca. 1580	Reconquest of Egypt by Theban princes
1468	Conquests of Thutmose III
ca. 1377–1360	Religious Revolution of Akhenaton
1296	Battle of Kadesh between Hittites and Egyptians
ca. 1260	Exodus of Hebrews from Egypt (?)
ca. 1004–965	Reign of King David in Israel
910–606	**Assyrian Empire**
760–700	Greek colonization of Sicily and southern Italy
753	Traditional date of founding of Rome
721	Fall of Samaria to Assyrians

THE GREEK AND ROMAN REPUBLICS

621	Constitution of Draco in Athens
606–509	Etruscan rule in Rome
594	Reforms of Solon in Athens
586	Fall of Jerusalem to Nebuchadnezzar
549	Cyrus becomes king of Persia
538	Return of Jews to Jerusalem
509	**Beginning of Roman Republic**
508	**Constitution of Cleisthenes in Athens**
494	First secession of plebs in Rome
490–479	Persian invasions of Greece
457–429	Ascendancy of Pericles in Athens
449	Twelve Tables in Rome
431–404	**Peloponnesian War**
338	Victory of Philip of Macedon at Chaeronea
336–323	Reign of Alexander the Great
327–290	Samnite Wars in Italy
301	Final division of Alexander's kingdom
281–272	Roman Wars with Pyrrhus
264–241	First Punic War
218–201	**Second Punic War**
167	Revolt of Maccabees against Antiochus IV of Syria
146	Macedonia becomes Roman province

66–62	Conquest and reorganization of Asia by Pompey
60	First Triumvirate
58–51	Conquest of Gaul by Caesar
44	Murder of Caesar
43	Second Triumvirate
31	**Battle of Actium—Beginning of reign of Augustus**

A.D.

THE ROMAN EMPIRE

14	Death of Augustus
33 (30?)	**Crucifixion of Jesus Christ**
69–96	Vespasian and the Flavian dynasty
96–180	The "Good Emperors"
235–284	"Barrack" emperors
284–305	Reign of Diocletian
312	Constantine becomes emperor of West
ca. 313	**"Edict of Milan"—Toleration of Christianity**
325	Council of Nicaea
330	Foundation of Constantinople
340–348	Conversion of Goths to Arian Christianity
ca. 400	Honorius removes Roman capital to Ravenna
451	Battle of Chalons—partial defeat of Attila the Hun
476	**Odoacer deposes last Roman emperor—"Fall of Rome"**

THE EARLY MIDDLE AGES

481	Clovis founds Merovingian kingdom
535–554	Reconquest of Italy by Justinian
590–604	Pontificate of Gregory I, the Great
622	**Flight of Mahomet from Mecca (Hegira)**
622–630	Persian Wars of Heraclius
635–715	Era of Muslim conquests
664	Synod of Whitby
726	Beginning of Iconoclastic Controversy
732	**Battle of Tours—Victory of Charles Martel over Muslims**
756	Donation of Pepin
768–814	Reign of Charlemagne
843	**Treaty of Verdun**
871–900	Alfred the Great of England
962	**Restoration of Empire under Otto I**
987	Foundation of French monarchy (Hugh Capet)
1018	Bulgaria incorporated into Byzantine Empire
1066	Norman Conquest of England
1077	**Henry IV does penance at Canossa**
1095	First Crusade proclaimed
1122	**Concordat of Worms**

1183	Treaty of Constance between Frederick Barbarossa and Lombard League
1189–1192	Third Crusade

THE LATER MIDDLE AGES

1198–1216	Pontificate of Innocent III
1204	Latin conquest of Constantinople (Fourth Crusade)
1215	**Magna Carta**
1220–1250	Reign of Frederick II
1236	Capture of Cordova by Christians
1268	Execution of last Hohenstaufen
1273	Rudolf of Hapsburg becomes Holy Roman Emperor
1295	Model Parliament of Edward I
1302	Summoning of States-General by Philip IV
1305–1376	**"Babylonian Captivity"** of the papacy
1337–1453	Hundred Years' War
1378–1417	Great Schism
1414–1418	Council of Constance
1453	**Fall of Constantinople to Turks**
1455–1485	Wars of the Roses
1469	Union of crowns of Aragon and Castile
1492	**Discovery of America by Columbus**

THE EARLY MODERN EPOCH

1497–1499	Voyage of Vasco da Gama to India
1517	**Ninety-five Theses of Martin Luther**
1519–1521	Conquest of Mexico by Cortes
1519–1522	First circumnavigation of world by Magellan and crew
1545–1563	**Council of Trent**
1555	Religious Peace of Augsburg
1581	Independence of Dutch Republic
1598	Edict of Nantes
1613	Beginning of Romanov dynasty in Russia
1618–1648	**Thirty Years' War**
1648	Peace of Westphalia
1649	Execution of Charles I of England
1683	Last siege of Vienna by Turks
1688–1689	**Glorious Revolution in England**
1689–1725	Reign of Peter the Great
1700–1721	Great Northern War
1701–1714	War of the Spanish Succession
1713	**Peace of Utrecht**
1740–1748	War of Austrian Succession
1756–1763	Seven Years' War
1772	First Partition of Poland
1775–1783	**American War of Independence**
1787	**American Constitution**

FROM THE FRENCH REVOLUTION TO THE FIRST WORLD WAR

1789	**Beginning of French Revolution**
1794	Fall of Robespierre
1804	Napoleon becomes emperor of French
1814–1815	**Congress of Vienna**
1830	July Revolution in France (revolutions in Belgium and Poland)
1832	First Reform Bill in England
1839–1840	First Opium War in China
1846–1848	United States-Mexican War
1848	**Year of Revolutions**
1853–1854	Visit of Commodore Perry to Japan
1859	Franco-Italian War with Austria
1861–1865	**United States Civil War**
1861	Emancipation of Russian serfs
1866	Austro-Prussian War
1867	British North America Act (Dominion of Canada)
1869	Opening of Suez Canal
1870–1871	**Franco-Prussian War**
1870	Unification of Italy
1871	Unification of Germany
1875	Beginning of French Third Republic
1882	British occupation of Egypt
1899–1902	Boer War
1904	Entente Cordiale between Britain and France
1904–1905	Russo-Japanese War
1908	Austrian annexation of Bosnia and Herzegovina
1914 (June)	**Murder of Archduke Francis Ferdinand**
1914 (July–August)	**Beginning of the First World War**

THE FIRST WORLD WAR AND THE LONG ARMISTICE

1917 (April)	United States declaration of war with Germany
1917 (November)	**Bolshevik Revolution in Russia**
1918 (March)	Treaty of Brest-Litovsk
1918 (November)	Armistice between Allies and Central Powers
1919 (June)	**Treaty of Versailles**
1920 (January)	Beginning of League of Nations
1920 (March)	Final rejection of Versailles treaty by United States Senate
1921–1927	New Economic Policy in Russia
1922 (October)	**Mussolini's "March on Rome"**
1923 (January)	Franco-Belgian invasion of Ruhr
1923 (November)	Hitler "Beer-Hall Putsch"
1925	Treaties of Locarno
1928	First Five Year Plan in Russia
1929	Stock-market crash in United States
1930–1935	**Great Depression**

1931	Statute of Westminster (complete independence of British dominions)
1931 (September)	Japanese invasion of Manchuria
1933 (January)	**Hitler becomes chancellor of Germany**
1933 (January)	Franklin Roosevelt becomes United States President
1935 (October)	Italian invasion of Ethiopia
1936 (July)	Beginning of Spanish Civil War
1936 (October)	Rome-Berlin Axis
1938 (March)	German Annexation of Austria
1938 (September)	Pact of Munich
1939 (March)	German occupation of Czechoslovakia
1939 (August)	**Nonaggression agreement between Russia and Germany**

THE SECOND WORLD WAR AND ITS AFTERMATH

1939 (September)	German invasion of Poland
1939 (November)– 1940 (March)	Russo-Finnish War
1940 (April)	German invasion of Norway
1940 (May)	German invasion of Holland and Belgium
1940 (June)	German occupation of Paris
1941 (June)	German invasion of Russia
1941 (December)	Japanese attack on Pearl Harbor
1942 (August)	Beginning of siege of Stalingrad by Germans
1942 (November)	Landing of United States forces in North Africa
1943 (September)	Surrender of Italy
1944 (June)	**Allied invasion of Normandy**
1944 (July)	Expulsion of Germans from Russia
1944 (August)	Liberation of Paris
1944 (October)	Decisive naval victory by United States over Japan
1945 (February)	Conference of Yalta
1945 (May)	**Unconditional surrender of Germany**
1945 (August 6)	**Atomic bomb dropped on Hiroshima**
1945 (August 14)	**Unconditional surrender of Japan**
1945 (October)	Establishment of United Nations
1947 (March)	Announcement of Truman Doctrine
1947 (June)	Announcement of Marshall Plan
1948 (February)	Communist coup in Czechoslovakia
1949 (April)	**Signing of North Atlantic Treaty (NATO)**
1949 (May)	Proclamation of basic law for Federal Republic of Germany
1949 (October)	Proclamation of People's Republic of China
1950 (June)	**Beginning of Korean War**
1950 (November)	Uniting for Peace Resolution passed by United Nations General Assembly
1953 (March)	Death of Stalin
1954 (October)	Signing of Western European Union treaty
1956 (October)	Invasion of Sinai peninsula by Israelis
1956 (November)	Hungarian revolt crushed by Russians

1957 (October)	Launching of "Sputnik" by Russians
1958 (January)	Beginning of European Common Market
1958 (May)	French army coup in Algeria—government of de Gaulle
1958 (September)	Referendum on French constitution—formation of French Community
1959 (January)	Castro takes over Cuban government
1960 (June)	Independence of Belgian Congo
1960 (July)	United States economic sanctions against Cuba
1960 (July)	Security Council authorizes United Nations force in Congo
1960 (November)	**Election of John F. Kennedy as United States president**
1961 (April)	Abortive invasion of Cuba by Cuban exiles
1961 (August)	Erection of wall between East and West Berlin
1961 (August)	Resumption of nuclear testing by Soviet Union
1962 (January)	Expulsion of Cuba from Organization of American States
1962 (July)	Independence of Algeria
1962 (September)	Netherlands abandons control of West Irian (Netherlands New Guinea)
1962 (October)	Confrontation of United States and Soviet Union over missiles in Cuba
1962 (Oct.–Nov.)	Frontier war in Himalayas between India and China
1962 (November)	Victory of de Gaulle party in French elections
1963 (January)	French veto of Britain's entry into European Common Market
1963 (April)	Formation of coalition government in Congo, marking formal end to secession of Katanga
1963 (April)	Encyclical *Pacem in Terris* issued by Pope John XXIII
1963 (August)	**Limited test-ban treaty signed**
1963 (October)	Adenauer retires from chancellorship of West Germany
1963 (November)	**Assassination of John F. Kennedy; succession of Lyndon B. Johnson as United States president**
1964 (October)	Election of Labor Government in England under Harold Wilson
1964 (October)	Fall of Khrushchev—replacement by Brezhnev and Kosygin
1964 (October)	Exploding of atomic device by People's Republic of China
1964 (November)	Landslide election of Lyndon B. Johnson as United States president
1965 (February)	Beginning of United States aerial attacks on North Vietnam
1965 (April)	Occupation of Dominican Republic by United States marines

EXAMINATION QUESTIONS

These essay questions have been designed to test the student's ability to isolate those factors that have been of greatest importance in Western civilization. If he prepares the answers thoroughly and has, in addition, an adequate command of the detailed facts given in his text, he should be in a position to answer satisfactorily most exam papers set in Western civilization courses. Obviously not all these questions are of equal weight, and few could be set in a single examination. (The figures in parentheses refer to pages in the Outline where information relating to each question may be found.)

1. Define the Neolithic Revolution and explain its significance in world history. (5–6)

2. Although ancient Egypt may be cited as an example of a long-lived and stable civilization, underneath the appearance of stability there was in reality much that changed between the Old and New Kingdoms. Trace this process of change and try to account for it. (7–15)

3. Give an account of the successive inhabitants of Mesopotamia in ancient times. What were their respective contributions to civilization? (15–20)

4. In what way did Hebrew monotheism help to solve the problems posed by earlier religions? (21–22)

5. Contrast the governmental systems of Athena and Sparta. Under which system would you prefer to live and why? What were the drawbacks of Athenian democracy? (26–30)

6. How did Athenian imperialism originate, and what were its immediate and long-term consequences for Athens? (30–32)

7. What were the political and cultural consequences of the conquests of Alexander the Great? (35–36, 41–43)

8. In what fields of thought did the Greeks make their greatest contributions to civilization? Mention some of the pioneers and in so doing show in what respects the Greek style of speculation was new in world history. (36–40)

9. It has often been said that the Romans acquired their empire unintentionally and attempted to rule it through institutions suitable only for a city-state. In the light of your knowledge of the history of the Roman Republic criticize or substantiate this remark. (49–57)

10. What were the steps taken by Augustus to legitimize his rule and take care of the problems involved in administering a large empire? (58–59, 62)

11. What were the conditions in the early Roman Empire favoring the rise

of such a religion as Christianity? How did the organization of the Christian Church fit it to be the successor of Rome? (69–73)

12. Describe the reforms of Diocletian and Constantine, and explain how they served to postpone the collapse of the Empire. (74–75)

13. For many centuries Constantinople remained the easternmost bastion of Western civilization. Describe the manner in which it was able to fulfill its task. (78–82)

14. Try to account for the success of Islam in building and maintaining its empire. What intellectual and cultural achievements may be placed to its credit? (82–85)

15. Trace the steps by which the Frankish (Merovingian) monarchy became a large empire in the time of Charlemagne. Describe the kind of empire over which he ruled and the means by which he administered it. (86–88)

16. Describe the major institutions of the feudal system and the conditions that made it a workable system for the transitional stage between the Roman Empire and the rise of national states. (93–96)

17. Why did the Church find itself so frequently at odds with the Holy Roman Empire during the Middle Ages? Trace the steps by which it became independent of the secular powers by the early thirteenth century. (98–101)

18. Consider the conditions in England favoring a strong monarchy in the eleventh century, and explain how and why King John was forced to yield some of his power to the barons in 1215. (103–104)

19. Criticize the effectiveness of the Crusades as a means for attaining the ends envisaged by the popes who called them. In what respects was medieval Europe affected by them? (108–111)

20. It has often been said that medieval culture was excessively influenced by authority and uninterested in the material world. Criticize this viewpoint. (112–114)

21. Describe the conditions which gave rise to the Conciliar Movement, and consider the Councils of the early fifteenth century as (a) an effort to solve current problems in Christendom, and (b) as an anticipation of the Protestant Reformation. Why did the movement fail? (116–117)

22. Explain in some detail why Germany and Italy were unable to unite into national states during the Middle Ages. (99–101, 124–125, 128)

23. What do you find in the history and achievements of the Italian Renaissance which justifies the use of the word Renaissance (rebirth)? (128–131)

24. Contrast the aims and achievements of the Spanish and Portuguese discoverers. What was the effect of the discoveries in their respective mother-countries? (134–136)

25. Explain what is meant by what is sometimes called the Commercial Revolution, and distinguish it from the Industrial Revolution which began in the eighteenth century and continues to the present day. (136–137)

26. Explain the role of Martin Luther in the Protestant Reformation, and give reasons why he, unlike earlier opponents of the Church, was able to survive to become the founder of an enduring church. (138–141)

27. How did the Catholic Church react to the Protestant Reformation, and how were its various moves calculated to arrest its progress? What role was played by the Catholic monarchies in the process? (145–150)

28. Contrast the methods used by the Tudor and the first two Stuart monarchs in dealing with Parliament, and try to discover how royal failures in this task led eventually to the execution of Charles I. (153–157)

29. In spite of the political skill of Charles II, Stuart rule ended in the establishment of a full constitutional monarchy. Trace the process to the death of Queen Anne in 1714. (157–158)

30. What major purpose can be discerned in the various wars fought by Louis XIV? What were the strengths of the political and economic system of seventeenth-century France that enabled him to sustain these wars? (161–163)

31. When Alfred North Whitehead called the seventeenth century the "century of genius," he was referring primarily to its scientific achievements. Give a brief account of these, and explain how they revolutionized modern man's view of the world. (170–173)

32. What is meant by "enlightened despotism?" Give a brief account of the most important of the enlightened despots and of their achievements. Why do you think enlightened despotism proved unable to stand against the new revolutionary ideas of the end of the eighteenth century? (177–184)

33. Contrast in general terms the aims and achievements of the American and French Revolutions. (190–197)

34. Consider Napoleon as (a) the heir of the French Revolution and (b) the last of the "enlightened despots." (197–199)

35. What were the social and political effects of the early Industrial Revolution, and to what new theories did they give rise? (210–216)

36. Trace systematically the breakdown of the "Metternich System" in the thirty-five years following the Congress of Vienna. (223–228)

37. Trace the progress of parliamentary reform in Britain in the century

following the Congress of Vienna. How did the new voters use their new power to improve their lot during this period? (228–230, 252–256)

38. Show how the Russian Revolution of 1917 was largely prepared by Tsarist policy in the nineteenth century. (242–245)

39. Consider how far inept diplomacy was to blame for the outbreak of the First World War. Briefly evaluate also other important factors in the international discord of the time. (247–248, 260–263)

40. What were the major factors in the upsurge of imperialism in the later part of the nineteenth century? Describe briefly the consequences in either the Far East, South East Asia, North Africa, or Sub-Saharan Africa. (264–282)

41. Consider how far the Fourteen Points of President Wilson were implemented in the Peace Treaties that followed World War I. What criticism would you offer of the Treaties as a settlement of the unsolved problems that contributed to the War? (287–290)

42. What obstacles did the Bolsheviks face in the years immediately following World War I, and how far were they solved by the year 1930? (292–293)

43. After World War I it was widely thought that "democracy" had proved itself to be the most effective form of government. Yet most European states abandoned it in the 1930's. Account for the phenomenon in general terms, and mention the countries which became totalitarian during the period. (294–300)

44. What justification is there for calling World War II "Hitler's War?" Explain in some detail. (305–308)

45. Give some account of the social consequences of the Industrial Revolution of the last fifty years, and make an attempt to trace, with a few examples, the effect of the Revolution on twentieth-century literature and thought. (310–311, 314–316)

46. What were the major problems confronting the victorious powers in 1945 in their efforts to achieve a stable and peaceful world, and why were they so difficult to solve? (325–329)

47. Describe the structure and organization of the United Nations and mention some of the interventions it has made in the postwar years. Go into some detail in describing one such intervention and evaluate its success or failure. (331–334)

48. Try to account for the retreat from colonialism after the War. Choose one country that won its independence before 1950 and another that won it during the period since, and explain the particular situation in these countries which resulted in the granting of independence. (334–344)

BIBLIOGRAPHY

The titles in this bibliography are divided into two sections, paperback and clothbound books. Paperback books are listed with the name of the series or publisher only. The clothbound books are listed with the name of the publisher and the date of the most recent edition. Preference is given in this bibliography to paperback books, since these are cheaper and more easily obtainable, though most college libraries should have at least some edition of all clothbound books recommended here.

CHAPTER 1: PREHISTORIC MAN

Paperback Books:
Childe, V. G. *Man Makes Himself.* Mentor.
Clark, Grahame. *World Prehistory: An Outline.* Cambridge.
Cleator, P. E. *Lost Languages.* Mentor.
Leakey, L. S. B. *Adam's Ancestors: The Evolution of Man and His Culture.* Torch.

Clothbound Books:
Ceram, C. W. *Gods, Graves, and Scholars.* Knopf, 1951.
Hawkes, Jacquetta, and Leonard Wooley. *Prehistory and the Beginnings of Civilization.* Vol. 1 of the UNESCO *History of Mankind.* Harper & Row, 1963.

CHAPTER 2: THE ANCIENT NEAR EASTERN CIVILIZATIONS

Paperback Books:
Albright, W. F. *From the Stone Age to Christianity.* Anchor.
Breasted, J. H. *Development of Religion and Thought in Ancient Egypt.* Torch.
De Burgh, W. G. *The Legacy of the Ancient World.* Penguin.
Frankfort, Henri. *The Birth of Civilization in the Near East.* Anchor.
Gurney, O. R. *The Hittites.* Penguin.
Hutchinson, R. W. *Prehistoric Crete.* Penguin.
Kramer, S. N. *History Begins at Sumer.* Anchor.
Neugebauer, Otto. *The Exact Sciences in Antiquity.* Torch.
Oesterley, W. O., and T. H. Robinson. *An Introduction to the Books of the Old Testament.* Meridian.
Olmstead, A. T. *A History of the Persian Empire.* Phoenix.
Orlinsky, H. M. *Ancient Israel.* Cornell.
Wilson, J. A. *The Culture of Ancient Egypt.* Phoenix.

Clothbound Books:
Breasted, J. H. *A History of Egypt.* Scribner, 1909.
Ceram, C. W. *The Secret of the Hittites.* Knopf, 1956.

Frankfort, Henri, *et al. The Intellectual Adventure of Ancient Man.* University of Chicago, 1946. Most of this book appears in *Before Philosophy* (Penguin).

Gordon, C. H. *The World of the Old Testament.* Doubleday, 1958.

Lods, Adolphe. *Israel from its Beginnings to the Middle of the Eighth Century.* Allenson, 1953.

Olmstead, A. T. *A History of Assyria.* University of Chicago, 1923.

Pritchard, J. B. *Ancient Near Eastern Texts Relating to the Old Testament.* Rev. ed. Princeton, 1955.

Weill, R. *Phoenicia and Western Asia to the Macedonian Conquest.* Harrap, 1940.

CHAPTER 3: THE CIVILIZATION OF THE ANCIENT GREEKS

Paperback Books:

Bowra, C. M. *Ancient Greek Literature.* Galaxy.

————. *The Greek Experience.* Mentor.

Cornford, F. M. *From Religion to Philosophy.* Torch.

Dickinson, G. L. *The Greek View of Life.* Collier and Ann Arbor.

Hadas, Moses. *Ancilla to Classical Reading.* Columbia.

Hamilton, Edith. *The Greek Way to Western Civilization.* Mentor.

Kitto, H. D. F. *The Greeks.* Penguin.

Robinson, C. A. *Hellas: A Short History of Ancient Greece.* Bacon.

Smith, Morton. *The Ancient Greeks.* Cornell.

Tarn, W. W. *Alexander the Great.* Beacon.

————. *Hellenistic Civilization.* Meridian.

Zimmern, Alfred. *The Greek Commonwealth: Politics and Economics in Fifth-Century Athens.* Galaxy.

Clothbound Books:

Bonnard, André. *Greek Civilization.* 3 vols. Macmillan, 1957.

Hadas, Moses. *Hellenistic Culture Fusion and Diffusion.* Columbia, 1959.

Jouguet, P. *Macedonian Imperialism and the Hellenization of the East.* Knopf, 1928.

Rostovtzeff, M. I. *Social and Economic History of the Hellenistic World.* Vols. 1 and 2. Oxford, 1941.

Sarton, George. *A History of Science: Hellenistic Science and Culture in the Last Three Centuries B. C.* Harvard, 1959.

Warbeke, J. M. *The Searching Mind of Greece.* Appleton-Century-Crofts, 1930.

CHAPTER 4: FROM CITY-STATE TO WORLD EMPIRE—THE EXPANSION OF ROME

Paperback Books:

Barrow, R. H. *The Romans.* Penguin.

Carcopino, J. *Daily Life in Ancient Rome.* Yale.

Cowell, F. R. *Cicero and the Roman Republic.* Penguin.

Dill, Samuel. *Roman Society from Nero to Marcus Aurelius.* Meridian.

Duff, J. W. *A Literary History of Rome.* 2 vols. ed. by A. M. Duff. Vol. 1, *From the Origins to the Close of the Golden Age.* Vol. 2, *The Silver Age: From Tiberius to Hadrian.* Barnes & Noble.

Grant, Michael. *The World of Rome.* Mentor.

Hamilton, Edith. *The Roman Way to Western Civilization.* Mentor.

Mackail, J. W. *Latin Literature.* Collier.

Mattingly, H. *Roman Imperial Civilization.* Anchor.

Mommsen, Theodor. *A History of Rome.* Wisdom Library and Meridian.

Rostovtzeff, M. I. *Rome.* Galaxy.

Starr, C. G. *The Emergence of Rome as Ruler of the Western World.* Cornell.

Syme, Ronald. *The Roman Revolution.* Oxford.

Clothbound Books:

Adcock, F. E. *Roman Political Ideas and Practice.* University of Michigan, 1959.

Buchan, John. *Augustus.* Houghton Mifflin, 1937.

Charlesworth, M. P. *The Roman Empire.* Oxford, 1951.

Frank, Tenney. *An Economic History of Rome.* 2nd ed. John Hopkins, 1927.

Grenier, C. *The Roman Spirit in Religion, Thought and Art.* Knopf, 1926.

McKendrick, Paul. *The Mute Stones Speak.* St. Martin's, 1960.

Marsh, F. B. *The Founding of the Roman Empire.* Barnes & Noble, 1960.

Rostovtzeff, M. I. *Social and Economic History of the Roman Empire.* 2nd ed. 2 vols. Oxford, 1957.

CHAPTER 5: THE RISE OF THE CHRISTIAN CHURCH AND THE FALL OF THE ROMAN EMPIRE

Paperback Books:

Bultmann, Rudolf. *Primitive Christianity in Its Contemporary Setting.* Meridian.

Burckhardt, Jacob. *The Age of Constantine the Great.* Anchor.

Craig, C. T. *The Beginning of Christianity.* Apex.

Dawson, Christopher. *The Making of Europe,* Meridian.

Deissmann, Adolf. *Paul: A Study in Social and Religious History.* Torch.

Dill, Samuel. *Roman Society in the Last Century of the Western Empire.* Meridian.

Duckett, Eleanor S. *The Gateway to the Middle Ages: Monasticism.* Ann Arbor.

Gibbon, Edward. *The Decline and Fall of the Roman Empire* (abridged). Vols. 1 and 2. Collier.

Lebreton, Jules, and Jacques Zeiller. *A History of the Early Church.* 4 vols. Collier.

Lot, Ferdinand. *The End of the Ancient World and the Beginnings of the Middle Ages.* Torch.

Tacitus. *On Britain and Germany.* Penguin.

Weiss, Johannes. *Earliest Christianity.* 2 vols. Torch.

Clothbound Books:

Duchesne, L. *Early History of the Christian Church.* 3 vols. Longmans, Green, 1947.

Latourette, K. S. *A History of Christianity.* Harper, 1953.

Moss, H. St. L. B. *The Birth of the Middle Ages, 395–814.* Oxford, 1935.

CHAPTER 6: THE BYZANTINE AND MUSLIM EMPIRES

Paperback Books:

Baynes, N. H., and H. St. L. B. Moss. *Byzantium.* Oxford.

Gibb, H. A. R. *Mohammedanism.* Galaxy.

Grunebaum, G. E. von. *Medieval Islam.* Phoenix.

Guerdan, René. *Byzantium.* Capricorn.

Guillaume, Alfred. *Islam.* 2nd ed. Penguin.

Hitti, Philip K. *The Arabs: A Short History.* Gateway.

Hussey, J. M. *The Byzantine World.* Torch.

Runciman, Steven. *Byzantine Civilization.* Meridian.

Talbot-Rice, David. *Byzantine Art.* Penguin.

Vasiliev, A. A. *A History of the Byzantine Empire.* 2 vols. Wisconsin.

Clothbound Books:

Baynes, N. H. *The Byzantine Empire.* Oxford University Press, 1943.

Cross, S. H. *Slavic Civilization.* Harvard, 1948.

Ostrogorsky, George. *A History of the Byzantine State.* Rutgers, 1957.

Spuler, B. *The Muslim World.* 2 vols. Humanities, 1960.

CHAPTER 7: THE EARLY MIDDLE AGES TO A.D. 1000

Paperback Books:

Bark, W. C. *Origins of the Medieval World.* Anchor.

Easton, S. C., and Helene Wieruszowski. *The Era of Charlemagne: Frankish State and Society.* Anvil.

Sayles, G. O. *The Medieval Foundations of England.* Perpetua.

Southern, R. W. *The Making of the Middle Ages.* Yale.

Stenton, Doris M. *English Society in the Early Middle Ages.* Penguin.

Wallace-Hadrill, J. M. *The Barbarian West: The Early Middle Ages.* Torch.

Clothbound Books:

Artz, F. B. *The Mind of the Middle Ages.* 2nd ed. Knopf, 1958.

Fichtenau, H. *The Carolingian Empire.* Dufour, 1957.

Haskins, C. H. *The Normans in European History.* Houghton Mifflin, 1915.

Laistner, M. L. W. *Thought and Letters in Western Europe.* 2nd ed. Cornell, 1957.

Taylor, H. O. *The Mediaeval Mind.* 2 vols. Harvard, 1925.

Thompson, J. W. *The Economic and Social History of the Middle Ages, 300–1300.* Appleton-Century-Crofts, 1928.

CHAPTER 8: THE HIGH MIDDLE AGES TO THE END OF THE THIRTEENTH CENTURY

Paperback Books:

Adams, Henry. *Mont-Saint-Michel and Chartres.* Anchor, Collier, Mentor.

Baldwin, M. W. *The Mediaeval Church,* Cornell.

Bryce, James. *The Holy Roman Empire.* Schocken.

Crombie, A. C. *Medieval and Early Modern Science.* 2 vols. Anchor.

Dawson, Christopher. *Religion and the Rise of Western Culture.* Image.

Fremantle, Anne. *The Age of Belief: The Medieval Philosophers.* Mentor.

Ganshof, F. L. *Feudalism.* Torch.

Gilson, Étienne. *Reason and Revelation in the Middle Ages.* Scribner.

Painter, Sidney. *The Rise of Feudal Monarchies.* Cornell.

Panofsky, Erwin. *Gothic Architecture and Scholasticism.* Meridian.

Pirenne, Henri. *Economic and Social History of Medieval Europe.* Harvest.

Power, Eileen. *Medieval People.* Rev. ed. Barnes & Noble.

Schachner, Nathan. *The Mediaeval Universities.* Perpetua.

Vignaux, Paul. *Philosophy in the Middle Ages.* Meridian.

Waddell, Helen. *The Wandering Scholars.* Anchor.

Clothbound Books:

Barlow, F. *The Feudal Kingdom of England, 1042–1216.* Longmans, Green, 1954.

Barraclough, Geoffrey, ed. *Medieval Germany, 911–1250.* 2 vols. Barnes & Noble, 1961.

Clough, S. B., and C. W. Cole. *Economic History of Europe.* 3rd ed. Heath, 1952. (Use also for subsequent chapters.)

Davis, H. W. C. *Medieval Europe.* 2nd ed. Oxford, 1960.

Fawtier, Robert. *The Capetian Kings of France.* St. Martin's, 1960.

Heaton, Herbert. *Economic History of Europe.* Rev. ed. Harper, 1948. (Use also for subsequent chapters.)

Morey, C. R. *Medieval Art.* Norton, 1942.

Petit-Dutaillis, C. *Feudal Monarchy in France and England from the 10th to the 13th Century.* Kegan, Paul, 1936.

Runciman, Steven. *History of the Crusades.* 3 vols. Cambridge, 1951–54.

Tellenbach, G. *Church, State and Christian Society at the Time of the Investiture Controversy.* Humanities, 1940.

Ullmann, Walter. *Growth of Papal Government in the Middle Ages.* Rev. ed. Barnes & Noble, 1963.

CHAPTER 9: THE LATE MIDDLE AGES TO 1500.

Paperback Books:

Butterfield, Herbert. *The Origins of Modern Science.* Rev. ed. Collier.

Cam, Helen. *England Before Elizabeth.* Torch.

Cheyney, E. P. *The Dawn of a New Era, 1250–1453.* Torch.

Haskins, G. L. *The Growth of English Representative Government.* Perpetua.

Huizinga, J. *The Waning of the Middle Ages.* Anchor.

Myers, A. R. *England in the Late Middle Ages.* Penguin.

Vernadsky, George. *A History of Russia.* Yale.

Clothbound Books:

Altamira, Rafael. *History of Spain.* Van Nostrand, 1949.

Flick, A. C. *The Decline of the Mediaeval Church.* 2 vols. Knopf, 1930.

Perroy, Edouard. *The Hundred Years' War.* Oxford, 1951.

Sabine, G. H. *History of Political Theory.* 3rd ed. Holt, Rinehart & Winston, 1962. (This excellent text may be used throughout. Especially good on this period.)

Tierney, Brian. *Foundations of the Conciliar Theory.* Cambridge, 1955.

CHAPTER 10: THE RENAISSANCE AND THE AGE OF DISCOVERY

Paperback Books:

Berenson, Bernard. *Italian Painters of the Renaissance.* Meridian.

Burckhardt, Jacob. *The Civilization of the Renaissance in Italy.* 2 vols. Torch.

Cassirer, Ernst, *et al.,* eds. *The Renaissance Philosophy of Man.* Phoenix.

Diaz del Castillo, Bernal. *The Discovery and Conquest of Mexico.* Evergreen.

Ferguson, W. K., *et al. The Renaissance: Six Essays.* Torch.

Haydn, Hiram. *The Counter-Renaissance.* Evergreen.

Matthews, G. T., ed. *News and Rumor in Renaissance Europe: The Fugger Newsletters.* Capricorn.

Symonds, J. A. *The Renaissance in Italy.* 3 vols. Capricorn.

Zweig, Stefan. *Erasmus of Rotterdam.* Compass.

Clothbound Books:

Brebner, J. B. *The Explorers of North America.* Macmillan, 1923.

Crow, J. A. *The Epic of Latin America.* Doubleday, 1946.

Ferguson, W. K. *The Renaissance in Historical Thought.* Houghton Mifflin, 1948.

Holand, Hjalmar. *Explorations in America Before Columbus.* Twayne, 1956.
Lucas, H. S. *The Renaissance and the Reformation.* Harper, 1934.
Packard, L. B. *The Commercial Revolution, 1400–1776.* Berkshire Studies, 1927.

CHAPTER 11: THE PROTESTANT REFORMATION AND THE WARS OF RELIGION

Paperback Books:
Bainton, R. H. *Here I Stand: A Life of Martin Luther.* Apex and Mentor.
Harkness, Georgia. *John Calvin: The Man and His Ethics.* Apex.
Mosse, G. L. *The Reformation.* 3rd ed. Holt, Rinehart & Winston.
Powicke, F. M. *The Reformation in England.* Oxford.
Smith, Preserved. *The Age of the Reformation.* 2 vols. Collier.
Weber, Max. *The Protestant Ethic and the Spirit of Capitalism.* Scribner.
Wedgwood, Cicely. *The Thirty Years War.* Anchor.

Clothbound Books:
Grimm, H. J. *The Reformation Era, 1500–1650.* Macmillan, 1954.
McElwee, William. *The Reign of Charles V, 1516–1558.* Macmillan, 1936.
Williams, G. H. *The Radical Reformation.* Westminster, 1962.

CHAPTER 12: THE EUROPEAN STATE SYSTEM IN THE 16th AND 17th CENTURIES

Paperback Books:
Bindoff, S. T. *Tudor England.* Penguin.
Burtt, E. A. *The Metaphysical Foundations of Modern Science.* Anchor.
Dampier, W. C. *A Shorter History of Science.* Meridian.
Friedrich, Carl J. *The Age of the Baroque, 1610–1660.* Torch.
Gooch, G. P. *English Democratic Ideas in the Seventeenth Century.* Torch.
Haller, William. *The Rise of Puritanism.* Torch.
Hoffding, Harald. *A History of Modern Philosophy.* 2 vols. Dover.
Klyuchevsky, Vasili. *Peter the Great.* Vintage.
Nef, J. U. *Industry and Government in France and England, 1540–1640.* Cornell.
Nussbaum, F. L. *The Triumph of Science and Reason, 1660–1685.* Torch.
Ogg, David. *Europe in the Seventeenth Century.* Collier.
Wolf, A. *A History of Science, Technology and Philosophy in the Sixteenth and Seventeenth Centuries.* 2 vols. Torch.

Clothbound Books:
Adams, G. B., and R. L. Schuyler. *Constitutional History of England.* Rev. ed. Holt, 1934.

Chrimes, S. B. *English Constitutional History.* 2nd ed. Oxford, 1953.

Firth, C. H. *Oliver Cromwell and the Rule of the Puritans in England.* Houghton Mifflin, 1934.

Mazour, A. G. *Russia: Tsarist and Communist.* Van Nostrand, 1962.

Randall, J. H., Jr. *The Making of the Modern Mind.* 2nd ed. Houghton Mifflin, 1940.

CHAPTER 13: THE EIGHTEENTH CENTURY—AGE OF ENLIGHTENMENT

Paperback Books:

Becker, Carl. *The Heavenly City of the Eighteenth Century Philosophers.* Yale.

Beloff, Max. *The Age of Absolutism, 1660–1815.* Torch.

Bredvold, L. I. *The Intellectual Milieu of John Dryden.* Ann Arbor.

Cassirer, Ernst. *The Philosophy of the Enlightenment.* Beacon.

Cobban, Alfred. *History of Modern France, 1715–1799.* Penguin.

Gershoy, Leo. *From Despotism to Revolution, 1763–1789.* Torch.

Roberts, Penfield. *The Quest for Security, 1715–1740.* Torch.

Robertson, C. G. *Chatham and the British Empire.* Collier.

Stephen, Leslie. *History of English Thought in the Eighteenth Century.* 2 vols. Harbinger.

Thomson, G. S. *Catherine the Great and the Expansion of Russia.* Collier.

Clothbound Books:

Bruun, Geoffrey. *The Enlightened Despots.* Berkshire Studies, 1929.

Buffinton, A. H. *The Second Hundred Years' War, 1689–1815.* Holt, 1929.

Kerner, R. *Bohemia in the Eighteenth Century.* Macmillan, 1932.

Lord, Robert. *The Second Partition of Poland.* Harvard, 1915.

Namier, L. B. *England in the Age of the American Revolution.* 2nd ed. St. Martin's, 1961.

CHAPTER 14: THE AMERICAN AND FRENCH REVOLUTIONS AND THEIR CONSEQUENCES

Paperback Books:

Alden, J. R. *The American Revolution, 1775–1783.* Torch.

Brinton, Crane. *A Decade of Revolution, 1789–1799.* Torch.

———. *The Lives of Talleyrand.* Norton.

Bruun, Geoffrey. *Europe and the French Imperium, 1799–1814.* Torch.

Burke, Edmund, and Thomas Paine. *Reflections on the Revolution in France* & *The Rights of Man.* Dolphin.

Butterfield, Herbert. *Napoleon.* Collier.

Gershoy, Leo. *The Era of the French Revolution, 1789–1799.* Anvil.

Geyl, Peter. *Napoleon: For and Against.* Yale.

Gipson, L. H. *The Coming of the Revolution, 1763–1775.* Torch.

Goodwin, Albert. *The French Revolution.* Torch.

Herold, J. C. *The Mind of Napoleon.* Collier.

Lefebvre, Georges. *The Coming of the French Revolution.* Vintage.

Markham, F. M. R. *Napoleon and the Awakening of Europe.* Collier.

Thompson, J. M. *Robespierre and the French Revolution.* Collier.

Tocqueville, Alexis de. *The Old Regime and the French Revolution.* Anchor.

Tolstoy, Leo. *War and Peace.* 2 vols. Penguin. Abridged versions, Bantam and Dell.

Clothbound Books:

Palmer, R. R. *The Age of the Democratic Revolution, 1760–1800.* Princeton, 1959.

Ritcheson, C. R. *British Politics and the American Revolution.* Oklahoma, 1954.

Thompson, James M. *Napoleon Bonaparte.* Oxford, 1952.

CHAPTER 15: THE EARLY INDUSTRIAL REVOLUTION

Paperback Books:

Berlin, Isaiah. *Karl Marx: His Life and Environment.* Galaxy.

Fremantle, Anne. *This Little Band of Prophets: The British Fabians.* Mentor.

Mantoux, Paul. *The Industrial Revolution in the Eighteenth Century.* Torch.

Marx, Karl, and Friedrich Engels. *The Communist Manifesto.* Gateway.

————. *Basic Writings on Politics and Philosophy.* Anchor.

Schumpeter, Joseph. *Capitalism, Socialism and Democracy.* Torch.

Toynbee, Arnold. *The Industrial Revolution.* Beacon.

Usher, A. P. *A History of Mechanical Inventions.* Beacon.

Wilson, Edmund. *To the Finland Station.* Anchor.

Clothbound Books:

Ashton, T. S. *The Industrial Revolution, 1760–1830.* Oxford, 1948.

Clough, Shepard B. *The Economic Development of Western Civilization.* McGraw-Hill, 1959.

Cole, G. D. H. *Socialist Thought.* Vols. 1 and 2. St. Martin's, 1953–1954.

Hammond, J. L., and B. Hammond. *The Rise of British Industry.* Harcourt, Brace, 1937.

Webb, Sidney, and Beatrice Webb. *A History of Trade Unionism.* Longmans, Green, 1957.

CHAPTER 16: REACTION, REFORM, AND REVOLUTION, 1815–1850.

Paperback Books:

Artz, F. B. *Reaction and Revolution, 1815–1832.* Torch.

Brunn, Geoffrey. *Nineteenth-Century European Civilization.* Galaxy.

Bury, J. P. T. *France, 1814–1940.* Perpetua.

Grund, F. J. *Aristocracy in America: Jacksonian Democracy.* Torch.

Halévy, Elie. *History of the English People.* Vols. 1–3. Barnes & Noble.

Hofstadter, Richard. *The American Political Tradition.* Vintage.

James, Marquis. *Andrew Jackson: Portrait of a President.* Universal.

Lipson, E. *Europe in the Nineteenth Century, 1815–1914.* Collier.

Madariaga, Salvador de. *Bolivar.* Collier.

May, Arthur. *The Age of Metternich.* Berkshire Studies.

Nicolson, Harold. *The Congress of Vienna.* Compass.

Robertson, Priscilla. *The Revolution of 1848: A Social History.* Torch.

Salvemini, G. *Mazzini.* Collier.

Schlesinger, Arthur M., Jr. *The Age of Jackson* (abridged). Mentor.

Tocqueville, Alexis de. *Democracy in America.* 2 vols. Vintage and Schocken.

Clothbound Books:

Hammond, J., and B. Hammond. *The Age of the Chartists, 1832–1854.* Longmans, Green, 1930.

Henderson, W. O. *The Zollverein.* 2nd ed. Quadrangle, 1959.

Herring, H. C. *A History of Latin America.* Knopf, 1955.

Veit, Valentine. *The German People: Their History and Civilization.* Knopf, 1946.

Woodhouse, C. M. *The Greek War of Independence.* Hutchinson, 1952.

Woodward, E. L. *The Age of Reform, 1815–1870.* Oxford University Press, 1938.

CHAPTER 17: NATIONALISM, REFORM, AND STEPS
TOWARD WAR, 1850–1914.

Paperback Books:

Albrecht-Carrié, René. *Italy from Napoleon to Mussolini.* Columbia.

Barker, Alan. *The Civil War in America.* Anchor.

Birrell, Francis. *Gladstone.* Collier.

Halévy, Elie. *History of the English People in the Nineteenth Century.* Vols. 4–6. Barnes & Noble.

Kohn, Hans. *Pan Slavism.* Vintage.

Leech, Margaret. *Reveille in Washington.* Universal.

Morrow, I. F. *Bismarck.* Collier.

Nichols, R. F. *The Disruption of American Democracy.* Collier.

Ruggiero, Guido de. *The History of European Liberalism.* Beacon.

Seton-Watson, Hugh. *The Decline of Imperial Russia, 1855–1914.* Praeger.

Shafer, Boyd. *Nationalism: Myth and Reality.* Harvest.

Taylor, A. J. P. *The Course of German History.* Capricorn.

Thomson, David. *England in the Nineteenth Century: 1815–1914.* Penguin.

Clothbound Books:

Binkley, R. C. *Realism and Nationalism, 1852–1871.* Harper, 1935.

Ensor, Robert. *England, 1870–1914.* Oxford, 1936.

Fay, S. B. *The Origins of the World War.* 2nd ed. Macmillan, 1938.

Hayes, Carlton J. H. *A Generation of Materialism, 1871–1900.* Harper. 1941.

Kann, R. A. *The Multiracial Empire.* 2 vols. Columbia, 1950.

Langer, W. L. *European Alliances and Alignments, 1871–1890.* Knopf, 1931.

Passant, E. J. *A Short History of Germany, 1850–1945.* Cambridge, 1959.

Taylor, A. J. P. *The Struggle for Mastery in Europe, 1848–1918.* Oxford, 1954.

Thompson, J. M. *Louis Napoleon and the Second Empire.* Noonday, 1955.

CHAPTER 18: THE GROWTH OF IMPERIALISM IN THE NINETEENTH CENTURY

Paperback Books:

Easton, S. C. *The Rise and Fall of Western Colonialism.* Praeger.

Fairbank, J. K. *The United States and China.* Compass.

Nehru, Jawaharlal. *The Discovery of India* (abridged). Anchor.

Schumpeter, J. A. *Imperialism and Social Classes.* Meridian.

Clothbound Books:

Burt, A. L. *The Evolution of the British Empire and Commonwealth.* Heath, 1956.

Carrington, C. E. *The British Overseas.* Cambridge, 1950.

Hobson, J. A. *Imperialism: A Study.* 5th ed. Macmillan, 1933.

Langer, W. L. *The Diplomacy of Imperialism, 1890–1902.* Knopf, 1935.

Lugard, F. D. *The Dual Mandate in British Tropical Africa.* 2nd ed. Shoe String, 1964.

Moon, Parker T. *Imperialism and World Politics.* Macmillan, 1926.

Snyder, L. L. *The Imperialism Reader.* Van Nostrand, 1962.

Thornton, A. P. *The Imperial Idea and Its Enemies.* St. Martin's, 1959.

CHAPTER 19: THE FIRST WORLD WAR AND THE PEACE TREATIES

Paperback Books:

Aron, Raymond. *The Century of Total War.* Beacon.

Falls, Cyril. *The Great War, 1914–1918.* Capricorn.

Farmer, Frances, ed. *The Wilson Reader.* Oceana.

Pares, Bernard. *The Fall of the Russian Monarchy.* Vintage.

Wolfe, Bertram. *Three Who Made a Revolution: Lenin, Trotsky, Stalin.* 4th ed. Dial.

Clothbound Books:

Bailey, T. A. *Wilson and the Peacemakers*. Macmillan, 1947.

Churchill, Winston. *The World Crisis*. 5 vols. Houghton Mifflin, 1923–1929.

Cobban, Alfred. *National Self-Determination*. Oxford, 1945.

Cruttwell, C. R. M. *A History of the Great War, 1914–1918*. 2nd ed. Oxford, 1936.

Gathorne-Hardy, G. *The Fourteen Points and the Treaty of Versailles*. Oxford, 1940.

Holborn, Hajo. *The Political Collapse of Europe*. Knopf, 1951.

Keynes, J. M. *The Economic Consequences of the Peace*. Harcourt, Brace, 1920.

Mantoux, Étienne. *The Carthaginian Peace; or the Economic Consequences of Mr. Keynes*. Scribner, 1952.

Nicolson, Harold. *Peacemaking, 1919*. Harcourt, Brace, 1939.

Walters, F. P. *A History of the League of Nations*. 2 vols. Oxford, 1952.

CHAPTER 20: THE LONG ARMISTICE

Paperback Books:

Arendt, Hannah. *The Origins of Totalitarianism*. Rev. ed. **Meridian.**

Brenan, Gerald. *The Spanish Labyrinth*. Cambridge.

Bullock, Alan. *Hitler: A Study in Tyranny* (abridged). Bantam.

Deutscher, Isaac. *Stalin: A Political Biography*. Vintage.

Kennan, George F. *American Diplomacy, 1900–1950*. Mentor.

———. *Russia and the West Under Lenin and Stalin*. Mentor.

Leuchtenburg, W. E. *The Perils of Prosperity, 1914–1932*. University of Chicago.

Luethy, Herbert. *France Against Herself*. Meridian.

Perkins, Dexter. *The New Age of Franklin Roosevelt, 1932–1945*. University of Chicago.

Rauch, George von. *A History of Soviet Russia*. 3rd ed.; rev. Praeger.

Seton-Watson, Hugh. *From Lenin to Khrushchev: A History of World Communism*. Praeger.

Shirer, W. L. *The Rise and Fall of the Third Reich*. Crest.

Shub, David. *Lenin* (abridged). Mentor.

Trotsky, Leon. *The Russian Revolution* (abridged). Anchor.

Clothbound Books:

Carr, E. H. *The Twenty Years' Crisis, 1919–1939*. Macmillan, 1946.

Gathorne-Hardy, G. M. *A Short History of International Affairs, 1920–1939*. 4th ed. Oxford, 1950.

Gedye, G. E. R. *Betrayal in Central Europe*. Harper, 1939.

Halperin, S. W. *Germany Tried Democracy*. Crowell, 1946.

Neumann, Sigmund. *The Future in Perspective*. Putnam, 1946.

Wheeler-Bennett, J. W. *Munich: Prologue to Tragedy.* Meredith, 1963.
Wolfers, Arnold. *Britain and France Between Two Wars.* Harcourt, Brace, 1940.

CHAPTER 21: A CENTURY OF MATERIAL PROGRESS AND ITS CULTURAL CONSEQUENCES

Paperback Books:
Barnett, Lincoln. *The Universe and Dr. Einstein.* Rev. ed. Mentor.
Barzun, Jacques. *Darwin, Marx, and Wagner.* Anchor.
Berle, Adolf A. Jr. *The Twentieth Century Capitalist Revolution.* Harvest.
Drucker, Peter. *The New Society: The Anatomy of Industrial Order.* Torch.
Einstein, Albert, and Leopold Infeld. *The Evolution of Physics.* Simon & Schuster.
Eiseley, Loren. *Darwin's Century.* Anchor.
Frankel, Charles. *The Case for Modern Man.* Beacon.
Heilbroner, Robert L. *The Future as History.* Evergreen.
Jones, Ernest. *The Life and Work of Sigmund Freud* (abridged). Anchor.
Riesman, David. *The Lonely Crowd.* Rev. ed. Yale.
Whyte, W. H., Jr. *The Organization Man.* Anchor.
Wilson, Edmund. *Axel's Castle.* Scribner.

Clothbound Books:
Asimov, Isaac. *The Intelligent Man's Guide to Science.* 2 vols. Basic Books, 1960.
Galbraith, J. K. *The Affluent Society.* Houghton Mifflin, 1958.
Levi, Albert W. *Philosophy and the Modern World.* University of Indiana, 1959.

(See also under Chapter 15 for books on Industrial Revolution.)

CHAPTER 22: THE SECOND WORLD WAR AND ITS AFTERMATH

Chamberlin, Waldo, and J. J. Hovet. *Chronology and Fact Book of the United Nations* (1941–1961). Oceana.
Churchill, Winston S. *The Second World War.* 6 vols. Bantam.
Courlander, Harold. *Shaping our Times: What the United Nations Is and Does.* Oceana.
Eisenhower, Dwight D. *Crusade in Europe.* Dolphin.
Feis, Herbert. *The Road to Pearl Harbor.* Atheneum.
Gross, Ernest A. *The United Nations: Structure for Peace.* Harper.
Hersey, John. *Hiroshima.* Bantam.
Montgomery, Bernard L. *Memoirs of Field-Marshal Montgomery.* Signet.

Clothbound Books:

Aron, Robert. *The Vichy Regime.* Macmillan, 1959.

Feis, Herbert. *Churchill, Roosevelt, Stalin.* Princeton, 1957.

Snyder, L. L. *The War: A Concise History, 1939–1945.* Messner, 1960.

Wilmot, Chester. *The Struggle for Europe: History of World War II.* Harper, 1952.

CHAPTER 23: THE POSTWAR WORLD

Paperback Books:

Agar, Herbert. *The Price of Power: America since 1945.* University of Chicago.

Carter, Gwendolyn. *Independence for Africa.* Praeger.

Dean, Vera M. *The Nature of the Non-Western World.* Mentor.

Easton, S. C. *The Rise and Fall of Western Colonialism.* Praeger.

Emerson, Rupert. *From Empire to Nation.* Beacon.

George, Dorothy. *England in Transition.* Penguin.

Harris, Richard. *Independence and After: Revolution in Undeveloped Countries.* Oxford.

Lukacs, John. *A History of the Cold War.* Anchor.

Millis, Walter. *Arms and Men.* Mentor.

Pickles, Dorothy. *The Fifth French Republic.* Rev. ed. Praeger.

Roberts, H. L. *Russia and America: Dangers and Prospects.* Mentor.

Schwartz, Harry. *The Red Phoenix: Russia since World War II.* Praeger.

Seton-Watson, Hugh. *Neither War nor Peace: The Struggle for Power in the Postwar World.* Praeger.

Smith, W. C. *Islam in Modern History.* Mentor.

Clothbound Books:

Feis, Herbert. *The China Tangle.* Princeton, 1953.

Frank, Isaiah. *The European Common Market.* Praeger, 1961.

Kahin, C. McT., ed. *Governments and Politics of Southeast Asia.* 2nd ed. Cornell, 1964.

Moore, Ben T. *NATO and the Future of Europe.* Harper, 1958.

Myrdal, Gunnar. *An International Economy: Problems and Prospects.* Harper, 1956.

Strachey, John. *The End of Empire.* Random House, 1960.

Truman, Harry S. *Memoirs.* 2 vols. Doubleday, 1955–1956.

INDEX